T0330028

IN CHINA'S WAKE

In China's Wake

HOW THE COMMODITY BOOM TRANSFORMED DEVELOPMENT STRATEGIES IN THE GLOBAL SOUTH

Nicholas Jepson

Columbia University Press
New York

Columbia University Press
Publishers Since 1893
New York   Chichester, West Sussex
cup.columbia.edu
Copyright © 2020 Columbia University Press
All rights reserved

Names: Jepson, Nicholas, author.
Title: In China's wake : how the commodity boom transformed development
strategies in the global south / Nicholas Jepson.
Description: New York : Columbia University Press, [2019] | Includes bibliographical
references and index.
Identifiers: LCCN 2019016862 | ISBN 9780231187961 (cloth : alk. paper) |
ISBN 9780231187978 (pbk. : alk. paper) | ISBN 9780231547598 (ebook)
Subjects: LCSH: Developing countries—Economic conditions. | Economic
development—Developing countries. | Natural resources—Developing countries. |
China—Commerce. | China—Foreign economic relations—Developing countries. |
Developing countries—Foreign economic relations—China.
Classification: LCC HC59.7 .J48 2019 | DDC 338.9009172/4—dc23
LC record available at https://lccn.loc.gov/2019016862

Columbia University Press books are printed on permanent and durable acid-free paper.
Printed in the United States of America

Cover image: © bergserg / Getty Images

Contents

Figures and Tables

Figures

Tables

Acknowledgments

This book began life back in 2011 as a half-formed idea for a PhD project comparing Bolivia's and Zambia's experiences of the commodity boom era. In Latin America, many of the "pink tide" governments seemed to be leveraging natural resource export booms in service of new policy initiatives and development strategies, in the process breaking with the liberal economic orthodoxy that had held sway across the region since the 1980s. My starting point was to wonder why this was happening in (some of) Latin America but no similar shifts had occurred among the resource-exporting states of sub-Saharan Africa. Zambia, where Michael Sata was about to win the presidency on a populist platform recalling aspects of some of the Latin American cases, looked like a promising place to begin.

In any event, Sata's Patriotic Front government failed to institute any pink tide–like political economic reorientation. But in my efforts to understand why Zambia did not go the way of Bolivia (or Ecuador or Argentina), I began to broaden the focus of my research—first, on how and why the ability of states to set their own development agendas appears to wax and wane during times of flux in the global political economy (with the rise of China playing the starring role in our current era's upheavals); and second, on the ways in which changing global conditions play out at the national level, as they alter the terrain for state–society relations in countries across the world. The result was a much wider project, encompassing

[xi]

fifteen resource-exporting states (including fieldwork in three—Zambia, Ecuador, and Jamaica), culminating initially in a dissertation submitted to the University of Bristol in late 2015.

Since then, what eventually would become this book has gone through a series of revisions and updates to reach its current form, particularly taking into account the end of the boom (an outcome that was not yet definite in 2015) and its effects in some of the countries surveyed. Nevertheless, the book's focus remains very much on the boom itself, understood in the abstract as a world-historical phenomenon, but one which has had profound, concrete impacts on the lives of a large percentage of the world's population, not least across the global South.

Over its various stages the majority of this book was researched and written at the universities of Bristol (School of Sociology, Politics, and International Studies) and Leeds (School of Politics and International Studies), and now completed at the University of Manchester's Global Development Institute. Thanks go to all these institutions for providing me the opportunity to work in stimulating and supportive research environments. I owe a debt of gratitude especially to my two PhD supervisors at Bristol, Jeff Henderson and Malcolm Fairbrother, for allowing me the leeway to pursue such an ambitious doctoral project. Both were extraordinarily generous with their time and support. More than anyone else, Jeff has provided steadfast guidance, assistance, and mentorship, both during my time at Bristol and beyond, without which neither the dissertation nor the book would have been possible. Malcolm's interventions continually pushed me to improve my work and were especially crucial in helping me to shape the methodological aspects of the book.

At Bristol, my research was supported by an Economic and Social Research Council +3 studentship, awarded through the South West Doctoral Training Centre, along with overseas fieldwork funding from the same source. A Santander Latin America travel grant partly financed fieldwork in Ecuador, and a University of Bristol alumni bursary supported me while writing up the dissertation. I am grateful to the University of Wisconsin–Madison's Sociology department and the University of California, Santa Barbara's Global Studies department for hosting me during visits in 2013 and 2014, respectively. Particular thanks go to Rich Appelbaum and Jan Nederveen Pieterse at UCSB and Gay Seidman at UW–Madison.

A large number of people have provided various forms of support, guidance, and other assistance in bringing this project to fruition (and with other aspects of my work). Among others, I owe thanks to Stephanie Barrientos, Pritish Behuria, Terrell Carver, Ryerson Christie, Peter Clegg, James Copestake, Victor Faessel, Bill Freund, Tigist Grieve, Sam Hickey, Rory Horner, David Hulme, Diana Mitlin, Khalid Nadvi, Sue Newman, Rebecca Schaaf, Seth Schindler, Tamer Söyler, Robert Wade, Sean Watson, Polly Wilding, and Neil Winn, as well as my interviewees in Ecuador, Jamaica, and Zambia and the four anonymous reviewers who gave very helpful critiques and comments. I also want to thank the two editors I have worked with at Columbia University Press: first, Bridget Flannery-McCoy, who took the book on and steered me expertly through the first steps; and second, Caelyn Cobb, who took over from Bridget and has since proven equally adept in guiding the book toward publication. Both have been extraordinarily patient and helpful throughout, as has Todd Manza, who copyedited the manuscript. All errors are my responsibility alone.

Finally, special thanks go to my parents, Sue and Paul, and my brother Richard, for their support all along the way.

Abbreviations

ANC	African National Congress
APRA	American Popular Revolutionary Alliance
BEE	Black Economic Empowerment
BNDES	Banco Nacional de Desenvolvimento Econômico e Social (National Bank for Economic and Social Development)
BRI	Belt and Road Initiative
BRIC	Brazil, Russia, India, and China
BRICS	Brazil, Russia, India, China, and South Africa
CONAIE	Confederación de Nacionalidades Indígenas del Ecuador (Confederation of Indigenous Nationalities of Ecuador)
CONFIEP	Confederacion Nacional de Instituciones Empresariales Privadas (National Confederation of Private Enterprise Institutions)
DDO	donor-dependent orthodoxy
ELN	Ejército de Liberación Nacional (National Liberation Army)
EO	extractivist-oligarchic
ER	extractivist-redistributive
FARC	Fuerzas Armadas Revolucionarias de Colombia (Revolutionary Armed Forces of Colombia)
FDI	foreign direct investment
FIESP	Federação das Indústrias do Estado de São Paulo (Industrial Federation of the State of Sao Paulo)

GDP	gross domestic product
GNI	gross national income
GNP	gross national product
HO	homegrown orthodoxy
IFI	international financial institution
IMF	International Monetary Fund
ISI	import substitution industrialization
JLP	Jamaica Labour Party
LPRP	Lao People's Revolutionary Party
MAS	Movimiento al Socialismo (Movement for Socialism)
MEC	minerals-energy complex
MMD	Movement for Multiparty Democracy
MPLA	Movimento Popular de Libertação de Angola (Popular Movement for the Liberation of Angola)
ND	neodevelopmentalist
NIEO	New International Economic Order
ODA	official development assistance
OECD	Organisation for Economic Co-operation and Development
OPEC	Organization of the Petroleum Exporting Countries
PAC	Programa de Aceleração do Crescimento (Growth Acceleration Program)
PDVSA	Petróleos de Venezuela, S.A. (Venezuelan Petroleum)
PF	Patriotic Front
PJJHD	Plan Jefes y Jefas de Hogares Desempleados (Unemployed Heads of Household Plan)
PNP	People's National Party (Jamaica)
PRC	People's Republic of China
PRSP	Poverty Reduction Strategy Paper
PT	Partido dos Trabalhadores (Workers' Party) (Brazil)
QCA	qualitative comparative analysis
RS	rentier state
SAP	structural adjustment program
SNMPE	Sociedad Nacional de Mineria, Petroleo y Energia (National Society of Mining, Petroleum, and Energy)
SOE	state-owned enterprise
TCC	transnational capitalist class
UNCTAD	United Nations Conference on Trade and Development
UNIP	United National Independence Party

WTO	World Trade Organization
YPF	Yacimientos Petrolíferos Fiscales (Treasury Oil Fields)
YPFB	Yacimientos Petroliferos Fiscales Bolivianos (Bolivian Treasury Oil Fields)

IN CHINA'S WAKE

Introduction

There is a strong case to be made that the rise of China is the most important political-economic process of the late twentieth and early twenty-first centuries. A country which is home to around one-fifth of the world's population has doubled its gross domestic product (GDP) every seven to eight years since the beginning of Deng Xiaoping's reforms, in 1978. In that year, China's economy was smaller than that of the Netherlands, in current U.S. dollar terms (World Bank, World Development Indicators). By 2017, it was the second only to that of the United States and was two and a half times bigger than that of Japan. In recent years, however, it has become increasingly clear that the consequences of an ascendant China's externalization may be of even greater significance than its remarkable domestic transformation. A now well-established literature has pointed to a crucial (though perhaps dysfunctional) symbiosis between the U.S. and Chinese economies as well as China's growing influence in various parts of the global South, as investor, trading partner, and creditor. Excited media reaction to these developments has portrayed China as anything from a new champion against the neocolonial designs of the United States to simply the latest (and most rapacious) manifestation of imperialism (Mawdsley 2008; Telesur 2015; Larmer 2017).

Most serious studies, of course, provide a more nuanced account of China's return to global prominence and its implications for development in the rest of the South. Nevertheless, with some important exceptions, a majority focus on the impact of direct relations between the People's Republic of China (PRC) and particular states or regions (Brautigam 2009; Gallagher and Porzecanski 2010; Fernandez Jilberto and Hogenboom 2012; Glassman 2010), whether in terms of loans, investments, trade, geopolitics, or migration (French 2015; Brautigam and Gallagher 2014; Mohan and Lampert 2013; Large 2013). In contrast, this book examines the impact of China's rise on the shape of the world economy as a whole. China has restructured some of central processes that power global capitalism, producing profound consequences for those states whose developmental prospects depend upon the functioning of these circuits. Nowhere is this strengthening of China's gravitational pull more evident than in commodity markets, and for this reason, this is where the book's focus lies.

The principal argument is that, over the period 2002 to 2013, such China-driven disruption to the structures of commodity markets shifted the circumstances of insertion into the global economy for dozens of Southern natural resource–exporting states. Ballooning Chinese import demand for a range of metals and minerals was the primary driver behind a boom in prices, which presented Southern resource exporters with access to significant new flows of revenue, largely under the discretionary control of their governments. In turn, this loosened the disciplinary power exercised by the international financial institutions (IFIs) and global capital markets and provided states with a level of policy autonomy that allowed (but did not compel) them to substantively break with neoliberal economic orthodoxy for the first time in a generation.

Despite the PRC's relative abundance of domestic resources, after around 2002, the import demands of an ever-expanding economy reached the point where they began to have a major impact upon global markets across a range of commodities, especially in the metals and energy sectors. More than any bilateral links of trade or finance, it is here that China's rise has had the most profound effect upon the global South and, arguably, upon the global political economy as a whole. With China in the driver's seat, the longest and most pronounced commodity boom in a century transformed developmental prospects for exporters of these products. As demand rose amid constricted supply, governments found themselves in a much-improved bargaining position with transnational resource firms, facilitating their appropriation of a larger proportion of the extractive surplus via taxes, royalties, or ownership. Where states moved to press these advantages (and it should be noted that not all did), a larger slice of an expanding revenue pie meant the securing of a large new fiscal resource, substantially lessening or entirely negating the need for engagement with IFIs, Organisation for Economic Co-operation and Development (OECD) donor countries, or global capital markets—the three main transmission belts of neoliberalizing policy discipline.

Largely freed from such constraints, and with burgeoning national accounts, these states possessed the autonomy to pursue nationally defined development models. In some cases, such as that of Ecuador, much of the resource surplus was directed toward redistribution. In other countries, such as Argentina, programs that recalled earlier developmentalist strategies, favoring domestic industrialists, were attempted. Angola's government funneled its oil wealth into massive reconstruction projects, which blurred the lines between elite predation and nascent accumulation. Finally, other states—for instance, Zambia or Peru—did not experience any definitive break, as dominant elites (whether capitalists or state managers themselves) saw no reason to shift course. Crucially, however, in all these states and several more, political-economic strategy throughout the boom years was set domestically and was no longer circumscribed from without.

Though there are several twentieth-century examples of economic ascent comparable in speed to the rise of China, it is the combination of scale and rapidity that marks the latter as uniquely significant in world history (Coates and Luu 2012). The growing global strength of China, and a rising South generally, has, since the beginning of the century, led various observers to contrast a dynamic PRC with a United States in apparent decline (Wallerstein 2003; Jacques 2009; National Intelligence Council 2012, 2017; Rachman 2016). To some, the U.S. position looked threatened, even in the early to mid-2000s, with the wars in Iraq and Afghanistan, spiraling debt, and heavy dependence on China—and other "Asian drivers"—as creditors and as markets (Kaplinsky and Messner 2008; Arrighi 2007; compare to Hung 2008). The global financial crisis of 2008 to 2009 and the related European debt crisis which followed served to speed up the sense of a changing balance of economic power, with the GDP share of emerging and developing economies having exceeded that of the advanced economies for the first time in 2007, and with China becoming the world's largest economy, at least in terms of purchasing power parity, by 2015 (International Monetary Fund n.d.).

Though an increasing number of states aspire to emerging power status, the sheer heft of China's rise, its thirst for imports, and its huge currency reserves has given it a far more significant role than any of the other Southern nations as an actor and investor in the developing world, something which has not escaped scholarly attention. Literature that addresses the global significance of China's rise has been slower to arrive than studies focused on regional interactions, though some important steps have been taken in the former direction (Arrighi 2007; Frank 1998; Hung 2009, 2016) and recognition of the distinctive features and potential impacts of China-centered globalization is growing (Pieterse 2011; Henderson 2008; Henderson, Appelbaum, and Ho 2013; Bonini 2012; Jenkins 2018). My intention here is to build upon this work by giving a more detailed delineation of the recent and potential future developmental implications of China's rise, couched in terms of a world-historical perspective, which can incorporate both a theoretical sense of how change occurs at the global or systemic level with an empirical investigation of the uneven and particular national manifestations produced by, and in reaction to, these broader shifts.

Commodity markets and the states that supply them are my chosen focus, since it is here that China's transformative impact on the world-system and the developmental fortunes of the South has been most obvious to date. No claims are advanced as to the future directions of these relationships. However, illustrating the connections between Chinese ascendancy and the commodity boom (and then, in turn, the boom's political-economic implications for resource exporters) may serve as a demonstration of larger potential shifts to come, should the PRC continue to develop at anything like the pace of recent decades.

In this regard, it is now widely, if not universally, thought that China's continued economic development depends upon navigating a process of rebalancing—of shifting away from currently high levels of export and investment dependence toward a larger role for domestic consumption (Yang 2014; Pieterse 2015), a topic that has been on the agenda within China for longer than many appreciate (Breslin 2011a, 2011b). Taken together with a somewhat slowing GDP growth rate (from an average of 8.9 percent in 2010–2013 to 6.9 percent in 2014–2018), the force China exerts on commodity markets is unlikely to continue to strengthen at the pace that was observed over the boom years. Nevertheless, the fate of many of these markets is now tightly bound to that of China, which at this point is the world's number one energy consumer and oil importer and accounts for more than half of world metal consumption (Enerdata 2018; World Bank Group 2018a). Economic growth in the PRC is more resource intensive than in most other countries and will likely continue to be so, even if resource intensity declines, as is expected with efforts to rebalance and improve efficiency (Crowson 2018; Humphreys 2018).

At this point, it remains to be seen how successful China's efforts to grapple with rebalancing and reducing emissions will be, leaving future trends in commodity prices very much uncertain. It may be that other large Southern countries are able to pick up the baton in terms of driving demand, though India, for example, currently has a much less energy- and materials-intensive economy than China's, at a comparable level of GDP (Humphreys 2018). A recent World Bank study focusing on China as part of an "emerging market 7" group of developing states projects a baseline scenario to 2027 in which global metals demand continues to grow, albeit somewhat more slowly than in recent years, while energy demand growth is maintained at similar rates (Baffes et al. 2018). Of course, these states, and the rest of the world, will need to plan their development around a need to limit carbon emissions to avoid catastrophic climate change, which may have significant negative consequences for fossil fuel markets in particular (International Energy Agency 2015).

Some evidence suggests that the well-beaten path to development, which relies on the growth of manufacturing industries, is becoming much more difficult to traverse (Rodrik 2016). If this is the case, then it may call into question some important commonplace assumptions about how development can be achieved—and may make natural resource sectors even more significant. The hypothesis formulated by Raul Prebisch (1949) and Hans Singer (1950), which posits that, over the long run, prices for commodities will continue to decline relative to prices for manufactured goods, is a key plank in the established wisdom that manufacturing constitutes a much more promising basis to foster development and growth.[1] This trend, though, went into reverse during the boom, and, as of 2016, commodity terms of trade, overall, remained better than at any time from the early 1980s until the boom (Farooki and Kaplinsky 2013; Geronimi, Anani, and Taranco 2017). Figure 0.1 illustrates the trend for four metals (copper, aluminum, zinc, and lead), showing that, for all except aluminum (a special case, which is discussed in more detail in chapters 1 and 9), gains since the early 2000s have been historically exceptional—and prices remain considerably higher than in the two decades prior to the boom.

While it is too soon to tell whether such a situation is likely to endure, this apparently gloomy outlook for manufacturing and promising conditions

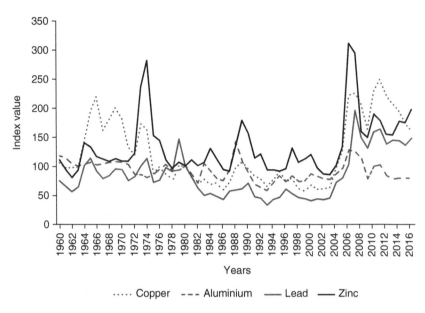

Figure 0.1 Terms of trade for selected metals versus manufactures, 1960–2016. Calculated from CEMOTEV "Primary Commodities" Access.

for some commodities have prompted a serious effort to consider how to best use extractive industries in support of diversification and industrialization, especially in the African context (Morris, Kaplinsky, and Kaplan 2012; Morris and Fessehaie 2014; Corkin 2012; Tordo et al. 2013; Ovadia 2016). This literature has grappled with some of the problems common with reliance on resource-powered growth, in that such sectors tend to be rather "enclavic" in nature. That is, they often create few jobs and operate as part of value chains in which most upstream activities (such as the manufacture of machinery) and downstream activities (such as processing and distribution) are undertaken in other parts of the world, leading to very few positive local impacts beyond the generation of revenue from extraction itself. In response, the literature recommends "local content" policies under which, as far as possible, backwards and forward linkages are created between the resource industry and the local economy—by, for example, stipulating minimum quotas for the proportion of goods and services to be supplied by domestic firms.

This book, however, is not principally aimed at identifying and mapping out the precise policy mix that resource-rich states ought to employ to make a success of their development. Nor is this a book about the "resource curse" thesis, which comes in various flavors but in most versions posits resource wealth as a developmental pathology, encouraging corruption and profligacy on the part of state elites (Auty 2002; Sachs and Warner 1995; Karl 1997; compare to Schrank 2004; Rosser 2007). The use and misuse of resource wealth—and strategies to maximize its developmental benefits—will certainly play an important role in the case studies presented in chapters 5 through 9. However, the main aims of this book are, first, to demonstrate the way in which the pull of Chinese commodity demand created the conditions for policy autonomy among resource-exporting states; second, to explain why, for better or worse, some of these states took advantage of their new circumstances to make a substantive break with neoliberal policy orthodoxy, while others did not; and third, to map out what I identify as five distinct patterns of policy response to the boom (three that involve a break with neoliberalism, two that do not), each corresponding to a particular complex of domestic forces, which can be categorized into five ideal types. In short, this is not, in the main, a book about which states succeeded and which failed in turning the boom to their developmental advantage, but about the nature of the forces—first at the global level and then at the local level—which created the space for the various attempts to do so.

Summary of Principal Arguments

My argument consists of two main claims. Claim A is derived from a view of the rise of China that is couched in a world-historical perspective and traces a path of causation from PRC industrialization and spiraling demand for resources to the disruption of world commodity markets, which in turn engenders change in the *global* structural conditions that constrain developmental possibilities among indebted resource-exporting states in the global South. Claim B entails a jump in scale to examine the ways in which *national* processes, actors, and structures respond to these shifting global conditions as they appear within the domestic sphere of resource-exporting countries.

Claim A. For states in the global South with substantial levels of public debt, a high export concentration in point-source natural resources (particularly fuels and minerals), imported in large and growing quantities by China, was a necessary but not sufficient condition for a break with neoliberal policy orientation during the years 2002 to 2013.

Claim B. For each resource-exporting state, whether such a break occurred—as well as its form and direction—depended primarily upon the dynamics of its domestic state–society relations.

The logical steps that underpin claim A are as follows:

1. Chinese demand was the principal force behind the commodities boom of 2002 to 2013.

2. Price increases were most significant in the metals, minerals, and fuel sectors, which can be linked to the profile of Chinese commodity demand and the nature of global supply constraints.[2]

3. High commodity prices tended to significantly improve resource-exporting states' fiscal and current account balances through increased sales and higher returns (and thus increased tax revenue) per unit.

4. Higher prices and constrained supply also made extractive industries more attractive for investment, even in regions previously ignored because of difficulties and high costs in extraction, poor infrastructure, or political instability. This strengthened the bargaining power of Southern governments relative to extractive firms and opened up the possibility of their retaining a greater percentage of the surplus from extraction. This was accomplished in many states by full or partial nationalization, joint ventures between parastatals and multinationals, or higher proportions of royalty and taxation revenues per unit on extracted products.

5. Governments that acted to maximize their resource revenues in this way saw markedly improved fiscal and balance of payments environments, ameliorating the need for engagement with IFIs. This effect was likely enhanced by the prospect of new investment and loans from China and other emerging economies, allowing governments to achieve better terms on loans and aid by triangulating between creditors and investors, both old and new.

6. This new fiscal space allowed governments of resource-exporting states to reject pressures toward neoliberalization—whether applied directly, via IFI and donor conditionality, or indirectly, via the preferences of global capital markets—and to adopt their own policies and national development strategies, which in many cases made for a substantive break with neoliberalization.

7. Not all resource-exporting states reacted to these new conditions by making such a break—meaning that natural resource exports were a necessary but not sufficient condition for this kind of shift. Reasons for this variation among resource-rich countries are taken up in the latter chapters of the book.

8. The argument for resource exports as a necessary condition for breaking with a neoliberalizing trajectory applies mostly to Southern states with high levels of public debt at the start of the boom, since these states were most dependent upon IFI loans and aid and therefore were most exposed to neoliberal discipline via the imposition of policy conditionality. States in the global South that have remained relatively debt free are likely to possess more leeway to autonomously set policy (as in the case of China itself).

9. Highly indebted Southern states that are not resource exporters, such as those that rely on exports of manufactured goods or agricultural products, did not experience these export price effects and so, all things being equal, will not have had any opportunities to move away from neoliberalism. One exception here is the special case of soybeans, which will be explored in chapter 5. Several agricultural commodities did experience a China-driven boom, to varying extents. But soy is the only one in which both the scale of impact *and* the particular structural features of the sector made it comparable to metals and fuels in terms of potential for generating policy autonomy.

Chapters 1 to 3 mainly concern claim A and aim to establish the theoretical and empirical basis for the steps outlined here. In first place, claim A relies upon the argument that commodity prices were substantially higher during the boom than in preceding decades and that this phenomenon was mainly due to rising Chinese demand. Chapter 1 looks at this claim by examining trends in China's industrialization and resource consumption, together with patterns in global commodity markets. The chapter also frames China's rise in a world-historical perspective, adopting Giovanni Arrighi's secular cycles of accumulation model as a lens through which the context of Chinese development and its consequences for the rest of the global South might be understood.

Having established the framework of overlapping cycles of global accumulation, chapter 2 applies this schema to trace the fortunes of resource exporters, and of Southern states more generally, through successive regimes of accumulation since the colonial era. I detail the features of the developmentalist consensus following World War II, under which Southern states exercised a degree of autonomy in setting developmental strategies and priorities behind walls of national regulation. I then discuss the circumstances leading to developmentalism's replacement by neoliberalism, which differed from the previous regime in attempting to regulate national political economies within far more constrictive parameters of liberalization.

For states that had become highly indebted during the 1970s—many resource exporters prominent among them—IFIs and international donors acted as the avatars of neoliberalization, pressuring for policy reform in exchange for loans and aid. Structural adjustment programs (SAPs) formalized these liberalizing constraints, which persisted (later in modified form, as Poverty Reduction Strategy Papers, or PRSPs) for as long as indebted states relied upon continuing lifelines from IFIs and donors. This sequence sets the scene for the onset of the commodity boom and claim A, where a hypothesized return to conditions of relative national autonomy appears to have been produced among hard commodity exporters by the fiscal consequences of the rise of China. Speculatively, it may be possible that these processes are merely one of the first indications that a larger reorientation of the global political economy is afoot, perhaps even of the same magnitude as that which produced the shift from Fordism–developmentalism to neoliberalism in the 1970s.[3] I return to these questions in the conclusion.

Chapter 3 assesses the merits of claim A through an application of the qualitative comparative analysis (QCA) Boolean analysis technique. QCA is a means of maximizing both the number of cases and the number of comparisons which can be made between cases, while maintaining a case-based approach that allows for an examination of each state in its own right (rather than a series of data points). Following a brief summary of the QCA process (which is discussed more extensively in the appendix), I then show that the findings support claim A—that a high export concentration in natural resources is a necessary condition for a break with neoliberalism on the part of a given Southern state. I also find that an absence of dependence on aid and concessional loans from OECD donors, or official development assistance (ODA), is a second necessary condition for this outcome, a theme I pick up again in chapter 8.

Chapters 4 through 9 explore the arguments around claim B, which states that whether a break with neoliberalism takes place—and the form and direction of any post-neoliberal turn that does occur—depends primarily upon the nature of relations between the state and social forces in a given country. I use this proposition as the basis for the formation of a typology of political-economic trajectories observed in resource-exporting states under the conditions of the commodity boom, which I introduce in chapter 4, before devoting a separate chapter to each of the five identified types. My concern is less with which of these possible paths may be better or worse for the countries in question than with mapping out their directions and how they came to be taken in the first place. The arguments that underpin this formulation are as follows:

1. Flowing from the consequences of claim A, highly indebted resource-exporting states in the global South have, since the beginning of the commodity boom, possessed a newfound ability to reorient their political-economic trajectories away from neoliberalization in pursuit of nationally defined development strategies. Any such shift depends upon successful efforts by the state to increase its share of extractive revenues, thus equipping itself with a substantial fiscal resource (and, often, hard currency reserves) that is independent of IFIs, donors, or capital markets.

2. During the neoliberal era of the 1980s and 1990s, the structural power of transnational forces acted to substantially shape and constrain both political-economic decision-making and the range of possible interactions among domestic social forces in Southern resource-exporting states. This is not to deny a role for local actors in struggles over the pace and form of neoliberalization, but it is an argument for pervasive parameterization toward neoliberal outcomes by IFIs, donors, and capital markets.

3. In effect, the autonomous fiscal resource provided by increasing state revenues from commodity exports may be employed as a kind of "force field," behind which domestic groups and configurations thereof struggle for ascendancy, free from the overriding structural leverage of transnational forces.[4]

4. The nature of the social group(s) able to gain political ascendancy in a given national space and to influence the flow of resource revenues to their own benefit will determine whether any break with neoliberalism occurs—and the direction it takes if it does.

5. Where productive and nationally oriented domestic capital gains primacy, a post-neoliberal settlement that directs extractive surplus toward

these groups is likely, producing a model with some similarities to the developmentalist projects of the post–World War II era, though with adjustments for the fact that multilateral economic regulation retains its neoliberal features. I label this configuration the *neodevelopmentalist type* (chapter 5).

6. Where movements based on popular class coalitions are able to win control of the state, the result is not a rejection of capitalism but a more favorable settlement with transnational extractive capital, with a significant proportion of extractive rents funneled toward social spending of various kinds and something of a move away from neoliberal regulatory forms. This trajectory is designated as the *extractivist-redistributive type* (chapter 6).

7. In cases where no large and autonomous local business class exists, reaction to the opportunities provided by the commodity boom depends principally upon the actions of state elites. Two distinct trajectories may result.

First, in those states where political elites are not influenced by a legacy of dependence upon flows of aid, state managers will be less cautious in attempting to control and allocate larger quantities of resource rents. In such cases, which in some respects resemble the rentier state model, rent-seeking and predation may be prevalent, but this does not rule out the operation of circuits of accumulation as a consequence of the level of resource revenue flowing through the global economy. This is the *extractivist-oligarchic type* (chapter 7).

In the other type of state-led case, a form of neoliberalism driven by the priorities of donor agencies will persist where political elites' power has historically been built upon a web of patronage flowing through the state from international aid, loans, and nongovernmental organization activities. Here, state managers will be reluctant to risk these relationships, which have to this point provided the material basis for their rule. This is the *donor-dependent orthodoxy type* (chapter 8).

8. In those states where a domestic capitalist class fraction with extensive ties to transnational (particularly Northern) capital attains or retains dominance, neoliberalism will persist, in line with the interests of this domestic–transnational alliance. This I call the *homegrown orthodoxy type* (chapter 9). Chapter 9 also considers the important case of Jamaica, an exporter of bauxite (the raw material used to produce aluminum). Because China, over the boom years, was able to meet a large proportion of its bauxite and aluminum demand with domestic sources, the aluminum

market did not experience the same boom conditions as was seen with other metals. Jamaica thus serves as a counterfactual case, demonstrating that the key condition enabling breaks with neoliberalism was not natural resources per se but a natural resource sector that experienced a surge in import demand from China.

Chapter 10 concludes by placing China's rise in the context of the *longue durée*, as a means of assessing its significance alongside other historical shifts in the topography of global capitalism and of pointing to possible future directions. Clearly, there is absolutely no guarantee that the PRC's long run of rapid growth will continue, and predictions of a so-called hard landing have become increasingly common in recent years. In the short to medium term, China faces worries over stock market turbulence and the inflation of a real estate bubble. On a longer timescale, the task of rebalancing the PRC's economy toward a domestic consumption–driven model seems more pressing than ever, though this involves multiple challenges. Should the current leadership or its successors succeed in squaring this circle, or in finding alternative means of sustaining rapid accumulation— massive infrastructural investment abroad appears to be a key new strategy—it seems likely that the processes highlighted in this research would constitute simply the first stirrings of a pervasive disruption to the circuits of capitalism across the world-system.

Even so, given the various barriers that lie ahead, it would be premature to assert that China will continue to grow at pace, pulling commodity exporters—and perhaps others—along in a manner that would foster their policy autonomy and bankroll their development strategies in the long run. As of 2018, with prices having softened in the past half decade, several natural resource exporters are finding themselves once again in need of external financial assistance—and once more exposed to the discipline of donors and IFIs. Nevertheless, China's pivotal role in the longest and largest commodity boom since the nineteenth century has established that resource exporters now depend upon this new pole of the global economy not just for markets or investment capital but also for their very ability to set policy independently of Northern demands.

CHAPTER I

World Markets in China's Wake

T here is no doubt that the world experienced a commodity boom in the years 2002 through 2013, with a brief dip in 2009 in response to the global financial crisis. Only two other periods in the past century may be described as commodity booms, though neither matches the 2000s vintage for either length or magnitude.[1] This would be true even if the 2002–2008 period were considered alone (Helbling 2008; Farooki 2012). It is hardly surprising that few analysts predicted the scale or durability of the boom (Conceição and Marone 2008), given the uniqueness of the period. During the initial boom years, analysts regularly predicted that the price cycle would likely soon come to an end (see, for example, International Monetary Fund 2006, chap. 5; United Nations Conference on Trade and Development 2006, 25; Suni 2007) or assumed that prices would not rise again following the global financial crisis (Bremmer and Johnston 2009).

The recovery of hard commodity prices in the 2009–2013 period, despite continued stagnation in the global North, is evidence that commodity price drivers had been transformed—to the extent that it makes less sense to speak of a temporary boom (as previously occurred in the early 1950s and mid-1970s) than of a commodities supercycle (a rise in prices over perhaps a decade or more), or possibly even a structural break (a longer-term shift in relative prices, in this case, between those for commodities and those for manufactured goods). The 2002–2013 boom may well be the first generalized commodities supercycle in recorded history (Farooki and Kaplinsky 2013, 57, 67–68; compare with Erten and Ocampo 2013).[2]

An analysis of China's evolving place in global commodity markets shows that it is now the central motor that has propelled this transformation for a range of raw materials, particularly most metals but, increasingly, fuels as well.[3] China's thirst for resources was the major driver of booming prices in these markets over the early twenty-first century, and their fortunes continue to be strongly bound to those of China even after the end of the boom.

These global shifts enabled resource-exporting states in the South to resist the disciplinary pressures of transnational capital and to institute alternative policies and development strategies during the boom years. In the first instance, this is obviously related to increased revenue from both higher prices and expanded volumes of sales. More than this, however, with many existing natural resource deposits nearing exhaustion, increasing global demand sparked a new wave of investment in extractive industries across the global South, with firms forced to consider locations that previously had been discounted owing to some combination of extraction costs, political instability, poor infrastructure, or geographic remoteness from the intended market (Klare 2012; Moyo 2012).

China and Chinese firms had a direct role to play in this, with major investments in the extractive industries of Mongolia, Brazil, Ecuador, the Democratic Republic of the Congo, Guinea, South Sudan, Papua New Guinea, and Angola, among many others.[4] Chinese investments have extended far beyond extractives, though, into transport, power generation, real estate, and agriculture—one estimate puts total investments in the South at more than $500 billion over the 2005–2013 period (Scissors 2018). China's state-owned banks lent $136 billion to African governments and state-owned enterprises (SOEs) alone from 2000 to 2017 (School of Advanced International Studies 2018).

The debate around China's direct impact on the rest of the global South—via investment, loans, construction, and trade—is already well advanced (Brautigam 2009, 2015; Lee 2017; Hurley, Morris, and Portelance 2018). The intention of this book is to focus instead on the rise of China's indirect impact on Southern resource-rich states via the changes wrought in global markets for their main exports. The result over the course of the commodity boom was not only higher absolute revenues for such states but also increases in their bargaining power relative to multinational firms and thus in their ability to retain a larger proportion of an expanding pie for the setting and realization of nationally defined development goals. To this end, some states pushed through full or quasi nationalizations of resource industries (Kaup 2010; Romero 2012), acquired larger stakes in their extractive operations (Krusekopf 2015), or signed much more favorable contracts with multinationals (Escribano 2013). At the very least, most upped their royalty and taxation rates on extraction (see Lungu 2008a; Nem Singh 2012). These moves, in turn, potentially provided Southern states with revenue streams outside the control of global capital and the international financial institutions (IFIs), creating space for greater discretion in policy making.

The China Effect on Commodity Markets

Figure 1.1 shows price indexes since 1960 for metals, energy, and agricultural commodities, in constant 2010 dollars. Prices began to rise for all three groups around 2002, with a steeper gradient in metals and energy. By the mid-2000s, real prices for metals and energy were higher than previous peaks (in the 1960s for metals and the 1970s for energy) and continued to climb until 2007–2008, at which point both categories experienced sharp

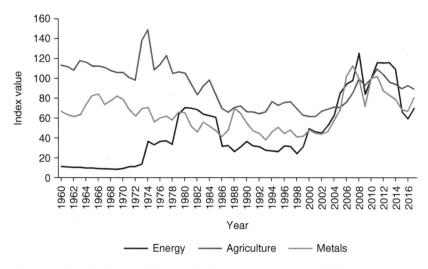

Figure 1.1 Historical commodity price indexes, in constant 2010 dollars.
Source: World Bank, Commodity Price Data—Pink Sheet Data.

dips, concurrent with the global financial crisis. Prices rebounded strongly before beginning to fall off in 2012 for metals and in 2014 for energy, with a slight strengthening in 2017, leaving both close to or above their previous peak levels, and certainly higher than in the years immediately preceding the boom. Surprisingly, the post-2008 resurgence came despite widespread economic torpor across most of the global North, providing a clue that commodity prices were now being driven by forces other than conditions in these traditionally dominant markets.

Copper, in particular, is a significant case in highlighting the power of China as a commodity demand driver. Copper is so widely used in cables, pipes, and almost all electronic devices, with few good substitutes,[5] that copper price movements have long tended to be good predictors of global economic activity, to the extent that it has earned the nickname "Dr. Copper" for its forecasting abilities (*Economist* 2011). Nevertheless, as figure 1.2 shows, copper price movements over the period correlate much more closely with shifts in net import demand from China than from the Group of Seven countries, particularly after 2006. Though the fall in price seen in 2009 coincides with declining G7 imports (while Chinese imports are largely stagnant), price movements thereafter closely mirror changes in Chinese imports rather than those of the G7.

Figure 1.2 Copper prices compared to net G7 and Chinese copper imports. Calculated from Chatham House Resourcetrade.earth database and World Bank, Commodity Price Data—Pink Sheet Data.

China's rapid, materials-intensive development in the 1995–2002 period already placed it as a highly significant consumer of most metals and as the most important factor in new demand growth (Yu 2011). However, China has substantial reserves of many commodities, and so much of the new demand in this earlier period was met by expanding domestic production. As this growth began to lag behind consumption, China was forced to import ever-larger quantities of key resources, the effects of which began to manifest themselves in rising global prices around the middle of the last decade.

Figure 1.3 gives an indication of China's evolving role as an importer in the three largest base metal markets (iron ore, copper, and aluminum). In 2002, China already accounted for 18 percent of global copper imports, but it was a less significant importer of the other two metals, where domestic reserves were greater. The most striking growth in terms of import share is seen in iron ore, where China's imports moved to 64 percent of the world total by 2013. In copper, the increase in share of imports is less pronounced but still significant, reaching 30 percent in 2013. However, this was in the context of a world market that grew much faster over the boom years, from $39.8 billion in 2002 to $227 billion in 2013 for copper, compared to movement from $122.7 billion to $163 billion for iron ore (Chatham House n.d.). China played a much more minor role in aluminum

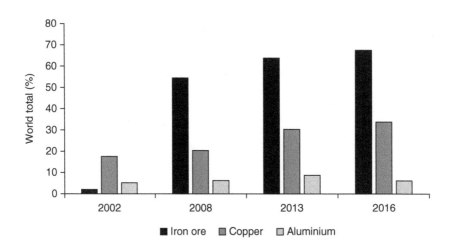

Figure 1.3 China base metal imports as a share of world total. Calculated from Chatham House Resourcetrade.earth database.

trade, with imports rising from 5.2 percent to 8.6 percent of world totals between 2002 and 2013. This is an important differential, which I will return to in chapters 9 and 10. Figures for 2016 are provided as evidence of China's continuing centrality to these commodity markets, even in a post-boom context.

Figure 1.4 provides another view of these markets by comparing the change in Chinese import demand for each metal against that of the rest of the world in dollar values, both over the whole period (2002–2013) and since the global financial crisis (2008–2013). Chinese demand was very clearly the most important driver of these markets in the postcrisis years in particular, compensating for weak performance elsewhere. Over the whole of the boom years, the iron ore sector again stands out, with imports to China surging by more than $100 billion, even while elsewhere they fell by $61.5 billion. Though rest of the world's demand for copper was relatively strong over 2002–2013, China alone accounted for a little under half the global total, while, again, China's role in aluminum appeared to be less significant.

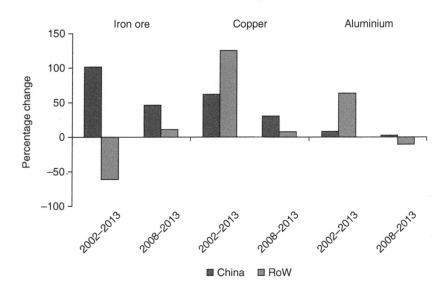

Figure 1.4 Chinese demand compared to that of the rest of the world (in billions of dollars). Change in industrial metals imports, 2002–2013, calculated from Chatham House Resourcetrade.earth database.

For energy commodities (principally oil, coal, and natural gas), the picture is somewhat different. China's share of global energy consumption rose substantially, up from 12 percent in 2002 to 22 percent in 2013, overtaking the United States to become the world's largest energy consumer from 2009 onward. Coal overwhelmingly remained China's most important fuel source, with the People's Republic of China accounting for more than half of global consumption in 2013 (Enerdata 2018). Even with oil making up less than one-fifth of China's energy usage, according to some estimates the PRC surpassed the United States in 2014 to become the world's largest oil importer (U.S. Energy Information Administration 2015), a significant milestone, given China's status as the world's fourth-largest oil producer and the fact that the country was still a net exporter in the early 1990s (Stang 2014).

Natural gas is a less important though growing factor in the Chinese energy mix. Consumption rose by an average of 15 percent per annum over the 2000s, and although this began from a low base, China became the third-largest market for gas in 2013 (U.S. Energy Information Administration 2015; Enerdata 2018). Even though, globally, the majority of natural gas is transported via pipelines and so is not traded on world markets, the high degree of substitutability between energy commodities, as compared to metals, means that price movements in natural gas are heavily influenced by the global oil (and, to a lesser extent, coal) trade.

Overall, China has become the major demand driver in energy markets over recent years, accounting for 55 percent of consumption growth from 2002 to 2013 and becoming the biggest net energy importer by 2012 (Enerdata 2018). It also seems likely that China's centrality within energy markets will be maintained in the future, with India's role also becoming increasingly significant (World Bank 2018). Until recently, trends in the PRC's energy intensity (measured as primary energy consumption divided by gross domestic product) were somewhat higher than those seen in South Korea at similar levels of GDP (see table 1.1).[6] Energy intensity in China has now begun to drop, suggesting that income elasticity of energy consumption may be starting to fall off, likely because of structural changes to the economy and efforts to increase efficiency in line with emissions targets. Nevertheless, energy intensity remains high today in comparison to other states at similar levels of GDP (table 1.2). An International Energy Agency (2017) projection, based on China's implementation of current policy plans, has China's energy intensity falling through 2040. However,

TABLE 1.1
South Korea and China energy intensity (in British thermal units) at comparable levels of gross domestic product

	South Korea			China		
Year	Energy intensity (1,000 Btu/dollars 2010 GDP purchasing power parity)	Per capita GDP (constant 2010 U.S. dollars)	Year	Energy intensity (1,000 Btu/dollars 2010 GDP purchasing power parity)	Per capita GDP (constant 2010 U.S. dollars)
1980	9.1	3,700	2007	9.0	3,488
1981	8.8	3,904	2008	8.6	3,805
1982	8.2	4,162	2009	8.5	4,142
1983	7.9	4,644	2010	8.3	4,561
1984	7.5	5,066	2011	8.3	4,972
1985	7.5	5,405	2012	8.1	5,336
1986	7.4	5,953	2013	7.5	5,722
1987	7.3	6,629	2014	7.0	6,108
1988	7.4	7,346	2015	6.6	6,497

Sources: World Bank, World Development Indicators; U.S. Energy Information Administration, "Open Data."

TABLE 1.2

Energy intensity for China and selected economies, 2015

Nation	2015 per capita GDP (constant 2011 U.S. dollar purchasing power parity)	2015 energy intensity (1,000 Btu/dollars 2010 GDP purchasing power parity)
China	13,570	6.6
Brazil	14,703	4.3
Indonesia	10,368	2.6
Thailand	15,252	4.9

Sources: World Bank, World Development Indicators; U.S. Energy Information Administration, "Open Data."

even assuming slowing GDP growth, these forecasts foresee the PRC becoming the largest consumer of oil and the biggest source of demand growth for natural gas globally, as these fuels (along with renewables) are increasingly adopted as somewhat cleaner alternatives to coal. We will revisit these issues in the concluding chapter.

China's Rise in World-Historical Perspective

Although empirical observation of the effects of China's growing global weight will be undertaken principally at the national level, I adopt a theoretical framing that views these national shifts as ultimately the product of transformation at the global level, requiring explanation in terms of systemic change. I rely heavily on Arrighi's formulation of the world-system, especially in its temporal aspect (Arrighi 1994; Arrighi and Silver 1999; Sewell 2012).[7] In particular, I use the idea of a series of overlapping secular cycles of accumulation as a kind of baseline to an ever-evolving global political economy and a basis for understanding China's rise within the current world-historical context.

According to this schema, the United States has been the central dynamo in the accumulation cycle that began at the end of the nineteenth century and superseded the previous, British-led phase during the first half of the twentieth (Arrighi 1994, 277–84). Despite the 2008 crash, the United States currently retains its position at the center of global capitalism, as the largest economy (at market exchange rates) and the holder of the world reserve currency (Hung 2008; World Bank n.d.). Nevertheless, since the turn of the twenty-first century, for the large numbers of Southern states whose economies depend upon the export of natural resources, it is China rather than the United States that now constitutes the primary driver for the most important processes of accumulation in which they participate.

Clearly, the implications of China's rise are not confined to commodity markets or resource-exporting states. Several authors have focused, in particular, on China's evolving relationships in Africa (for example, Brautigam 2009, 2015; Mohan and Lampert 2013), Latin America (Jilberto and Hogenboom 2012; Gallagher 2016; Fornes and Mendez 2018), and Southeast Asia (Glassman 2010; Reilly 2012). More broadly, China and Chinese institutions' growing influence are evident in development finance (Brautigam and Gallagher 2014; Kaplan 2016; Chin and Gallagher 2019) and investment (Kaplinsky and Morris 2009; Gonzalez-Vicente 2012), as an economic competitor (Álvarez and Claro 2009; Jenkins 2012; Edwards and Jenkins 2015), and as a possible economic model (Zhao 2010; Breslin 2011b). The scale of China's reach and impact is already clear in reconfigurations of global production networks (Asmeh and Nadvi 2013; Gereffi 2014) and is beginning to be felt in currency markets (Prasad 2017; Subacchi 2017) and in the security domain (Alden and Large 2015).[8]

Most recently, China's growing world role has become even more prominent with the rollout of the hugely ambitious Belt and Road Initiative (BRI), an umbrella term covering a wide range of projects—in transport, energy, communications, and industrial production—centered on Eurasia but extending into parts of Africa, Latin America, and the Pacific (Cai 2017). Linked to BRI is the increasing penetration of Chinese capital into Europe, including, for example, Chinese SOEs' purchase of ports, amounting to around one-tenth of European capacity (Johnson 2018), and substantial investment in advanced manufacturing, with a view to technological upgrading (Drahokoupil 2017, 8–9).

As much as the PRC's global significance across these fields is now widely acknowledged, a linked debate exists—both within and beyond academia—on the more speculative terrain of what these shifts may augur for the future. Of particular interest has been the question of whether China might at some stage challenge the U.S.-centered (or more broadly "Western") global economic and geopolitical order. (A small sample of a by now vast literature on this includes Arrighi [2007]; Ikenberry [2008]; Jacques

[2009]; Hung [2016]; Nye [2015]; and Rachman [2016].) Another strand of discussion places China at the head of a group of emerging powers in a "rise of the rest" (Amsden 2001; Zakaria 2008), these days most often identified with Brazil, Russia, India, China, and (since 2010) South Africa (BRICS), though sometimes extended to other large Southern states such as Mexico, Indonesia, Nigeria, and Turkey (Pieterse 2011; BBC 2014). Such talk was boosted significantly in the aftermath of the 2008 crisis, which shook confidence in the Anglo-American model of capitalism while throwing into relief the relative economic successes of the four original BRIC countries, whose economies were said to all diverge from Washington Consensus policy in various ways (Ban and Blyth 2013). In 2009, the BRICs (later joined by South Africa) became a formal institution, organizing regular summits and eventually inaugurating the New Development Bank and the Contingent Reserve Arrangement. Some see these institutions, along with the China-led Asian Infrastructure Investment Bank, as potential Southern-led alternatives to the IFIs (Griffith-Jones 2014; Stuenkel 2016, chap. 4) and as part of an emerging BRICS collective financial statecraft (Roberts, Armijo, and Katada 2018). Others are much more skeptical, relating the BRICS' role to the older idea (not coincidentally associated with Brazil) of large developing states as "sub-imperialist" powers (Garcia and Bond 2017). Somewhat similar arguments are also made with regard to China itself, with its rise seen as potentially buttressing rather than ending the era of U.S. hegemony (Hung 2016, 173–4; Fischer 2015).

These latter works are perhaps more reflective of the current tone of a debate that has cooled somewhat on the extent to which China and other rising powers have the potential to upend the global order. While the geographies of global trade, production, and finance have all become much more "polycentric" or "pluripolar" in recent years (Horner and Nadvi 2018; Grabel 2018), excited talk of North–South convergence (Spence 2011) and the rise of the BRICS (Carmody 2013) has been dampened in recent years by recession in Brazil and Russia, political turmoil in South Africa and Brazil, and slowing GDP growth in China (Bremmer 2017; Roubini 2014; Tisdall 2016). At the time of this writing, balance of payments crises in Turkey, Argentina, and Pakistan threaten to spread to a host of other emerging markets (Jones 2018; Jamal 2019), and an incipient U.S.–China trade war could cause serious economic disruption at a global level (Kuo 2018). China itself faces major challenges in resolving the mounting contradictions in its economic model (Pieterse 2015; Hung 2016, chap. 7), while it is simultaneously being touted as the potential leader of a new round of globalization, especially through the BRI (Liu and Dunford 2016; Warner 2017).

Such swings between optimism and skepticism should demonstrate the dangers of presentism and of reading long-term trends from what may be relatively unenduring phenomena. The remainder of this book, therefore, is aimed at highlighting the new centrality of China as a driver of transformations in the structure of the global political economy, by revealing the scope and scale of effects stemming from shifts that have already occurred. The direct relations between China and the rest of the global South—along dimensions of finance, investment, and trade, among others—have clearly become highly significant over the past two decades. These will all necessarily play a part in the analysis to come. My focus, however, will be on commodity markets, the area in which the extent of PRC's gravitational pull is perhaps most readily apparent but in which the second-order implications of these changes, in opening new space for policy autonomy on the part of resource-exporting states, have yet to be systematically laid out.

It is clearly too soon to make the leap to claims of impending Chinese hegemony, and I do not seek to assert that these dynamics represent the beginnings of a Chinese-led cycle of accumulation.[9] But if we were to ask what the embryonic stages of such a shift might look like, the evolving contours of the relationship between the PRC and the global economy certainly appear somewhat similar to previous episodes (Bonini 2012). There are, of course, also instances where rapid growth of a single large economy has rewired key components of the global political-economic circuitry without that economy rising to hegemonic status, most notably in the case of twentieth-century Japan (Bunker and Ciccantell 2007). For current purposes, attention to the ways in which such shifts have played out in the past can lay the groundwork for an initial thinking through of the kinds of changes we might expect to detect among Southern resource-exporting states during the commodity boom years.

Change in the periphery is often sidelined in sweeping world-historical accounts, which prefer to focus on the rise and fall of hegemons and imply that such cycles simply leave the world outside core centers of accumulation in a state of unchanging or perhaps increasing exploitation. Of those studies which do concentrate on the South, Bunker and Ciccantell (2005), examining very long-term change in the Brazilian Amazon, assume a deepening peripheralization of raw materials–producing areas with each new accumulation cycle, in a manner rather reminiscent of Frank's (1966) original development of underdevelopment thesis. However, for O'Hearn (2005), development or ascendancy within the world-system for a given state is blocked at each historical conjuncture by a range of barriers to accumulation, a situation faced by aspiring hegemon and periphery alike. Advance, stagnation, or decline for all states in common then comes as a result of more or less successful iterative attempts to solve the various problems of accumulation.

This allows for agency on the part of peripheral governments, despite a certain parameterizing of available options by systemic constraints, partially constructed and imposed through the actions of both the ascendant economy and the current hegemon, though loosened somewhat in periods of systemic shift. In this, O'Hearn builds on Haydu's (1998) earlier work on reiterative problem solving and on Senghaas's (1985) study of small European states that were able to "piggyback" on British accumulation processes in the nineteenth century. This belies some of the more familiar static conceptions of the world-system, in which exceptional individual cases of ascendancy have no bearing on the relative positions of peripheral nations, which are condemned to underdevelopment by the very fact of their low position in the hierarchy. It is worth quoting O'Hearn's alternative formulation at length here, since it meshes extremely well with the notion that underpins my central argument, of the loosening of neoliberal external constraints via Chinese disruption of global commodity markets:

The precise nature of an outcome of, say, crisis and recovery, hegemonic shift, and local position within the newly organized world-system is contingent, not only on relative positions of regional actors but on the strategies they choose at crucial junctures. In particular, localities are not just subjugated into a path-dependent position of underdevelopment. Rather, they have limited options, some of which are worse and some of which are less worse and, just possibly, some of which are actually better. These switching points are probably more likely to occur during periods of hegemonic shift when world-system positions are changing and some localities are being reintegrated into new roles that are defined by the new regional or hegemonic powers. In these situations, it may even be possible for certain regions to "hook on" to core accumulation processes and to achieve upward mobility within the world-system. (O'Hearn 2005, 133)

China may not (yet) be rising to hegemonic status, but it is already far more than a regional power, and there can be no doubt that the world's economic center of gravity has shifted substantially in the first two decades of the twenty-first century. Nowhere is this more evident than in commodity markets, especially in metals and minerals. With prices having declined, albeit not to preboom levels, causing severe political and economic disruption in many resource exporters, it is not clear that the commodity boom represents a switching point of the kind described by O'Hearn. Even if the boom has definitively ended, however, the period stands as a kind of prototype of exactly the kind of spatially uneven reconfiguration we would expect to see play out alongside any future process of hegemonic shift or other equally large-scale systemic transformation.[10]

Taking up O'Hearn's points, the rest of this book serves as a theoretical exploration and empirical illustration of the way in which constraints on local actors are differentially tightened and relaxed by such shifts, the boom allowing (though not compelling) Southern resource exporters to "hook on" to China-centered accumulation processes and achieve, if not upward mobility, then at least a far greater degree of freedom from the disciplinary structural power of the IFIs and the whims of global capital flows. The new resource-powered spaces of nationally autonomous decision-making that arose during the 2002–2013 period were breaks with previous economic orthodoxy, which would have been all but impossible in the prior decade. With the end of the boom, some of these experiments have been defeated electorally (as in Argentina) or descended into chaos (as in Venezuela), though others (such as Bolivia and Kazakhstan) have more or less endured, to varying degrees. But even if commodity prices encounter a precipitous and enduring fall in the near future, the range of policy heterodoxy and development strategies that the commodity boom unleashed surely would be worthy of study, even in the event that, as with the New Economic International Order in the 1970s, they prove to be relatively fleeting phenomena.

Chapter 2 takes the world-historical framework elaborated in this chapter and attempts to incorporate its insights into an examination of the fortunes of commodity-exporting states, and of the global South more broadly, across multiple eras of successive global regimes. In tracing the shifting developmental constraints and openings that have waxed and waned for resource exporters in each era, the aim is twofold. First, the goal is to illuminate the specifications and sources of neoliberal discipline under which such states have labored in recent decades. Second, understanding the newfound ability of resource-exporting states to transcend neoliberal conditionality under the circumstances of the 2002–2013 commodity boom requires an understanding of the distinct regulatory forms of pre-neoliberal regimes—particularly of the post–World War II settlement that I refer to as Fordism–developmentalism, under which the scope for nationally autonomous policy making was far wider.

CHAPTER II

Natural Resources and Development Under Shifting Global Regimes

I n the global South, notions of development have been bound up with commodity production and export ever since the colonial era.[1] Although the exploitation of natural resources and crops was not always a primary motivation for European imperialism (Hobsbawm 1989, 66–68), in most cases, much of the "development" seen in colonial possessions consisted of building the necessary infrastructure to produce, transport, store, and export primary commodities (Rodney 1972, 209). For Immanuel Wallerstein, commenting on the identification of the French term *mise en valuer* ("making into value") with the colonial concept of development, development "was a set of concrete actions effectuated by Europeans to exploit and draw profit from the resources of the non-European world" (Wallerstein 2005, 1263).

Such processes are linked to the idea of a "civilizing" European mission, most easily identified with the "white man's burden" of the scramble for Africa but also very much visible in the earlier colonizations of the Americas. Though the civilizing trope is most obviously associated with social change, particularly with the spread of Christianity, economic development (that is, the exploitation of locally available resources) also could be seen as a task fundamental to human advancement, following Enlightenment principles. Exploitation of untapped minerals and agricultural land, while clearly advancing the material interests of the colonizers, could be dressed up as a progressive historical mission, borne by Europeans in the face of a seeming inability of locals to carry out the task.[2] Key to the success of this mission was the coercive power of Europeans to expand territorial claims and to exploit people and resources found in other areas of the globe. By the end of the nineteenth century, the result was the incorporation—unevenly and largely on European terms—of most of Africa, Asia, and the Americas into a global system of production and trade (Wolf 1982).

This situation set the initial conditions around which the problems of development (as now understood) have crystallized. A policy of "making into value" of the resources contained in areas of the world newly integrated into the global system—whether under formal colonial control or not—lined up closely with Ricardo's notion of comparative advantage. The South, trading with a technologically advantaged industrializing North, was comparatively well endowed with land, natural resources, and, in some cases, the potential for cheap labor.[3]

For many critical scholars, the persistence beyond independence of this colonial division of labor, whereby manufactured goods produced in the metropole (or center) are exchanged for primary commodities grown or extracted in the colony (or periphery), lies at the root of explaining global disparities of wealth and income among regions.[4] In Latin America, this argument had been anticipated in the stance of economic nationalists during the nineteenth century (Grosfoguel 2000), though it was in the decades following World War II that its intellectual underpinnings were fully fleshed out, in the form of structuralism.

Central to the structuralist case was the Prebisch–Singer thesis that terms of trade for commodities (and for commodity-exporting states) tend to decline over time. The basis of this claim is a low income elasticity of demand for commodities, especially when compared to manufactured goods. As incomes increase, demand for commodities (which are more likely to be necessities) grows slowly, while that for manufactured goods (approximating a category of luxuries) rises more quickly, with a consequent impact on relative prices. Thus, rising income in a commodity-exporting peripheral state results in ever-larger volumes of manufactured imports, creating trade deficits that, as relative prices continue to erode, require ever greater quantities of commodity exports to make up the shortfall. For center countries, the opposite holds: as incomes grow, imports of commodities increase, but the cost of these is amply covered by the trend toward higher prices for manufactured goods.[5] A second structuralist argument, again empirically based, relates to the instability generated by the reliance of most peripheral states on a narrow range of commodity exports, leaving them vulnerable to price swings, unlike industrialized economies, which tend toward diversified exports and thus are less exposed to price movements in any one market (Prebisch 1949; Singer 1950, 1984; Saad-Filho 2005).

For structuralists, then, peripheral pursuit of comparative advantage by maximizing production in primary products is a self-defeating strategy, which is bound to widen rather than to close the gap with the industrialized center. The proposed alternative strategy of import substitution industrialization (ISI) had its antecedents in mercantilism and in Friedrich List's infant industry protection but was new insofar as it presented an explicit program for correcting the North–South developmental imbalance. Given the limitations of commodity-based development shown in the Prebisch–Singer thesis, industrialization seemed the only path capable of reversing these inequalities. Establishing and expanding manufacturing industries would, in principle, correct for declining terms of trade, diversify the economy, and, by generating formal employment and urbanization, create an internal market of consumers, reducing reliance upon the vagaries of the world market. In fact, a concentration on developing domestic markets was crucial to the whole effort, since, initially at least, there seemed little possibility of penetrating the markets of the center. Given low productivity levels and a lack of technology, peripheral goods were likely to be of poor quality, with high production costs, and stood little chance of competing with center states' manufactures on equal terms.

The solution was to turn inward, satisfying national demand for previously imported manufactures with domestic production. Since local firms tended to be just as unable to compete at home as they were abroad, and because they lacked the requisite capital and technology to develop spontaneously, state intervention was required in order that domestic infant industries could be protected and incubated before being (eventually) readied for competition. A mixture of tariffs, multiple exchange rates, subsidies, demand management, infrastructure development, and cheap credit generally were the most important ingredients of ISI strategies (Baer 1972; Hirschman 1968). In many areas, Northern manufacturing firms were invited to produce for the domestic market behind high tariff walls (Cooper 2002, 100). In the face of low levels of domestic private capital, the state often was the only national entity capable of marshaling large concentrations of capital. States would therefore also intervene more directly, sometimes as monopsony buyers and marketers of exports (with the goal of saving for industrialization efforts) and also as owners of state-owned enterprises, particularly in heavy industries such as steel.

In Latin America, and to a lesser extent elsewhere, ISI had in fact preceded its postwar formalization, as a strategic policy response to the unequal global division of labor (Saad-Filho 2005, 130–31). Basic industrialization proceeded with little planning, initially as a consequence of rising demand for bulky, low-technology goods, which were uneconomical to import, and then as the Great Depression and World War II reduced the flow of manufactured imports to most areas of the South and thus stimulated domestic production to meet demand. However, the post–World War II period saw the first systematic effort to understand and counter inequitable features inherent to the global division of labor. In many ways, this turn was a natural complement to decolonization in much of Asia and Africa, bringing to the fore the notion of a third world as a complex of regions with shared characteristics and facing similar obstacles. Political independence for many states joined a rising tide of nationalist aspiration in the South, with the "second independence" of economic autonomy a priority goal for many (see, for instance, Freund 1981). In this era, the idea of development still very much corresponded with an Enlightenment belief in progress, though this now meant industrialization—large-scale socioeconomic transformation that would catapult Southern states to levels of material prosperity similar to those seen in the developed states of the North.

From the North, the influence of modernization theory meant that developing countries tended to be viewed simply as less advanced versions of their developed world counterparts, with states following each other in replicating a series of nearly identical steps on a road to development. The end goal, and developed status, was a society and economy that looked like those of Western Europe and, especially, of the United States (Bernstein 1971; Robinson 2002). Supported by the international financial institutions (especially the World Bank), the proposition of development in the image of a prosperous United States was a key plank of post–World War II U.S. hegemony in the South and served as a bulwark against Soviet influence and more radical third world nationalism (Arrighi and Silver 1999, chap. 3). Though development was therefore a quasi-universal project, state managers in each case were afforded relative freedom to manage the process at the national level. A variety of different development strategies could, in this way, be accommodated within a U.S.-led global regime, which set fixed exchange rates and used the International Monetary Fund (IMF) as a means of propping up the system through short-term loans (McMichael 1996).

The Soviet Union did, however, provide another possible model for Southern states, particularly given an impressive initial post–World War II record of industrial growth and its lack of colonial past.[6] U.S. efforts in the South often were clearly framed in terms of Cold War geopolitical competition. Nonetheless, state socialist countries (and those claiming to aspire to such status) tended to hold a view of development that stressed socioeconomic transformation via industrialization, managed at the national level. Though obviously diverging on matters such as property relations, state socialist developmentalism shared several features with predominant views in the West and, most importantly, could be accommodated within the postwar Bretton Woods regime.

Of course, not all states readily accepted U.S. or Soviet tutelage, and significant variations occurred in terms of both intention and implementation, even among those pledged to one sponsor or the other.[7] Nevertheless, combined with intellectual contributions from the South itself—importantly Latin American structuralism—a certain synthesis of development ideas coalesced into an "industrialization consensus" (Ocampo 2014, 296), a "development project" (McMichael 1996; 2000), or "embedded liberalism" (Ruggie 1982), which permitted various forms of government intervention in markets and showed a tolerance of national variation contrasting rather sharply with later neoliberalism.

Developmentalism, in this sense, can be viewed as half of a global regime of accumulation, with Fordism–Keynesianism as its Northern mirror. The latter proffered a class compromise that allowed wages to rise with productivity gains and, in most cases, instituted welfare states of one kind or another. High mass consumption as a norm, demand management, and automatic stabilizers helped to dampen both cyclical downturns and the likelihood of political radicalism. Analogous to class compromise in the North was an emerging North–South settlement. First, decolonization met the nationalist aspirations of Southern elites while institutionalizing the nation-state as the universal political unit underpinning the post–World War II international political and economic order. Such states were necessary for development projects to be delegated to national authorities, allowing for the prospect that economic as well as political autonomy might at some point be achieved (though the former was rarely realized). Third, access to the global market and, with it, Northern-style consumption was extended, though, unlike in the developed world, this reached only a minority of most Southern populations (George and Sabelli 1994, 147).

Although at this point structuralism and associated theories began to see specialization in natural resources as fundamentally incompatible with development, it was still envisaged that extractive industries would play an important role in supporting peripheral industrialization. Taxation of resource exports—usually large volumes produced by a small number of foreign companies at a limited number of locations—represented a far easier means of generating revenue than, for example, relying on tax receipts from households or domestic businesses, both logistically and given the small size of formal sectors in much of the South. The ability of the state to act as landlord was thus a means to concentrate relatively large quantities of capital, which could then be deployed toward ISI projects.

Again, these kinds of arrangements might be thought of as indicative of a North–South compromise. Southern states' demand for a larger slice of the pie was tolerable, so long as the pie continued to expand, which it did both generally (in terms of global growth) and more narrowly (in natural resource sectors), buoyed by postwar reconstruction and then the rise of Japan and Germany. Cold War fears also played a role in shaping Northern flexibility on this point. In Chile, for example—the home of *cepalista* structuralism—the imposition of royalty payments and profit taxes of 50 to 60 percent in the copper sector did lead the U.S. firms Anaconda and Kennecott to register complaints in Washington. However, geopolitical considerations in the wake of the Cuban Revolution dissuaded U.S. authorities from any kind of intervention, and both companies were still able to post average profits of 14 to 18 percent from 1955 to 1965 (Hellinger 2004a).

Even where partial nationalization took place, as, in the case of copper, occurred in both Chile and Zambia during the 1960s, such moves tended to be tolerated, provided that transnational extractive capital continued to maintain a profit (Larmer 2010). Indeed, as Larmer points out in relation to Zambia, the acquisition of a share of natural resource firms by states was often viewed in a positive light by transnational corporations. Governments' broader developmentalist goals were not necessarily out of line with profit maximization, and their involvement in the running of extractive enterprises might well help guard against more radical demands.

Breakdown of the Developmentalist Consensus

The United States was forced to abandon central features of the Fordist–developmentalist regime owing to an exhaustion of the potential for continued material expansion under Fordism and mounting pressures stemming from an associated growth of financialization. Productivity gains, which had allowed for both rising profits and wages, began to encounter diminishing returns, even as unionized labor was still powerful enough to continue pushing up pay and expanding welfare provisions. Meanwhile, sponsorship of nationally managed accumulation on the part of key allies, which underpinned U.S. hegemony, served to eventually undermine itself. Capital from the most successful examples of these national projects, West Germany and Japan, was able to adopt U.S. technological and organizational advances in combination with cheaper labor (Brenner 2003, 14–15).

By the late 1960s, increasing competition brought falling profit levels, particularly in the United States, which responded with a devaluation that signaled the first crack in the Bretton Woods system of fixed exchange rates. Concurrently, the growing Eurodollar market offered a means to deposit dollars outside U.S. restrictions. American businesses, allowed to operate within Europe with few restrictions, soon saw the advantages of banking in the less constrictive Eurodollar market rather than back in the United States. This essentially represented large-scale capital flight, coming in the midst of a fiscal crisis brought about by the twin expansionary currents of Lyndon Johnson's Great Society social spending and the Vietnam War (Strange 1987, 6–7).

Initially, U.S. responses to the crisis aimed at salvaging what was left of the Fordist regime by attempting to reflate the global economy back toward a path of material expansion. This course, though, contained within itself the seeds of its own destruction. The loose monetary policies of the 1970s, as well as the first of two oil shocks, produced stagflation, together with a massive increase in global liquidity, which eventually led to the continuance of U.S. hegemony by other, less stable means—namely, by an acceptance of the primacy of finance capital and a successful attempt to at least temporarily reassert U.S. power through an alliance with and channeling of such forces (Arrighi 1994, 300–10). Despite its apparent freeing of the United States from the balance of payments constraint, the movement away from the Bretton Woods fixed dollar–gold system to one of floating exchange rates, completed by 1973, widened the growing tendential gap between returns on productive and financial capital by opening up significant arbitrage possibilities. This growing systemic bias toward financialization meant that the loose monetary policies of the mid-1970s, bringing with them a liquidity designed to reinvigorate the U.S. economy, instead ended up largely fueling the growth of offshore banking in London and elsewhere.

Compounding both the crisis of U.S. hegemony and the associated growth of dollar liquidity beyond U.S. control was the oil shock of 1973. For commodity exporters, an inflationary environment and depreciating dollar in the early 1970s served to reduce export sector returns, particularly because all major commodities were priced in dollar terms. In this context, the Organization of the Petroleum Exporting Countries (OPEC) decided to collectively hike oil prices, beginning in 1971 but seen most dramatically in the 1973 oil shock, when prices quadrupled in a few months. Partly, of course, this was a political decision led by Middle Eastern states in response to U.S. support for Israel in the Yom Kippur War. More broadly, it represented a new assertiveness, both political and economic, on the part of Southern states emboldened by an apparent waning of U.S. hegemony, symbolized by defeat in Vietnam.

Higher oil prices reverberated through to other sectors, and the effect was strengthened by loose American monetary policy, which promoted a flight from dollar holdings into commodity speculation (Arrighi 2003). Though prices increased across the board, this was accompanied by both greater volatility in the face of global economic turbulence and rising production costs in point-source commodities as easily accessible deposits were exhausted. Attempts were made to copy the OPEC model in other industries, such as copper, and a wave of extractive industry nationalizations, tending toward outright expropriation, moved across sub-Saharan Africa and Latin America, reflecting a desire on behalf of Southern governments to maximize and stabilize rates of surplus retention to be used in increasingly ambitious development programs (Shafer 1983; Toye 2014).

This somewhat more radical trend among commodity exporters culminated in the Declaration for a New International Economic Order (NIEO), advanced by the Group of 77 developing commodity producers and adopted by the UN General Assembly in 1974 (Cox 1979). NIEO demands had their antecedents in the commodity stabilization fund, which Keynes had proposed during the Bretton Woods negotiations, in various ad hoc producer–consumer agreements during the post–World War II years, and, of course, in the United Nations Conference on Trade and Development (UNCTAD), the body from which the NIEO proposals emerged.

Nevertheless, the NIEO was explicitly positioned as a rejection of and alternative to the Bretton Woods settlement and thus to the moderate developmentalist compromise upon which U.S. hegemony in the South rested (Agarwarla 1983, 1–3). The new configuration was to be based on a managed system of stable and high prices for commodities, supported by producer cartels, coupled with freedom for Southern governments to regulate the operations of multinationals, including their expropriation and nationalization, where this was deemed appropriate. These demands coincided with various attempts on the part of national authorities, both North and South, to escape the bounds of the developmentalist consensus (Harvey 2005, 12–13). In the South, the likes of Jamaica and Peru sought to turn apparent mineral bonanzas toward a thorough restructuring of their political economies (Becker 1982; Stephens 1987).

Had American attempts to kick-start a new round of global material expansion in the 1970s worked, it is possible that the ensuing demand for primary products might have strengthened the position of the commodity exporters and helped them achieve many of their aims. Emboldened by the success of OPEC in gaining control over production levels and pricing of oil, international agreements were sought for twenty commodities, though only five were ever concluded (in coffee, tin, cocoa, sugar, and rubber). Of these, only the International Coffee Agreement included OPEC-like producer quotas, through which prices could be controlled. All five lapsed or were broken up during the 1980s and 1990s (Gilbert 2006). In part, this failure rested on the divergent interests of most commodity producers and OPEC, which the G77 had hoped would contribute generously to a buffer fund to guard against commodity shocks (Love 2010; Toye 2014).

OPEC, at times, acted in solidarity with the other commodity producers—in 1976, for instance, it threatened to hike oil prices, should the developed world not also contribute to these buffer funds. High oil prices, though, acted as a drag on oil-importing commodity producers and were a major component of recession in the North, dampening demand for resources such as copper and iron ore, which were used as industrial inputs in energy-intensive production. As the decade wore on, these negative pressures on commodity markets began to outweigh gains arising from the flight from dollars into commodities, which in any case was concentrated in oil and gold.

As the long period of global material expansion started to run into the sand, raw materials prices declined in the late 1970s, while oil remained strong into the 1980s.[8] Oil fed financial expansion by injecting massive amounts of liquidity, in the form of petrodollars, into the global financial system. Cheap and plentiful capital, aggressively pushed by Northern banks, was too tempting to resist for many Southern resource exporters, particularly those which had initiated more radical and ambitious development projects during the brief commodities boom (Arrighi 2002; Frieden 1981; Fraser 2010, 6–9). As the export revenues to cover this kind of expansionary fiscal stance dried up, international capital markets were tapped, in the belief that the recession would be a temporary blip in a fundamental restructuring of North–South economic relations. This already rather ragged illusion was finally shattered in 1979, with the so-called Volcker shock, the decision by Federal Reserve Chairman Paul Volcker to hike U.S. interest rates in the face of runaway inflation and a declining dollar, ratcheted up with further increases over the next three years.

For the by now heavily indebted global South, this was a double, crippling blow. On the one hand, credit-sensitive industries in the North, such as construction and manufacturing, were badly hit, together with effective consumer demand, as unemployment in the United States and Europe spiraled, further reducing demand for raw material exports. Even more importantly, the bandage of cheap credit, which had seen natural resource producers through the volatile late 1970s, evaporated as Southern states were placed in the unenviable and untenable position of having to compete with the United States for capital flows. For the United States, a year before the election of Ronald Reagan, this was the decisive turning point in the abandonment of the Fordist–Keynesian settlement and the embrace of an embryonic regime of accumulation that would become fully articulated as global neoliberalism. On another level, it represented the switch from a U.S. policy generally directed in the interests of productive capital to an implicit recognition of—and alliance with—the power of finance capital (Arrighi 1994, 316–19).

Global Neoliberalism

The rise of neoliberalism has been exhaustively chronicled (as a small sample, see Harvey 2005; Gill 1995; Fourcade-Gourinchas and Babb 2002; Wade 2006; Duménil and Lévy 2004; Overbeek 1993). Most recently, Slobodian (2018, 30–31) pinpointed its origins in the Austrian chamber of commerce of 1920s Vienna—and in a postimperial concern to place property and the market beyond the reach of the new democratic nation-states. Neoliberalism then emerged more prominently as a heterodox body of economic thought, following World War II. As applied to policy, neoliberal approaches were foreshadowed before the 1970s, as in the U.S. aid plan to Bolivia in the 1950s (Young 2013), though it was only with the crisis of Fordism–developmentalism that neoliberalism began to gain wider acceptance in both intellectual and political circles.

As is well known, neoliberalism's first full-fledged foray into the South came with the ascendancy, beginning around 1975, of University of Chicago–trained economists in Chile during the Pinochet dictatorship (Valdés 1995). Indeed, it is from Chilean intellectuals' use of the Spanish term *neoliberalismo* that the English label "neoliberalism" was widely adopted in reference to Pinochet-like programs of reform, usually with negative connotations (Boas and Gans-Morse 2009). In the North, the 1979 election of Margaret Thatcher in the United Kingdom and, especially, that of Ronald Reagan in the United States, one year later, proved decisive in terms of shifting global momentum toward a thoroughgoing—though never complete—restructuring of global and national regulatory forms around neoliberal principles (Harvey 2005, 9).

Neoliberalism as a phenomenon is notoriously difficult to define, given the divergence between neoclassical theory and neoliberal policy sets as actually applied, the distinction to be made between at least two temporal phases of neoliberal regulatory programs, and a multiplicity of national forms as neoliberalization has been superimposed over existing domestic dynamics, producing a range of varying tendencies and contradictions around the world (Brenner, Peck, and Theodore 2010). There also is the complicating factor that few self-describe as neoliberal and that the term is almost always used by critics (see, however, Ostry, Loungani, and Furceri 2016). Nevertheless, in broad terms, neoliberal approaches build on neoclassical assumptions of individual utility maximization to promote an ideal in which naturally occurring markets should, as far as possible, be left unhindered to do their work as efficient arbiters of the distribution of goods and services.

It is relatively uncomplicated to trace a direct line from these principles to major policy recommendations—privatization, the removal of ISI-style state support for industry, the liberalization of trade and capital flows, an economy-wide lifting of regulations, and the so-called flexibilization of labor markets. Of course, as many observers have pointed out, the state–market juxtaposition that serves as a basis for these kinds of changes is in most respects a false dichotomy, since all require action on the part of the state, both to implement and then to maintain the new structures (Weiss 2010; Harrison 2005). Indeed, even the IFIs, which spearheaded neoliberalization in most of the South, have at various points been criticized on the basis of free market principles, given that, from the 1980s on, their very rationale became one of intervention (Babb 2009, 85–90).

In line with intellectual trends in the United States, the World Bank and the IMF gradually adopted neoliberal ideas over the course of the 1970s. This led to a new diagnosis of the crisis and stagnation that had afflicted much of the South from the second half of that decade. The externalist case, that unequal global economic structures and a vulnerability to trends in the North had hamstrung Southern developmental efforts, was now roundly rejected, whether in its strong (dependency) or soft (structuralist) version. In its place, the internalist case, that Southern governments had themselves been the architects of their own failure, was presented. The new explanation, too, had a softer version—that well-meaning but wrongheaded policies had brought inefficiencies and perverse incentives—and a harder variation—that developmentalism had served as a vehicle for the establishment of patronage networks, cementing the position of corrupt, antidevelopment elites (Arrighi 2002). As Arrighi points out, there were undoubtedly elements of truth to both sets of charges. ISI was also undeniably problematic as a development strategy (Chibber 2002; Saad-Filho 2005), though problems of clientelism, inefficiency, and corruption were not, in most cases, satisfactorily tackled by neoliberal reform (Szeftel 2000; Roberts 1995; Aspinall 2013).

In any case, the problems in many zones of the South culminated in 1982, with the Mexican debt crisis, as it became obvious that, under the impact of U.S. interest rate hikes, states were struggling to pay debts racked up during the preceding petrodollar-fueled period of high global liquidity (Strange 1987). Many Southern states thus required large loans from IFIs (with the World Bank moving into budget support) just at the point where an internalist, neoclassical-inspired vision of the cause of this indebtedness had become embedded in these institutions. The result was a major extension of IFI missions, taking on the restructuring of Southern political economies along neoliberal lines via the lever of conditionality, meaning lending in exchange for policy reform, which became the basis for the now notorious structural adjustment programs demanded of more than one hundred countries between 1983 and 2005 (Saad-Filho 2005).[9]

Given neoliberalism's inherent neoclassical assumptions, the common IFI claim of technocratic ideological neutrality is, to say the least, dubious (Hay 2004; Wade 2010). Even if such assertions on the status of adjustment policies in the abstract were to be accepted, however, SAPs were, in practice, inherently political projects that sought, in more or less explicit ways, to alter the balance of forces among domestic groups. Stemming especially from the work of Robert Bates (1981), the hard variant of the internalist critique claimed that corrupt Southern elites, as beneficiaries of the distortionary effects of "bad" developmentalist policies, could not be simply persuaded to adopt "sound" policy, since this would reduce their access to patronage resources and so hinder their ability to maintain a position at the apex of society. SAPs, therefore, should be purposefully used to undermine these sectors, together with allied elements (an urban elite, in Bates's work on sub-Saharan Africa), via a dismantling of the state apparatus (Arrighi 2002).

Of course, it is important to point out that neoliberalization in the global South was not simply a case of external policy imposition and coercion, nor was it ever evenly or universally applied. First, many domestic elites, especially given the large proportion educated in the United States (or, to a lesser extent, in the United Kingdom), were increasingly convinced by free market logic, or else sided with IFIs to gain political advantage over rivals or to push through unpopular policies (Chwieroth 2007; Teichman 2004; Vreeland 2003). Second, many states in the global South—overwhelmingly those not compelled by debt to accept SAPs—tended toward some combination of largely bypassing the liberalizing trend, avoiding reform until comparatively late, or taking up liberalization gradually and on their own terms. Third, various forms of resistance, disengagement, or defiance of SAPs and the neoliberal agenda more broadly were common across the South, both from elites and the masses (with the latter often giving rise to anti-IMF riots), though such action succeeded mostly in slowing rather than reversing the tide (Wade 2003; Whitfield and Fraser 2010).

Even given these caveats, in my view it makes sense to regard neoliberalism as a global regime of accumulation, following Fordism–developmentalism and corresponding to the phase of financial expansion in a U.S.-led world economic cycle. In this manner, neoliberalism, as with Fordism, should be seen essentially as a tendential externalization of a particular temporal phase of the U.S. political economy (compare Henderson, Appelbaum, and Ho 2013). During the Bretton Woods era, an internally focused, continent-size United States operated relatively independently of the global economy, at least in comparison to the previous hegemonic power, the United Kingdom (Arrighi 1994, 289). A global regime that allowed for post–World War II reconstruction, Keynesian class compromise, and autonomous national developmentalism, therefore, not only furthered U.S. Cold War security interests but also did little to impinge upon U.S. accumulation. This remained true until the success of the leading national accumulation projects (in West Germany and Japan), together with the growth of international finance, began to breach the walls of regulation that separated nationally autonomous spheres (Arrighi 1994, 314).

Following the crisis-prone 1970s, the U.S. embrace of financialization required global as well as domestic restructuring if it was to be employed as a basis for continued U.S. hegemony. In contrast to the fraying developmentalist foundation of relatively protected national spaces of accumulation, taking advantage of the benefits of financialization and neoliberalization called for a global scene in which capital could move freely across the globe. The continuing internationalization of U.S. finance capital (Krippner 2005) built upon the results of the Volcker shock, which reversed capital flows back toward the United States, and the mix of consensual and coerced opening to capital movements around the world, which facilitated the process.

If neoliberalism, considered on a national level, tended to entail a redistribution of income upward (Duménil and Lévy 2001), this was partly built upon another form of redistribution at the global level, as capital shifted back from South to North, with the IFIs as the ultimate guarantors of this process.[10] For this reason, Makki (2004) labels global neoliberalism a "tributary regime." In keeping with Arrighi's notion of financial phases of accumulation cycles, redistribution upward on multiple scales masked slug-gish expansion of the global economy as a whole, with world gross domestic product growth slowing substantially, from an average of 5.5 percent per year in the crisis-prone 1970s to 2.3 percent in the 1980s and 1.1 percent in the 1990s (Wade 2004). Large swaths of the global South were reduced to near stasis for long stretches during the 1980s and 1990s, and Latin America, sub-Saharan Africa, and West Asia's per capita GNP levels, as a proportion of those in the core, declined over the same period (Arrighi, Silver, and Brewer 2003).[11]

In broad terms, those regions and states that did not embrace liberalization so readily or early, particularly in East Asia, bucked these disappointing tendencies and registered relative developmental successes (Henderson 2011). Such unevenness in both reform efforts and economic outcomes provides some ammunition for the critique of claims that neoliberalism might be thought of as a global regime (Brenner, Peck, and Theodore 2010). This line of argument contends that an understanding of neoliberalism as a global disciplinary force inadequately accounts for its variegated nature by positing global unevenness not as a constituent feature of neoliberalization itself but as an addendum to an otherwise unidirectional world-historical force. The point that neoliberalizing pressure (both internal and external to a given state) superimposed upon existing political-economic landscapes will produce differential outcomes, unintended consequences, and countervailing forces in different locations is well taken. The second half of this book attempts, in part, to address these concerns via a rescaling of analysis to the national level.

Indeed, in many respects, the notion of a variegated, constitutively uneven process of global neoliberalization is an excellent fit with the overall theoretical stance adopted in this research, of an open-ended world-system conceived of as the outcome of a historical process of part–part and part–whole interaction (McMichael 1990, 2000). If both approaches attempt to incorporate reciprocal rather than unidirectional interaction among global locations, however, it should be noted that the form and level of reciprocity seen in such relationships is to a large degree determined by differentials in political and economic power. Against the backdrop of competition for mobile capital, states in the global South will tend to be much less able to defy, resist, or modify pressures toward the neoliberalization of their political economies than many of the less risky investment destinations of their Northern counterparts. When the scope is limited to those Southern states that accumulated high burdens of debt during the 1970s, thus leaving themselves dependent upon IFI support, the direction of influence is much closer to being unidirectional in nature.

This is not to say, however, that neoliberalization, even when advanced through SAP policy conditionality, is ever entirely determinative of political-economic outcomes. Instead, the global neoliberal regime and its attendant regulatory institutions are best thought of as disciplinary in nature, producing, to borrow a term from Brenner, Peck, and Theodore (2010), a parameterization of national government policies, with the lever of debt allowing for a narrowing of space between parameter walls in those cases most beholden to the IFIs.[12] In fact, Fordism–developmentalism might also be regarded as (unevenly) establishing a set of looser parameters for each national state. Within this space, developmentalist projects in the South and Keynesian settlements in the North could be accommodated though efforts such as the NIEO, which attempted to challenge the structures upon which the global regime rested, breached the parameters, and so tended toward destabilization.

Neoliberalism, though, is distinct in that a greater level of discipline is exercised at the global level—whether directly, by IFIs, or indirectly, via capital markets—with less discretion left to national authorities. For this reason, though neoliberal forms show a good deal of temporal and spatial variation, particularly in the North, the neoliberal era has lacked the variety of national political-economic orientations seen during the Fordist–developmentalist period. The examination of post-neoliberal turns that makes up the second half of this research suggests that, with the weakening of neoliberal disciplinary power and the concurrent opening of policy choices seen over the commodity boom years, we witnessed the reemergence of a broader range of distinct developmental strategies in the global South.

This conceptualization provides a basis for the claims upon which this book's arguments rest. All things remaining equal, in highly indebted states of the global South, a break with a neoliberalizing political-economic trajectory, expressed via governmental policy orientation, was not possible—at least, not without prompting a ruinous isolation from the circuits of the global economy. As detailed in chapter 1, the rise of China and the disruptive influence that its spiraling resource import demand has had on global commodity markets since 2003 provided an escape route from neoliberal parameterization for those states that export these commodities, allowing for a range of possible approaches that, while certainly not limitless, more closely mirrored the degree of scope for the independent, domestic setting of policy priorities seen during the developmentalist era.

CHAPTER III

The Rise of China as a Necessary Condition for Post-Neoliberal Breaks

A fundamental proposition of this book is that, after decades of breakneck growth, the relative weight of China within the world economy has now reached a stage where the People's Republic has become a major driver of the global accumulation process. Further, as a medium-income state that is still urbanizing and industrializing at pace, the sources and characteristics of Chinese growth are very different from that of the other main engines of world capitalism, found in the global North. This means that as the gravitational pull exercised by the Chinese economy on the rest of the world strengthens, its potential to disrupt and transform the coordinates of the larger capitalist whole comes increasingly to the fore. Should swift Chinese growth continue in the medium to long term, particularly if combined with the kind of relative stagnation in the North that has been seen since 2008, the evidence for China-driven structural change is likely to appear in a variety of forms.

For now, though, the clearest example of Chinese-led global political-economic transformation remains the commodity boom of the years 2002 to 2013. Having set out the empirical case for Chinese import demand as the primary source of the boom, in chapter 1, I now turn to focus on the other side of this equation and to investigate the political-economic consequences for those resource-exporting states that found themselves pulled along in China's wake.

To begin, I will recap the argument that underpins the primary hypothesis, concerning the connection between the commodity boom and the ability of resource-exporting states to break with neoliberal policy orientations. In this section, I endeavor to draw out the implications of the conceptual framework for the rest of the analysis in this book. Of particular importance is the rationale behind the decision to use national indicators (principally in terms of policy change) to measure the impact of a global phenomenon (China-driven reshaping of commodity markets).

In addition, I will draw on the theoretical model discussed in previous chapters to begin more tightly specifying the hypothesis. In this regard, I argue that direct interaction with China (via trade or loans) was not required for a natural resource–exporting state to leverage its resource revenues toward policy autonomy and a break with neoliberalism. Instead, the key necessary condition is that a given state's main exports were commodities in which a resource-hungry China has raised prices and demand across the global market. It therefore is of little importance whether an exporter of such products was selling directly to China or to other partners. I also address precisely what I mean by policy autonomy and how this differs from the notion of policy space in existing literature. Following these observations, I turn toward the analysis itself, with an application of the qualitative comparative analysis technique to test the hypothesis that a high concentration of exports of natural resources subject to the Chinese demand shock during the commodity boom years was a necessary (but not sufficient) condition for a given (highly indebted) state to break with neoliberalism.[1]

National Policy Autonomy Under Boom Conditions

In line with the theoretical and historical framing of the research set out in chapters 1 and 2, China-driven changes in commodity markets are fundamentally conceptualized as a global shift within a single world division of labor, but also, importantly, as a phenomenon that is first manifest at the nation-state level. In line with this logic, neoliberalism is here understood as a tendential global regime of accumulation that, however, has been primarily implemented by national authorities. For all that such implementation has been uneven across time and space, the neoliberal orientation of a particular economy is reflected in and substantially driven by policies set by its government. It follows, then, that a national economy in which the overall thrust of policy changes, to stand in contradiction to neoliberal orthodoxy, can no longer, in an important sense, be considered as belonging to the neoliberal fold. It is for these reasons that the analysis in the remainder of this book is primarily framed at the national level. While the ultimate unit of analysis remains the global political economy, the state is adopted as the unit of observation, and both neoliberalism and breaks from it are defined in terms of national policy orientation.

Chapter 2 detailed the tightened constraints that national authorities, particularly in the South, faced in setting policies during the neoliberal era of the 1980s and 1990s. Some governments, of course, wholeheartedly embraced neoliberalization and needed little prompting from external sources to do so. Many others, though, found their options increasingly limited by such forces, whether they arrived in the form of international financial institution conditionality, policy priorities mandated by international donors, or more indirect disciplinary pressure exercised through the preferences of global capital markets. All three of these phenomena might be thought of as channels through which a larger shift in the shape of global accumulation was transmitted to the national authorities of the global South.

Clearly, such change was not blanket or uniform, and many Southern states stalled, resisted, or avoided externally imposed neoliberal discipline in a variety of ways, with varying degrees of success. Nevertheless, as the 1980s and 1990s wore on, the trend was toward shrinking space for Southern governments to propose and implement policies that ran counter to a liberalizing trajectory. This was especially the case in states rendered vulnerable to the three channels of neoliberal influence mentioned. High levels of sovereign indebtedness necessitated negotiations with the IFIs, aid dependence afforded donors direct participation in the policy process, and the fight to attract scarce mobile capital forced states to compete as destinations for investment.

Many states in the South, then, have been increasingly circumscribed within a neoliberalizing trajectory as the unfavorable circumstances of their insertion into the global economy have pushed their acceptance of these transnational demands.[2] No matter the source of neoliberalization, though (and of course domestic constituencies have also played at least some role in all cases), its implementation is always manifested in terms of national policy change, along the familiar axes of deregulation, privatization, and liberalization, together with corresponding shifts in monetary and fiscal policy.

The notion advanced here is that China's effect upon natural resources markets produced, for exporters of these goods, a new, much more favorable shift in their circumstances of insertion into the global economy. With China driving substantial increases in both demand and prices, resource-exporting states were given the possibility of capturing a greater share of the extractive surplus—a larger slice of an expanding pie. With this new potential revenue stream not subject, for the most part, to the whims of IFIs, donors, or capital markets, states that were able to leverage their resource wealth in the conditions of the commodity boom now possessed the capacity to escape externally imposed neoliberal constraints, in a double sense. First, greatly expanded flows of resource revenues often meant that states previously dependent upon IFIs, donors, and capital markets no longer needed to accept the demands for liberalizing policies that, in varying forms, accompanied these sources of funding. The second, linked point is that beyond lifting or reducing debt and aid dependence, new revenue flows had the potential to create sufficient fiscal space for development strategies of various stripes, involving increased public spending, in contrast to the austerity and retrenchment often prescribed by the dire state of national accounts prior to the commodity boom.

If neoliberalism can be thought of as a global shift reflected through changes in national policy, then, a similar framing applies to the commodity boom. A rising China disrupted and altered the dynamics of world markets for a range of extractive commodities, in turn creating the global conditions that provided exporters of these goods with the wherewithal to escape neoliberal constraints in favor of their own nationally defined development agendas. Again, the primary site of change lies at the global level, and yet its results may be observed at the national scale. Given this, for the purposes of this book, a break with neoliberalism is defined as a substantive change in a state's political-economic orientation away from neoliberal goals and means, as indicated by the overall set of policies adopted. I will comment on this definition in more detail later and then discuss its operationalization as a key component of the QCA.

Importantly, though, the theorization applied here relies upon a logic of China-driven change on a global scale (via commodity markets), which is then reflected in the external conditions encountered by resource-exporting states. The resultant policy autonomy does not, therefore, rely upon direct Chinese interaction with these states, whether in the form of investments and loans or of bilateral trade links. The implication, in terms of formulating the hypothesis, is that it does not matter whether or not a resource-exporting state traded directly with China. As long as the state in question had a high level of export concentration in commodity markets that were subject to the China effect on prices and demand, the posited mechanism through which these resource exports allowed for a break with neoliberalism remained the same. For example, in 2012, the PRC accounted for less than 3 percent of Bolivian exports (United Nations Comtrade n.d.). However, because Bolivia's main exports—natural gas and various metal ores—are classes of goods in which China's growing demand drove boom conditions from 2002 to 2013, the hypothetical policy autonomy provided by such export sectors should also extend to Bolivia.

The evident disconnect between orthodox prescriptions of development policy and those successfully pursued by the "Asian Tigers" (Wade 1990; Amsden 1994) helped to stimulate a debate on the degree of policy space open to developing countries by the early to mid-2000s (Wade 2003; Gallagher 2005; Mayer 2009). Much of this literature focused on the extent to which trade regulations being negotiated at the World Trade Organization (WTO) at the time might serve to remove as options policies that were crucial to many successful efforts at "late" development—whether, in Fredrich List's phase, rich countries were "kicking away the ladder" after themselves (Chang 2002). One way of framing these issues has been to argue that policy space needs to be divided into two components: de jure (formal policy sovereignty) and de facto (the ability to achieve goals via use of policy instruments) (Mayer 2009). In this view, while de jure policy space is limited by participation in international agreements such as the WTO, the effects of globalization and international integration on de facto policy space pull in different directions. For example, capital market liberalization may reduce policy space through the greater need to set monetary policy in relation to global market conditions rather than in furtherance of domestic goals. On the other hand, the effectiveness of policy instruments will be increased by trade integration, which facilitates easier access to a larger market, and the restraints that multilateral rules place upon states pursuing "beggar thy neighbor" policies.

While these may be reasonable arguments in some ways, my own focus is not on whether particular policy instruments are *effective* in meeting their desired targets but on whether it is *feasible* for a given state to select them in the first place. This is therefore a less expansive notion than that which appears in much of the literature, and for this reason I use the term "policy autonomy" rather than "policy space" to denote it. In my usage, policy autonomy encompasses the formal de jure authority of states to implement favored policies. It also incorporates the question of the extent to which creditors, donors, and investors exercise disciplinary power over policy choice—whether these groups' power to withdraw financing in response to negatively received policy changes effectively constitutes a veto over such policies being pursued. This means that I am interested in the conditions under which it is practicable for a state to pursue policies that deviate from those favored by IFIs, donors, and creditors. I depart from some of the policy space literature in leaving aside questions of whether particular policies are likely to prove successful or not in the long run.

The argument here is built on the observation that an external veto on policy has effectively been exercised on a number of occasions, when states' attempts to implement heterodox programs were met with the removal of IFI, creditor, and/or donor support, the economic consequences of which pushed governments to change course (Baer and Beckerman 1989; Gwynne and Kay 2000; Kayizzi-Mugerwa 1990). But the power of external "capital controllers" (Winters 1996) to exert such disciplinary force clearly is not invariant or all-constraining. First, the extent to which a state is reliant upon gaining or maintaining access to such funds will condition the amount of damage that can be wreaked by their withdrawal. This is why commodity boom conditions, in providing an alternative stream of funding largely independent of creditors and donors, weaken the disciplinary force which their exit can threaten. Second, my contentions around the ability of governments to break with orthodox policy prescriptions are not posed at the level of individual policies. It seems clear that states always retain some flexibility in their policy agendas and that external reactions to singular policy changes may vary with a variety of contextual factors (Fairfield 2015, chap. 6). Instead, my claim is that, of those states subject to neoliberalizing policy discipline, only those that benefited from the 2002–2013 China-driven commodity boom then possessed the policy autonomy to break with orthodoxy at the level of their policy orientation overall.

Qualitative Comparative Analysis

I use qualitative comparative analysis to test the hypothesis that the China-driven commodity boom opened the way for the exercise of policy autonomy among Southern resource-exporting states. QCA mimics the thickness of qualitative case-based comparative studies but enables the comparison of a much larger number of cases than is typically possible with such methods, by following individual case-based analysis with the reduction of each case to a configuration of conditions (akin to variables), which then may be simultaneously compared across a relatively large number of cases. Crucially, for my purposes, the logic of causality and comparison on which QCA is based makes it very suitable for testing hypothesized necessary causes.

I apply QCA to a set of eighteen country cases from across the South, all with relatively high levels of indebtedness at the beginning of the boom and with populations above 10 million.[3] Following on the discussion of neoliberalism as it translates from global regime to national policy constraints (chapter 2), I define a break with neoliberalism as a given state's

TABLE 3.1

Qualitative comparative analysis data by case

Nation	BRK	RES	CFF	POR	ODA	FDI	ENG
Angola	1	1	1	0	0	0	1
Argentina	1	1	0	0	0	0	0
Bolivia	1	1	1	0	0	1	1
Brazil	1	1	0	1	0	0	0
Ecuador	1	1	1	0	0	0	1
Ethiopia	0	0	1	0	1	0	0
Ghana	0	0	1	1	1	1	0
Indonesia	0	1	0	1	0	0	1
Kazakhstan	1	1	0	0	0	1	1
Malawi	0	0	1	0	1	0	0
Malaysia	0	0	0	1	0	1	0
Peru	0	1	0	1	0	1	0
Philippines	0	0	0	0	0	0	0
Senegal	0	0	0	1	0	0	0
Tanzania	0	0	1	0	1	1	0
Uganda	0	0	1	0	1	1	0
Venezuela	1	1	1	1	0	0	1
Zambia	0	1	1	1	1	1	0

adoption of an overall policy trajectory that, during the neoliberal era of the 1980s and 1990s, would not have been acceptable to IFIs or donors and thus would have been impossible to enact without a highly damaging rupture with creditors or Development Assistance Committee members.[4]

Alongside my hypothesized necessary condition, RES (the presence of a high export concentration in natural resources subject to the China demand shock), I test a number of other conditions of possible causal significance. These are CFF (high levels of Chinese financial flows to the state concerned), POR (significant outflows of portfolio investment), ODA (high levels of dependence on official development assistance), FDI (high levels of foreign direct investment), and ENG (high export concentration in energy commodities, in particular, rather than in resources more broadly). The cases considered and the values assigned to them on each of the conditions (1 indicating the presence of a condition, 0 indicating its absence) can be seen in table 3.1. Performing a QCA analysis of necessary conditions for the outcome BRK gives the results shown in table 3.2.

Table 3.2 shows the results of testing for the presence and absence (~ before a condition indicates its absence) of all conditions in respect of the outcome (BRK). Consistency scores measure necessity—a score of 1 means

TABLE 3.2

Analysis of necessary conditions for the outcome BRK

Condition Tested	Consistency Score
RES	1.00
ENG	0.71
CFF	0.57
POR	0.29
ODA	0.00
FDI	0.29
~RES	0.00
~CFF	0.43
~POR	0.71
~ODA	1.00
~FDI	0.71
~ENG	0.29

Source: Calculations using fsQCA.

that a condition was necessary for the occurrence of the outcome (a break with neoliberalism). Since the condition RES has a consistency score of 1, this means that, as hypothesized, the presence of a high export concentration in resources subject to the China-demand shock of the boom years is a necessary condition for breaks with neoliberalism to have taken place in this period. Significantly also, ~ODA (a lack of dependence on official development assistance) was also a necessary condition for a break to occur, a finding to which I will return in chapter 8, in particular, where the impact of aid dependence on several resource-exporting cases is explored in more detail.

Building from this base, the following chapters examine resource-exporting states in more detail. I begin with the resource exporters from the QCA set examined here. However, I increase the number of cases considered, from the ten resource exporters included in the QCA analysis to fifteen, by relaxing the scoping conditions on indebtedness and population, adding Jamaica, Laos, Mongolia, South Africa, and Colombia to this new set of cases, for the purposes of typology formation.

CHAPTER IV

A Typology of Political-Economic Trajectories
Under Commodity Boom Conditions

P revious chapters have made the case that, during the commodity
boom, natural resource exports presented an escape route from previous neoliberalizing constraints. I argue that both these neoliberal parameters and the China-driven changes in commodity markets that
allowed for their transcendence operate primarily as global systemic conditions, forming and transforming through complex (and unequal) part–
part and part–whole relations within a world-system not reducible to interactions among national societies. Nevertheless, it is at the national level
that pressure toward neoliberalization and the exit hatch opened by the
commodity boom have been manifested, as consequences flowing from
shifting circumstances of national insertion into the global market.

Of course, there is no direct or mechanical correspondence between
global dynamics and local political economy formation (Cardoso and
Faletto 1979, xv). This notion, in fact, is the basis for the framing of my
first hypothesis in terms of resource exports as a necessary cause—the
opportunity for local actors to pursue a non-neoliberal path was opened
by global processes, but there was no globally generated imperative for any
particular resource-rich state to do so. Building on this analysis, then, two
obvious questions present themselves: Under what circumstances might a
break with a neoliberalizing course occur in a given Southern resource-
exporting state, given commodity boom conditions? And what form(s)
might such breaks take?[1] Since it is not possible to read answers to either

question from analysis of global shifts, a change in scale to consider intranational forces is required.

A theoretical problem presents itself at this stage, however. The notion of systemic change at the global level derives from the premise of a single world capitalism, which should, by most accounts, be fundamentally incompatible with an analysis of discrete national societies.[2] My intention is to manage the jump in scale from global to national by arguing that global structures essentially manifest themselves in the local sphere as a kind of topography over which intranational relations play out.[3] Each Southern state faces unequal circumstances of insertion into the global economy, which unevenly constrain or empower certain domestic social forces (including transnational capital operating within the domestic sphere) and limit the spectrum of viable policy choices. When global economic structural change acts to alter these circumstances of insertion—trade relationships, investment patterns, or the workings of global markets, for instance—the economic basis for action waxes and wanes differentially across the various groups of local actors.

Such global shifts do not arrive in a national vacuum but are superimposed upon existing patterns of uneven social relations. Thus, while it is possible to see commonalities in the effects of the 1970s oil boom on, say, Nigeria, Venezuela, and Indonesia, their very different internal social dynamics prior to the boom made for distinct directions of travel when the impact of rising prices began to be felt (Freund 1978; Coronil 1997, chap. 6; Robison 1988). Shifts in the global market might therefore be thought of as forming and reforming the landscape on which local groups relate to one another, though with their composition, relative strength, and orientation being the result of many previous rounds of interaction among themselves, played out as partly contingent processes, on terrain corresponding to past iterations of global structural conditions.

At times, global reconfigurations may be sufficiently broad as to have a major impact in almost all countries, as with the turn away from Fordism–developmentalism and toward neoliberalism, discussed in chapter 2. In other instances, the domestic effects of world structural change may be largely concentrated among particular kinds of states, as with the China-led commodity boom beginning in 2002. By enhancing the potential for natural resource–exporting states to capture a greater proportion of rising commodity rents, the possibility of using these flows to transcend externally derived neoliberal constraints was opened, clearing the way for domestic actors to reassert their autonomy in defining the state's political-economic orientation.

Processes of neoliberalization, as well as prior historical periods, clearly left an indelible mark in terms of shaping the starting points, alliances, and orientations of various local groups at the beginning of the commodity boom years. It is also obvious that the boom did not act to remove all constraints presented by global economic conditions—many of the states surveyed were still to a greater or lesser extent dependent upon foreign capital and could not entirely ignore its preferences. Nevertheless, as will become evident through a consideration of the cases, commodity boom conditions among Southern resource exporters were more akin to the relative national autonomy, within broad limits, of the Fordist–developmentalist period than to the far more circumscribed policy choices associated with the neoliberal era.

Forming the Typology

The typology presented in chapters 5 through 9, and summarized here, revolves around the central argument that, in the context of greater national policy autonomy experienced during the commodity boom years, local social and state–society relations were the main shaper and driver of the form of political-economic orientation adopted in a given state, whether or not this involved a break with neoliberal orthodoxy.[4] Where breaks occurred, this was, in the main, a result of pressure from domestic actors who succeeded in deploying commodity revenues toward the implementation of policy programs that favored their particular interests. Three broad types of distinct post-neoliberal turn are observed, associated with a leading role, respectively, for industrial capitalists (neodevelopmentalist type), popular class coalitions (extractivist-redistributive), or clientelistic state bureaucracies (extractivist-oligarchic). The remaining two types represent commodity boom trajectories where neoliberalization persisted, even if the impact of the commodity boom meant that state–society relations could not be described as static or unchanged from the previous period. In one of these two types (the homegrown orthodoxy type), continued neoliberalization was driven by externally oriented local capitalist fractions with extensive transnational links. In the other (donor-dependent orthodoxy), it was driven by state managers upholding a status quo that preserved their positions at the head of a nexus of patronage relations interconnected to international donors.

The summary of the typology shown in tables 4.1 and 4.2 provides details of the relative strength of domestic actors for each category, brief comments on the political-economic structure and overall policy orientation associated with the different types, and a list of cases considered as broadly corresponding with the ideotypical characteristics identified with a given type.[5] Each type relates to a policy orientation underpinned by a pattern of social relations that emerged during the commodity boom years (approximately 2002 to 2013), though where breaks with neoliberalization occurred, they did not necessarily do so at the beginning of the period (since boom conditions enabled rather than compelled the occurrence of such shifts). The end of the commodity boom brought back conditions that were hostile to post-neoliberal experiments, which is why the typology here is limited to the period from 2002 to 2013, as the earliest and latest points at which a commodity-fueled break would have been possible. After the boom, the various cases of post-neoliberal break have met disparate fates, some hanging on with variable degrees of success or failure, while most have turned back in broadly neoliberal directions, as is discussed in the following chapters.

The task of forming the typology of resource-exporting states does not lend itself to the reduction of each case's characteristics to dichotomous values indicating the presence or absence of each feature, as in the qualitative comparative analysis used in the chapter 3. This is because, with the exception of aid dependence, all of the variables along which a type is defined (capitalist strength, popular class strength, political-economic structure, and political-economic model) are multifaceted and difficult to distill into singular values. I therefore assign cases to types based on a qualitative assessment of similarity between ideotypical form and the characteristics of a particular case across all five variables. The notion of family resemblance is a guiding principle in the sense that, while a match between a given case and the ideal type for any one variable is not necessary for type membership, a close correspondence across the majority of variables is required.

In each of the typology chapters, I provide a table that summarizes the features of the ideal type and the cases belonging to this type across the five variables. As an example, table 4.3 shows this summary for the extractivist-oligarchic type, to which chapter 7 is devoted. As can be seen, Angola is a close, though in some instances not exact, match with the ideal type across

TABLE 4.1
Typology of commodity boom political–economic trajectories among Southern resource-exporting states

Oligarchic-Extractivist	Redistributive-Extractivist	Neodevelopmentalist	Donor-Dependent Orthodoxy	Homegrown Orthodoxy
Angola (oil)	Ecuador (oil)	Brazil (iron ore, soy, oil)	Mongolia (copper, coal)	Peru (copper, zinc)
Kazakhstan (oil, copper)	Venezuela (oil)	Argentina (soy, oil)	Zambia (copper, cobalt)	South Africa (platinum, coal)
	Bolivia (natural gas, tin)		Laos (copper, coal)	Colombia (oil, coal)
				Indonesia (natural gas, coal, oil, copper)

Note: Main exports of listed countries are in parentheses.

TABLE 4.2
Political-economic structure of ideal types under commodity boom conditions, 2002–2013

	Oligarchic-Extractivist	Redistributive-Extractivist	Neodevelopmentalist	Donor-Dependent Orthodoxy	Homegrown Orthodoxy
Capitalists	Highly dependent upon and fused with state	Autonomous but weak and divided geographically and/or in orientation	Autonomous, relatively strong. Dominant fraction nationally oriented	Highly dependent upon and fused with state	Autonomous, relatively strong, externally oriented
Popular classes	Weak	Relatively strong	Moderate/strong, but subordinate	Weak	Weak/moderate
History of aid dependence	No	No	No	Yes	No
Political-economic structure	Access to state resources confers economic power (through access to resource rents). Capitalist class therefore overlaps to large extent with governing party and bureaucracy. Patronage-based politics. Little disciplinary power exercised by international financial institutions—little pressure to appear democratic or follow neoliberal policies.	Coalition of urban formal and informal workers and middle classes provide bases of support for governing party. Sometimes tacit agreements with sections of bourgeoisie. Partnership with Northern extractive capital, though on improved terms.	More domestically oriented faction of business is dominant political force, in alliance with subordinate urban formal labor and middle classes. These groups in opposition to more externally oriented capital (e.g., finance, agro-export).	As with authoritarian-extractivist type, access to state resources confers economic power (historically, in large part, through access to aid flows). Capitalist class weak outside state patronage. Legacy of dependence on aid as significant proportion of revenue and thus donors highly influential.	Relatively unified export-oriented capitalist fraction with strong ties to and reliance upon foreign capital dominates political formation. Foreign capital markets and/or International Monetary Fund still powerful in domestic policy agenda. Popular class groups atomized and weak/lack legitimacy.

Policy orientation/ development model				
Disjuncture between avowed developmentalist model and reality, which tends more towards patronage distribution. State/ quasi-state, or private domestically owned (or joint venture) resources fund capital-intensive development concentrated on urban centers, highly noninclusive development initiatives which tend toward predation. Infrastructure, prestige projects, takes Gulf States/ Singapore/China as purported models.	State-owned or heavily taxed resources fund redistribution, education, and health spending. Limited nationalizations. Involves dispossession in extractive areas, tends to favor urban population. Few concerted efforts at diversification or industrialization.	Attempts to leverage larger domestic markets and industrial bases. State-owned or private domestic/joint venture resource sector. Rents fund targeted poverty alleviation, extension of services to poor. Also subsidize national firms (who are meant to compete at home and abroad). Corporatist approach to labor, substantial minimum wage hikes.	Primacy of donors means political-economic trajectory heavily influenced by their priorities. Departs from "pure" neoliberalism in emphasizing education, health, and, latterly, infrastructure. Palliative rather than developmental approach to poverty. Foreign-owned or joint venture resource sector. Low effective taxation on natural resources means little surplus retained nationally.	Continuing liberalization, though with some moves toward expanded social provision, as with conditional cash transfer schemes. Incremental increases in natural resource taxation, largely private owned. Emphasis on attracting foreign direct investment.

TABLE 4.3
Oligarchic–extractivist ideal type and cases

	Ideal Type	Angola	Kazakhstan
Capitalists	Weak. Highly dependent upon and fused with state	Few "true" capitalists—public funding funneled into developmental schemes that provide flows of rent to elites, little of which (though perhaps some) appears to have laid ground for accumulation. Main domestic capitalist actor is state-owned oil enterprise Sonangol.	Two-tiered oligarchy, with first stratum composed of inner circle close to president, allocated control of natural resource industries. Emergent second tier bearing closer resemblance to capitalist class but increasingly co-opted by state.
Popular classes	Weak	Weak. Nascent urban middle class, but nurtured by and dependent upon state patronage.	Weak. Occasional agitation from unionized energy workers, but no broader movement. Crackdown following shootings of oil workers in 2011.
Legacy of aid dependence	No	No	No
Political-economic structure	Access to state resources confers economic power (through access to resource rents). Capitalist class therefore overlaps to large extent with governing party and bureaucracy. Patronage-based politics. Little disciplinary power exercised by international financial institutions—little pressure to appear democratic or to follow neoliberal policies.	Dominant authoritarian presidency with wide range of de facto discretionary powers. Oil revenue allocated via Sonangol as patronage to narrow elite. Lines between state and private realms blurred. Deal signed with International Monetary Fund in 2009 but no policy conditionality other than limited demands for greater transparency.	Paternalistic authoritarian president tops "power vertical" system. Large overlap between apex of state and private elite. Business ownership depends upon patronage, particularly in most profitable sectors.

Model			
Disjuncture between avowed developmentalist model and reality, which tends more towards distribution of rents to elites. State/quasi-state or private domestically owned (or joint venture) resources fund capital-intensive development concentrated on urban centers, highly noninclusive development initiatives which tend toward predation. Infrastructure, prestige projects, takes Gulf States/ Singapore/China as purported models.	Official development strategy evokes high modernist vision of development. Huge road- and rail-building program. Ambitious projects in industrialization, agriculture, and housing serve as vehicles for predation, though some nascent accumulation may be occurring. Elite enrichment justified as creation of national bourgeoisie. Much of country virtually untouched by new development efforts.	Developmental success major part of regime legitimacy. Use of "snow leopard" motif invites comparisons with Asian tigers. Shift from post-Soviet neoliberalism toward state capitalism, particularly since 2008, under auspices of state holding company Samruk–Kazyna. Large-scale development plan including petrochemicals, infrastructure, and housing. Samruk–Kazyna also used to distribute patronage to elites.

all variables. Kazakhstan, however, presents greater variation from the ideal type, particularly on the "capitalists" variable.

As is explained more fully in chapter 7, the ideotypical feature here is a weakness of domestic private capital to the point that the local political economy is instead dominated by the distribution of patronage resources, which flow from the state. This results in a ruling political elite that straddles the formal public–private divide (and may, for instance, include business owners) but that does not constitute a true capitalist class, since their position tends to be based more upon access to and distribution of rents than the accumulation of capital. The Kazakhstani case does not exactly follow this pattern, in the sense that a group of capitalists somewhat independent of the state has begun to emerge. Even on this variable, though, the situation observed in Kazakhstan, of a quasi-capitalist upper elite dependent upon ties to the presidency, with the addition of a somewhat more independent second capitalist tier, still follows the ideotypical model in most respects. Nevertheless, even if Kazakhstan were judged as not matching the ideal characteristic on this variable, the case does correspond more closely along the other variables, as can be seen in table 4.3.

Conceptualizing Social Forces

Prior to presenting the typology over the following chapters, some attention must be devoted to explaining the class and class fraction categories used in its formation. Despite a long and respected tradition (Cardoso and Faletto 1979; Paige 1978; Evans 1979; Rueschemeyer, Stephens, and Stephens 1992) and occasional newer examples (Achcar 2013; Allinson 2015), class analysis of peripheral social formations has declined in prominence over recent years, at least among English-language authors. Where class analysis has been conducted in relation to the global South, the perhaps most widely read works of recent years have concentrated on the purported formation of a transnational capitalist class (TCC) as the most significant contemporary process (Robinson 2001, 2004; Sklair 2001).

The claim, particularly associated with William Robinson, that a united transnational capitalist class not only exists but is in the process of forming a transnational state via the International Monetary Fund, the WTO, and the like, is justly criticized in many quarters as rather overblown (Block

2001; McMichael 2001). Nevertheless, as a relatively contemporary theoretical current that concerns shifts in national–transnational class dynamics, TCC writings are a natural first port of call for the following analysis, even if their main proposition runs counter to my argument for a renewed foregrounding of the domestic during the commodity boom years (at least in resource-exporting states). By critically combining insights from TCC theorists with earlier views on peripheral classes and the state, I seek to construct a model capable of accounting for the forms of inter- and intraclass struggles seen across my range of cases. For resource-exporting states in the South, these struggles primarily revolve around control of the extractive surplus, whether this is direct (in the form of profits) or indirect (through state redistribution via taxation).

I argue for the saliency of three major dimensions to this struggle, which, taken together, play a primary role in determining the leading social actors in a particular state and thus the political-economic direction pursued under commodity boom conditions. First, the degree to which leading capitalist sectors are oriented toward and integrated with transnational capital is significant, as TCC scholars argue, though this orientation cannot be reduced to a simple dichotomy between nationally and transnationally oriented elements, as is the tendency in TCC literature. Second, domestic historical, geographic, and contingent factors all have a role to play in the relative strength and unity of the various classes, class fractions, and other social actors, meaning that the preferences and strategies of any one group cannot simply be determined via reference to their objective interests. Third, as discussed previously, world-historical conditions present domestic actors with an uneven topography with which all must contend, unevenly narrowing or widening the parameters of possible action for each group.

TCC scholars see the turn toward the globalization of circuits of production and exchange from the 1970s as part of an incipient process of transnational capitalist class formation (Sklair 2001; Robinson 2001; Robinson and Harris 2000), through which leading capitalist firms free themselves from ties to particular nation-states. While space does not permit a thorough interrogation of these claims, a useful departure point for current purposes is the TCC notion of national versus transnational orientation as the primary axis of intracapitalist conflict in the neoliberal era (Robinson 2008, 170). Here "descendent" capitalist fractions whose interests correspond with the development of nationally bounded capitalisms (such as import-substituting industry) fight a losing battle with an "ascendant" bourgeoisie whose objectives lie in the extension of a global capitalism unfettered by national borders.

Problematically, however, these accounts tend to both underestimate geographic unevenness and run the risk of assuming an automatic correspondence between basis of accumulation and intracapitalist alliance formation. Kaup's (2013c) mapping of neoliberal and counter-neoliberal turns in Bolivia is helpful on both points. First, as he points out, there is a need to consider distinct "spatialities of power" among capitalist fractions, drawing a distinction between "*global* elites that participate in *local* circuits of accumulation and *local* elites that participate in *global* circuits of accumulation" (102, emphasis in original). The global elites can use their spatially diffuse power base to avoid (via shifting location) or minimize (via appeal to global institutions such as the WTO) the risks posed by local class conflict. Local elites may not be reliant upon local markets and might perhaps benefit from similar protection by global institutions. They do, though, tend to be more intimately interwoven with and dependent upon local class relations as well as a domestic productive base. As Kaup notes, a failure on the part of local, transnationally oriented capitalists to deal with domestic opposition, whether from rival fractions or popular classes, may result in a catastrophic loss of power and influence.

A second problem for TCC theories, in the context of Southern social formations, is a too-neat division of local capital into national and transnational wings, which fails to adequately account for the dimensions of intraclass relations during the neoliberal era or to help illuminate their shifts during the commodity boom years. In many respects, as Kaup notes, the TCC schema maps onto older delineations of peripheral capitalist classes (see, particularly, Poulantzas 1975). Most obviously, a national bourgeoisie is identified by both theoretical traditions. With a domestic base of accumulation, this fraction is expected to push for a domestically oriented economic strategy broadly in line with the postwar developmentalist settlement.[6]

Set against this group, the domestic representatives of the transnational capitalist class, as described in the TCC literature, are essentially equivalent to a combination of two of Poulantzas's postulated groups: the comprador bourgeoisie—which has no domestic basis of accumulation and therefore acts primarily as agent for foreign capital—and the internal bourgeoisie—which possesses some domestic base but still relies upon global circuits of capital. Following either of the TCC or the national–internal–comprador models, then, potentially fits with a picture of an intraclass conflict (national versus TCC, or national versus comprador and internal), manifested in each case as a struggle for state policies favorable to each fraction's interests (that is, developmentalism versus neoliberalism).[7]

Chibber (2003, 2005) makes the point, however, that while intraclass differentiation on the basis of distinct linkages to core capital is not ruled out, many peripheral capitalists "seem to have been happy to play both roles simultaneously—trying to protect their domestic market, while striving for lasting ties with metropolitan firms" (Chibber 2005, 2). In this way, most peripheral capital might be best characterized as part of an internal bourgeoisie, or at least as occupying some intermediate location along a national–comprador continuum. If such is accepted, then the shift from developmentalist to neoliberal national settlements across the South, which began in the 1970s, cannot realistically be framed, as TCC scholarship would have it, as solely or primarily a conflict of domestically versus transnationally oriented capitalist fractions.

This has major implications for typology formation, given my characterization of the commodity boom as, for resource exporters, a diminution of transnational disciplinary power and a renewed foregrounding of domestic power struggles as determinative. Applying TCC arguments to these shifts would tend to suggest that commodity boom–driven breaks with neoliberalism represent a simple reversal in the tide of transnational versus domestic struggle, to now once again favor the national bourgeoisie. If, however, most groupings of capital do not easily fit into such a dichotomy, how might they be distinguished from one another, and how does this translate into the favoring of particular development strategies?

Returning to Kaup, it seems clear that other potential axes of struggle are possible, in addition to that of the domestic–transnational. In Bolivia, which lacks a strong urban industrial sector as in some of its larger neighbors, the group that benefited most from developmentalist-like policies of subsidies, infrastructure investment, and easy credit were lowland agriculturalists— hardly a national bourgeoisie. In the 1980s, economic crisis and structural adjustment provided an avenue for a rival highland mining elite to gain political ascendancy by hitching themselves to an IFI-supported neoliberalization process, which brought partnerships with foreign extractive capital but also crucially removed state support from their lowland counterparts.

While objective interest clearly has some bearing on this kind of sequence, a legacy of partly contingent historical struggle seems to play the decisive role. Kaup's argument here is that in an extractive economy like Bolivia's, the intracapitalist struggle that occurs is really about access to the material benefits that flow from the resource sector, whether directly, in the form of profits, or indirectly, via state revenues recycled into subsidies, loans, government procurement, and other forms of spending.

However, Kaup seems to see this share of the extractive surplus as a kind of fixed prize, up for grabs to the (current) winner of the domestic class struggle. The problem is that this argument leaves out important world-historical dimensions to intracapitalist struggle in resource-exporting states—structural shifts both in commodity markets and in the global political-economic terrain more generally—which place constraints on the distribution of extractive revenues. In every case examined as part of the typology, the conditions of the neoliberal era largely ruled out the launching of any new effort to funnel extractive revenues, via the state, to a particular branch of the domestic bourgeoisie. First, low commodity prices significantly reduced both the absolute size of the surplus and the power of the state to bargain for a larger relative share. Second, increasing levels of debt meant less capacity for public spending and a growing reliance upon IFIs insistent upon adherence to structural adjustment programs and their successors. Third, IFI conditionalities generally stipulated that the state would work to reduce its claims on extractive revenue through privatization and lowering of taxes in the sector. Fourth, even had state coffers borne developmentalist or redistributive spending, agreements with IFIs—together with new sets of global rules—mostly ruled out preferential treatment for domestic firms and pressured governments to cut back on social spending.

Seen in these terms, those fractions of domestic capital that benefited from the shift toward neoliberalization did so in one of two ways. The most obvious benefit was the lowering of the tax burden and the opening up of the sector to domestic bourgeoisies with direct interests in the extractive industries. In other cases, the situation was more of a negative-sum game. Where little in the way of domestic ownership in resource industries existed (or was created), the main consequence of neoliberalization, in terms of extraction, was a diminution of the proportion of extractive surplus that was retained in the domestic sphere via government revenue. In these instances, capitalist fractions would gain primarily in relative terms, via the ensuing paucity of state resources with which rival groups could be supported through subsidies, easy credit, and the like.[8] In Bolivia, both effects are observed. An existing mining bourgeoisie was granted greater access to deposits previously reserved for the state-owned enterprise COMIBOL, but it also was strengthened, in relative terms, by a withdrawal of protective tariffs and subsidies from sectors associated with lowland agrocapital.

The rise of China and the subsequent commodity boom was highly significant for resource-exporting peripheral states, principally because the result was to put the extractive surplus in play once again, negating the four points outlined here and extending the possibility of its control to a larger array of domestic social groups. First, high commodity prices meant a larger absolute surplus and greater state bargaining power over the size of its share. Second, increased commodity revenues lifted or lessened IFI and aid dependence (and their attendant conditionalities) and provided an autonomous fiscal resource for public spending. Third, the lifting of conditionalities allowed states a free hand to bargain with extractive firms, unencumbered by the demands of IFIs. Fourth, with potentially healthy fiscal positions and less constriction by IFI agreements, resource-exporting states were potentially in position to launch programs aimed at national development or redistribution.[9] In other words, they may have had a newfound ability to appropriate and employ a significant chunk of the extractive surplus in favor of one or more fractions of the domestic bourgeoisie in a way that was not possible under neoliberal conditions.

If the use of the state as a means of channeling extractive surplus to particular kinds of capitalists was ruled out under neoliberalism and reentered the realm of possibility during the commodity boom, a similar logic applies to popular classes.[10] Neoliberal constraints significantly narrowed the scope for social spending, pushed governments to reduce the size of public sector payrolls, and undermined the organizational capacity of workers via labor flexibilization programs. Popular mobilization was still a potentially powerful force in some cases, though, and Latin America, especially, saw several instances of leaders elected through their channeling of anti-neoliberal populism (Weyland 2003; de la Torre 1997). However, most of these presidents quickly reversed their stance upon election (Stokes 2001, 2–5) or faced punishment by IFIs and markets, followed by economic chaos.[11] Again, within the context of a high levels of indebtedness, a break with neoliberalism (rather than an attempt to resist or blunt its advance) was simply not possible for Southern states—even if popular class led movements were able to secure electoral victories—while global neoliberal conditions persisted.

If the commodity boom opened the door for post-neoliberal turns, though, what were the implications for a popular class movement that was able to gain state power? In the case of Bolivia, Kaup sees the Movimiento al Socialismo (Movement for Socialism, or MAS) as rather timid and, in fact, as working to secure the position of transnational (particularly extractive) capital in Bolivia. A more detailed examination of Evo Morales's program appears in chapter 6. For now, it is worth noting that the MAS in government certainly has been less radical than some observers had hoped (Webber 2010), and it most definitely entered into partnership with transnational extractive firms, albeit on terms more favorable to the state.

Nevertheless, my argument is that, while Bolivia under Morales remains clearly capitalist, its trajectory over the boom years (and hung on to since) was no longer wedded to neoliberalism. A larger role for the state in extraction, and consequently greater revenues, funded new social spending and, for example, public investment in transport and rural electrification. This pattern was reflected even more strongly in Ecuador and Venezuela, the other resource-exporting states that saw popular mobilization come to the fore during the commodity boom. Governments grounded in such movements still faced clear limits on their policy choices (and, especially in Venezuela, would run into serious contradictions of their own), but they were still relatively unconstrained in comparison with the previous neoliberal period.

The final domestic social force of causal significance in the typology is the state itself, as has already been noted in the brief discussion of Angola and Kazakhstan. Clearly, rulers and state managers have had a role to play in all of the countries surveyed. But in cases where large domestic capital is either absent or lacks the capability to operate autonomously of the state, the power of those political elites with control over the latter is foregrounded. Political clientelism is a feature of all polities, North and South, but becomes more dominant as a logic of governance depending on the extent that the state represents the only significant nexus of accumulation and rents in the domestic economy.[12]

The next five chapters each focus on one of my types and follow a similar structure in doing so. After a short introduction, I give a description of the given ideal type, principally in terms of political-economic path during the course of the commodity boom. For three of the types (neo-developmentalist, extractivist-redistributive, and extractivist-oligarchic), the goal is to illustrate, in general terms, each distinct form of divergence from previous neoliberalization, highlighting the linkages between the reconfiguration of domestic class relations and policy change. For the other two chapters/types (donor-dependent orthodoxy and homegrown orthodoxy), the aims are similar but are geared toward an understanding of these two distinct forms of overall neoliberal continuity.

In each chapter, I then examine the impact of the commodity boom on the circumstances of insertion into the world economy, for cases belonging to the type under discussion, looking at trends in the global markets for their resource exports and, in turn, outcomes in terms of changes in government revenue and expenditure. For some cases—as with Angola, for instance—there have been substantial direct linkages with China, both in terms of Chinese investment and loans and bilateral trade. However, while these connections, where present, are noted in my account, it should be remembered that it is not necessary for any resource-exporting state to deal directly with the People's Republic in any way in order to take advantage of China's effect on its extractive export sectors. Chinese demand has driven price increases in markets for commodities that are traded globally, which has similar consequences for all resource exporters, whether their main export destination is China or anywhere else.

The next sections in each typology chapter deal with the domestic political economies of those cases that correspond to the given type. Owing to space limitations, I select one case as an exemplar of the type and give a detailed examination of its trajectory during the commodity boom, while also providing necessarily shorter summaries of the other cases. I discuss Jamaica alongside cases of the homegrown orthodoxy type, since its political-economic orientation most closely resembles this ideotypical configuration. As is detailed at length in chapter 9, however, Jamaica does not strictly belong in this type, or indeed in the typology as a whole. The Caribbean nation is the only case, of all those considered, in which the resource export sector (for bauxite/alumina) was not subject to the surge of Chinese demand that drove the potential for post-neoliberal openings in other resource-rich states. Jamaica is therefore a crucial counterfactual case, used to probe the unusual empirical situation of a contemporary resource exporter largely bypassed by the China-led commodity boom.

CHAPTER V

Neodevelopmentalist Type

Argentina and Brazil

This chapter focuses on neodevelopmentalism, perhaps the most distinctively novel form of divergence from neoliberalism to emerge over the years of the commodity boom. Among the three types of post-neoliberal turn included in the typology, neodevelopmentalism is unique in that its practical application is tethered to a relatively comprehensive preexisting theoretical paradigm, standing in contrast to the rather ad hoc evolution of policy orientation and after-the-fact theorization that often seems to characterize the other forms of post-neoliberalism, discussed in chapters 6 and 7.

Following an introductory summary of the main arguments, I provide an outline of the theoretical model of neodevelopmentalism and its associated policy recommendations, noting the various breaks and continuities with the equivalent neoliberal agenda. I then consider the interplay between international market conditions and policy change in the two cases I see as belonging to this type, Argentina and Brazil, demonstrating that the space for their post-neoliberal policy reorientations was created by China-led price movements in global markets for their respective resource exports. I devote particular attention to the case of soy, a major export sector for both Argentina and Brazil, arguing for its inclusion (uniquely, among agricultural goods) alongside minerals and fuels as a commodity for which Chinese demand has fundamentally altered the shape of the global market.

Next, I focus on the domestic political-economic trajectories of the two cases, highlighting correspondences and divergences from the neodevelopmentalist template. Brazil represents the wellspring of neodevelopmentalist thought, but it also is the state most commonly identified as the paradigm's primary—or sometimes only—proponent (Carrillo 2014). Alongside an increasing tendency toward the practical application of neodevelopmentalist ideas from 2006 until 2016, however, elements of the previous neoliberal settlement were retained (Ban 2013), an uneasy coexistence that tended to partially undermine the neodevelopmentalist project (and, after the boom, would contribute to its downfall).

Perhaps surprisingly, given the relative lack of discussion of Argentina as a neodevelopmentalist case (though see Wylde 2011, 2016; Feliz 2011), it is the Argentinian governments of Nestor Kirchner (2003–2007) and his successor and wife, Cristina Fernandez de Kirchner (2007–2015), that most fully and unambiguously implemented a neodevelopmentalist strategy. For this reason, I use Argentina as the exemplar case for the type, accordingly providing a longer treatment of its post-neoliberal turn than that given over to the Brazilian case.

Viewed from one angle, neodevelopmentalism as a notional policy orientation represents a middle path between classic Latin American structuralism and the neoliberalism that held sway over the region during the 1980s and 1990s (Morais and Saad-Filho 2011, 2012).[1] Another perspective is that neodevelopmentalism is an attempt to adapt old structuralist goals to the demands of a liberalized global economy (Bresser-Pereira 2012). In so doing, its proponents seek to apply the lessons of the successful developmental experiences of the newly industrialized East Asian countries, replacing pre-neoliberal domestic-focused import substitution industrialization strategies with a stress on competitiveness at home and abroad (Kröger 2012; Hochstetler and Montero 2013).

Although market mechanisms are viewed as often highly efficient arbiters of distribution, the neodevelopmentalist state is expected to intervene in a variety of ways to nudge markets toward favorable developmental outcomes. Without resorting to ISI-style protectionism, neodevelopmentalists advocate an active industrial policy, focusing on directed credit, subsidies, and infrastructural development as well as support for consumption (via, for example, wage increases) in an effort to build the domestic market.

Local productive capital, of course, benefits from state-supported consumption, but it is also pushed to internationalize where possible, as occurred in the Asian Tiger cases. Perhaps scarred from the fiscal crises that marked the end of the ISI period and much of the neoliberal era, the need to deliver primary surpluses is often emphasized (Boschi and Gaitan 2009).

The neodevelopmentalist approach is posited as a general development strategy, meaning that its principles are not intended to apply solely or in particular to the conditions of the commodity boom.[2] As will become clear in discussion of the two cases belonging to this type, however, any attempt to roll out a neodevelopmentalist program under neoliberal conditions would have faced grave difficulties, at least in the context of a highly indebted resource-exporting state.[3] This is, first, because the neodevelopmentalist stress on fiscal restraint seems impossible to balance with the need to support firms and consumers via industrial policy and subsidies while simultaneously meeting high debt service requirements. Second, any need to engage with the international financial institutions to manage these debts would entail adherence to a set of conditionalities that would tend to rule out most of the signature neodevelopmentalist policies. With the onset of the commodity boom, though, any natural resource–exporting state potentially had access to a revenue stream that might be turned toward easing fiscal problems sufficiently to deliver a primary or even a net budget surplus while paying for the interventionist elements of a neodevelopmentalist program. Achieving this feat would then reduce or eliminate the need for IFI support, freeing the state in question from policy conditionalities.

Argentina and Brazil both utilized the benefits of the commodity boom as a foundation for policy autonomy, though in ways that certainly have differed—as, relatedly, have the forms of their experiments with neodevelopmentalism. Some accounts concur with the link between the boom and political-economic shifts in Brazil and Argentina, but essentially characterize these as instances of "institutional erosion" and "reform backsliding," reflected in declining scores on World Bank Worldwide Governance Indicators (Wise and Chonn Ching 2018, 10). Such a framing effectively ignores the possibility that there was any purposive strategy behind the patterns of policy change seen in Argentina and Brazil over the period, beyond mere graft and populist expediency.[4]

It is also the case that many of the indicators on which several of the Worldwide Governance Indicators are based present particular forms of political and economic policy—the absence of price controls or subsidies, for example—as though they were apolitical matters of best practice. Further, they rely on subjective judgments along these lines. For instance, the indicator for regulatory quality draws in part on the Institute for Management and Development's World Competitiveness ranking, which asks businesspeople to score countries on the extent to which labor regulations impede business and corporate taxes discourage entrepreneurship (World Bank Group n.d.). That the Worldwide Governance Indicators seem to show Argentina and Brazil as both failing in governance terms, then, is in fact consistent with an argument that both were breaking with neoliberalism during this period. Here, I do not begin from the assumption that such breaks are inherently negative but instead aim to understand specifics of the two countries' trajectories, in a manner that parses commodity boom-era changes as more than just a linear reversing away from reform.

Argentina, emerging from International Monetary Fund tutelage, economic depression, and then debt default in 2002, used a subsequent currency devaluation to kick-start an export revival. This move happened to coincide with the beginnings of a boom in Chinese demand for soy (including soybeans, meal, and oil), Argentina's main export. Profitability levels in the Argentinian soy sector were thus massively enhanced, resulting in rising foreign currency earnings and also opening space for the government to access soy revenues directly by imposing substantial export taxes (an effort that would eventually meet with pushback from agro-exporter groups). Taken together, these new current account and fiscal inflows allowed the Argentinian governments of Nestor Kirchner and then Cristina Fernandez de Kirchner to avoid any reengagement with the IMF and global capital markets, eliminating impediments to the implementation of neodevelopmentalist policies.

Neoliberalization in Brazil had not advanced as far as in many of its neighbors prior to the boom, and the country had hung on to substantial portions of its industrial base throughout. Some elements of developmentalist thought and policy were also preserved in the economic bureaucracy (Hochstetler and Montero 2013). The neoliberal turn therefore contained elements of continuity from the previous era, but the shift toward neodevelopmentalism during the commodity boom years was also rather more gradual than that seen in Argentina. Persistent neoliberal influence in policy-making circles meant a continued focus on inflation targeting. The principal tool employed to manage inflation—an overvalued currency—ran against neodevelopmentalist prescriptions and reduced the benefits accruing to Brazil from the boom in prices and demand for its resource exports (soybeans, iron ore, and oil, among others).

Nevertheless, the much-improved external position for the country, which developed during Luiz Inácio Lula da Silva's first term, beginning in 2003, allowed the government to clear its debts with the IMF and thus to end the fund's influence on policy formation by 2005. Though Lula would largely continue to maintain an orthodox macroeconomic framework (with some partial departures under his successor, Dilma Rousseff), this should not obscure the significance of the developmentalist industrial policy implemented after 2006, encompassing directed credit, production subsidies, and a revival of public infrastructure spending (Weisbrot, Johnston, and Lefebvre 2014; Doctor 2015; Kröger 2012). Without a devaluation-induced boost to export competitiveness, it was the China-driven boom in Brazil's resource exports that both insulated the country from the need to listen to IFI advice and paid for its neodevelopmentalist strategy.

If the conditions of the resource boom opened the space for the two states to pursue their variations upon the neodevelopmentalist project, the question remains why these paths were taken, as opposed to another form of post-neoliberal turn or even the maintenance of a neoliberal orientation. At the beginning of the commodity boom, maintaining a neoliberal orientation was certainly a possibility in both cases. On the eve of the 2002 elections in Brazil, Lula had pledged support, in writing, for a neoliberal agenda. Even in Argentina, where anger with the socioeconomic impact of an IMF-sponsored austerity program had led to government ouster and default, two of the three leading (though eventually losing) candidates in the 2003 election advocated a free market program.[5] As with the other cases across the typology, I ascribe the fact of Brazil and Argentina's departures from neoliberalism, as well as their particular form, to domestic factors, particularly the changing relations among class fractions under commodity boom conditions.

The 2000s in Argentina and Brazil saw a resurgence of the political power of a domestic productive bourgeoisie, primarily at the expense of foreign transnational and domestic finance capital, though via somewhat different routes in each case. The neodevelopmentalist stress on support for domestic producers does, of course, correspond with this shift. In ways that hark back to the institutional arrangements of the Getúlio Vargas and Juan Perón eras, class compromise and corporatism led to formal labor taking a subordinate but relatively favored role in the new ruling coalition.

Neodevelopmentalism as a Political-Economic Model

Neodevelopmentalism displays certain obvious similarities with neoliberalism. First, as policy paradigms, both have drawn upon distinct intellectual programs grown from fundamental beliefs about how individuals, markets, and states interact and function within capitalism. This makes neodevelopmentalism unique among my post-neoliberal regime types as being substantially based on an existing canon of literature and a fully formed, off-the-shelf theoretical model. In Argentina and Brazil, these ideas and assumptions were picked up, elaborated, and partially implemented by governments, serving as suitable vehicles for particular kinds of development projects. Although a simple translation of neodevelopmentalist principles into policy did not take hold in either case, it is still instructive to begin by briefly surveying neodevelopmentalism as an intellectual program.

The most prominent research surrounding neodevelopmentalism is primarily Brazilian, concentrated especially within the Getulio Vargas Foundation in São Paolo and the State University of Rio de Janeiro. There are clear similarities between the lines of thought found in these Brazilian schools and a wider reinvigoration of the debate over the proper role of the state in development. This debate has included a renewed focus on industrial policy (Chang 2002; Wade 2010, 2012), growing interest in the application of developmental state concepts in new contexts (de Waal 2013; Ashman, Fine, and Newman 2010), and, in mainstream circles, the "new structural economics" promoted by, among others, Justin Lin (2011, 2012). While there is insufficient scope within the present research to do justice to any of these arguments, it is worth noting that cross-fertilization between Brazilian authors and broader trends in developmentalism has certainly occurred. The culmination of this exchange is embodied in the 2010 manifesto entitled "Ten Theses on New Developmentalism," composed in São Paolo and signed by a host of prominent scholars from around the world (Bresser-Pereira 2012).

However, building on Latin American developmental experiences, and those of larger, earlier urbanizing and industrializing states of the region in particular, Brazilian neodevelopmentalist thought has a dynamic of its own.[6] Ebenau and Liberatore (2013) give a useful and concise synthesis of the platform, which encompasses a capable bureaucracy with relative policy and fiscal independence; state support for firms in improving competitiveness and pushing toward internationalization; a broad concept of macroeconomic stability, encompassing "competitiveness," essentially meaning the maintenance of an exchange rate conducive to export growth; a concern for inclusivity in development, in the sense of ensuring relatively equitable distribution of gains secured as competitiveness improves; and a major stress on neodevelopmentalism as a national(ist) project, with broad support needed from across domestic society.

Perhaps the most important and obvious departure from neoliberalism here is a de-emphasis on inflation in favor of a more encompassing idea of macroeconomic stability to the advantage of productive rather than finance capital (Morais and Saad-Filho 2011). Though inflation is not ignored, maintaining a competitive and stable exchange rate is more highly valued, along with great concern for the state of the balance of payments. Inherited from neoliberalism is a relatively conservative approach to fiscal policy: though leeway for infrastructure and some social spending is expected, a primary surplus is considered necessary for the effective functioning of the model. The design of social programs associated with neodevelopmentalism has come to mesh with second-generation World Bank models, mostly a system of conditional cash transfers, which tend to cost a fraction of traditional welfare payments and thus are helpful in maintaining fiscal discipline while pushing often rather large numbers of recipients above the absolute poverty line.

At the same time, increased competitiveness (stemming from government support and macroeconomic policy) is meant to create a virtuous circle of formal job growth, pulling workers out of the less productive informal sector and further increasing competitiveness. Both sectoral and firm-specific industrial policy is advocated, particularly with a view to technological upgrading, though the extent to which this is meant to conform to or defy existing comparative advantage is sometimes unclear. Ebenau and Liberatore's (2013) final point, regarding the building of a broad consensus around a common national development project, echoes the structuralist era and certainly represents an appeal to nationalism as a reaction against the transnationalization of the neoliberal era (with particular resonance in Argentina) (see also Bresser-Pereira 2015). Nevertheless, this nationalism clearly has been informed by oft-made comparisons between pre-neoliberal development strategies, contrasting successful export-oriented industrialization programs (such as that of South Korea) with the more ambivalent ISI experiences typical of Latin America (see, for example, Kohli 2004, chap. 4; Gereffi 1989; Jenkins 1991). For this reason, in neo-developmentalism, the import substitution of the old structuralism is transformed, particularly in the context of a liberalized global economy, into a kind of mercantilism, led by the national champions of domestic productive capital, at home and abroad. As in former experiences of structuralism, particularly in Brazil and Argentina, the mass political base for this project is sustained by wage policies that favor the urban formal working class, allowing for class compromise premised on "growth with equity" as well as driving effective domestic demand (Boito and Saad-Filho 2016).

External Market Conditions and Their Economic Implications

I include Argentina and Brazil in the typology of resource exporters partly on the basis of both countries' important soybean sector. Soy is, of course, not an obvious product to bracket with the minerals, fuels, and metals otherwise examined in this research, and I do not count any other agricultural goods as natural resource exports for the purposes of the typology. Since the beginning of the commodity boom, however, soy has exhibited certain characteristics that merit its consideration alongside nonrenewable natural resource exports as a possible source of leverage for post-neoliberal turns. Most importantly, the global soy market has been affected by Chinese demand to an extent which is unique among agricultural products and is far more reminiscent of the observed trend for metals such as copper. Figure 5.1 shows the rapid growth in Chinese import demand for soybeans over the 2000–2016 period, particularly coinciding with the boom in prices from 2006 on.

Although soy is consumed as a human foodstuff in China, the vast majority of import demand growth seen since the early 2000s stems from meat consumption trends, which have risen in tandem with Chinese incomes. Changes in livestock-raising techniques, beginning in the 1980s, meant an increasing use of soy as an animal feedstock. This, combined with a shift of Chinese farmers away from soy toward higher-yield corn, has left an increasing shortfall in domestic soy supply as more chicken, beef, and

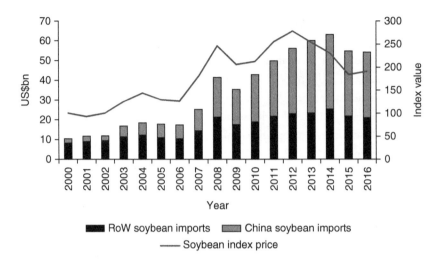

Figure 5.1 China compared to the rest of the world: soybean imports and soybean index prices, 2000–2016. Calculated from Chatham House Resourcetrade.earth database and World Bank, Commodity Price Data—Pink Sheet Data.

especially pork is added to Chinese diets (Hansen and Gale 2014). By contrast, demand for major grains such as rice has been largely met through domestic supply in recent years.[7]

On the producer side, since the 1990s, shifts in the soy industries of Brazil and Argentina (the second- and third-largest producers after the United States) make these countries' sectors particularly comparable to natural resource extraction in other cases. The adoption of genetic modification and biotechnology in seeds and fertilizers, no-tillage production techniques, and the use of satellite data have given the Brazilian and Argentinian soy industries a capital- and technology-intensive character that is out of step with the majority of the labor-intensive, low-tech agriculture in the global South (McFarlane and O'Connor 2014).

Growing economies of scale have seen an increasing concentration of capital and ownership in both countries. Large Northern transnational corporations, such as Cargill and Bunge, have joined domestic groups like Maggi (in Brazil) and Lucci (in Argentina) in displacing smaller farmers, with the result that the top 3 percent of producers own 50 percent of the land planted with soy in Argentina (GRAIN 2013). (In Brazil, the top 5 percent of producers own 59 percent of the land planted with soy.) Rather than dealing with a large number of household or small-scale producers, then, the Argentinian and Brazilian governments are faced with a small number of dominant large producers—similar to, though less extreme than, the enclave nature of a typical extractive industry.[8] Combined with the scale of price and demand effects from China, this allowed the Argentinian state, in particular, to effectively act in a rentier capacity, appropriating and allocating a share of the soy surplus in a manner that mirrored the behavior of other governments with regard to extractive industry rents. Although the upper limit to the state's take from soy appears to be relatively smaller than that seen in, say, equivalent oil or gas sectors, Argentina's export taxes yielded 20 to 25 percent of tax receipts between 2008 and 2011, with soy accounting for around two-thirds of the total (Richardson 2012, 27, 74).

Successively higher levels of soy export taxes were a key source of the greater revenue streams that allowed increased subsidies and social spending in Argentina after 2003. In 2010, for example, 10 percent of spending was allocated to energy and transport subsidies, which had the dual effect of lowering domestic production costs and supporting consumption (Bril-Mascarenhas and Post 2015). A portion of the soy export tax was, in fact, specifically allocated to food producers selling on the domestic market, again in an effort to free up wages for consumption, as well as to dampen inflationary pressure (Richardson 2009).

Brazilian governments generally eschewed these tactics, instead seeking to maximize soy production, minimize costs, and seek market access through diplomatic initiatives at the WTO (see, for instance, *Financial Times* 2013). Brazilian neodevelopmentalism did encompass state support of the agricultural sector to some extent, however, with $10 billion in farm support allocated in 2010 and a system of directed credit meant to encourage expansion and support smaller farmers (Korves 2013; Organisation for Economic Co-operation and Development 2015). Combined with new farming techniques and massive infrastructure expenditure, these measures enabled soy production to move beyond its original heartland in the South and Southeast regions and into the Central-West and even Amazonia (with the consequence of accelerating deforestation) (Garrett, Lambin, and Naylor 2013).

Brazil is unusual among those typology cases deemed to have departed from a neoliberal path. Outside the country's oil industry, moves to directly capture commodity revenue through either state participation or upping tax and royalty payments—which tended to provide the most fundamental first step toward realizing post-neoliberal ambitions elsewhere—were entirely absent. As a result, both import and export taxes, across all sectors, accounted for less than 5 percent of Brazilian government revenue (Kaplan 2014).

In Brazil (and Argentina), however, the effect of Chinese demand on global markets for their resource exports had another important effect. External commodity boom conditions beginning in 2003, magnified via previous devaluations in both Brazil (in 1999) and Argentina (in 2002), stimulated resource export volumes and values, significantly adding to hard currency earnings. Coming immediately after the 2002 crisis in Argentina (and its major spillover effects on Brazilian creditworthiness), the resource boom's overwhelmingly positive impact on the health of the current account supplied the requisite room for maneuver in breaking with neo-liberal policies, even if this manifested somewhat differently in the two cases. Figure 5.2 gives some indication of the scale of this change, with export purchasing power in both states following the familiar path of commodity market movements—substantial increases beginning in 2002–2003, continuing until a downturn with the global financial crisis in 2008,

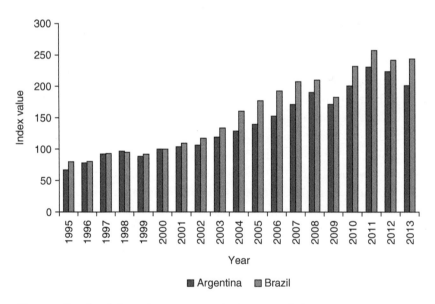

Figure 5.2 Brazil and Argentina export purchasing power index, 1995–2013.
Source: United Nations Conference on Trade and Development, UNCTADStat data center.

but then rebounding more strongly and quickly than would be plausible if driven by still-stagnating Northern markets.

As a result of this strong export performance, Brazil moved from a current account deficit equivalent to 100 percent of exports in 1999 into surplus by late 2003 (Serrano and Summa 2011). Along with substantial levels of capital inflows (partially a consequence of high interest rates), this external turnaround was a prerequisite for Lula's decision to clear all of Brazil's debts to the IMF in 2005. In freeing Brazil from formal policy conditionality, this move opened the way for the turn toward neodevelopmentalism produced by the political realignments that accompanied Lula's reelection in 2006 (Loureiro and Saad-Filho 2019).

Even during Lula's second term, as well as under his Partido dos Trabalhadores (Workers' Party, or PT) successor, Rousseff, Brazil's macroeconomic orientation remained for the most part orthodox. An appreciating currency seems likely to have been at least partially the result of the boom in iron ore and soybean exports, producing "Dutch disease" effects, which undermined any efforts at development of more technologically sophisticated industry (Jenkins 2012). Persistent overvaluation of the real chimed with the PT governments' continuing preoccupation with inflation, resulting in an absence of policy measures to tackle the problem.

For commodity export sectors, lack of devaluation after 1999, and thus relative lack of competitiveness, left no room for Argentinian-style export taxes on the soy sector. Nevertheless, the impact of the commodity boom, in compensating for the overvalued real and driving export expansion in soy, iron ore, and other minerals, allowed for a fourfold increase in international reserves from 2004 to 2009 (International Monetary Fund n.d.). Brazil's markedly improved solvency from the dark days of the 1999 currency crisis led to falling debt spreads and a decline in debt service requirements. The key role that the export boom played in this process is highlighted in figure 5.3, as debt service, both as a percentage of exports and of gross national income (GNI), continued to fall since the beginning of the boom in 2002–2003.

The PT governments, then, adopted a cautious set of policies that effectively ruled out the possibility of direct appropriation and distribution of large shares of resource export revenues, the mechanism which was the main wellspring of the ability to transcend neoliberal constraints in other cases. Instead, though, Brazil depended upon the commodity boom in order to simultaneously pursue two otherwise contradictory agendas: an

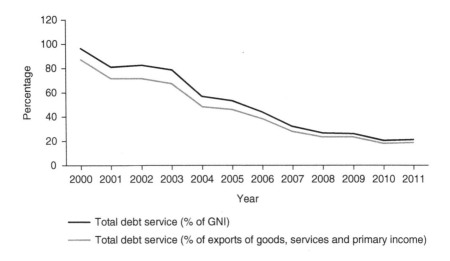

Figure 5.3 Brazil's debt service, 2000–2011.
Source: World Bank, Commodity Price Data—Pink Sheet Data.

orthodox neoliberal macro framework combined with neodevelopmentalist industrial and social policies. In 2002, Lula's likely victory in the upcoming presidential elections precipitated a wave of anxiety both domestically and abroad, with concerns that the Workers' Party candidate planned debt default and sweeping nationalizations (Mollo and Saad-Filho 2006; Anderson 2011). After a bout of capital flight, stock market turbulence, and currency depreciation, Lula made a written public commitment to continue with the neoliberal orientation of the Fernando Henrique Cardoso government and with IMF-mandated reforms, including central bank independence.

In 2006, by contrast, the fruits of an export-led (and particularly commodity-led) recovery—rising reserves, a positive current account balance, and improved tax receipts—could be parlayed into a more ambitious domestic developmental agenda. Even at this point, elements inside and outside the government pushed for a policy of generating ever-higher primary surpluses, with the goal of aggressively reducing debt-to-GDP ratios further (Serrano and Summa 2011). Nevertheless, since IMF obligations could no longer magnify the force of these voices, Lula now possessed the leeway to embark upon a neodevelopmentalist agenda. Increased social spending, successive minimum wage hikes, public investment initiatives, and a doubling of lending from development bank Banco Nacional de Desenvolvimento Econômico e Social (National Bank for Economic and Social Development, or BNDES), to 4 percent of GDP, helped the domestic market take over as the main economic engine. GDP grew by an average of 4.5 percent per year during Lula's second term, despite the impact of the global financial crisis (World Bank n.d.; Doctor 2015).

In comparison to Argentina's policies over the same period, Brazil's record suggests that the PT's continuing preoccupation with inflation (and maintenance of an overvalued real through high interest rates) may have closed off avenues for revenue and export maximization, which otherwise might have allowed for a much more comprehensive realization of neo-developmentalist goals. By the time interest rates were tentatively reduced under Rousseff, the boat had perhaps been missed on these opportunities, as I discuss further in the following section. In Argentina, pursuit of export competitiveness via an undervalued peso was, initially at least, more sur-vival strategy than development model, given the country's isolation from capital markets following the 2002 debt default. However, given devalua-tion and advances in productivity, it quickly became apparent that, under commodity boom conditions, soy could be taxed at rates akin to rates in natural resource industries, without excessively damaging profitability or competitiveness. The fiscal benefits to the government may have been pro-portionately smaller than those accruing to a typical oil exporter, but, when seen in context, this should not lead to the conclusion reached in some quarters (for example, Weisbrot et al. 2011) that the importance of soy for Argentina's economic recovery has been exaggerated.

Export tax revenues from soybeans and their products, in fact, appear to have been more crucial than their simple weight in fiscal accounts would suggest. Indeed, they were a key source of the subsidies that helped to revive the domestic market following devaluation and drive a consumer boom (Richardson 2009; Kaplan 2014). This redistribution from exporters to domestic producers was the cornerstone of the evolving Argentinian eco-nomic model under the Kirchners. These also are exactly the kinds of poli-cies that would not have been permissible within an IMF program. The independent fiscal resource provided by soy exports, therefore, played an important role in deferring the need for a postdefault rapprochement with creditors, which would have threatened the government's ability to pur-sue its particular variation on neodevelopmentalism. Had the commodity boom not begun shortly following default and devaluation, then, it seems extremely unlikely that anything like the policy orientation initiated under Nestor Kirchner and deepened under Cristina Fernandez de Kirchner could have been constructed.

Brazil

Brazil's turn toward neodevelopmentalism during the commodity boom essentially entailed a gradual shift in influence at the level of policy, in favor of more nationally inclined segments of capital, along with their allies in popular sectors and within the arms of the state. Brazil never experienced a process of neoliberalization as extreme as that seen in most of its neighbors, and it inherited a rather ragged but still substantive legacy from the ISI era in the form of a significant industrial base, a relatively large number of state-owned enterprises, and a persistence of developmentalist thinking among elements of the bureaucracy (Hochstetler and Montero 2013).

Over the commodity boom years, large domestic capital can be broadly categorized into two (partially overlapping and partially contingent) blocs. A more internationally integrated fraction, consisting of much of the services sector (especially finance), media, and some manufacturing, tended to favor a neoliberal policy orientation, which in the Brazilian context meant inflation targeting, high interest rates, free capital movement, a floating exchange rate (with an overvalued currency), privatizations, and central bank independence (Morais and Saad-Filho 2011). Another fraction was made up of state-owned enterprises, elements of manufacturing (especially those with a domestic base of accumulation, such as in food processing), construction, and agribusiness. These sectors tended to support more interventionist measures via active industrial policies as well as, in many cases, the extension of domestic demand through wage increases (Loureiro and Saad-Filho 2019; Bresser-Pereira 2015).

Boom conditions essentially allowed for a compromise between these two blocs. For example, high interest rates (on average, the fifth highest in the world over the period 2003 to 2015, according to Weisbrot et al. [2017]) combined with a floating exchange rate targeted inflation while resulting in an overvalued real. Meanwhile, negative effects of such a regime on investment and competitiveness could be compensated for, to some extent, by the extension of cheap credit via BNDES, subsidies, industrial policy, and wage hikes. In fiscal policy, too, tax revenue from the export boom helped the Lula presidency (2002–2010) to maintain a primary surplus while increasing public spending. Lula and his successor, Rousseff, successively deepened the developmentalist elements of the policy mix, in an effort to wring faster growth from the economy, but Rousseff would eventually run into the limits of this strategy and see her political coalition collapse along with it, as the commodity boom petered out.

Lula's first administration (2002–2006) is perhaps better characterized as fundamentally neoliberal in orientation, rather than neodevelopmentalist, even if some important changes during this period laid the groundwork for more full-fledged reorientation, from 2006 on. Nevertheless, Lula's first government essentially continued in the same vein as his predecessor, Cardoso, with contractionary monetary and fiscal policies targeted primarily at price stability. While no new privatizations occurred, none of the previous sell-offs, such as the unpopular sale of mining giant Vale in the late 1990s, were reversed. Some rather pioneering social programs, such as Fome Zero (Zero Hunger) and Bolsa Familia (Family Allowance), did originate during this period, and these formed the flagship of the international promotion of Brazil as a potential developmental model in the rest of the global South, part of a campaign initially aimed at gaining a permanent UN Security Council seat (Muggah and Hamann 2012; Dauvergne and Farias 2012).

Lula's perhaps reluctant embrace of neoliberalism had, in fact, occurred in several stages. Following each of his three unsuccessful presidential campaigns (in 1989, 1994, and 1998), Lula successively dropped numerous elements of what originally had been a rather radical socialist platform, in an effort to broaden his electoral appeal. Even so, the 2002 campaign, with Lula emerging as the front-runner, was widely seen as a referendum on Cardoso's unpopular experiment with neoliberalism (Hunter and Power 2005). Although elements of the previous ISI model had been dismantled during the 1980s, Cardoso's 1994 Real Plan was the first time that a comprehensive set of neoliberal-inspired policies had been applied in Brazil (Mollo and Saad-Filho 2006). The program contained the usual roll call of measures, including liberalization of trade and of markets for capital and labor, a slew of privatizations, and shrinking of the state apparatus. Hyperinflation was successfully curbed, but at the expense of an overvalued currency (pegged to the U.S. dollar), and interest rates remained above 30 percent from 1995 to 1999 (Amann and Baer 2000). This combination was initially relatively successful, though it depended upon massive capital inflows to compensate for the persistent current account deficits produced by the new exchange rate.

As the enthusiasm felt among capital markets for developing economies soured in the wake of the 1997 Asian crisis, the real came under sustained pressure, and devaluation ensued in 1999, though not before the agreement with the IMF of a $40 billion structural adjustment package (Ferrari-Filho and De Paula 2003). A postdevaluation revival was short-lived, as Brazil was caught up in the fallout from a not-dissimilar crisis in neighboring Argentina. At this point, the economic record of Cardoso's plan seemed mixed at best, certainly when placed alongside the austerity measures, which had been an integral part of the strategy and which only intensified as the government sought to placate nervous creditors.

Given this backdrop, Lula, as the most prominent opposition candidate, seemed to be in a promising position in the run-up to the 2002 election. However, despite having substantially moderated his platform over the years, speculation was rife, particularly among a fiercely anti-PT media, that Lula would suspend public debt repayments if elected. Both the Brazilian stock market and international investors responded poorly to the prospect of a PT victory, putting Lula under pressure to affirm his commitment to repaying creditors and respecting agreements with the IFIs.[9] The resulting "letter to the Brazilian people," in which Lula acceded to the demands, stands as something of an irony: a candidate who looked likely to win in large part because of the unpopularity of his predecessor's economic policies was now required to endorse exactly these measures.

The incident serves as a useful illustration of the difficulties of successfully adopting and implementing a policy platform running counter to neoliberal orthodoxy prior to the effects of the commodity boom being felt. As described previously, it was only after the boom revived export markets, from 2004 on, that Brazil found itself with a sufficiently strong external position for post-neoliberal divergence to become feasible. The decision by Lula (and continued by Rousseff) to take this path as it opened up, however, depended upon a domestic political realignment, which occurred over the course of the PT's first term and came to a head with Lula's reelection in 2006.

Lula's acceptance of IMF terms and his enthusiasm for maintaining growing primary budget surpluses tended to alienate the traditional leftist base of the PT, which increasingly became attracted to the alternative paradigm offered by neodevelopmentalist ideas. In 2005, opposition parties, still suspicious of Lula, even given a degree of policy convergence, revealed a scandal involving cash for congressional votes in support of the PT (Boito and Berringer 2014). This was almost successful in toppling the government and did result in the resignation of several senior figures, including finance minister Antonio Palocci.

Eroding trust in a party that had always attempted to set itself apart from the pervasive corruption of Brazilian politics, the scandal left Lula relying for reelection upon segments of the population more likely to favor a neodevelopmentalist agenda. Principally, this meant new PT supporters, especially in the Northeast and peri-urban zones, who had benefited from conditional cash transfers (Hunter and Power 2007; Bresser-Pereira 2012), as well as nationally inclined segments of capital, who were as disappointed with the fruits of neoliberalism as Lula himself appeared to be and were seeking more governmental support. After paying off the total outstanding debt to the IMF in 2005—just as happened in Argentina—Lula won the 2006 election easily, reconfigured his administration by placing heterodox economists in key posts, and announced a shift toward a policy of "national economic development."

Many important interventions were undertaken during this second term, which departed from neoliberal orthodoxy and which were continued by Lula's successor, Dilma Rousseff. Perhaps most ambitious of these was the Programa de Aceleração do Crescimento (Growth Acceleration Program, or PAC), a $236 billion package of public infrastructure investment, followed up with PAC II, under Rousseff, worth another $525 billion (Morais and Saad-Filho 2012). The state-owned BNDES was not new, having been created under Cardoso, a reminder of the continuing weight of developmentalist voices even during the Brazilian neoliberal era. Nevertheless, it came to prominence during Lula's second term, when BNDES massively expanded its credit lines to the point that, by 2012, it was lending more annually than the World Bank (Doctor 2015; Cameron and Stanley 2017). This went some way to compensating for a lack of private investment as interest rates remained high.

The minimum wage was raised several times, helping to reintegrate organized labor into the PT coalition while simultaneously expanding domestic markets (Seidman 2010). Significant sections of informal labor were regularized and brought into the formal sphere, also entailing wage increases. Along with subsidizing national capital in the domestic sphere, a mix of support for state enterprises and encouragement of the concentration of private capital, combined with Brasilia's diplomatic backing, led to the emergence of transnationalized Brazilian "national champions" such as Petrobras (oil), Odebrecht (construction), Gerdau (steel), and AmBev (beverages).[10] Meanwhile, conditional cash transfers were hugely expanded, with Bolsa Familia reaching 11.4 million households by 2010 (Morais and Saad-Filho 2012). While overvaluation of the real under both Lula and Rousseff never presented the same advantages to commodity exporters as devaluation had in Argentina, neither did PT governments ever attempt to impose the kinds of export taxes seen in Brazil's southern neighbor, and Lula's facilitation of an expanding agricultural frontier allowed for a continuing concentration of landownership in the hands of large agribusiness (Anderson 2011).

Rousseff, Lula's former chief of staff and handpicked successor, entered office in 2011, committed to a more ambitious developmentalist program. The next two years brought a reduction in interest rates, from 12.5 percent to a record low of 7.5 percent by the beginning of 2013 (prompting depreciation of the real), tax rebates for industry, a quadrupling of BNDES outlays, public–private partnership opportunities offered on generous terms, and price controls on energy (Singer 2017). These measures were so strongly tied to the interests of industrialists that they were often referred to as the "FIESP agenda," after the Federação das Indústrias do Estado de São Paulo (Industrial Federation of the State of Sao Paulo). Nevertheless, it was during this period that "despite the evident convergence between the government's program and the interests of the industrial sector, the industrialists . . . gradually moved away from Rousseff, and slowly and steadily aligned with the rent-seeking opposition bloc. It was as if, with every gesture made by the government to favor them, there grew among the industrialists the vision that it was all about 'interventionism'" (Singer 2017, 361).

Disappointing results of Rousseff's agenda in the face of a worsening external environment likely helped to push key segments of capital away from the PT and back behind a return to more conventional neoliberalism. A wave of mass protests began in 2013, triggered initially by increases in public transport prices but soon growing and tilting toward an anticorruption agenda fueled by the *lava jato* (car wash) scandal. Though *lava jato* implicated a range of businesspeople and senior figures from across the political landscape, media coverage, popular anger, and the efforts of prosecutors were especially directed toward the PT government, just as prices for key commodity exports started to plateau and then decline. Alhough Rousseff was reelected in 2014, she would be impeached and ousted from power two years later (on the basis of a relatively minor budget reporting offense) and replaced by an interim government committed to neoliberalization and redoubled austerity.

Neoliberal Argentina

After unsuccessful heterodox experiments in the immediate postdictatorship era of the 1980s, Carlos Menem, a populist right-wing Peronist, was elected in 1989, under conditions of hyperinflation, and Argentina adopted an ambitious and radical neoliberal restructuring program throughout the 1990s (Riggirozzi 2009, 94–96; Azpiazu, Basualdo, and Nochteff 1998). This included sweeping privatizations (including of the pensions system), unilateral liberalization of trade and capital movements, and the flexibilization of labor markets. A key variant on the standard structural adjustment package negotiated with the IMF was the convertibility plan, which stopped just short of dollarization by pegging the peso to the U.S. dollar at 1:1 and mandating an 80 percent reserve requirement in U.S. dollars. The plan met its primary goal by reducing inflation from 200 percent to 5 percent in two years, and GDP growth in the Menem years was robust, save for one year of recession, in 1995.

With an artificially strong peso, cheap imports of consumer goods flooded in, leading to the closure of many small and medium-size domestic companies. Large enterprises, however, tended to benefit enormously in terms of productivity, a result of new imported capital goods and falling labor costs as a result of flexibilization (Feliz 2012). This is important in the sense that, although the 1990s certainly saw an increasing penetration of foreign capital (both productive and financial) in the Argentinian economy, the domestic productive sphere, even if now relatively subordinate, had in nominal terms increased its unity and capacity, allowing it to begin to play a much more influential role when conjunctural circumstances swung in its favor during the early 2000s.[11]

One of the predictable impacts of neoliberalization in Argentina was a huge increase in unemployment. Privatized and newly concentrated industries laid off workers, adding to the large numbers left jobless as their employers were forced out by cheap imports and larger firms. Compounding this, decentralization had shifted to the provinces the burden of many aspects of public provision of health, education, and social programs, with this restructuring resulting in the shedding of two hundred thousand jobs (Grugel and Riggirozzi 2007). Repeated rioting had been the consequence, even from the early years of *menemismo*, with this unrest eventually solidifying into the *piquetero* movement of the unemployed, which organized a sustained bout of social conflict over eight months of 1997. The piqueteros had become powerful actors by the time of the 2001 debt default, meaning that postcrisis strategies had to work at containing or co-opting the more radical demands for change present in some of the various organizations falling under this broad label (Dinerstein 2003).

The Mexican crisis of 1994 had already shown the fragility of Argentinian neoliberalism before the impact of the linked East Asian, Russian, and Brazilian crises, between 1997 and 1999, signaled the beginning of the end. Menem's fiscal policies were hardly expansive, as is occasionally claimed (Mussa 2002). In fact, Argentina ran a primary surplus in every year of the 1990s. Nevertheless, in conditions of apparent macroeconomic stability under a neoliberal regime, Paris Club investors and IFIs were eager to sustain an increasing spiral of debt, engendered by an overvalued peso, the racking up of ever-wider trade deficits, and the lack of policy instruments available to combat successive crisis-driven rounds of capital flight. When Brazil, Argentina's biggest export market, devalued the real in 1999, Argentinian exports became even less competitive and the convertibility regime appeared increasingly unsustainable.

Unsurprisingly, the 1999 elections saw victory for the opposition candidate, Fernando de la Rua. Despite promising reforms, de la Rua was unable to resist policy pressure, principally from the IMF, which had funneled substantial sums into propping up the convertibility regime and would not at this stage countenance its abandonment. By 2001, recession had turned to depression as de la Rua cut public sector wages by 13 percent as part of a "zero deficit plan." In November of the same year, the IMF abandoned the government, which at this point imposed a daily cash withdrawal limit (the *corralito*) as it worried about runs on the banks. Unrest had already been widespread, especially among the unemployed and newly impoverished, but this restriction brought the middle classes out to the streets en masse, prompting the declaration of a state of emergency, which ended with thirty-six killed by the police, including seven children, and de la

Rua then fleeing in the presidential helicopter. The next two weeks saw a succession of five different presidents, until eventually the leader of the National Chamber of Deputies, Eduardo Duhalde, was able to restore a semblance of order (Munck 2001, 2003; MacEwan 2002).

Post-Neoliberal Argentina

In contrast to the gradual change seen in Brazil, Argentina's debt default signaled a sudden loss of power for financial capital—both domestic and transnational—within the domestic sphere, meaning that these groups had little influence on how policy evolved in the postdefault environment. In the immediate aftermath, caretaker president Duhalde (a Peronist) enacted a series of emergency measures designed to contain the social impact of the economic catastrophe and to limit political instability. Though seemingly rather ad hoc and designed to address temporary, specific problems, these policies would form the basis for a rather more programmatic neo-developmentalist orientation under the Kirchners.

The transitional period under Duhalde is thus of great significance as the genesis of a new political coalition that would set the terms of Argentina's political-economic path for the next decade or more. Initially important were a heterodox group of economists from the University of Buenos Aires, the Grupo Fenix, together with the Grupo Productivo, a lobbying organization of powerful industrialists set up in the 1990s to influence the privatization process (now thoroughly disillusioned with the neoliberal creed), and the piquetero movements, which carried the threat of widespread unrest (Riggirozzi 2009 103; Gak 2011). All agreed with Duhalde that resolving the crisis required rebooting domestic production—far above any need to placate investors and creditors, whose voices were at this point greatly diminished.

Absolutely key to all subsequent policy was the abandonment of convertibility, in January 2002. The newly floating peso settled quickly to a rate of approximately 3:1 against the U.S. dollar. Default was declared on a large proportion of the public debt and much private domestic debt converted to the public sphere. "Pesification" of dollar-denominated paper at the old 1:1 rate meant 66 percent haircuts for creditors, and this, together with partial default and the state's assumption of private debt, significantly reduced the power of financial capital in Argentina, at the cost of access to international credit markets.

Meanwhile, devaluation brought both a slump in imports (and, initially, in consumption in general) and the emergence of newly competitive exports, setting up conditions for renewed accumulation as all sectors entered trade surplus. This formed the hinge upon which the fundamental reorientation of the Argentinian economy, from debt-driven to export-driven, turned. It seems doubtful, though, that the ensuing loosening of the balance of payments constraint would have been sustained without the commodities boom of the 2000s. Certainly, the neodevelopmentalist project, which was essentially paid for with commodity export rents, seems unlikely to have emerged without the boom.

This becomes obvious upon considering the evolving role of soy in both economic recovery and policy reorientation. Following devaluation, rents from the export commodity sector were leveraged as a major source of revenues with which to maintain fiscal solvency. With these industries now highly competitive internationally (soy being the largest and most profitable), Duhalde was able to impose a 10 percent export tax without threatening producer profitability (Fairfield 2011). Though ostensibly a temporary emergency measure, this taxing of, essentially, elements of the rural bourgeoisie by a Peronist president recreated a central historical fault line in the Argentinian political economy, one that had endured from Perón's first administration up until the return of democracy in 1983 (Richardson 2009). Here, as in O'Donnell's (1978) classic analysis, an urban-populist coalition of workers and national bourgeoisie, joined by transnationally oriented capital, backs a government that restricts exports of agricultural goods to the detriment of the large Pampean landowners. These goods would have been mostly beef and wheat, both classified as wage goods, owing to the substantial share of workers' incomes taken up by their consumption. By restricting exports, increasing domestic supply, and depressing prices, real wages were effectively increased while nominal wages were contained, serving the interests of both workers and industrialists.

Generally, such an arrangement would eventually run into a balance of payments crisis, given lost export earnings, at which point a new grouping of the rural landlords and export-oriented capital would take over, devaluing the currency, cutting back on support for the domestic market, and moving strongly toward the maximization of agricultural production for export. When this resulted in stagflation, a new crisis would ensue, and groups resembling the first coalition would resume power.

In Richardson's (2009) view, the rise of soy as a monocrop over the 1990s and 2000s, to a large extent displacing wheat and beef production, allowed a reconfigured populist coalition to break the cycle, in the early 2000s. Very little soy is consumed domestically in Argentina; therefore, provided the sector remains profitable, it is possible to impose export taxes (known as *retenciones*) not with the goal of reducing exports but to directly capture a portion of the surplus for the state, without harming export earnings, thus avoiding the usual balance of payments constraint.[12] A portion of the retenciones could then be redeployed into production and consumption subsidies, with outcomes analogous to the earlier grain and meat export restrictions, effectively boosting real wages while reducing pressure on employers to raise nominal wage levels. Soaring Chinese demand and ever-increasing soy prices gave Duhalde's successors great leeway to up the level of the retenciones without threatening the industry's profitability, allowing for the redistributive arrangement to continue and expand in scope.

With the election of Nestor Kirchner, in 2003, the populist coalition solidified and Duhalde's emergency taxes became permanent fixtures, repeatedly increased as exporters' profits rose—to 20 percent in 2003, and twice in 2007, to 27.5 percent and then to 35 percent, as the most intensive phase of the boom kicked in.[13] At first glance, the overall inability of large agribusiness to resist these measures is surprising, given their enduring centrality to the Argentinian economy and the growth of the sector across the decade. Fairfield (2011) convincingly argues, though, that the rural bourgeoisie lacked both the instrumental and the structural power to substantially influence government under the Kirchners. Rural exporters had few if any ties to government and had in fact been relatively isolated from politics even under Menem and de la Rua. Compounding this was a lack of unity and homogeneity within the sector, which was divided into four representative associations based on size of holding. Structurally, and perhaps counterintuitively, Argentinian agribusiness was fatally weakened by its continued ability to reap often record profits in spite of repeated tax increases, given the devalued peso[14] and high international prices; policy makers had few reasons to believe that further taxes might threaten investment levels, whether domestic or transnational.[15]

The Components of Argentinian Neodevelopmentalism

In spite of benefiting greatly from devaluation, Argentinian agribusiness resented what they correctly saw as redistribution from the rural export-oriented motor of the economy to the government's urban constituencies under *kirchnerismo*. This is true in several senses, to the extent that this process really represents the foundation stone upon which the Argentinian form of neodevelopmentalism was built. Export orientation and the taxing of agro-industrial sectors provided the main source of foreign exchange; allowed for sustained primary surpluses in spite of expanding spending; funded investment, subsidies, and social programs; and facilitated management of the exchange rate.

One such piece of the neodevelopmentalist project—and, like export taxes, one which had its genesis in the emergency measures of 2002—was post-neoliberal social policy. Concerned by the militancy of some piquetero groups in conditions of double-digit negative GDP growth and continuing social instability, Duhalde created the Plan Jefes y Jefas de Hogares Desempleados (Unemployed Heads of Household Plan, or PJJHD) (Feliz 2012; Dinerstein et al. 2008). This provided an income transfer of $40 a month, on the condition that the beneficiary engage in some kind of community work, such as small-scale public works or artisanal food production.[16] The complementary Plan Manos a la Obra (Hands to Work Plan) provided access to the equipment necessary for the PJJHD schemes.

While these schemes to some extent undoubtedly descended into clientelism, with the unemployed often essentially working for local politicians in exchange for a stipend, the goal of the PJJHD was seemingly simply to draw the sting from the movements of the unemployed.[17] This was successful in the sense of temporarily diffusing some of the worst unrest, though Duhalde was in fact forced to call new elections early, after the shooting of two piquetero protesters by police during a protest in June 2003. Just as Duhalde's emergency economic policies had, without any great strategic intent, shaped the conditions under which capital would come to be reintegrated into the emerging neodevelopmentalist regime, so too had Duhalde's social interventions set the tone for a Nestor Kirchner's neocorporatist approach to labor and social policy in the subsequent years.

The PJJHD was gradually replaced by two schemes, the Plan Familias Para la Inclusión Social (Family Social Inclusion Plan) and the Plan de

Capacitación y Empleo (Training and Employment Plan). Despite the declining participation of the World Bank in funding the programs, a post–Washington Consensus influence is obvious, particularly for the first of the two (Feliz 2012; Wylde 2011). Plan Familias, designed for those unable to work, includes the kinds of stipulations common to most conditional cash transfer programs—medical checkups and regular school attendance for dependents. The Training and Employment Plan, in contrast, required attendance at training programs and evidence that the recipient was searching for work. More important in containing the social threat posed by the unemployed (combined with stimulating jobs growth) was the transformation of the Hands to Work Plan into new schemes meant to address inadequate housing and utility provision, under which beneficiaries would work as cheap construction labor, with the government providing tools and building materials. Workers were required to form cooperatives to secure these supplies, channeling groups of potentially disruptive unemployed into bureaucratic channels, where local authorities could favor those groups and individuals that proved more pliable (Feliz 2012).

With respect to formal labor, both Kirchners deployed a classically corporatist–Peronist strategy, similar in orientation to their social policy. Formal workers, the core base of popular support for the government, saw benefits, but they were increasingly demobilized and directed through bureaucratic channels to access these benefits. Nevertheless, concessions to influential private sector unions such as the Confederación General de Trabajo (General Confederation of Labor), led by the powerful truckers' union, saw considerable increases in both minimum and real average wages (Cook and Bazler 2013).[18] Much of Menem's flexibilization package was repealed, and a return to collective bargaining allowed advancements for labor while largely removing the threat of radicalism and unrest. In dollar terms, however, wages remained low, facilitating the continuing profitability of even structurally uncompetitive firms (particularly manufacturers). Informal workers arguably did better than under the original Peronist coalitions, given the new provision of social programs, though workers' pay in the public sector rose consistently slower than inflation, a consequence of the priority placed on the need to maintain a primary budget surplus, at least under Nestor Kirchner.

This concern for primary surplus is very much in keeping with a neo-developmentalist approach, in which a broad macroeconomic stability is prized above a concern with narrow monetary policy. In the Argentinian case, although the government was not attempting to win the approval of international credit markets—given that these were effectively closed off after the 2002 default—a primary fiscal surplus was necessary to permit the settling of the remaining debt on advantageous terms. This was a key policy priority and a source of political legitimacy for Nestor Kirchner, who had come to power mainly on a platform of rejection of the IMF and a promise of "serious capitalism," in contrast to the "speculative capitalism" of the 1990s (Wylde 2011).

With the economy booming by 2005, and with a concurrent rise in international reserves, Nestor Kirchner was in a strong position vis-à-vis international creditors. He succeeded in securing a deal for payment of thirty-five cents on the dollar for most of the Paris Club debt and paid off all outstanding IMF debt, enabling Argentina to leave the fund, at least in de facto terms (Stiglitz 2006; Dieter 2006). While settling the IMF debt may have been of mostly symbolic importance, it is still the case that the commodity boom had provided a means for the economy to operate successfully, independently of transnational financial capital, allowing for the setting of a thoroughly non-neoliberal development strategy.[19]

Following devaluation, the main instrument of this strategy was the maintenance of a stable and competitive exchange rate. The stimulation this afforded to exports helped to build up international reserves, allowing for control of the exchange rate and, absent the possibility of deficit financing, providing a hedge against possible decreases in commodity prices. These factors, combined with the ability to tax export commodities heavily and thus allow for fiscal stability despite a relatively expansive stance, facilitated the macroeconomic stability sought by neodevelopmentalists, at least during the Nestor Kirchner administration. Moreover, in keeping with neodevelopmentalist doctrine, and unlike Brazil, interest rates were kept low in order to stimulate investment (Ebenau and Liberatore 2013).[20]

Against this backdrop, the government was able to roll out what amounted to an industrial policy, essentially consisting of a redistribution from the most profitable fraction of capital (agro-exporters) to the least (industrial manufacturing), further supporting the competitiveness of manufacturing, on top of the already hugely positive impact of the exchange rate regime. In contrast to Brazil, however, these interventions were less direct and explicit, meaning that they often have not been understood as industrial policy as such.[21]

Once again, some of these policies originated in immediate postcrisis measures, which were later adapted to more programmatic use under the Kirchners. For example, price controls on privatized (mostly foreign-owned) utilities and transport were initially meant to simply alleviate suffering and slow the inevitable round of postdevaluation inflation. Under Nestor Kirchner, however, these became instruments for the recuperation of domestic markets by freeing up income for consumption.[22]

While it was by no means as ambitious as the Brazilian PAC, Argentinian infrastructure spending increased fivefold by 2008, fueling a boom in construction (Wylde 2011). In the absence of a development bank, the government worked informally with the central bank to encourage an emphasis on credit for long-term productive purposes (Hornbeck 2013).[23] As we have seen, taxes on the export of wheat and beef—and even temporary export bans, as in previous eras—effectively functioned as wage subsidies. In this sense, informal government pressure on banks to ease credit, or negotiations with supermarkets to voluntarily control the price of basic goods, also may be thought of as forms of industrial policy. In almost all cases, the central goal was to support the profitability of a structurally uncompetitive domestic industrial sector, with the corollary of maintaining sufficient popular class support to ensure political legitimacy for this project, presented in nationalist-developmentalist terms.

This aim, in fact, is somewhat distinct from the ideotypical neodevelopmentalist strategy, whereby domestic industry is promoted and supported in order that technological upgrading and higher-value-added production may be achieved. The only area in which such policies were attempted in earnest was in the agro-industrial sector. Differentials in tariff rates on primary products (for example, soy) compared to their processed derivatives (such as soy oil or pellets) acted to equalize profit rates for exports in these categories and thus to encourage greater exports of lightly processed agricultural manufactures (Peine 2013). As a consequence, Argentina, the third-largest exporter of soy products overall, became the world's number one in both soy oil and meal (Hansen and Gale 2014).

Any technology-intensive manufacturing that exists in Argentina, such as the important auto industry, which mostly exports to Brazil, is part of a highly integrated global supply chain and is heavily dependent upon imports. This is part of the generally weak integration of the Argentinian productive structure (Ebenau and Liberatore 2013). With imported industrial inputs becoming expensive following devaluation, it is perhaps unsurprising that the auto sector was once again in trade deficit by 2011.

Manufacturing generally seems to have run into contradictions during the presidency of Cristina Fernandez de Kirchner (2007–2015).[24] As productivity began to stagnate, profits were gradually undermined by continuing formal sector wage increases (Feliz 2015). In order to placate industrial capital and maintain profitability, the prices of consumer goods from this sector were allowed to rise, fueling inflation, which was hidden by manipulation of official statistics. Inflation began to eat into the real exchange rate and the government increasingly struggled to balance wage demands, domestic firms' profitability, and exporters' international competitiveness, primarily by extending subsidies. Subsidy spending moved from $1.6 billion to $18.1 billion (or 4 percent of GDP) from 2006 to 2011 (Hornbeck 2013).

In 2008, the defeat of the proposed move to a variable windfall tax on agricultural exports denied the government extra resources with which to fund increased spending and hold down utility prices in the context of rising inflation. A partial substitute for these revenues was found through the renationalization of pension funds in the same year, until, in 2010, the government turned to the unusual solution of earmarking a portion of the central bank's dollar reserves for the repayment of outstanding international debt (Kaplan 2014). The bank's governor was removed after objecting, marking another step in a process of eroding separation between the bank and the government during the postcrisis years. Even if the return of the bank to political control remained tacit, a 2012 charter made its policy orientation explicit, with its mandate being to "promote monetary stability, financial stability, employment, and economic development with social equity" (cited in Hornbeck 2013, 7), in contrast to the narrow inflation-targeting mandate of the typical neoliberal central bank. This is perhaps the clearest statement of the extent to which Argentina's policy trajectory moved from a neoliberal path under the Kirchners. It is also revealing in that these priorities self-consciously reflect those of the neodevelopmentalist model.

By 2014, there were indications that the government was considering a return to borrowing on the international market (Schiipani and Rodrigues 2014), simply out of necessity; dwindling foreign reserves, by this point, were being depleted by the twin tasks of covering fiscal deficits and maintaining the stability of the peso. The government agreed on $5 billion in compensation to former owner Repsol for the expropriation of oil company Yacimientos Petrolíferos Fiscales (Treasury Oil Fields, or YPF) and began negotiations with the IMF regarding compliance with its norms on data reporting. These moves may well have been intended to start the process of regaining investor confidence, though repeated threats to strip Argentina of its G20 membership also may have been a factor. In any case, later in 2014, a New York court ruled in favor of a so-called vulture fund, which had bought up a portion of debt owed to the holdout creditors—those who had rejected the broadly successful 2005 renegotiation of bonds that followed the 2002 default.[25] Since the ruling prohibited the government from meeting payments on the rescheduled debt unless the vulture funds were also repaid, Argentina then entered its second, though far less consequential, default in twelve years (Mander 2014). This cut off the possibility of renewed borrowing on international markets.

In this regard, it is interesting that the Kirchner government, over time, seems to have become increasingly interested in direct Chinese assistance as a means of preventing the neodevelopmentalist project from stalling. In 2010, a $10 billion loan was obtained from China Development Bank for a renovation of Argentina's mostly defunct rail network, and further infrastructure deals with Chinese policy banks followed, including three loans totaling $7 billion, signed immediately after the vulture fund ruling (Gallagher and Myers 2018). Perhaps even more significant was the concurrent announcement of an $11 billion currency swap with China, providing a much-needed source of foreign exchange (Kaplan 2014). Nevertheless, with the economy entering recession in 2014, *kirchnerista* candidate Daniel Scioli lost the 2015 presidential election to Buenos Aires mayor Mauricio Macri, who would return Argentina to a neoliberal agenda—and also to the IMF, agreeing to a $50 billion loan in 2018 (Gillespie 2018).

Conclusion

Neodevelopmentalism as an intellectual agenda is a significant addition to the important tradition of Latin American development thought, reflecting its geographic roots through a preoccupation with correcting for the historical failures of the ISI strategies pursued across the region. In another sense, though, neodevelopmentalist proposals seek to manage the difficult task of implementing a somewhat interventionist model of development, while simultaneously maintaining trade and fiscal surpluses, in an effort to avoid ruffling transnational feathers within the reality of a neoliberal global regime. Both the Brazilian and Argentinian varieties of neodevelopmentalism, however, emerged during the particular circumstances of the commodity boom, which provided a boost both to government revenue and to the current account, substantially lessening the difficulties of combining a conservative fiscal policy with an expanding public role in the economy.

Empirically, at least, this leaves unanswered the question of whether sustaining such a balancing act would have been possible under the trickier neoliberal conditions that, after all, the model had been specifically crafted to navigate. We do, though, have the evidence of what happened after the end of the boom, when, in both cases, neoliberal governments retook control of the state in the midst of decaying economic conditions. Counterfactually, too, there is good reason to suppose that, in the Brazilian and Argentinian cases, the successful rollout of any program that departed from neoliberal norms in any substantive way would have remained infeasible without the onset of the commodity boom.

This is true even in the case of the less radical plan instituted in Brazil. The lack of an export boom would have prevented Lula from clearing the IMF debt in 2005, leaving the PT government still committed to the deal between the fund and Cardoso in 2002 (as, indeed, was the intention behind this agreement). The takeoff in exports during Lula's first term is generally held as being responsible for the return to growth in Brazil (Bacha and Fishlow 2011; Anderson 2011), meaning that its absence may well have resulted in continuing stagnation and perhaps even a worsening of the debt situation and IFI dependence. Had the PT managed to win a second term under such circumstances, there likely would have been scope for expansion of the relatively cheap Bolsa Familia program, which remains an important part of Lula's legacy. However, any of the more ambitious initiatives that marked 2006 as a major turning point in Brazil's divergence from neoliberalism—the expansion of BNDES and Petrobras, the PAC, or continued wage increases—would seem to be highly unlikely.

Postdefault governments in Argentina, cut adrift from the capital markets, had less of a need to maintain macroeconomic credibility in the eyes of external investors.[26] The simple fact of this isolation, however, does not, on its own, account for an ability to set policy autonomously. Without the boom in soy exports, in particular, it is hard to see how any postcrisis administration in Argentina would have managed default without returning to further borrowing. This most likely would have taken the form of some kind of IMF-sponsored restructuring package, requiring further rounds of austerity and offering zero scope for the consumption and production subsidies seen under Nestor Kirchner, let alone for the more ambitious policy moves of his successor.

Instead, in terms of the direct fiscal contribution from the retenciones, the buildup of international reserves, and the more generalized economic impact of the takeoff in exports, soy was the crucial factor. Soy both paid for a sizable proportion of the new social and industrial policies and insulated the Kirchners from the need to turn back to the IFIs and capital markets. In later years, *kirchnerismo* ran into contradictions, as ever-greater subsidies were instituted to balance rising inflationary pressures, wage demands, and profitability, presenting particular challenges after the failed attempt to further increase agricultural export taxes in 2008.

It requires no great insight to suggest that the combination of measures implemented to bridge these gaps and maintain the economic model—the nationalization of pension funds and the expropriation of YPF shares, or the diversion of central bank reserves to plug budget holes—would not have been feasible under IFI supervision or for a state looking to return to the bond markets. Indeed, return to the bond markets is exactly the outcome that these policies were designed to avoid. Without the commodity boom, though, there would have been no neodevelopmentalist settlement to protect.

The main purpose of these typological chapters is to understand the form, character, and objectives of each political-economic type, as well as the internal and external dynamics that have produced these trajectories. Passing judgment on the relative success or failure of each state's development strategy, or the validity of the models upon which they are based, is therefore largely outside the scope of this research. However, it is worth commenting upon a basic irony, encountered in both the Argentinian and Brazilian cases, which illustrates the gap between the neodevelopmentalist ideal and their actual development paths, as well as the paramount importance of commodity boom conditions in papering over the resulting cracks—which were then brutally exposed after the end of the boom.

Neodevelopmentalist theory retains the structuralist belief in achieving development via industrial upgrading, moving up the production chain via improvements in technology, skills, and labor productivity. The irony for both Argentina and Brazil is that the policy autonomy and fiscal resources required to pursue this development strategy became available not through the initiation of some self-sustaining virtuous circle of growing competitiveness in industry but because of a major turnaround in the fortunes of their commodity exports. A historic inability to move beyond these sectors, which lie at the very bottom of their respective production chains, was, of course, a major component of the structuralist diagnosis of underdevelopment, something which is echoed in neodevelopmentalist accounts.

It may be that, eventually, the industrial policies that were enabled by commodity boom conditions in both countries will prove to have laid the groundwork for the kind of transformation of the productive structure at which such policies purport to aim. For now, though, a more reasonable assessment seems to be that the commodity boom, for the most part, simply allowed the Brazilian and Argentinian governments to keep uncompetitive manufacturing industries on life support (Carrillo 2014; Feliz 2015). Such concerns have not gone unnoticed, particularly in Brazil, where the worry is about "reprimarization," a regression to a previous role within the global division of labor as a primary commodity exporter—with China driving this process as it devours resources and sends back cheap manufactures (Curado 2015; Gallagher and Porzecanski 2010, chap. 3).[27]

The dependence on commodity exports, which for decades (or even centuries) has often been identified as the main obstacle to Latin American development, clearly continues for Brazil and Argentina, and has even deepened in recent years. When commodity prices began to drop significantly, the vulnerabilities of both Brazil and Argentina to such volatility was once again exposed, threatening to undo any social and economic gains made over the boom years. Political and economic turbulence has brought an end to the two states' emergent neodevelopmentalism, at least for now— and, in the Brazilian case, it led to a major political crisis, which set the table for a resurgent far right. Whether the neodevelopmentalist experiments were inherently flawed or might have proved more resilient, had they been better implemented, remains an open question. Nevertheless, as this chapter has shown, had Chinese import demand not sparked the commodity boom, neither Argentina nor Brazil would have had the economic strength to resist the demands of creditors and begin these experiments in the first place.

CHAPTER VI

Extractivist-Redistributive Type

Ecuador, Bolivia, and Venezuela

Grouping together the governments of Hugo Chavez (Venezuela, 1998–2013), Evo Morales (Bolivia, 2005–), and Rafael Correa (Ecuador, 2006–2017) is hardly an original proposition. The Latin American "pink tide" of the 2000s brought a debate in the literature over the nature of the regions' new left-leaning administrations. The most influential characterization here was of Venezuela, Ecuador, and Bolivia as representatives of a "bad" populist left, as contrasted with a "good" left composed of more sensible moderates, as in Brazil, Chile, and Uruguay (Petkoff 2005; Casteñeda 2006; Weyland 2009). At this point, debate has certainly moved on from this reductionism, influenced no doubt by the rather divergent fortunes that the three more radical Andean cases have experienced since the end of the commodity boom.

My intention here is not to regress to a bad/good or radical/reformist dichotomy. Instead, I suggest a different justification for bracketing Ecuador, Venezuela, and Bolivia, in terms of their political-economic trajectories over the commodity boom years. This is based on commonalities in these countries' circumstances of insertion into the global economy and, crucially, the domestic class configurations that shaped and were shaped by these external linkages. For the extractivist-redistributive (ER) type, uniquely in the typology, the key social force that lay behind a distinctive form of post-neoliberal turn was the popular classes. Indeed, I argue that the ER type existed in three variants over the boom years, and that these differences stem from divergent priorities among their leading popular sector actors. I label these variants "communitarian" (Venezuela), "social movement" (Bolivia), and "technocratic" (Ecuador). However, in all cases strong executives launched redistributive projects on the twin foundations of a growing resource surplus and nearly constant mass mobilization, with mass mobilization employed in conjunction with repeated plebiscites as a means of pushing through the government's agenda in the face of elite resistance.

Here, I discuss the ER trajectory as an ideal type, drawing on notions of populism, which is useful for understanding the emergence of ER governments but does not tell the whole story. The centrality of redistribution to the ER agenda is noted as reflecting ER leaders' reliance on support from marginalized groups—from the urban informal sector, for instance—where the main axis of struggle revolves around exclusion from, rather than exploitation by, the circuits of capitalism.

Following a brief summary of the ER developmental agenda and its possible contradictions with the priority given to redistribution, I move to examine how conditions changed for the main export sectors in each case over the 2002–2013 period. As fuel exporters, all three ER states experienced a marked turnaround from the very low price levels of the 1990s, with China constituting an increasingly hefty driver of global demand. My aim here is to point out the linkages among this China effect on fuel commodities markets, the ensuing enhanced capabilities of ER governments to maximize extractive revenues, and, in turn, the governments' ability to fund new forms of social expenditure.

Finally, I address the domestic political-economic paths taken by each of the three cases during the boom, using Ecuador as the exemplar case for the type. Differences in how redistribution and development were conceived of by authorities in each ER state are key to understanding how the distinctive character of leading popular sectors in each country produced political-economic differentiation among them. In Venezuela (communitarian variant), the government faced the only nationally unified capitalist class of the three cases, which intensified struggle and made the initially poorly rooted governing party seek greater engagement with and organization of core supporters through participatory mechanisms.[1] This, combined with a reluctance to rely upon the traditional arms of the liberal democratic state, led to a growing resort to community organization both as the bedrock of *chavismo* and as a source of informal structures through which to deliver social policy (along with patronage distribution to key elites, including the military).

In Bolivia (social movement variant), the origins of the ruling Movimiento al Socialismo in locally focused social movements, combined with institutional features that favored decentralization, produced a similar focus on municipal administration of social funds. In Ecuador (technocratic variant), by contrast, the collapse of the indigenous social movement bloc Confederación de Nacionalidades Indígenas del Ecuador (Confederation of Indigenous Nationalities of Ecuador, or CONAIE) after it supported the disastrous presidency of Lucio Gutiérrez meant that it was not a major actor in the political movements that brought Rafael Correa to power in Ecuador. Here, urban middle and professional classes took a leading role in government, giving a far more centralized, bureaucratic, and technocratic flavor to policy goals and orientation. In some senses, these three divergent outcomes appear to represent varying trade-offs between mass participation and a coherent national development project.

The Extractive-Redistributive Type: Ideotypical Characteristics

Central to the understanding of the ER type regime is the issue of populism. Roberts (2007, 5) provides a fairly standard, broad definition of Latin American populism as "the top-down political mobilization of mass constituencies by personalistic leaders who challenge elite groups on behalf of an ill-defined *pueblo*, or 'the people.'"[2] Typically, ER regimes are associated with populism in a pejorative sense (Hawkins 2003; Levitsky and Loxton 2013). The term is meant to indicate the "seduction" (de la Torre 2010) of the populace by a charismatic demagogue with little in the way of coherent policy propositions, who instead generates support by portraying themselves as the embodiment of the will of the people in an ethical-symbolic sense, contrasted with the corruption and immorality of the old oligarchy. This Manichean worldview then leads to a majoritarianism that lends itself to the dismantling of liberal democratic checks and balances and their replacement by creeping authoritarianism.

Although this critique is undoubtedly rooted in reality, the extent of its validity depends upon one's particular conception of democracy. Chavez, Correa, and Morales certainly relied upon majoritarianism—both in the polls and on the streets—as a primary means of driving through their agendas and as a lever against the power of domestic capital. Since the state—previously the almost exclusive territory of elites of various kinds—was not conceived of as neutral territory by any of the three leaders, it is hardly surprising that efforts were made in all cases to dismantle or bypass liberal democratic institutions.[3] Given the increasing concentration of authority in the executive branch under all three presidents, combined with their personalistic and charismatic styles, there clearly were dangers associated with these processes, which might plausibly lead to a wide range of political outcomes (Laclau 1977, 170–75; Parker 2001).

Nevertheless, as Lander (2005) points out, populism of this sort has served as a vehicle for the inclusion of large proportions of populations previously marginalized under heterogeneous, hierarchical, and exclusionary societies. If the classical Latin American populist era of Juan Perón and Getúlio Vargas saw the integration of new urban populations, particularly formal workers, then pink tide populist processes were primarily about the political participation of those marginalized under neoliberalism—principally urban, informal populations hugely swelled in numbers by the impact of liberalization. The form that this participation took—expression through populist mechanisms—reflected the fact that the dominant political base in each state lay largely outside the formal sector and was not easily organized along bottom-up lines (Ellner 2012).[4]

Populism is also an appropriate fit for ER regimes, since their most salient social dynamic—of mass marginalization—chimes with the appeal to a *pueblo* (people) in binary opposition to, first, a domestic oligarchy, and secondarily, global neoliberalism. As Kaup (2013b, chap. 1) points out in reference to Bolivia, this in turn requires attention to the differences between processes of exploitation and marginalization within capitalism. In all three ER states, economic stagnation and then liberalization had the effect of excluding large numbers of people from participation in circuits of accumulation, whether through increasing urban unemployment, through accumulation by dispossession in the countryside, or through peasant marginalization in the face of cheaper, liberalized food imports. As a result, the primary axis of popular struggle revolved around exclusion from processes of accumulation (particularly pronounced in these states with enclavic resource industries) rather than around levels of exploitation *within* these processes.

Therborn (2012, 15) notes that taking account of popular marginalization as well as exploitation requires a revised notion of class in order to be comprehensible, and thus he settles on "the popular classes in all their diversity, the *plebeians*" (emphasis in original). Clearly, this broad whole contains contradictory elements, and different sectors within the popular classes of each state varied in prominence (though with a general urban preponderance in all three). Nevertheless, the fundamental notion of ER regimes as an attempted corrective to exclusion rather than exploitation serves as an effective lens through which their political styles, strategies, and policies may be understood.

One ideotypical characteristic of ER states, reflective of an inclusionary orientation, was the use of mobilization and repeated elections and referenda to force through changes to political structure. Correa and Morales undoubtedly took their cues from the experiences of Chavez in Venezuela here. All three leaders prioritized a "refounding" of their nations through use of constituent assemblies to draw up new constitutions, followed by various referenda on further constitutional or institutional change. These electoral contests, which generally delivered strong mandates to the three governments, were meant to demonstrate the "will of the people" as a legitimization, which overrode liberal democratic checks and balances and facilitated a majoritarian rather than consensus-building governance style. Regular electoral events were used as rallying points, which kept supporters almost continually mobilized and sustained momentum for incumbents.

Economic policy aspired toward developmentalist goals, at least in principle. However, these were often sidelined in practice, partly owing to the prioritization of redistribution and partly because of tensions with those sectors of capital that would have been the main beneficiaries—even if, in Bolivia and Ecuador, relations with domestic capital became gradually more accommodative toward the end of the period (Wolff 2016). Overvalued exchange rates, designed to minimize inflation and increase mass consumption, undercut local producers and had an especially detrimental impact on agriculture. Some efforts were undertaken to diversify away from economic dependence on hydrocarbon production, which was perhaps most promising in Ecuador, but the results were generally disappointing.

Instead, and in keeping with the theme of demarginalization, emphasis was on maximizing and redistributing resource rents in a broadly programmatic rather than clientelistic manner (even if clientelistic practices were undoubtedly at play in all three cases, too). As a result, the state took a greater role in extraction, through very much in continued partnership with transnational capital, which was required in order to provide investment and technology. In an era of high commodity prices, transnational extractive firms generally accepted the new terms proposed by governments, if not without protest, and continued to operate profitably in ER states, in spite of the regular and sometimes strident anti-imperialist rhetoric of their governments. Nevertheless, while productive structures have hardly been diversified, economic (as well as political) relations shifted away from dependence on the global North. Chinese capital, both in terms of direct investment and oil-for-loans deals, is now of vital importance in Venezuela, Ecuador, and, to a lesser extent, Bolivia. Russian, Brazilian, Iranian, South Korean, Indian, and even Belarusian capital have all had a presence in one or more of the three states.

External Market Conditions

All of the ER states are primarily fuel exporters, with oil accounting for 55 percent of Ecuadorian exports and 91 percent of Venezuelan exports in 2012 (Chatham House n.d.). In Bolivia, natural gas made up half the total value of exports that same year, with zinc, tin, and lead together adding another 10 percent to the country's export concentration in natural resources. Focusing on hydrocarbons, figure 6.1 shows price indexes for oil, natural gas, and fuels as a whole (a measure that also includes coal). As can be seen, oil prices began to rise around 1999, earlier than increases in other commodities, though from a historically low level. After a drop associated with the September 11, 2001, attacks, a stronger upward price trend began, around the start of the commodity boom proper, from 2003. The chart also reveals the tendency toward price co-movement among fuel commodities, particularly in the 2003–2009 period. Although China is certainly not the only determinant of fuel prices, it clearly is now the central demand driver in this commodity class, as was discussed in detail in chapter 1.

While oil is traded freely on world markets and thus shows relatively little variation in geographic pricing, the situation for natural gas is somewhat more complicated, with implications for Bolivian exports. Though

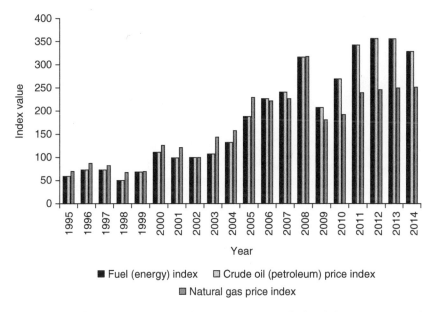

Figure 6.1 Fuel commodity price indexes, 1995–2014. Calculated from International Monetary Fund, World Economic Outlook Database.

there has been a recent growth in the trade of liquid natural gas, which can be shipped around the world freely, most gas is still transported via pipeline, and prices are thus dependent upon localized supply contracts rather than market trading. That said, movements in prices for possible energy substitutes, primarily oil, do have a major influence upon the prices of piped natural gas (Cameron and Stanley 2017). In the context of high and rising energy prices, Evo Morales was able to renegotiate Bolivia's gas supply contracts with Brazil and Argentina—by far Bolivia's two largest export markets. In the Brazilian case, the new variable rate was initially set at four times the previous level, which had been agreed upon in the 1990s (Kaup 2008). As a result of higher prices and a Morales move to appropriate a larger share of the surplus for the state, the fiscal contribution of hydrocarbon revenue rocketed from 9.8 percent of Bolivia's gross domestic product in 2005 to 35 percent in 2013, even in the context of a fast-growing economy (Johnston and Lefebvre 2014).

As in Bolivia, rapidly growing fuel export sectors fed substantial increases in both revenue and expenditure in Venezuela and Ecuador (figures 6.2 and 6.3). From 2004 to 2009, for example, oil accounted for fully 62 percent

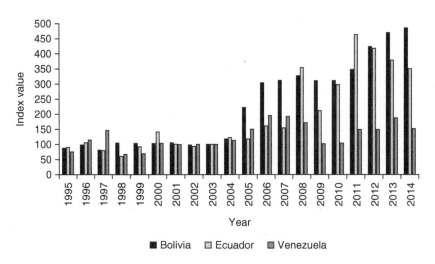

Figure 6.2 Bolivia, Ecuador, and Venezuela resource revenue index (in real), 1995–2014.

Source: Economic Commission for Latin America and the Caribbean, CEPALSTAT.

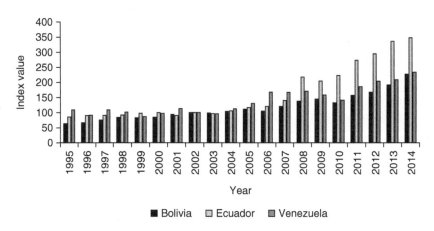

Figure 6.3 Bolivia, Ecuador, and Venezuela general government expenditure indexes (in real), 1995–2014. Calculated from Economic Commission for Latin America and the Caribbean, CEPALSTAT; International Monetary Fund, World Economic Outlook Database.

of Venezuelan central government revenues, a period during which $60 billion was plowed into social services provided by the community *misiones*, which we will discuss (Kaplan 2014). Although the relative increase in Venezuelan expenditures (shown in figure 6.3) appears moderate compared with its ER counterparts, it should be noted that these figures do not reflect the substantial spending on the part of the state-owned oil enterprise Petróleos de Venezuela, S.A. (Venezuelan Petroleum, or PDVSA), which, since the early 2000s, has been directed toward a developmental role.

In Ecuador, the share of oil in government accounts was somewhat lower, but still hugely significant, at 34 percent of total revenues in 2009 (Weisbrot, Johnston, and Lefebvre 2013). In 2007, Ecuador raised its windfall profits tax to 99 percent as a means of forcing transnational firms to the negotiating table. By 2010, all the transnationals had either signed new contracts, which paid a flat fee of between $16 and $41 per barrel, or had withdrawn from the country. Companies such as Petrobras (Brazil), Noble (United States), and the China National Petroleum Company all pulled out, with their operations taken over by the SOE Petroamazonas. Many transnational corporations accepted the new terms, however, including Repsol (Spain), ENAP (a state-owned Chilean enterprise), and—interestingly, given China National Petroleum's withdrawal—private Chinese firms Andes Petroleum and PetroOriental (Escribano 2013). In addition to the Human Development Bond, which we will discuss, Ecuadorian social spending rose from 5 percent of GDP in 2006, the year of Correa's election, to more than 9 percent for the years 2010 to 2012, which included a doubling of education spending (Weisbrot, Johnston, and Lefebvre 2013).

Venezuela

Although Venezuela under Hugo Chavez (and now his successor, Nicolas Maduro) has clearly been home to the most radical experiment of all the ER regimes, it is easy to forget that such a course represents a major break from the first years of Chavez's presidency, when the agenda, at least in economic terms, was still indistinct. Railing first against a moribund domestic political class, through an overhaul of institutional structures and the harnessing of popular mobilization, Chavez began to build a framework around which a more radical project eventually emerged. It also provided an example that Correa and Morales would later follow.

Venezuela had been a late and erratic neoliberal reformer, and even during the 1990s, governments had attempted to partially reverse neoliberal policy when oil prices had allowed it (Coronil 1997, 375–82; Hellinger 2004b, 32–40). Chavez seems to have long been influenced by leftist thought, and the initial program of his Movimiento Quinta Republica (Fifth Republic

Movement), in 1997, did advocate some greater degree of state intervention in the economy, with, for example, a proportion of oil revenues to be directed in support of a failing agricultural sector (Lander and Navarrete 2007). Nevertheless, by the time of the 1998 presidential campaign, the message had become less clear as the Fifth Republic Movement admitted various new centrist factions, resulting in compromise and deliberate ambiguity in policy wording (Ellner 2001).[5]

Once Chavez was in office, the brakes were applied on new privatizations, but fiscal conservatism and orthodoxy were embraced. It is perhaps illustrative of the now oft-forgotten evolution of Chavez's policies that, eighteen months into his first term, the question of whether the new government would evolve in a neoliberal, populist, or radical direction was still being posed by Ellner (2001), who later was a (qualified) supporter of *chavismo*.

It is difficult to discern whether Chavez had radical plans in mind from the start, though historically low oil prices in 1998 meant that the economic basis for any such program was initially lacking (Buxton 2008). The government's early diplomatic focus on the revival of OPEC as a means of constricting oil supplies suggests an appreciation that low oil prices constituted a major barrier to government action (Parker 2003). Only the increasing resistance of economic elites, as Chavez strove to gain greater control of the state, prompted a turn away from economic orthodoxy and liberal democratic norms. This was first played out in the struggle over the national oil company PDVSA, after which the Chavez government became more radical in both goals and means.

The first two years of Chavez's "Bolivarian Revolution," then, reflected a desire to address the concerns of his popular base while (necessarily) working within the constraints of a neoliberal global conjuncture. However, the wave of popular sentiment upon which Chavez was elected was primarily anti-oligarchic rather than anti-neoliberal, and for this reason the anti-oligarchic message was overwhelmingly emphasized as the new government's primary purpose, leaving political-economic change somewhat sidelined (Buxton 2008). The main target was the Puntofijo system of governance, in place since 1958, which allowed for elections within the two-party social democrat/Christian democrat system but allocated positions in the bureaucracy and other arms of the state equitably between the two parties, ensuring their joint domination over Venezuelan political life. The flip side to this arrangement was a class compromise referred to as "sowing the oil," meaning that oil revenue would be allocated in a manner that guaranteed rising incomes for all classes, as a response to the threat of a communist urban guerrilla movement in the 1960s.[6]

As in many resource-based economies, commodity price increases in the 1970s saw a move toward greater state involvement in the economy and a more expansive fiscal posture. Volatile oil prices over the decade were treated as temporary blips, and debt was expanded to cover the shortfalls, a situation which worsened during the 1980s, when prices continued to decline. Previous boom conditions had encouraged an overreliance on the petroleum sector, which meant that, by the 1980s, the rest of the economy— which had been systematically neglected—offered little prospect of recovery. Agricultural collapse, in particular, meant a mass migration to the cities and the creation of a new informal urban class, which found no voice in either hegemonic party.[7] With real per capita incomes 8 percent lower in 1997 than in 1971, the broad majority of the population saw a deterioration in their circumstances over time.

Widespread marginalization and impoverishment,[8] contrasted with a long-standing popular belief that oil could and should drive national and social development, led to widespread disillusionment with *puntofijismo*, manifested in rioting in 1989 and two attempted coups in 1992 (one led by then Lieutenant Colonel Hugo Chavez). The exhaustion of the Puntofijo Pact eventually fatally weakened the domestic capitalists who ultimately lay behind the two major parties, without a sustained period of neoliberalization having promoted an alternative capitalist fraction, as occurred in Bolivia.[9] The situation thus was ripe for the emergence of an outsider candidate capable of mobilizing disenfranchised but unorganized popular sectors. That this was only tangentially related to the matter of neoliberalism was evidenced by the candidacy, in the elections of 1998, of the pro-neoliberal Irene Sáez, who was the initial front-runner until she accepted the endorsement of one of the traditional parties.

Given the stranglehold these parties had long maintained on the state, it is no surprise that some of Chavez's first moves in power were aimed at short-circuiting their interests by overhauling or bypassing various parts of the state apparatus, most prominently with the election of a constituent assembly and the new constitution that resulted, though there also were struggles over the composition of the Supreme Court. For the first two years, however, economic policy remained largely orthodox, with commitments made to private property and timely debt repayments and with macroeconomic policy based on International Monetary Fund advice (Vera 2001).[10] Projects to give property titles to landless groups looked somewhat more radical but in fact were largely based on Hernando de Soto's ideas about incorporating the poor into private property regimes (Parker 2005).

Lack of change in the economic sphere during the first years of *chavismo* seems to have simply been a function of the prioritization of institutional change. This does not mean that there was any radical anticapitalist plan waiting to be unveiled, but neither does it necessarily suggest an absence of desire to move away from neoliberalization. Chavez, in fact, seems to have initially envisaged a development project that involved a key role for the domestic bourgeoisie (Lander 2007; Ellner 2004) and that would have furnished them with subsidies and protection in much the same manner as they enjoyed under *puntofijismo*. Polarization in Venezuela—meaning Chavez was unable to carry domestic capital along with him—seems to have reached a critical point with his moves to gain control of PDVSA. It was the successful, though fraught, battle for government control of oil that both prompted Chavez to radicalize (in the face of opposition from the bourgeoisie) and allowed the *chavista* project to survive, with the *chavista* project hinging on the upswing in oil prices that occurred over the period of struggle (Buxton 2008).

Though it was state-owned, PDVSA had, by 1998, become almost entirely autonomous from the government, was involved in various joint ventures with transnational oil companies, and was itself a transnational conglomerate, with investments in U.S.-based Citgo Petroleum and several refineries (Parker 2005). Given this, it is hardly surprising that PDVSA operated essentially as a private firm would, attempting to limit its fiscal contribution to the state through transfer pricing and lobbying for tax cuts. It had also, contrary to official OPEC policy, adopted a strategy of maximizing production volumes, which of course contributed to the low price of oil as well as integrating Venezuela more tightly with the U.S. market and alienating OPEC partners.

Chavez's moves to bring PDVSA under greater state control and to reorient the company toward a less commercial ethos brought conflict with its executives and drove a wedge between the government and the domestic capitalist class.[11] PDVSA promoted a policy of continuing the opening of the sector to foreign private capital and presented itself as a bastion of technocratic efficiency, contrasted with the shortsighted populism of *chavismo*.[12] The management and professional staff of PDVSA became key actors in the various attempts to unseat Chavez in 2001 to 2003, associated with the peak business association Federación de Cámaras y Asociaciones de Comercio y Producción de Venezuela (Venezuelan Federation of Chambers and Associations of Commerce and Production).[13]

Though Chavez survived these conflicts, the polarization that they wrought drove much of the middle class into the arms of the opposition and definitively ruled out compromise with domestic capital, spurring radicalization along a number of axes. Capital strikes and lockouts over this period brought greater state participation in the economy—out of the necessity to maintain support for the government by minimizing shortages of goods rather than out of any great ideological commitment. One of the most prominent of these measures was the establishment of a government chain of informal supermarkets to provide subsidized goods in poor areas, as food distribution almost ground to a halt toward the end of 2002 (Clark 2010). This was a hugely popular move, which was made permanent as the Mision Mercal, pointing to another dynamic of radicalization—the need for Chavez to rely more heavily upon his base, in the absence of middle-class support.

The first years of his administration, under conditions of low oil prices and relatively little government control over hydrocarbon revenues, had provided little funding for any prospective social programs for the poor.[14] There was therefore a danger that the political and rhetorical changes that had proved so popular with these sectors—manifested in the huge mobilization that succeeded in bringing Chavez back to power after the attempted coup in April 2002—might have taken Chavez only so far, in the absence of more inclusionary social policies. A need to link directly to this base as a means of maintaining and enhancing its mobilization potential combined with a distrust of the institutions of the liberal state to produce programs designed to be implemented at a community level. These were collectively known as the *misiones*,[15] which were administered by informal neighborhood organizations with relatively little oversight from above and mostly funded directly from the reformed PDVSA.[16] Thirty thousand community councils also were eventually established, with the task of implementing public work schemes in their locality (Ellner 2013).[17]

Meanwhile, lockouts over the 2001–2003 period of unrest led several groups of workers to take over their companies and restart production, progressing from this to successfully demanding expropriation by the state. Increasingly intractable opposition from capitalists continued to drive further radicalization in subsequent years, as price and exchange controls increased in scope in order to combat the inflationary impact of shortages and limit what became a consistent flow of capital flight. In addition to expropriations driven from below, state ownership of a growing proportion of the economy mainly reflected a desire to establish a position of strength against domestic capital in fighting price speculation, smuggling, and induced shortages.[18]

These policies would have been simply unsustainable without the government's successful battle for control of PDVSA, but, more fundamentally, even this would have counted for little without the upsurge in oil prices that immediately followed in subsequent years. This provided the economic base for the state to fill the gaps left by striking capital, to arrange for the emergency import of basic consumer goods, and to establish the *misiones*, which formed the foundation of continuing popular support for the government. In this context, it is no surprise that the wheels of the *chavista* project began to fall off as oil prices started to drop, around 2014.

Bolivia

Bolivia differs from Venezuela in the makeup of both its elite and its popular sectors, which have had a large impact on its post-neoliberal trajectory (Ellner 2012). Unlike in Venezuela, a Bolivian capitalist class divided roughly along sectoral lines, and more clearly by geography, meant that the leading opposition movement manifested itself in demands for regional autonomy (or even independence). Though, as with the other ER cases, popular mobilization (and subsequent governmental orientation) revolved around questions of marginalization, in Bolivia the process was rather different, with an alliance of heterogeneous (though ethnically linked) social movements gaining momentum, first locally and then nationally, before coming to power under the banner of Evo Morales's MAS in 2005.

The local character of many of these movements tended to persist, reinforced by the dispersion of a large proportion of gas revenues at the municipal level, which made the formulation and implementation of a coherent national development program under Morales difficult. The situation was made more challenging by the low level of state capacity in Bolivia, which began the commodity boom as the poorest country in South

America and in which several governance functions were carried out by donors and nongovernmental organizations until 2005. It is therefore unsurprising that post-neoliberal change in Bolivia was more modest than that seen in Ecuador and Venezuela, even though the Morales government has advanced a number of important policies that would have been unthinkable under previous neoliberal administrations and has proved more successful at preserving its project under the stress of falling commodity prices in the postboom years.

Kaup (2012, 2013c) posits that both post-neoliberalism and counter-neoliberalization in Bolivia can be traced to local class conflicts and that both have resulted in the consolidation of the power of the transnational capital within the country. In the first case, economic elites centered around mining interests in the highlands were able, in the 1980s and 1990s, to ally with global capital to push through a neoliberalizing agenda, at the expense of a lowland agro-industrial fraction. The agro-industrial fraction had enjoyed special privileges, particularly under General Hugo Banzer Suarez in the 1970s, which included, effectively, a redistribution of windfall commodity revenues from highland to lowland elites (Kaup 2012, 44–47). A neoliberal program that reversed this arrangement by dramatically lowering the government's take from extractive revenues clearly suited mining interests, which also benefited enormously from the opening of the sector to foreign investment.

According to Kaup (2013a, 2013c), the even greater fractionalization of domestic capital which ensued created spaces for the emergence of the popular classes as a significant political actor, first in high-profile acts of anti-neoliberal protest, such as the Cochabamba "gas war," and culminating in the historic election of Evo Morales as the first indigenous president of Bolivia (in South America's only majority-indigenous state). Essentially, internal wrangling between a geographically segmented economic elite weakened local capital in general, to the point where popular class ascendancy was possible. For Kaup, though, the limits to this victory are heavily circumscribed by the dominance of transnational capital in the context of a globalized economy. The MAS and its supporters "have struggled to be included in—and to receive some of the benefits of—Bolivia's extractive export-oriented economy . . . The Morales government has thus become the local actor participating in global circuits of accumulation. It has become the internal bourgeoisie, or perhaps better put, the internal proletariat and peasantry" (Kaup 2013c, 115).

This assessment appears accurate, at least in the sense that Bolivia's development strategy since 2006 has concentrated on the redistribution of the proceeds of extraction rather than the development of domestic industry. Here, the notion of internal popular classes is certainly a useful way to conceptualize the MAS in government. Nevertheless, Kaup's pessimism seems somewhat unwarranted. It is difficult to see how landlocked Bolivia, the poorest state in South America and with a population of fewer than 11 million (World Bank n.d.), would realistically manage to carve out a significantly more autonomous path of development at present than has been achieved under Morales, particularly given the levels of investment that will be required in the medium term to sustain the hydrocarbon sector (Cunha Filho, Gonçalves, and Déa 2010).

Some attempts were made to set up state-controlled basic industries such as food processing and paper production, though progress seems to have been limited. Probably of more significance was the inauguration, in 2013, of the first Bolivian natural gas separation plant, built by an Argentinian firm, which is slated to produce enough liquefied petroleum gas to supply the domestic market (*Latin American Herald Tribune* 2013). Further expansion of extractive frontiers, including a focus on beneficiation of raw materials, has been a priority, though results have generally been somewhat disappointing. The exploitation of the vast iron ore deposit (perhaps the world's largest) at El Mutun, on the Brazilian border, by the Indian company Jindal Steel, was meant to amount to a $2.1 billion investment and to include on-site sponge iron and steel plants. The development was subject to repeated delays and mutual accusations of bad faith on the part of the government and the firm, and in 2012 Jindal finally withdrew (Dube 2014a). Much has been made of the considerable potential for lithium extraction from the Salar de Uyuni salt flats, since lithium is a vital component of advanced battery technology, which may well power most of the world's auto fleet if a transition from fossil fuels occurs. With a quarter of the world's known reserves, Bolivia shifted between trying to find foreign partners (while insisting that any deal should include all stages of production taking place domestically) and trying to develop the industry alone, with apparently little success (Valle and Holmes 2013; Alper 2017).[19]

High levels of overall dependence on foreign capital have largely been a function of the weakness of the national gas company, Yacimientos Petroliferos Fiscales Bolivianos (Bolivian Treasury Oil Fields, or YPFB), which had been starved of investment during the 1980s and then privatized in the 1990s.[20] The subsequent renationalization of the Bolivian gas industry under Morales amounted to the state buying back majority control of the half of YPFB then owned by multinationals, substantially ramping up the state's tax take from the rest of the extractive sector, and negotiating much higher gas prices with main customers Argentina and Brazil. Such efforts may not have met the expectations of large numbers of MAS supporters in Bolivia and beyond (Veltmeyer 2012; Kennemore and Weeks 2011). Nevertheless, they were a sharp turn away from neoliberal policies, which would have been almost impossible under the global structural conditions of the 1990s, no matter the balance of domestic forces. They also represented a substantially better deal for the state vis-à-vis transnational capital.

As a result, government revenue from the Bolivian gas industry had increased sevenfold by 2012 (Fuentes 2012), allowing for a doubling of state spending. Some of this revenue was channeled into the Bono Juancito Pinto, a scholarship program for primary school children, and the Renta Dignidad, a universal noncontributory pension scheme for those over age sixty (Silva 2013).[21] Much of the new surplus, however, was diverted to municipal levels. This reflects the grounding of the MAS government in a mosaic of locally rooted social movements, to which it is fundamentally beholden. It also meshes with Bolivian institutional characteristics, especially the legacy of the Popular Participation Law of the 1990s, which had, in the spirit of decentralization, given municipalities more of a voice in the allocation of public spending. Many MAS supporters had first gained power at this level, and continued to hold it, but had been starved of funds, making a redirection of royalty and tax payments into their hands an obvious policy choice for MAS, though the decision may also have been related to low state capacity at the national level. With the nationalization of the electricity and water sectors, service delivery tended to be coordinated at the local level and was aimed at decommodifying provision. This had some promising results, such as the increase in rural electrification, from 20 percent of households to 50 percent (Fuentes 2015).

At the same time, handing gas and mining rents to local governments was a politically convenient way for Morales to undermine opposition from the lowland agro-exporter class, which at one stage posed a serious threat to the government. Despite losing the 2005 election to Morales, these interests operated from a position of relative strength after the election, owing to changes under which departmental prefects were now elected rather than appointed from the center (Bebbington and Bebbington 2010; Eaton 2011). The eastern Media Luna departments also contained the bulk of gas reserves and benefited from a complicated revenue sharing agreement, which made prefects in general—and those in the lowlands in particular—the major recipients of the increasing hydrocarbon revenue flows during the first years of the Morales government, until a large proportion of these funds were redirected to municipal levels.

Feeling threatened by an indigenous highland-based government, white and mestizo agricultural elites were able to mobilize support from a large proportion of savannah residents, who identified primarily along geographic rather than ethnic lines, in contrast to the self-consciously indigenous (and, to a lesser extent, Andean) character of the MAS government (Kohl 2010). A referendum on regional autonomy, in 2006, was an overall victory for Morales but also indicated strong support for regionalism in the Media Luna, leading to increasing tensions and resulting in racially inflected paramilitary violence, and even an abortive coup attempt, in 2008. Public opinion, even in the savannah, swung against the autonomy movement after a massacre of eighteen peasants in Pando department, in 2008. This, together with the momentum from his victory in a presidential recall referendum, allowed Morales to push through a bill on a plebiscite for the new constitution, in 2009 (Postero 2010).

Undoubtedly, the underlying issue for the lowland elites had been the prospect of land redistribution, in a state where, at the time of Morales's election, land ownership was among the least equitable in the world and semifeudalism remained entrenched in some areas (Weisbrot and Sandoval 2008). In order to end the standoff, Morales was willing to compromise on this issue by agreeing to protect existing landowners and only redistribute "idle" plots.[22] Perhaps, had Morales not offered this concession, or had landowners proved more intractable, conflict might have taken a direction similar to that seen in Venezuela, prompting a more radical approach from the government in order to keep goods and services moving in the face of opposition from capital. This seems unlikely, though, since the geographically fractured nature of the Bolivian capitalist class did not allow for a national anti-MAS movement, which might have drawn in more actors, such as the army (which, as an inherently nationalist organization, continued to support the government, despite natural sympathies with the lowland elites).

Ecuador

No Ecuadorian government made any substantive effort toward a sustained break with a neoliberal policy agenda between the beginnings of neoliberalization, in 1981, and the election of Rafael Correa, in 2006. During this period, a cultural and economic cleavage with deep historical roots—between the coastal area (centered around the commercial capital of Guayaquil) and the highlands (especially the political capital, Quito, and the surrounding Pichincha province)—combined with an electoral system that encouraged institutional instability and intra-elite conflict (Conaghan 1988, chap. 6) to produce a regular churn of presidents (table 6.1). The periodic rise of populist outsider candidates included a handful of avowedly anti-neoliberal figures. However, when they had successfully secured power, each would then reverse course and accede to the policy restrictions imposed by the conditionality of the international financial institutions, echoing the phenomenon of "neoliberalism by surprise," which was notorious across Latin America during this period (Stokes 2001; Campello 2015). Whether any of these presidents were ever personally committed to their espoused policy goals is questionable, though room to maneuver was in any case very much constrained by dependence upon IFI support and approval.

An important example of this kind of process is the election of former colonel Lucio Gutierrez, in 2002. Gutierrez's election is significant because his brief term in office coincided with the beginnings of the commodity boom, meaning that, at first glance, a shift away from neoliberalism under his watch should at least have been possible. Gutierrez's record in office, while hardly supporting the notion that he would have instituted a new direction of travel for Ecuador had he been able, still provides good evidence for the centrality of the commodity boom in enabling such shifts.

Gutierrez had been the leader of a group of young army officers who, allied with CONAIE, the indigenous federation of social movements, had deposed technocratic president Jamil Mahuad[23] in 2000, during the worst economic crisis in Ecuadorian history (Fitch 2005; Zamosc 2007).[24] Gutierrez was definitively from outside the party structure—and, being from the Amazon, was not tied to either of the rival regions of littoral and Andes. Seemingly, the stage was set for a break with neoliberalism in Ecuador. At a moment when Chavez's government in Venezuela was moving left, following the 2002 coup attempt, many commentators interpreted

TABLE 6.1
Ecuadorian presidents since 1992

Years	President	Party	Orientation	Reason for Leaving Office
1992–1996	Sixto Duran Ballen	Republican Unity	Right (coast)	Democratic succession
1996–1997	Abdala Bucaram	Partido Roldosista Ecuatoriano	Populist (coast)	Removed by Congress after economic/anticorruption protests
1997–1998	Fabian Alcaron	Frente Radical Alfarista	Centrist (highlands)	Caretaker—democratic succession
1998–2000	Jamil Mahuad	Union Democrata Cristiana/ Democracia Popular	Technocratic (highlands)	Military/indigenous coup amid economic crisis
2000–2003	Gustavo Noboa	Union Democrata Cristiana	Center right (coast)	Caretaker—democratic succession
2003–2005	Lucio Gutierrez	Partido Sociedad Patriotica	Populist (Amazon/ highlands)	Urban working/middle class coup, corruption/political crisis
2005–2007	Alfredo Palacio	No party affiliation (former head of Supreme Court)	Technocratic (coast)	Caretaker—democratic succession
2007–2017	Rafael Correa	Alianza PAIS	Leftist/populist (national [urban])	Democratic succession
2017–Present	Lenin Moreno	Alianza PAIS	Left/center, increasingly moving to the right (national [urban])	In office

Gutierrez's electoral victory as a sign of rising Andean (and, more broadly, Latin American) populist leftism (Hakim 2003). Though this is not entirely inaccurate, in the case of Gutierrez, the judgment was certainly premature.

Although supported by a slightly different coalition of forces, Gutierrez's appeals to the populace were similar to those that helped win popular support for Correa several years later, with initial policy proposals that certainly went further than those of Chavez prior to his election. These included promises to limit foreign debt payments, to renationalize parts of the economy, to remove the U.S. military base at Manta, and to increase social expenditures. As a reaction to the financial crisis and the unstable rule by shifting oligarchical fractions that led up to it, the election of Gutierrez certainly should be viewed as an ascendancy to state power by popular class groups. That he ended up reversing course and embracing a wholly neoliberal program even before assuming office demonstrates the enduring disciplinary power of international financial capital just prior to the impact of the commodity boom in Ecuador, which would give Correa far greater room to maneuver, four years later.

This is not immediately obvious when considering the internal and external situation in 2002. The traditional parties, and thus, elites (mostly, but not limited to, the capitalist classes), were the target of the 2005 protests that would eventually bring down Gutierrez (following his collusion with them over granting amnesty to ex-president Abdala Bucaram, exiled in Panama). But the main blow to the influence of the bourgeoisie had come during the 1999–2000 economic crisis, which also led to the ouster of a president, Jamil Mahuad, who had allowed several oligarchs to escape to Miami with their funds intact just before their banks collapsed (hence the emergence of Gutierrez as an "anti-elite" candidate).[25]

Thus, had Gutierrez pressed on with his original redistributive agenda, he would have had the advantages of a weakened capitalist class, already aware of the potential power of mass mobilization against them, and status as an outsider with few ties to these traditional powers—not substantially different in these respects from the situation faced by Correa in 2006. It therefore seems unlikely that the bourgeoisie would have possessed any greater political capacity to stop these hypothetical efforts than they had later, when confronted with Correa's plan to remodel the economy. The crucial difference lies in the fact that Gutierrez never possessed the economic means to meet his promises of social spending, and thus he never built the popular support that served as the solid wall from behind which Correa could launch his ambitious agenda.

Correa's sustained popularity, which he was able to deploy as a weapon through almost constant mobilizations, cementing and extending his mandate and forcing structural reform by arranging various referenda and elections (once a year, on average, after taking office), hinged on his ability to deliver promised social spending.[26] Thus, with regard to Gutiérrez (or a hypothetical leftist president at the time), the question is whether he would have been able to do the same, had he not abandoned his election promises of redistribution.[27] Subsequently, Gutiérrez, and the current representative of his Partido Sociedad Patriotica (Patriotic Society Party),[28] maintained that the deal with the IMF, which Gutiérrez signed in August 2003, was absolutely unavoidable, given budget arrears of $700 million—mostly comprising salaries owed to the army (a key base of support) and other public sector workers. Ecuador had been shunned by the IMF since Mahuad's suspension of debt repayments during the 1999–2000 crisis, and Gustavo Noboa's caretaker government had already begun a reform process, which had been dismissed as insufficient by the fund (BBC 2003). Even though the terms insisted upon were typically harsh, it does seem that government officials genuinely believed that the $240 million standby loan, eventually granted during Gutiérrez's first year in office, was necessary to head off an impending default.[29]

Against this must be set the fact that Gutiérrez assumed the presidency in 2003, when oil prices were already high and, having survived a coup attempt, Chavez was beginning to advance a more radical agenda in Venezuela. Thus, the international environment seemed rather accommodating to deviations from neoliberalism. Indeed, in 2005, during Correa's brief tenure as finance minister under caretaker president Alfredo Palacio, a break with IMF terms resulted in the suspension of a $100 million loan from the World Bank, but Ecuador turned to the bond market and was able to raise $650 million, albeit at a very high interest rate (Weisbrot, Sandoval, and Cadena 2006). The suspension of relations with the IFIs had come as a consequence of the reorganization of an oil stabilization fund, which had been set up just before Guiterrez's election, in the hopes of pleasing IMF managers. By law, this mandated that 70 percent of oil revenues were to be spent on buying back debt, with a maximum of 10 percent set aside for social spending. The social spending limit was tripled under the new arrangement. If this could be reformed in 2005, then, at least in principle, why could this not be done by Gutiérrez two years earlier?

It should not be discounted that two years of extra economic growth and distance from the debacle of 1999 to 2000 would undoubtedly have facilitated Ecuador's return to international capital markets, which may have been simply impossible in 2003. By 2003, however, oil was providing leftward-moving Venezuela with 69 percent of its export revenue; in Ecuador's case, the figure was proportionately half that. A new pipeline, which came on line in late 2003, significantly boosted Ecuador's export volumes, and this, combined with continuing price increases, meant that export receipts boomed, from $2.9 billion in 2003 to $6.5 billion two years later (figure 6.4). By the time Correa began his mandate, in 2006, the figure was $7.7 billion, accounting for 50 percent of exports. Taken together with the debt repayments and buybacks, which had continued (albeit at a reduced pace), Correa was in a far stronger position than Gutiérrez to reject IMF demands.

Correa's ability to channel oil revenues into social spending gave him a cushion of mass popularity, allowing him to take on an economic elite which, while weak, would nevertheless probably have been capable of derailing his agenda under the old congressional system, given that he

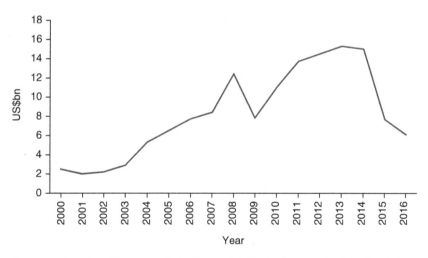

Figure 6.4 Ecuador oil exports (in billions of dollars), 2000–2016. Calculated from Chatham House Resourcetrade.earth database.

would have required the acquiescence of several of the old parties to rule. Correa instituted media laws, which changed ownership structures, and he calmed the previously vociferous criticism emanating from opposition newspapers by establishing dubious laws against so-called media lynching.

In addition to new financial taxes, Correa's increasing political strength was manifested in much-improved tax collection across the board, addressing a traditional weakness in Latin American economies. For instance, during the first quarter of 2012, the Ecuadorian Internal Revenue Service, Servicio de Rentas Internas, reported a 34 percent increase in tax revenue over the same period for the previous year. Much of this burden fell on the grupos economicos who previously had avoided much of their tax obligations. As part of the fulfillment of a populist election promise, in May 2013, the Servicio de Rentas Internas published a list of debtor companies. Among those listed was Exportadora Bananera Noboa, owned by the country's richest individual (and perennial presidential candidate), Álvaro Noboa.

The achievements in extending and rationalizing the tax system point to important features of Correa's government, which mark it as somewhat different from those in Venezuela and Bolivia. In Venezuela, the firing of thousands of mostly white-collar PDVSA employees was a major step in a process of polarization that saw the middle classes generally line up against *chavismo*, while in Bolivia the grassroots and ethnic origins of the MAS have served to partially exclude middle sectors. In contrast, the middle classes have been one of the main cores of support for Correa, starting with the urban *forajido* (outlaw) movement in Quito, which ousted Gutiérrez. This was reflected in the greater participation of middle-class professionals in Correa's government and civil service (solidified with increasing numbers employed by the state). This alleviated most of the suspicion around bureaucracy or technocracy encountered in the Bolivian and Venezuelan cases and resulted in a greater reliance upon the central state to achieve the government's policy goals and drive economic development. To some of Correa's critics, especially in Ecuadorian social movements, this meant a privileging of economic growth and efficiency over participation and empowerment (Becker 2013).

De la Torre (2013) is highly critical of this "technopopulism"—for him a novel combination of top-down, populist manipulation of the urban masses and an unaccountable rule by experts. Certainly, there was technocratic orientation to Correa's government, which was filled with figures from academia and nongovernmental organizations who had been alienated by the experience of neoliberalism. As de la Torre points out, the majority of the top posts were filled by individuals with postgraduate education—in a country of 15.5 million, where only 358 university professors have PhDs. By contrast, in Venezuela, a more developed state, with a population of 30 million, only seven of the twenty-nine most senior government appointees had any postgraduate training (as of 2013). Correa himself holds a PhD in economics from the University of Illinois Urbana–Champaign.[30]

Whereas the ER governments in Bolivia and Venezuela largely sought to bypass the state and to prioritize participation by diverting funds to local levels, the Ecuadorian state was extended and reoriented with the creation of the powerful new Secretaria Nacional de Planificacion y Desarrollo (National Secretariat of Planning and Development), which has responsibility for the design and implementation of the overarching National Development Plan as well as for reform of the state and the training of bureaucrats.[31] A representative of the National Secretariat, very much versed in developmental state concepts, commented that the institution had been designed with the experiences of the East Asian newly industrialized countries in mind.[32] Certainly, this institutional structure seems to have enabled the assembly of a more coherent national development vision and to have diverged from the neoliberal norm, in which finance ministers are able to dominate line ministries (Phillips et al. 2006).

Redistributive goals similar to those encountered in Venezuela and Bolivia found expression through a greater reliance upon nationally administered schemes than in the other two states. The Bono de Desarrollo Humano (Human Development Bond), which has been augmented several times since its introduction in 2006 (it stood at $80 in 2013 and increased again under new president Lenin Moreno), is a conditional cash transfer that provides a monthly stipend to the poorest 40 percent of the population. Social spending overall increased from 4.8 percent of GDP in 2006 to more than 9 percent of GDP from 2009 to 2011, including a doubling of education spending (Ray and Kozameh 2012).

Social and developmental spending, while clearly highly dependent upon oil revenues, also sprang from government's increasing ability to control and regulate the financial sector. This industry, primarily identified with the coastal *grupos*, had been substantially weakened by the 1999–2000 financial crisis, and it remains highly unpopular, making it a relatively easy target for Correa's government.[33] Indeed, after opposition candidate (and banker) Guillermo Lasso pledged to increase the Human Development Bond, as part of his 2013 presidential election campaign, Correa responded by suggesting a further increase, to be paid for through a tax on financial institutions.[34]

Reregulation of the financial sector had begun much earlier, however. The central bank was placed back under executive control in 2007, and this institution was used to lower interest rates as a means of extending credit. Though Correa's government may have been less focused on small-scale community initiatives than were the governments of Bolivia or Venezuela, the Popular Finance Program, established in 2008, led to a huge surge in loans to small businesses and cooperatives, as part of an attempt to both support and regulate the informal financial sector. Of perhaps greatest structural import was the barring of financial institutions from owning any other firms, whether inside or outside the financial sector.[35]

Also highly significant were regulations designed to stem capital flight and to promote domestic investment—in an environment unlikely to stimulate large amounts of foreign direct investment (FDI), at least from traditional sources. Banks were required to hold 60 percent of their liquid assets within the country and were taxed at 5 percent on any capital leaving the country (with this latter accounting for a full 10 percent of government revenues). The government also mandated that the central bank repatriate $2 billion in international reserves held abroad. This helped fund $3.5 billion of public investment in construction, agriculture, industry, and mortgage lending from 2009 to 2012, part of a coordinated response to the global financial crisis (Weisbrot, Johnston, and Lefebvre 2013).

The financial sector was unable to count upon any help from IFIs or transnational financial capital in putting effective pressure on the government. In 2008, the decision was made to default upon and declare illegal $3.2 billion of external debt, and then to buy almost all of it back at 35 percent of face value, saving $300 million per year in interest payments alone (Kennemore and Weeks 2011; Weisbrot, Johnston, and Lefebvre 2013). Effectively cutting Ecuador off from international capital markets in this way may have appeared risky, but it did have the effect of insulating Ecuador from any policy leverage on the part of the markets or the IFIs.[36] Meanwhile, Northern FDI dropped considerably, compensated for by public investment and, increasingly, flows from China.

Though Correa periodically complained about China's negotiating stances (*El Comercio* 2009), huge amounts of Chinese oil-backed loans and investments flooded into Ecuador after 2009.[37] The majority of these have gone to fund infrastructure megaprojects, including the $12 billion Pacifico oil refinery (Mfula 2013), the $2 billion Coca Codo Sinclair hydroelectric dam, and the similarly priced El Mirador copper mine, along with a host of oil exploration projects in the Amazon (Escribano 2013; Gallagher and Myers 2018).[38] China has been willing to fill in the gaps left by a lack of Northern investment in oil, and even more so in other sectors of the economy, leading to growing concerns around Ecuadorian dependence on China. One former high-ranking opposition party official took the view that this would be a point of political weakness for the government, as "part of Correa's strategy when he won [in 2006] was to say that Ecuador had become a colony of the United States and that the people should not accept this. Fine, but now we are becoming a colony of China, something which is more frightening for the average person."[39] The one government official I interviewed denied that Ecuador's relationship with China posed any serious problems, echoing Correa's public statements that if any country should worry about a growing dependence on the People's Republic of China, it was the United States.[40]

Toward the end of Correa's time in office, though, the Ecuadorian government began to again pursue investors from more traditional sources. An indication of this may be seen in the relaxing of the terms of the county's mining code, which previously had set aside 70 percent of profits to the state. This move was made in response to the disappointing level of interest in Ecuador's substantial copper and gold deposits and to Canadian mining firm Kinross's 2013 pullout from developing the large Fruta del Norte gold deposit (*El Comercio* 2014; *El Telégrafo* 2014). Exploiting Ecuador's largely untapped mineral resources was seen as vital, amid increasing concern that oil production was beginning to peak.

It is likely that Correa would have been able to pursue many of his social policies and to increase the presence of the state in the economy without the need for large amounts of Chinese (or, say, Venezuelan) capital, as occurred in Bolivia. But his more ambitious goals were probably impossible without external financing. The Pacifico refinery project alone is valued at one-seventh of annual GDP, for instance. When interviewed in 2013, a representative of the Association of Private Bankers in Quito was of the opinion that global liquidity was at such high levels that the government, should it wish, could have returned to international bond issuance, as has occurred in the case of many developing countries.[41] This was perhaps surprising, for a country that had selectively defaulted on its international obligations in 2008, but as commodity prices began to fall, the government did indeed return to the bond markets, to the tune of \$2 billion in 2014 (Rodrigues and Schipani 2014).

An important facet of the technocratic bent of Correa's government was a railing against what government supporters label "corporatism" (Becker 2013). In the Ecuadorian context, this is meant to evoke memories of the corporatist access to the state by business groups in the pre-Correa era. In reality, however, it was deployed against any "special interests," such as social movements or indigenous groups, which were portrayed as advancing narrow, sectional causes in defiance of the national interest—national interest being primarily determined by the new peak bureaucracy, which was able to stand above such concerns and map out a developmental future on a national scale. In terms of developmental ambition and cohesion, this structure seemed to offer advantages over those in Venezuela and Bolivia. Nevertheless, it also led to an increasing authoritarianism, with anti-mining protesters criminalized as terrorists.[42]

Perhaps in response to the more developmentalist bent of Correa, when compared with the other ER regimes, there were signs in 2013 that certain sectors of capital were content to reach a somewhat uneasy truce with Correa. An official from the Guayaquil Chamber of Industry was in no way hostile toward the government, despite lingering concerns.[43] New laws that prohibited private banks from owning companies in the real economy not only greatly reduced the power of domestic banks but also may well have partially severed the links between the financial elite and their counterparts in the industrial and agro-export sectors. The official from the Association of Private Banks, unsurprisingly, expressed a complete feeling of exclusion from the government: "In any democratic society, business leaders are able to influence the government—different sectors make proposals and it is for the politicians to make a judgment between them. We have tried to talk to the president, to the National Assembly, but no one wants to listen."[44]

Having witnessed events in Bolivia and Venezuela, however, there seemed to be a sense among the economic elites that any attempt to confront state power would be unrealistic. Interviewees from the commercial and industrial sectors talked of how relations with government had greatly improved, after early years of instability and uncertainty.[45] While most voiced significant concerns, usually relating to dependence on China and a lack of private foreign investment, there appeared to be a sense of pragmatic optimism among these groups, a feeling that the government was now willing to work with them. This rapprochement, which appears to have continued (Wolff 2016), is likely to now have been strengthened through a shift to the right under Correa's successor, Lenin Moreno.

Conclusion

There is a tendency in some recent scholarship relating to Latin America (Webber 2010; Kennemore and Weeks 2011; Veltmeyer 2013) to claim that cases such as Ecuador and Bolivia (and sometimes even Venezuela) have not deviated from a neoliberal logic, because their "neoextractivist" strategies continue to advance accumulation by dispossession. This was seen in Ecuador's decision to open up the Yasuní Ishpingo-Tambococha-Tiputini rainforest reserve to oil drilling, following an unsuccessful campaign asking for Northern compensation, amounting to half the value of estimated reserves, in exchange for leaving the oil in the ground (Vaughan 2014). The process will undoubtedly have a huge environmental impact in an area of exceptional biodiversity and will involve the displacement of Shuar and other indigenous groups. And clearly, in the context of climate change, any development strategy based on the exploitation of fossil fuels must surely have a limited shelf life.

There may be disappointment, on the part of some observers, with the dissonance between sometimes avowedly socialist rhetoric and a capitalist reality, particularly with regard to the governments of Ecuador and Bolivia, which have made a great show of enshrining constitutional rights not only for indigenous groups but also for Pachamama. But neoliberalism should not be confused with capitalism in general. Post-neoliberal turns in Ecuador and Bolivia certainly involved the deepening and widening of capitalism and capitalist social relations in ways that entailed exploitation and dispossession. Nevertheless, the character of this expansion—or development—in ER states was linked to export-oriented national popular projects of redistribution, expanded social services, infrastructure development, reregulation, increased taxation, and, in some cases, expropriation, all of which were most certainly off the menu during the neoliberal era and all of which signal that these three states have made a turn away from this particular form of capitalism, even while moving onto a path of renewed accumulation by somewhat different means.

Seen with the benefit of postboom hindsight, Morales in Bolivia has proved the most successful in consolidating his country's break with neoliberalization, even through a period of declining commodity prices and a regional realignment rightward. Even so, at the time of this writing, Morales's position is less certain than it has been for many years. In late 2018, Bolivia's Supreme Electoral Tribunal cleared the way for the president to stand for a fourth term, despite this ruling running counter to the result of a 2016 referendum (Achtenberg 2018). With a loose coalition of unlikely allies (encompassing parts of the MAS's former social movement base, along with lowland middle classes and elites) opposing Morales, the election result is by no means certain.

Ecuador has experienced more difficult economic conditions, not helped by a major earthquake, which hit the northern coastal region in 2016. Governing party candidate Lenin Moreno won only a narrow victory in the 2017 elections and lost the governing party's majority in Congress. It appears that Moreno was chosen as the presidential candidate in a deliberate electoral strategy to present a more conciliatory figure for Ecuadorian elites, in comparison to the combative Correa (Vivanco 2018). But, seemingly hastened by a personal falling out with Correa, Moreno has since presided over a significant shift rightward, realigning foreign policy toward the United States, reengaging with the IMF, and instituting austerity measures. There also have been efforts to remove Correa loyalists from positions of influence. The extent to which these changes have been driven by Moreno's own personal agenda and how much has been a response to economic and/or legislative pressures is at this point hard to untangle (Becker and Riofrancos 2018). Even so, while Correa's term was far from perfect, his ten-year period of relative stability and progress on most development indicators marks a major advance on the previous decade of multiple crises, during which not a single elected president completed their term.

Of the three ER cases, however, Venezuela has clearly suffered the most since the end of the boom prices (Hetland 2017; Buxton 2016). The impact of declining oil prices was amplified greatly by a fixed exchange rate system (originally imposed to stem capital flight in the mid-2000s), which produced a huge gap between official and black market rates for dollars, driving up the cost of imports and sparking hyperinflation (while access to dollars at the official rate quickly became a source of profitable arbitrage for state-linked elites) (Velasco 2016). U.S. sanctions have exacerbated matters, with restrictions on the country's ability to trade or raise finance in dollars making the prospect of economic recovery seem increasingly distant. This dire situation has led to mass outward migration, which, in turn, has prompted xenophobic reaction in some of Venezuela's neighbors.

The Venezuelan opposition has claimed fraud in every election since the beginning of the Chavez period—mostly with little basis in fact. But it now seems clear that, since 2016, the Maduro government has increasingly resorted to unfair electoral practices—barring main opposition candidates from the 2018 presidential election, canceling a 2016 recall referendum, and effectively dissolving the opposition-controlled National Assembly (Hetland 2019). At the time of this writing, the United States, together with allied governments in Brazil and Colombia, has sought to put pressure on Maduro by recognizing National Assembly leader Juan Guaidó as interim president and talking up the possibility of military intervention (Toro 2019).

CHAPTER VII

Extractivist-Oligarchic Type

Angola and Kazakhstan

I n comparison with the other four types presented in this research, the extractivist-oligarchic (EO) type shares most features with the donor-dependent orthodoxy (DDO) type—to be discussed in chapter 8—and yet EO cases are not donor-dependent, nor did they follow orthodox policy prescriptions during the commodity boom years. As in the DDO configuration, and unlike the remaining three types, EO denotes states that lack a large domestic capitalist class with substantial autonomy from the state. As with DDO, in EO cases, access to the state and thence to networks of transnational capital is the major source of both economic and political power, where rule is secured through leveraging control of the state to appropriate and distribute resources along networks of patron–client relations.[1]

The most salient difference between EO and DDO types, in terms of explaining their distinct trajectories over the boom years, lies in their differing levels of engagement with the transnational vectors from which state managers' economic resources flow, particularly in the preboom years. In DDO type cases, since at least the 1990s, the most important source of capital flowing through the state came in the form of aid. Aid dependence brought high levels of conditionality, and, in the context of very low levels of state capacity, many elements of neoliberal reform programs were directly devised and supervised by donors. As we will discuss in chapter 8, without strong, organized domestic capitalist or popular voices to press for change, DDO state managers have found it difficult, or perhaps undesirable, to articulate and implement any substantive reorientations away from neoliberal trajectories, since this would involve a break with the priorities of donors, upon whose financing streams political elites have long depended to cement their power. Importantly, unlike DDO cases, neither Kazakhstan nor Angola entered the period of the commodity boom with state structures dependent on donor funding and technical capacity. In consequence, while the two EO states arguably may be seriously lacking in any coherent development strategy, their actions are less constrained by a neoliberal bureaucratic imprint left by decades of donor tutelage.

After a brief introduction, I will begin by outlining the features of the EO trajectory, noting its similarities to the rentier state model. As with some of the classic cases of oil-based rentierism, it may well be that, under commodity boom conditions, the sheer quantity of extractive surplus that flows through the domestic economy is sufficient to spark a true process of accumulation, rather than simple distribution, even if this is accompanied by predictably high levels of waste and predation (Ovadia 2016, 2018).

Next, I will turn to the impact of the commodity boom in the two EO cases, Angola and Kazakhstan, showing that increases in oil prices and production volumes have been largely responsible for massively increasing government revenues and expenditures in both states. It is this fiscal capacity to set policy, independent of external pressures, that has enabled the distinctive blending of developmental and predatory policies and behaviors, together with a blurring of the lines between public and private sectors, that has come to define the political economy of Kazakhstan and Angola. Finally, I focus on the domestic political economy of the two cases, with a more extended discussion of Angola (used as the exemplar case here), detailing its political-economic path since emerging from civil war in 2002.

The most striking ideotypical feature of EO states is a strongly stated developmentalist orientation, outwardly reflected by often impressive investment in infrastructure and urban centers, behind which lies a pervasive (though perhaps mutating) system of clientelistic rent distribution that undergirds the logic of governance. The scale and quantity of development projects, along with the opportunities for rent-seeking which they bring, were turbocharged during the boom years by an accelerating flow of resource revenues. To some degree, these processes seem to have brought genuine accumulation, too.

Echoing a political-economic pattern seen across many locations and eras—including a number of Southern states during the neoliberal period—patronage flows out from a powerful central authority, facilitating the enrichment of a thin stratum of elites. For EO type states under commodity boom conditions, though, this equation has been modified by the centrality of a high modernist vision of development, the articulation of which forms a key part of government efforts to maintain hegemony. The result is that a focus on large-scale infrastructure development—for instance, in housing, transport, or urban transformation—provides a convenient channel through which to reward allies and maintain loyalties, although this channel, for all its inefficiency and predation, still produced tangible, if highly uneven, improvements.

As will be seen more clearly in discussion of the two cases, without the vast increases in resource revenues (relative to gross domestic product) brought by the commodity boom, this EO model would not have been viable. This is not to say that a less predatory system, not grounded in patronage relations, would have otherwise emerged. However, the sheer scale of government-funded initiatives seen in the EO cases simply would not have been possible during a sustained period of low hydrocarbon prices. Dependence upon international financial institution support—likely in such a context, given high levels of government indebtedness—would have effectively ruled out the officially promoted policy package, with its starring role for publicly led investment.

With access to abundant resource revenues, though, road networks were overhauled, cities were created or reconstructed, and new industrial ventures were pursued, in programs that all appear to lie somewhat along a continuum between developmental and predatory intent. In some senses, these characteristics recall—or, in the worst cases, perhaps parody—the ambitious plans for industrialization and modernization advocated by Southern states during the era of post–World War II decolonization. In other ways, there is a self-conscious appropriation of contemporary intellectual tropes, particularly the linguistic trappings of the developmental state concept. In this way, for example, even the highly inequitable sharing of the spoils gained from export revenues can be presented as state nurturing of a rising national bourgeoisie (Power 2012).

Importantly, state-owned extractive companies themselves were very much run along commercial, profit-oriented lines, particularly in hydrocarbons, meaning that the rents that underpinned the model continued to flow as long as export prices remained sufficiently high. Thus, both states came under increasing economic pressure with the end of the boom, but they have responded somewhat differently. While Kazakhstan has cut spending in some areas, it also sought to prop up its overall economic model with stimulus amounting to 12 percent of GDP from 2014 to 2017 (Brown 2018). Angola, meanwhile, has been more severely affected and appears to have embarked upon a more orthodox stabilization program, involving a raft of privatizations (International Monetary Fund 2018; CNBC Africa 2018).

The two cases took rather different paths through the neoliberal era and into a reassertion of policy autonomy in the 2000s. Neoliberalism and its constraints, to some extent, skipped Angola, which was embroiled in civil war from the time of its independence, in 1973, until 2002. Though some efforts were made to organize a conference with donors, following the end of hostilities, a combination of rising oil prices and Chinese investment allowed the victorious Movimento Popular de Libertação de Angola (Popular Movement for the Liberation of Angola, or MPLA) to overcome a postwar fiscal crisis without engaging IFIs and traditional donors.

In contrast, Kazakhstan, formerly part of the Soviet Union, entered a period of economic liberalization following its independence, in 1991. The reforms were encouraged and financially supported by the IFIs (Cooley 2003), with the speed and extent of the process lying somewhere between shock therapy in Russia and recalcitrance in Turkmenistan (Pomfret and Anderson 2001). In terms of the lasting effects of neoliberalization, though, Kazakhstan differed from the otherwise broadly comparable postsocialist DDO case of Mongolia in two crucial respects, which together account for Kazakhstan breaking with a liberalizing path while Mongolia did not.

First, Kazakhstan possessed (and retained) important state-owned gas and oil companies, which continued to provide a key source of external rents and would, during the boom years, present an easier means for the state to enter into partnerships with transnational extractive companies, on better terms (Vivoda 2009). Second, Kazakhstan's relationship with Northern interests and IFIs never could be primarily characterized as that of donor–recipient, as table 7.1 shows. Thus, because Kazakhstan was far less reliant than the likes of Mongolia on international extractive companies and donors as a source of technical capacity and, probably more importantly, less dependent on donors as a wellspring of government financing, during the mid-2000s, Kazakhstan was able to turn decisively away from its previous trajectory of neoliberalization.

TABLE 7.1

Official development assistance as a percentage of gross national income

	1991	1996	2001	2006	2011
Angola*	2.8	7.8	3.8	0.5	0.2
Kazakhstan	0.1 (1993)	0.6	0.8	0.2	0.1
Mongolia	3.0	15.0	16.9	6.1	4.4

*Angola's official development assistance receipts did temporarily increase in the mid-1990s, peaking at 23 percent of gross national income in 1994, though this was overwhelmingly composed of humanitarian aid related to an internationally brokered peace deal, which was not sustained.

Source: World Bank, World Development Indicators.

This external autonomy is, in both cases, combined with a central state that is far more powerful than weak capitalists or any other domestic groups, producing political-economic orientations in both EO states that act to strengthen the direct participation of the state (and state-owned enterprises) in the economy and to distribute patronage to key allies. (Similar trends were observed elsewhere, in earlier booms; see, for example, Winters [1996] on Indonesia.) This is broadly consistent with several accounts that view Kazakhstan, along with other energy-exporting Central Asian states, as new examples of the rentier state (such as Franke, Gawrich, and Alakbarov 2009; Robinson 2007), and with others that consider it self-evident that postwar Angola also fills the bill (Sidaway 2007; Wiig and Kolstad 2012).

There are clear indications, in both cases, that an oligarchy connected to the upper reaches of the state controls the internal distribution of hydro-carbon rents, funneling a large proportion to its own consumption and prestige projects (particularly the radical overhaul of urban landscapes in Luanda and Astana). A further share is diverted toward co-opting potential internal threats via distribution of patronage resources, such as through the incorporation of former rebel commanders into patron–client networks in Angola. In Kazakhstan, a serious opposition from organized interest groups, including an emerging capitalist strata, is more dangerous. As a result, the government has acted to co-opt business groups and quell occasional urban unrest by extending access to rents to a second tier of elites (Junisbai 2010, 2012; Isaacs 2013).

The Extractivist–Oligarchic Ideal Type

In spite of the developmentalist trappings, in several respects, the closest conceptual comparator to the EO type is the rentier state (RS). First suggested by Mahdavy (1970), in relation to prerevolutionary Iran, and most prominently developed by Beblawi and Luciani (1987), rentier states are usually defined by their reliance upon external sources of revenue, accruing principally to the government, which controls the consumption and distribution of these flows. The state therefore essentially acts as landlord or gatekeeper, pocketing unearned rents rather than levying taxes on productive activity.[2]

Much of the literature on rentier states is linked to notions of the resource curse (Karl 1997; Yates 1996; Jensen and Wantchekon 2004; among many others), with the claim that predation and poor institutional quality tend to arise through the lack of need to extract taxation from domestic sources. In this account, freedom from the need to levy taxes blocks the emergence of the classic liberal social contract of tax revenues supplied consensually by the citizenry in exchange for representation and government accountability (Ross 2001). Unconstrained by the need to respond to taxpayer demands, government tends to become inefficient, corrupt, and perhaps authoritarian (Skocpol 1982). Worse, state managers can divert a portion of their rents toward establishing a system of patronage through which any potentially restful social groups can be bought off and pacified. Given a seemingly guaranteed revenue stream, there also are few incentives for state managers to encourage economic diversification or, more broadly, development of the economy, particularly since such processes may well serve to create alternative bases of power on the domestic scene.

One of the most striking aspects of this schema is its degree of compatibility, despite a rather different theoretical heritage, with much of the conceptual apparatus I employ to explain links between domestic class configuration and political-economic regime type. A retooling of the rentier state model along these lines, in fact, is extremely useful in demonstrating these connections for the EO type.[3] The RS departure point—that the lack of state reliance upon taxation removes a key lever of social pressure with which to influence the behavior of state managers—may be modified to note, instead, that the lack of dependence on the actions of domestic capital precludes the application of domestic capitalist structural power in influencing the state. Indeed, Ross (2001) notes that rentier states operate "autonomously" from society.[4]

Where rentier states' autonomy ends, though, is in the circumstances of their insertion into the global market for their commodity exports.[5] This is clearly seen in many of the cases discussed in other chapters (not least with regard to the donor-dependent orthodoxy type), given the ability of IFIs, donors, and capital markets to advance neoliberal conditionalities during an era of low commodity prices. Some states with particularly high export volumes and relatively capable parastatal extractive companies—such as Venezuela—certainly were able to use resource rents as a means of delaying or minimizing reforms during much of the neoliberal period (Coronil 1997, 370; Hertog 2010). Even in these cases, though, a liberalizing direction of travel was clear in the years prior to the commodity boom.

At this point, the significance of a legacy of aid dependence becomes crucial for unraveling the distinct trajectories of EO and DDO states under boom conditions. For those rentier-like states that, during the neoliberal era, came to rely heavily upon aid in order to fulfill basic state functions, there clearly was an impact on the shape and culture of the bureaucracy, through such measures as insisted-upon organizational reform, direct donor input into spending choices and staff training, and others. Probably more importantly, however—and as will be discussed in more detail in chapter 8—as aid flows rather than resource revenues became the major source of rents captured by the state, aid correspondingly replaced export revenue as the nexus of the distribution and patronage networks underpinning the authority of political elites (see, for instance, Szeftel 2000; Moore 2004). Understandably, then, while state elites in DDO cases are undoubtedly aware of the potential for capturing a larger proportion of the extractive surplus, and in some instances have made rather inconsistent attempts to do so, they are reluctant to endanger existing flows of aid rents by explicitly abandoning their donor-led development agenda.

Without aid rents to protect, state managers in the EO cases, unlike their DDO counterparts, entered the boom without the need to hedge their bets between resource revenue maximization and maintaining the favor of donors. While, again, this difference does not necessarily translate into a more coherent approach to development, EO governments under conditions of high export prices are left with a relatively free hand when it comes to setting policy. In effect, then, the revenues flowing into state coffers during the commodity boom have allowed EO type state managers the kind of policy autonomy (from both domestic society and external capital) commonly associated with the rentier state, for better or worse.

There are further parallels between EO cases and their West Asian comparators, which go beyond, and in some senses confound, the RS model. Although the sincerity of EO governments' developmental agendas is at the very least questionable, the sheer volume of commodity rent passing through the domestic economy may well be enough to spark true processes of accumulation rather than simple distribution of the extractive surplus.

Interestingly, this situation seems to recall the historical political-economic path already taken by the Gulf monarchies. Hanieh (2011, chap. 2) provides an account in which the circulation of sufficiently large quantities of oil rents spurs a twin-track process of capitalist formation. Here, rulers' distribution of real estate and high-level public sector jobs to relatives, prominent allies, and older merchant families, while initially allocative or even parasitic, eventually proved to be the basis for future accumulation. Beyond this inner circle, emerging business groups generally were not permitted any direct control over extractive sectors, but they did begin to provide ancillary services around the oil and gas industries—in construction, basic manufacturing, or transport, for instance.

With the enrichment of bureaucrats through payments for contracts (from both internal and external sources) and states moving to offer interest-free loans to nascent capitalists (including those outside the rulers' inner circles), discerning a clear separation between state and capital, as well as predation and accumulation, became difficult. Nevertheless, and confounding expectations, most of the Gulf states now house successful downstream industries, usually state owned, which serve primarily as vehicles for "true" capital accumulation rather than patrimonial rent allocation (Hertog 2010).[6] Hanieh's (2011, 15) comparison here is with Engels's description of the Russian state as providing a hothouse for the growth of the capitalist class. While there are marked differences, particularly in the sense that the dominance of capital-intensive extraction in the Gulf has not involved the creation of a working class,[7] the other side of the ledger, where the state incubates nascent capitalists via subsidies and the granting of concessions, is rather similar.[8]

Though such processes are less advanced in Kazakhstan, and particularly in Angola, they do appear to have been occurring to some degree during the boom, with high prices acting as an accelerant in the formation of capitalist classes overlapping with and highly dependent upon the state. In both cases, hydrocarbon rents are directly channeled into a mix of allocative and accumulative activities, through state-owned companies answerable directly to the president. In Angola, this has prompted the rise of a new post–civil war economic elite, which, while seemingly harboring little interest in long-term productive investment, represents a shift from the pure predation of exchange rate manipulation and war profiteering of the 1990s (Soares de Oliveira 2015, chap. 1). In Kazakhstan, post-Soviet upheaval did allow for the emergence of a somewhat more independent group of capitalists, who were not linked to extraction and had fewer ties to state officials. Although this group has periodically been a source of opposition to the government, its role increasingly appears analogous to that of the second-tier Gulf capitalists—excluded from energy sectors but otherwise appeased via a share of government contracts.

External Market Conditions and
Their Political-Economic Implications

Crude oil dominates the export profile of both Angola and Kazakhstan, though to a lesser extent in Kazakhstan, which also exports minor amounts of copper, zinc, and natural gas as well as wheat. With most production occurring offshore, the Angolan oil sector was not unduly disturbed by the country's long civil war, and petroleum has accounted for more than 90 percent of exports since the early 1990s (United Nations Conference on Trade and Development n.d.). In Kazakhstan, the average has been above 50 percent since 2005 (table 7.2), with a large boost possible in the future as production at the Kashagan Field ramps up.[9]

TABLE 7.2
Oil as a percentage of total merchandise export value

	2000	2002	2004	2006	2008	2010	2012
Angola	96	96.2	97.6	97.4	96.2	96.2	98.1
Kazakhstan	51	51.2	46	52.4	50.3	58.8	55.3

Source: Observatory of Economic Complexity.

Although both cases possessed important oil sectors prior to the 2000s, a clear line can be traced between the boom in oil prices, expanding export receipts for the two states, and huge increases in government revenue and expenditure over the same period. Figure 7.1 shows the progression of total merchandise export values in Angola and Kazakhstan since 1998, together with that of the average international spot price per barrel of crude oil. As can be seen, the three curves follow similar trends, with an initial increase in oil prices during the late 1990s, reflected in export revenue movements (though weakly), followed by a stronger correspondence among indicators over the course of the commodity boom proper, beginning in 2003.

The relative weight of hydrocarbons in the export sectors of both cases suggests that the commodity boom would be associated with positive economic trends in Angola and Kazakhstan. However, establishing a connection between oil prices and government revenues and expenditures provides much stronger evidence linking change in commodity markets to a newfound capacity to implement independent development strategies. Comprehensive and accurate figures relating to the importance of oil revenues in government accounts are complicated, in the cases of Kazakhstan and Angola, by the fact that parastatals (Samruk-Kazyna and Sonangol)

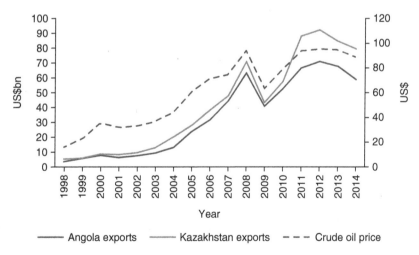

Figure 7.1 Angola's and Kazakhstan's total merchandise exports relative to oil prices, 1998–2014.
Sources: United Nations Conference on Trade and Development, UNCTADStat data center; World Bank, Commodity Price Data—Pink Sheet Data.

control a large proportion of these funds and directly allocate them to development projects, bypassing the regular budget process.

Nevertheless, IMF estimates of oil revenue as a percentage of total revenue in Angola are 80% for 2011 and 75% in 2013, while equivalent figures are 53% (2011) and 47% (2013) for Kazakhstan (International Monetary Fund 2014a; 2017). Given that export revenue, powered by the resource boom, rose so quickly and that oil payments have played such a large role in public finances, it is hardly surprising that government spending expanded rapidly in both EO states since 2003. Figure 7.2 illustrates this in the case of Angola, showing an index value for both general government revenue and expenditure, drawn from IMF statistics, which may well underestimate their growth, again because of the likely omission of many Sonangol activities. Adjusted for inflation, revenue had, by 2005, doubled from its 2000 level, and had tripled by 2011, after a dip in 2009, following the global financial crisis. Similar trends are observed in expenditure, though it is worth noting that the eventual decision on the part of the Angolan authorities to turn to the International Monetary Fund, in 2009, came after the growth in spending had begun to outstrip that of revenue and was not fully adjusted downward to compensate for the postcrisis blip in receipts. While the ensuing $1.4 billion loan from the fund did not come with particularly stringent policy conditionalities attached, these events prefigured the greater

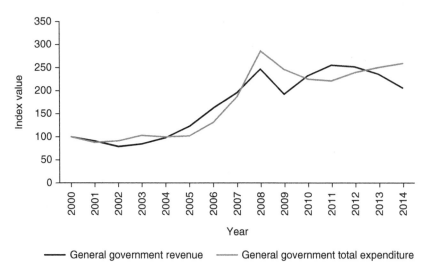

Figure 7.2 Angola revenue and expenditure indexes (in real), 2000–2014. Calculated from International Monetary Fund, World Economic Outlook Database.

apparent shift in policy that has more recently come with a more sustained drop in oil prices (International Monetary Fund 2018).

The argument for a connection between the commodity boom and the ability of resource-rich states to break with neoliberal constraints rests primarily upon the impact of Chinese demand on the structure of global commodity markets rather than necessarily upon any direct bilateral trade links. However, it is interesting to note that, in this regard, China has played a rather important direct role in the expansion of Kazakhstani and Angolan resource exports. A key plank of Kazakhstani foreign policy following independence has been the desire to balance Russian, Chinese, and Western influence, something which extends to external economic relations. While it is therefore no surprise to find that no one market dominates Kazakhstan's exports, China's share has grown steadily since 2000, becoming Kazakhstan's number one export destination by 2008. By 2012, one-fifth of Kazakhstani exports went to China—more than double the proportion that went to Russia, in second place (United Nations Comtrade n.d.).

The reentry of China into Angola has been a major focal point of recent media and academic interest in China–Africa relations, and the signing of a \$2 billion oil-backed loan deal with China's Eximbank, in 2004, was of major significance. Indeed, the "Angola model" has become the standard term for the system of commodity-backed loans for infrastructure that were advanced by Chinese policy banks to many Southern governments in subsequent years (Brautigam 2009, 73–77; Brautigam and Gallagher 2014; Tan-Mullins, Mohan, and Power 2010). The terms of this loan and of similar deals with the Angolan government have led to the involvement of both public and private Chinese entities in Angolan construction and infrastructure, though, perhaps surprisingly, Chinese firms are only peripheral players in the extraction of the country's oil (Corkin 2011).

Where the bilateral relationship certainly has strengthened is in trade. The Chinese share of Angolan oil exports jumped, following the end of the civil war, from 16.5 percent in 2002 to 41 percent two years later, and China has been the number one buyer of Angolan oil every year since 2008 (with a 62 percent share in 2008) (Observatory of Economic Complexity n.d.). Viewed from the other side, Angola is now the second largest supplier of petroleum to China, after Saudi Arabia (Weimer and Vines 2012). Nevertheless, though China has been an important trade partner and, in the Angolan case, creditor in the commodity boom period, it is the takeoff in the oil market, combined with particular domestic conjunctural factors—the end of the Angolan Civil War, new extractive projects in Kazakhstan—that have allowed both EO states the fiscal leeway to assemble their distinctive post-neoliberal orientations.

Angola

The pace of change in Angola since the end of civil war, in 2002, has been remarkable, with the economy becoming sub-Saharan Africa's third largest by 2005 and GDP growth peaking at 23.2 percent two years later (World Bank n.d.). This is despite a deeply troubled twentieth-century history. A liberation struggle against Portuguese colonialism began in 1961 but was only ended by the outbreak of revolution in Lisbon in 1974. By the time Angolan independence was declared, a year later, three domestic factions were fighting for control.

Though the ostensibly socialist MPLA held the capital, Luanda, throughout, the civil war grew larger in scale and duration as it morphed into a Cold War proxy conflict. The Soviet Union sent significant military aid to the MPLA, and the United States provided military assistance to the União Nacional para a Independência Total de Angola (National Union for the Total Independence of Angola, or UNITA), based in the diamond-producing highlands. The conflict escalated to the point of direct military involvement on the part of both Cuba and apartheid South Africa, but it continued for more than a decade after the end of the Cold War and the withdrawal of foreign forces, ending only with the death of UNITA leader Jonas Savimbi in 2002. Aside from low-level conflict in the enclave of Cabinda, thereafter President José Eduardo dos Santos ruled largely unchallenged until he stepped down in 2017.

During the 1990s, both sides in the civil war financed their war efforts almost entirely through the sale of oil (in the case of the MPLA) or diamonds (UNITA) (le Billon 2001). However, there clearly was huge capacity for the expansion of oil production under peacetime conditions, and it is the realization of this potential—with rapid growth in oil exports, from $5.9 billion in 2002 to $63.2 billion in 2012 (Observatory of Economic Complexity n.d.)—which was almost single-handedly responsible for the booming economy.

Having developed a "parallel state" apparatus centered on national oil company Sonangol during the 1990s (Soares de Oliveira 2007), the victorious MPLA leaders entered peacetime at a moment of rising prices and with an ideal vehicle through which to maximize their take from the growing oil revenue. These advantages, together with the involvement of China and other nontraditional donors, afforded President dos Santos the leeway to manage Angola's reengagement with the world largely on Angolan terms. This, in turn, left the government free to pursue a state-led, high modernist development model, which, in many senses, may be more rhetorical than substantive but nevertheless brought an impressive reconstruction of infrastructure (Power 2012; Soares de Oliveira 2015, 72–82). Clearly, though, much economic activity is blighted by elite predation, and development plans often actively exclude the vast majority of the population (Ovadia 2013).

At the end of the war, any ambitious development schemes seemed a distant prospect. With an impending fiscal crisis, it might have seemed inevitable that the government would establish an orthodox relationship with Northern donors and creditors and thus enact the neoliberal reforms that such an arrangement would require. While the government negotiated with the international financial institutions and repeatedly called for a donor conference in the initial postwar years, however, international demands that Angola submit to an IMF monitoring program and account for apparently missing oil revenue were largely ignored. Though clearly much of the Angolan objection can be ascribed to a reluctance to demystify opaque oil financing, Power (2012) points out that another concern was the prospect of neoliberal paring back of the state administration at a time when a primary MPLA goal was the territorial consolidation of its rule. More generally, the postwar government had an understandable sensitivity about questions of sovereignty and, crucially, unlike the majority of sub-Saharan states, this was Angola's first real encounter with conditionality, the initial stages of which had also been resisted, in various ways, by several neighboring states during the 1980s (Mosley et al. 1991).

Had the situation persisted, Angola, too, might have been forced to reluctantly engage with donor demands. Instead, a combination of rising oil prices, new deepwater fields coming on line, and the arrival of a new creditor, in the shape of China, allowed the government to largely define its own approach to economic management.[10] The involvement of China is by far the most prominent of these factors noted in the literature, and not without reason. Oil-backed loans from China's Eximbank (and later from the International Commercial Bank of China), beginning with a $2 billion deal in 2004 (Brautigam and Gallagher 2014), have become the paradigmatic examples of China's now widespread practice of offering commodity-backed loans to Southern states—the Angola model.

As Brautigam (2009, 275) points out, the first Chinese loan was not entirely novel, in that Angola had already contracted large amounts of oil-backed debt, mainly owed to Northern banks, over the 1990s. This said, the Eximbank deal was different in important respects. First, the terms were far more generous than those previously offered by Northern commercial banks, with low interest rates and a much longer repayment period. Second, this loan and the subsequent commodity-backed credits were tied to infrastructure projects, with the stipulation that 70 percent of ensuing contracts would be awarded to Chinese firms (Soares de Oliveira 2015, 56).

It is quite clear that large-scale loans from Chinese policy banks, to the tune of perhaps $20 billion by 2014 (Brautigam and Gallagher 2014), have been a major part of the post–civil war Angolan development story. For dos Santos, however, this was not simply about shifting dependence away from the global North and toward China. As in Kazakhstan, as we will see, the new Chinese presence was rather astutely parlayed into a greater freedom of government action, with a larger array of potential international partners and thus enhanced bargaining power for the Angolan side in choosing with whom to engage. Indeed, within a year of the first Eximbank deal, Angola secured two loans from British and French banks, totaling $4.35 billion and with commercial rate, though reasonable, terms (Brautigam 2009, 276).

Despite the political importance of oil-backed loans from the People's Republic of China, these did not lead to Chinese dominance, even in the oil sector, where Chinese companies were granted only limited access in comparison with more technically advanced Western firms (Soares de Oliveira 2015, 174). In line with the MPLA aim of diversification of partners, capital from other sources, including Brazil, Portugal, and Israel, is also very active in Angola, with the Brazilian construction firm Odebrecht becoming the largest private employer in the country.

Interestingly, Brautigam (2011, 277) cites a comment from the Angolan finance ministry that the 2002–2004 engagement with the IMF was primarily sought as a means of gaining an IMF seal of approval, which would then allow the government to continue raising capital from Northern banks at reasonable rates. The fact that such loans were forthcoming, as were the British and French credits, only a few years after rejecting the IMFs advances, points to rising production volumes and prices in the oil sector as a more fundamental basis of Angola's ability to maintain policy independence than direct Chinese engagement alone. Though it is perhaps possible that Chinese activities in Angola over the mid-2000s brought something of a spotlight to Angola, which might have helped to enthuse Northern banks, this is hardly the sort of green light for banks and capital markets that a positive assessment from the IMF usually provides. The fact that, even without IFI endorsement, Northern finance flooded into Angola over the next decade is surely evidence of the power of the commodity boom to attract capital inflows to resource-rich locations—even to a historically unstable, low-income state with poor infrastructure and little evidence of "sound" institutions or policy beyond a basic orthodox macroeconomic framework.

In 2009, following the global financial crisis, Angola did turn to the IMF for a $1.4 billion loan. However, even at this point of relative economic weakness, the comparatively lax conditions asked of Angola are striking, with the MPLA government essentially disregarding requested reforms that were not to their liking (Soares de Oliveira 2015, 178). The desire on the part of the fund to establish a presence in Angola, which by this point had become Africa's third-largest economy, shows a major shift in bargaining power from the early post–civil war years. As Soares de Oliveira points out, the IMF had gone from a complete refusal to engage, on the basis of $4.22 billion hole in government finances as of 2001, to sympathetic concern (but little condemnation) over a $32 billion gap (or 25 percent of GDP) ten years later.

The rising level of unaccounted-for funds are the direct result of the growth of a parallel state system, which bypasses the formal institutions of public administration (Soares de Oliveira 2007; Shaxston 2007). During the civil war, the state-owned Sonangol possessed a much higher credit rating than the government itself—largely because of the offshore location of the majority of its oil reserves—and thus became the main recipient of international loans. Oil-backed financing, coordinated through Sonangol, thus became the main means of funding the civil war in the 1990s.

During the postwar period, the company rose to become Africa's second largest, with a range of subsidiaries across shipping, banking, insurance, and real estate, along with overseas interests in Portugal, Brazil, Iraq, Venezuela, South Sudan, Algeria, and Cuba (Soares de Oliveira 2015, 185). Sonangol and the Gabinete de Reconstrução Nacional (National Reconstruction Cabinet), responsible for allocating the majority of (quasi) public funds, are both very much under the direct control of the presidency and clearly serve as vehicles for the enrichment of a thin stratum of MPLA elites and their allies (Ovadia 2013). Nevertheless, Sonangol itself appears to be run with a high level of technical competence, and it is undeniable that large-scale reconstruction efforts have taken place, particularly in infrastructure, since 2002. It may well be possible to ascribe many of the developmental advances that have occurred to little more than a side effect of the opportunities for enrichment arising from project deals, particularly when these include joint ventures with foreign partners. Even so, and somewhat similar to the experience of the Gulf states, the lines between predatory rentierism and accumulation, as well as between the state and private enterprise, are increasingly difficult to discern.

However, even if the MPLA ran a narrow, clientelistic system during the latter years of the civil war, there appears to have been a realization that a somewhat broader-based nation-building and development project was now necessary to secure the foundations of their rule. The concentration of efforts and funding in infrastructure, especially on the reconstruction and extension of the road and rail networks, to the tune of $4.3 billion per year, or 14 percent of GDP from 2004 to 2010 (Pushak and Foster 2011), is likely to have been of most benefit to a broad swath of the population. Overall, however, rural areas and the peri-urban *musseques* (slums) were ignored in favor of an aspiring urban middle class, encompassing perhaps a half million of the country's 20 million inhabitants. Improvements for this social layer came through the provision of house and car ownership, the extension of pensions, and a doubling of the number of civil servants, to four hundred thousand (Soares de Oliveira 2015, 82–83). The growing number of Angolans with disposable income added a second layer to the elite-driven urban gentrification, seen most obviously around Luanda's seafront, with the development of new supermarkets, shopping centers, and restaurants to a modernizing blueprint and with Dubai held up as a reference point (Power 2012).

With regard to the nascent middle classes, it is again difficult to mark a clear distinction between the extension of clientelistic networks as the basis for regime stability and a process of genuine class formation. Although it may not fit with a traditional RS schema, in this, Angola seemed to be following in the footsteps of several Gulf States that were largely excluded from fruits of the oil boom, though with a much larger domestic population. Hanieh's (2011) evocation of Engels's state as hothouse is particularly appropriate here, though with oil revenue utilized as fertilizer and the government very much in control of the process. As Soares de Oliveira (2015, 83) puts it, "The MPLA wants to internalize the process of class formation: through a limited distribution of the oil rent, it seeks to engineer the rise of a loyal and dependent state class rather than create the conditions for the spontaneous emergence of an unattached and unreliable middle class."

One of the more interesting aspects of the trajectory of Angolan development over the boom years was the manner in which its claimed intellectual basis shifted and solidified behind a kind of high modernist developmentalism quite at odds with neoliberal norms, and certainly with donor preferences (Sogge 2011; Soares de Oliveira 2011). The justification for favoring a relatively narrow band of society was premised on the creation of a so-called national bourgeoisie, with this term variously used to describe the enrichment of a small number of oligarchs (with, for example, 85 percent of Angolan banking credit being directed to around two hundred individuals) as well as in the somewhat broader sense of the creation of an urban consumer class. Rentierism and multilevel patronage thus could be justified in developmental terms, drawing on a multifaceted spectrum of influences, ranging from the final years of Portuguese colonialism to the Marxist roots of the MPLA to the image of Brazil as an idealized model society. While there is little suggestion that the Chinese model was interrogated in any depth by Angolan officials, the emphasis on experimentation and state-led megaprojects is familiar. The national bourgeoisie trope also seems very reminiscent of the desire to promote a black capitalist class in postapartheid South Africa (see chapter 9).

Beyond infrastructure provision and Sonangol, there were relatively few indications of long-term development planning on the part of government or capital. Several large-scale projects, which resemble pre-neoliberal industrialization efforts, were undertaken, chiming with the claimed developmentalist orientation of the state. Most prominent is the special economic zone outside Luanda. The special economic zone scheme, in its first phase, involves the development of seventy-three state industries, described by Soares de Oliveira as "a sort of theme park of import substitution industrialization" (Soares de Oliveira 2015, 63)—an apt summation of the government's approach to development as a whole.

While the costs associated with the special economic zone are difficult to ascertain, its workings are emblematic of the kinds of initiatives pursued since the end of the civil war. The various factories that comprise the facility were publicly funded, but they were developed by foreign firms as turnkey projects and then handed over to the government upon completion. That most of these factories either failed to produce anything or else ran at a loss seems to be due to a lack of interest in long-term planning in favor of the use of such schemes for short-term enrichment of favored insiders, beginning with the various contracts involved in the construction of the venture. Next, after a completed project was handed over to the government, it often would be quickly privatized, commencing another round of rent-seeking. According to Soares de Oliveira (2015, 63–71), this pattern was been repeated across a range of initiatives that, on a surface level, resembled familiar state-led developmentalism. These included kibbutz-style agricultural schemes, Chinese built-housing complexes, and a state-run network designed to purchase and distribute food from small producers, which apparently devolved into a conventional, privately run supermarket chain.

Kazakhstan

Although it was possessed of both a much higher per capita GDP and more autonomous capitalist elements, Kazakhstan's experience of the boom shared many important features with that of Angola and the EO ideal type. With the collapse of the Soviet Union, in 1991, Kazakh Communist Party leader Nursultan Nazarbayev took over as president of the newly independent country and remained at the helm of an increasingly authoritarian state up until 2019. Nazarbayev's paternalistic rule was apparently popular, with its legitimacy built upon an ability to deliver relatively rapid economic growth after the 1990s falloff common to almost all post-Soviet states (Koch 2013).

During this initial period after independence, neoliberal reform and privatization produced a new class of oligarch (Spechler 2008), though, in contrast to neighboring Russia, the state retained control of most strategic industries. Thus, the new capitalists, from early on, depended heavily on their ties to the presidency (Libman 2010), in a system resembling the "power vertical" of Putin's Russia (Isaacs 2010), rather than relying on loans from domestic capital, as with the Yeltsin government. The *finansovo-promyshlenye gruppy*, or financial-industrial groups, which emerged in the decade or so following the collapse of the Soviet Union, may be divided into two tiers (Junisbai 2010). The outer grouping consists of oligarchs who are permitted to accrue large fortunes in a more-or-less competitive environment. However, these figures were not allowed to own firms in the hydrocarbon or mineral sectors, Kazakhstan's most profitable industries, these being reserved for an inner circle around President Nazarbayev. At various points, the emergent capitalists of the second tier agitated for change and even formed opposition parties, though these efforts were rebuffed. Moreover, Nazarbayev demonstrated, several times, that the position of oligarchs in both tiers was dependent upon his personal patronage, even while he allocated oil wealth toward both strata of the elite to stave off potential destabilization (Isaacs 2008; Ostrowski 2009).

Borrowing the motif of the Asian tiger economies, Nazarbayev's stated goal for Kazakhstan—to become a Central Asian "snow leopard"—from the beginning associated regime legitimacy with developmental ambition. Initially, these efforts looked toward the World Bank's neoliberal narrative of development in the newly industrialized countries—published not long after Kazakhstan's independence—as a blueprint, with the state's role mainly being to prepare the ground for an effectively functioning market economy (World Bank 1993; Stark and Ahrens 2012).

However, with oil exports tied to Russian pipeline infrastructure and expansion of capacity dependent upon Western oil companies, Kazakhstani frustration with the inability to recoup revenue from extractive industries grew. Such feelings intensified in the early 2000s, as oil prices began to rise and huge new discoveries, such as the Kashagan Field (the largest outside West Asia), were made. A stronger bargaining position for the government prompted a reassertion of state participation through the stipulation of a minimum 50 percent share for oil parastatal KazMunaiGaz in joint ventures with foreign firms, as well as increasing attempts to broaden the range of investors as a means of reducing reliance upon any one Russian, Chinese, or Western firm (Domjan and Stone 2010).

A large proportion of hydrocarbon revenues was diverted toward a reorientation of the economy along a more state-led path, particularly following the 2008 financial crisis, though discerning between sincere developmental ambition and the need to allocate resources among supporters and potential enemies of the government is difficult. In many senses, this question may be somewhat moot, however. As with Sonangol in Angola, there appears to have been a recognition at the highest level of the state, if not among many individual members of the elite, that the best way to secure sufficient revenue for distribution of patronage was to run the main engine of accumulation/enrichment, the national oil company, according to commercial, profit-making principles (Franke, Gawrich, and Alakbarov 2009; Domjan and Stone 2010). While islands of efficiency may not extend much beyond Sonangol in Angola, there are some indications that, in Kazakhstan, other areas of the state may tend more toward the longer-term end of the accumulation–rent continuum. This is perhaps a reflection of a relatively stronger bureaucratic tradition, inherited from Soviet times, though, again, the lines between profit seeking and patronage seeking remained blurred over the whole period (Cummings and Nørgaard 2004).

Several sovereign wealth funds were set up during the boom years, including the National Oil Fund, which acts as a source of savings with which to stabilize the economy, and, most importantly, Samruk-Kazyna, which evolved from the unification of state holding companies into an apparent vehicle for development via government investments and loans and now manages $77.5 billion of assets (Grigoryan 2016).[11] Samruk-Kazyna plays an important role in industrialization, diversification efforts, and infrastructure expansion and apparently has been modeled on the Singaporean sovereign wealth fund Temask, though with more of an active developmental function (Kemme 2012). However, Samruk-Kazyna also has been used to extend loans to failing companies owned by members of the elite—particularly during the post-2008 recession—and has been criticized for the politically motivated appointment of senior figures and for largesse in payment of bonuses in recent years (Peyrouse 2012). As in Angola, the state parlays its control of resource rents into a dual, not always contradictory role as both development actor and guarantor of a national network of elite patronage.

Conclusion

In several senses, Angola and Kazakhstan may appear to be little more than some of the latest additions to the extensive roll call of rentier states, with the size of their resource sectors, relative to the rest of the economy, resulting in political-economic structures distorted and dominated by the struggle for control and distribution of extractive rents. These dynamics are in no way unique to the commodity boom period and can equally be applied to a range of states across the global South and in a variety of eras. There are good reasons, however, to argue for the designation of the EO type as representing a distinct form of rentierism that would not have been possible without the China-led resource boom.

Many of the structural adjustment initiatives of the 1980s and 1990s were partly geared toward tackling the perceived problems of rent-seeking behavior particularly associated with rentier states (Evans 1989). Nevertheless, the proposed solution, of shrinking the size, reach, and power of the state apparatus, tended to simply shift the focus of rentierism rather than eradicating it. I discuss this phenomenon in more detail in chapter 8, where I show, for instance, that even in a case such as Zambia, where privatization of the copper industry removed the major source of rent from state control, distribution of patronage, now increasingly derived from aid flows, continued to drive the country's political economy to a great extent, even if patronage networks now increasingly encompassed private as well as public office holders. In other cases, even during a neoliberal era of generally low prices and pressure to limit state participation in extraction, natural resource revenue was not dislodged from its position as the central source of rents. Neoliberalism, therefore, proved very much compatible with rentierism, even if dismantling state bureaucracies altered its institutional shell.

The circumstances of the commodity boom enabled the emergence of the particular form of rentierism seen in the EO type, which appears rather distinct from the kind of rentier state that would be expected under neoliberalism. While much of the developmentalist rhetoric emanating from the governments in Astana and Luanda was primarily intended to confer legitimacy upon the respective regimes, it also tended to draw from visions of economic transformation that ran contrary to neoliberal views. Similarly, although the ensuing development initiatives may have been vehicles for elite enrichment, these vehicles look rather different from those that would be expected under a regime seeking to appeal to neoliberal sensibilities. The leading role played by Sonangol in Angola, and increasingly by Samruk-Kazyna in Kazakhstan, gave a quasi state capitalist character to the functioning of both economies, in keeping with their economic priorities, which seemed to hark back to an older, modernization-inflected understanding of development.

The contrast between these features and the prevailing orthodoxy is particularly striking in the case of Angola. For all the World Bank's renewed enthusiasm for infrastructure in recent years, it seems safe to say that most of the Angolan government's major publicly funded schemes—the special economic zone, suburban housing development, airport construction, state-owned supermarkets, or the sheer scale of road and rail investment—would not have found their way into any Poverty Reduction Strategy Paper. This is not necessarily meant as praise of Angola's development strategy; after all, there seems little evidence of even an attempt to improve the lives of the majority of the population. There is no doubt, however, that the conditions of the commodity boom allowed both Angola and Kazakhstan to assert policy autonomy, with sufficient fiscal resources to pursue strategies of their own making.

CHAPTER VIII

Donor-Dependent Orthodoxy Type

Zambia, Laos, and Mongolia

The three states that I place within the donor-dependent ortho-doxy type have been heavily reliant upon aid and concessional finance from international financial institutions and bilateral donors since at least the 1990s, even if the share of aid as a percentage of gross domestic product has tended to decline somewhat since the early 2000s. Since none of these states had access to international capital markets until recently, this aid dependence, in a context of high levels of debt, constituted the main channel of transnational influence over their political-economic orientations during the neoliberal era. This is not to suggest that neoliberalizing policies were simply foisted upon helpless and unwilling states and societies. Indeed, there is considerable variation in the governments' receptiveness to liberalizing measures—both among the cases and within them, over time, and at different levels of power. Most of the postsocialist Mongolian governments, for example, were enthusiastically committed to a neoliberal program, even if this support has become more ambivalent over the period of the commodity boom. Laos, conversely, no doubt influenced by events in China, has pursued neoliberalizing reform reluctantly and only after sustained pressure from IFIs.[1]

Nevertheless, even as levels of aid dependence have lessened among the DDO states in recent years, the long-running ability of donors and IFIs to set the parameters of policy orientation, particularly through so-called participatory processes, has left a lasting legacy for the political economies of the DDO states. Ruling elites sit atop systems that employ post–Washington Consensus types of institutional structures and policy orientations while allowing for the maintenance of patron–client networks that reach down from the central state. With direct donor influence waning and booming natural resource sectors offering the possibility of greatly enhanced government revenues, a turn away from neoliberal orthodoxy might be expected—at the very least, in pursuit of further opportunities for elite predation, if not necessarily in the form of a full-fledged alternative development agenda. Such moves have occurred, in largely opportunistic and piecemeal fashion, though there is little evidence of any full-scale reorientation away from neoliberalism.

In the extractivist-oligarchic case of Angola, after decades of civil war, the regime was essentially presented with the option of embracing neoliberalism in 2002. The offer was rejected, with the help of rising oil revenues, and, drawing on a range of influences, Angola carved an independent political-economic path that looked rather different from the donor-led neoliberalism observed in most of its neighbors. DDO states, by contrast, entering the commodity boom with such neoliberalism as a default setting, deviated from this path—which, for the most part, allowed elites to retain their privileged positions—only cautiously, and with isolated policies. With no strong domestic capitalist class or unified popular classes present—save for the partial exception of Zambia—no local group had the means and motivation to force the issue. Thus, while political competition may well have occurred, this tended toward a battle for control of, inclusion in, and perhaps expansion of, networks of patronage distribution rather than for a reconfiguration of political-economic orientation overall.

I first will discuss the circumstances that led IFIs and donors to reform their structural adjustment programs, even if the resulting changes lay mainly in the domain of implementation rather than in policy or underlying ideals. The new so-called participatory agenda set the tone for donor and IFI-led neoliberalization during the late 1990s and into the 2000s, particularly for low-income states, where aid usually accounted for a large share of the national budget, limiting the scope for policy choice. I then note that a trend of declining aid dependence among DDO states would seem to have lifted this constraint during the 2000s, and yet, with the commodity boom arriving at the same time, the fact that none really attempted a full departure from a neoliberal agenda appears to be something of a puzzle. Here, I point to the salience of class formation, or the lack thereof. An absence of unified social interests opposed to neoliberalism resulted in few pressures on DDO governments to change tack from a status quo that largely benefited their ruling elites.

Next, I will move to show how the China-prompted commodity boom, as in the other types, presented an opportunity for DDO states to increase their resource revenues in a manner that would have laid the groundwork for any post-neoliberal turn, although this opportunity was largely passed over by states of this type. In this and the subsequent sections on domestic politics, I focus particularly on Zambia, which is used as the exemplar of the DDO type. Zambia, in fact, is an important case in terms of demonstrating my argument for a correspondence between lack of class formation and lack of social pressure against a government's preexisting neoliberal orientation, since here, in a departure from the ideal type, a limited degree of class formation helped bring to power a government that moved, if tentatively, further from neoliberal doctrine than seen in either of the other cases.

Aid Dependence and the Ideotypical Trajectory of the Donor-Dependent Orthodoxy Type

Though tending to decline in recent years, official development assistance has long provided a large proportion of government revenues in many of the poorest states of the global South.[2] Given these states' aid dependence, conditionality on the part of bilateral and multilateral donors has been a powerful lever through which to facilitate the adoption of a broadly liberalizing set of policies—at least in letter, if not, sometimes, in spirit. The packaging, scope, and emphasis of these programs has evolved since their original formulation, in the 1980s, as World Bank and International Monetary Fund structural adjustment programs. This shift, involving conditionalities which appear to be more flexible and to give more space to poverty alleviation but which require greater levels of commitment in an expanded number of policy areas, marks the DDO type as different from the homegrown orthodoxy cases I will discuss in chapter 9. In homegrown orthodoxy cases, a continuing neoliberal course is driven primarily by domestic capitalists, with correspondingly less attention paid to the concerns of international development professionals and no real need to demonstrate country ownership of or participation in the program.

For IFIs and donors, however, "ownership" and "participation" have become paramount concepts around which a more acceptable means of demanding adherence to policy conditionality has emerged since the late 1990s, in response to an incipient crisis of legitimacy in the SAP process.[3] In the first place, IFIs began to face growing criticism—even from some influential mainstream economists, most famously Stiglitz (2002)—of their "boilerplate" approaches, whereby structural adjustment programs tended to be viewed as an insistence upon a fixed set of policies derived from neo-classical assumptions, while paying no attention to particular country circumstances. Second, once signed up, governments of all political stripes found it exceedingly difficult to change course, at least at the policy level, even in response to increasing incidences of what became known as IMF riots, in dozens of states.[4] SAPs not only looked undemocratic but also seemed to create the prospect of social instability significant enough to interfere with their implementation.

The response from the IFIs was to adopt the participatory approach, involving consultations with local civil society groups, that was already used by most bilateral donors. This culminated in the replacement of SAPs with Poverty Reduction Strategy Papers, along with a shift toward some-what longer-term development goals and general budget rather than proj-ect support. A high degree of policy continuity with the pre-PRSP era, however, suggested that these new procedures allowed little added room for host governments to pursue strategies deviating from the liberalizing norm (Zack-Williams and Mohan 2005).

In policy terms, IFI and donor thinking evolved somewhat over the past four decades, with the post–Asian financial crisis years seeing an increas-ing interest in institutional reform, greater nods toward poverty allevia-tion, and a renewed focus on infrastructure development. Nonetheless, all of these tended to be seen as adaptations necessitated by the realization that SAPs were not applied in a vacuum but instead encountered local circum-stances, which often seemed to lead to some combination of incomplete implementation, social instability, or, most importantly, disappointing eco-nomic performance. Rather than question the appropriateness of the underlying model, however, IFIs tended to understand these failures in terms of local barriers to the smooth functioning of a liberal market econ-omy (Babb 2013).[5] Since ignoring these factors had largely proved unsuc-cessful, they were to be engaged with and corrected for. The ensuing "good governance" agenda, encapsulated by the World Bank's Country Policy and Institutional Assessments (Pushak and Foster 2011), conflated Weberian notions of bureaucratic institutional quality and neoliberal policies into an expansive, depoliticized agenda for reform.[6] Hence, lowering import tariffs was presented as equally representative of unarguable best practice as meritocratic recruitment in the civil service.

Poverty alleviation, also bound up within this technocratic framework, was acknowledged as a sort of market externality, requiring palliative action in the form of social safety nets or, more recently, conditional cash transfer schemes.[7] These approaches certainly may be interpreted as efforts to promote participation of the poor in both consumer and labor markets (Cammack 2004). At least as important, however, seems to have been a concern with the riots and resistance prompted by the original SAPs and the difficulties these revealed in terms of pursuing a neoliberalizing policy agenda within a democratic framework (Fraser 2005). Though they were no doubt reflective of a sincere overall desire to promote development and reduce poverty, IFI and donor programs of the era reveal a perceived need to build "reform coalitions," drawn from all levels of society, which would embrace the liberalization process, thereby forestalling the possibilities of social instability or reluctant implementation that would threaten its success.[8]

Beyond their antipoverty measures, the introduction of PRSPs represented an attempt to build reform coalitions as much through process as through policy, particularly in the primacy afforded to the new watchwords of ownership and participation. These terms were often taken to mean a greater voice for recipient country governments and societies, since they denoted a much larger role for local actors in the preparation of the PRSP (Cornwall and Brock 2005). It seems quite clear, however, that this held true only to the extent that domestic contributors agreed with the fundamental assumptions of the IFIs.

That participation of this sort mostly involved a selective inclusion of those civil society groups able and willing to articulate their perspectives in a form palatable to Northern nongovernmental organizations, bilateral donors, and IFIs has been ably demonstrated elsewhere (Craig and Porter 2003; Ruckert 2007; Harrison 2004). Participants were aware that the final document produced was subject to IFI approval, meaning that the bounds of what constituted acceptable participation were well understood. The result was to undermine the notion of ownership—domestic actors "owned" a program in the narrow sense that they were involved in its production. In so doing, government and civil society demonstrated a commitment to the aims of the PRSP, which forestalled any accusations of external imposition upon an unwilling host. The paradox here is that the PRSP process actually demanded more of governments than did the old SAPs—under the PRSP system they were required to express their own enthusiasm for the program rather than simply acquiesce to its demands.

All of this is made explicit in IFI documentation. An IMF report from the early stages of the participatory era, for example, understands ownership as "a situation in which the policy content of the program is similar to what the country itself would have chosen in the absence of IMF involvement. This is because the country shares with the IMF both the objectives of the program as well as an understanding of the appropriate economic model linking those objectives to economic policies . . . The country 'owns' the program in the sense that it is committed to the spirit of the program, rather than just complying with it" (Khan and Sharma 2003).[9]

Given the evolution of IFI and donor process and, to a much lesser extent, policy, within the parameters of a fundamentally unchanging liberalizing orientation, it is hardly surprising that aid-dependent states have remained committed to this agenda. However, since the early 2000s, Laos and Mongolia have seen a huge expansion in their previously marginal natural resource production, and Zambia's existing but stagnant copper sector has been reinvigorated. These industries have powered rapid growth—and rising government revenue—as a whole, meaning a significant reduction in ODA as a proportion of gross national income over the past decade.

As the weight of ODA has declined, the increasing proportion of government revenue and national budget expenditure not subject to approval by external actors has increased. Such changing circumstances would seem to hold out the possibility for these states to break with IFI and donor preferences and to pursue more nationally defined, non-neoliberalizing policy orientations. Indeed, this is exactly what has occurred in the case of Bolivia, examined in chapter 6. As shown in table 8.1, Bolivia was somewhat less aid dependent at the beginning of the commodity boom that any of the DDO type states. Nevertheless, ODA as a percentage of GNI in Bolivia on the eve of Evo Morales's election in 2006 stood at 7.7 percent, which clearly did not represent an insurmountable obstacle for the implementation of a relatively radical program that ran counter to the agendas advanced by donors and IFIs. All the DDO states had lower ODA dependence rates than this by 2010, at the latest, suggesting that aid dependence alone cannot account for their continued adherence (for the most part) to a neoliberal

TABLE 8.1

Official development assistance received (percentage of gross national income), 2002–2012

State	2002	2004	2006	2008	2010	2012
Bolivia	9	7	7.7	3.9	3.9	2.6
Laos	16.2	11.9	11.1	9.6	6.2	4.7
Mongolia	14.9	13	6.1	4.5	5.4	4.8
Zambia	18.4	22.4	15.4	8.4	6.2	4.7

Source: World Bank, World Development Indicators.

agenda. However, no departures from this path were likely to occur without powerful domestic voices demanding such a change of course—whether this came from domestic capitalists, popular movements, or state managers themselves. With the partial exception of Zambia, these voices have remained largely unheard in each of the DDO type states, in stark contrast to the mobilizations that preceded Morales's election in Bolivia.

In explaining these divergent outcomes, the most consequential difference between Bolivia and the DDO cases appears to lie in the strength of domestic social forces outside the state. Though Bolivia has the lowest per capita GDP in South America, capitalist social relations are more fully developed than in the DDO cases. The neoliberal era in Bolivia represented, fundamentally, an alliance between the highland mining capitalist fraction and transnational capital, which usurped the formerly dominant lowland agro-industrialists (Kaup 2013c).

The other product of neoliberalism in Bolivia was a growth in popular mobilizations, which began locally but were increasingly stitched together at national level by Morales's Movimiento al Socialismo (Kohl 2010; Albro 2005). Though appeals to ethnicity had some salience in this process, the core of the movement (including large numbers of individuals who did not identify as indigenous) was built from the informal urban sector and rural peasants and revolved around perceptions of exclusion (Ellner 2012). As Kaup (2013c) shows, by the time of Morales's election, the intracapitalist struggle had taken enough out of both the highland and lowland elites to allow the MAS to gain power, with the commodity boom providing the fiscal resources needed for the new government to stabilize and to address many of the demands of its social movement base.[10]

By contrast, capitalist development in the DDO states surveyed here is less deeply rooted. This has had three major impacts on the ways in which neoliberalization has played out in these cases. First, in the absence of any significant domestic capitalist class, state managers and allied elites leverage access to the state—and thus connections to networks of international capital—as the main means of domestic accumulation (and rent-seeking). Second, without large inward flows of transnational capital, aid (or ODA) has been the main source of rent and profit for state-connected elites during the neoliberal era, and the major channel through which neoliberalizing discipline has been transmitted to governments.[11] Third, the persistence of vertical patronage relations has resulted in segmentation and atomization of popular class groups, making the building of a MAS-like national movement infeasible.

As a result of these characteristics, with the coming of the commodity boom, any change of course away from a liberalizing trajectory would need to come not as a response to popular pressure or to pressure from powerful domestic capitalist groups, as in other types, but from the state managers themselves. Such moves were certainly possible during the boom—as in Zambia's renationalization of telecommunications and railways—when state elites perceived a likely benefit, whether in terms of accumulation, rent-seeking, or increased patronage resources. However, without national popular movements to apply pressure, and with generally low levels of state capacity, the articulation and implementation of any coherent alternative vision of development is extremely difficult, meaning that those changes that do occur are likely to be unprogrammatic, partial, and piecemeal. The case of Zambia is extremely useful in demonstrating this claim, since it stands as a partial exception to the DDO type's lack of capitalist class formation, together with a corresponding partial exception to continued neoliberalization.

External Market Conditions

By 2012, the exports of Zambia, Laos, and Mongolia were heavily concentrated in mineral sectors, as can be seen in table 8.2. Copper has long been the dominant Zambian export, even during the lean periods of the 1990s, when a combination of low prices and mismanagement meant that the mines of the Copperbelt ran at a loss. In the other two cases, major extractive

TABLE 8.2

Natural resources as a proportion of total exports

State	2005	2012
Laos	18%	52%
Mongolia	41%	89%
Zambia	78%	79%

Source: Observatory of Economic Complexity.

projects only really began in the 2000s, meaning that these sectors became progressively more important over the course of the decade.

Mongolia's and Laos's status as relative newcomers to resource export has somewhat ambiguous implications for their bargaining power with extractive firms. On the one hand, the two states begin with a blank slate, in contrast to the Zambian situation, where altering levels of mining taxation—effectively close to zero percent in many cases—required the repudiation of agreements signed by previous governments. On the other hand, the long-established Zambian mines are still viable and need little extra investment beyond maintenance and renovation, whereas entirely new ventures require investor commitment to developing large-scale projects from scratch in an untested and unfamiliar environment that is most likely lacking in necessary infrastructure. Certainly, the multiple rounds of struggle between successive Mongolian governments and Rio Tinto over the ownership and revenue split relating to the huge Oyu Tolgoi copper deposit, discovered in 2001, is indicative of some of these issues (Reuters 2015; Neems 2015; *Mining Journal* 2019).

The 2009 Oyu Tolgoi deal, however, under which the Mongolian government assumed an ownership share of 34 percent, is indicative of the improved terms that transnational mining firms were prepared to offer under commodity boom conditions, particularly when contrasted to the terms of Zambia's copper sector privatization during the 2000s, which provided little in the way of direct benefits for the treasury and included so many loopholes and concessions that tax avoidance on the part of mining firms was made easy. Royalty payments on extracted ore were set at 0.6 percent in secret agreements with individual companies—well below the official 3 percent rate. The privatization had only reluctantly been agreed to by the government, after donors withheld $530 million in aid and the

IFIs raised the prospect of debt relief upon success of the process (Dymond 2007).

When the commodity boom kicked in, only three years after privatization, Zambian exports took off, driven by copper. As I detailed in chapter 1, Chinese consumption accounted for more than two-thirds of the growth in demand for copper during the years 2002 to 2007, and then, kick-started by its postcrisis stimulus package, single-handedly kept the world market for copper buoyant until the end of the boom, in spite of declining demand elsewhere. Export destinations for Zambian copper are difficult to determine, since large quantities are, for example, officially exported to Switzerland as part of a transfer-pricing tax avoidance scheme, even if none of this copper is physically transported to its supposed destination.[12] Nevertheless, while the proportion of Zambian copper that found its way into Chinese infrastructure and manufacturing cannot be ascertained, it is clear that the People's Republic of China has altered the prospects for the Zambian mining industry beyond recognition, compared to the dark days of the 1990s.

In spite of these favorable conditions, successive Zambian governments have made only tentative steps toward capturing a share of these spiraling export revenues. Over the 2000–2007 period, hamstrung by the terms of the privatization process, mineral revenues provided just 0.3 percent of government totals, despite extractives making up more than 70 percent of exports and 20 percent of GDP (International Monetary Fund 2012). With the rise of the Patriotic Front (PF) applying pressure to the Movement for Multiparty Democracy (MMD) government, the royalty rate was raised, which, together with production and price increases, resulted in a 50 percent increase in mineral revenues from 2009 to 2010, followed by a near-doubling in 2011 (Moore Stephens 2014). While undoubtedly positive, the improvements came from a very low base and represented a major downscaling of ambition from the 25 to 75 percent variable windfall profits tax proposed in 2008 (Lungu 2008a).

Although the subsequent PF government raised the royalty rate again, to 6 percent, measures beyond this change to the taxation regime focused on effective auditing of mining companies in an effort to make sure that current liabilities were paid in full. This has been a major problem in the past, with one report estimating a total of $4.9 billion in illicit capital flight, mostly from mis-invoicing of copper sales, from 2000 to 2010 (Global

Financial Integrity 2012). The tax initiative was facilitated by technical assistance from Norway, which provided staff to improve the capabilities of the underresourced Zambian Revenue Authority.[13]

As with Zambia's membership in the Extractive Industries Transparency Initiative, this focus on transparency and full collection of existing taxes, rather than any attempt to more fundamentally shift the relationship between the Zambian state and extractive firms, is illustrative of the continuing influence of donors in Zambia. But it also points to one of the major hurdles faced by all three DDO states in attempting to harness the potential of the commodity boom: the problem of state capacity. In addition to a tradition of reliance upon donors, DDO states are all relatively small, impoverished, and often face shortages of skilled personnel. The circumstances that led to the abandonment of the copper windfall tax offer a revealing example here.

In 2007, Norway funded a team of consultants to examine the dubious individual agreements with mining firms that had been signed at privatization, with the recommendation of gradual and moderate reform, for fear of legal repercussions. When the Zambian government rejected these proposals and attempted to act independently by instead instituting the windfall tax the following year, mistakes in the design of the new system meant that, in some circumstances, firms could be liable for tax rates of more than 100 percent. This provided grounds for mining companies to protest and launch challenges, which, combined with the impact of the 2008 crisis, led the government to back down and abandon its plans.[14] Though the comparison is of course not exact, it is interesting to note that Zambia's GDP in 2014 amounted to $27 billion (World Bank n.d.), while Glencore, just one of the transnational mining firms with which the government must negotiate, reported revenues of more than eight times this amount during the same year (Hulme and Wilson 2014). Similarly, the equivalent figures for Mongolia and Rio Tinto are $12 billion and $47.7 billion, respectively.

Clearly, a similar mismatch arises in a case such as Angola (belonging to the EO type) when it deals with even larger oil giants, such as Chevron or the China National Petroleum Company. However, as discussed in chapter 7, Angola entered the commodity boom with the advantage of Sonangol, an apparently efficient and well-run state-owned oil enterprise, which leaves the country less than completely dependent upon transnational firms for resource extraction. Perhaps equally important, however, although

Angolan administration may rely heavily upon foreign consultants for technical expertise—and likely wastes large sums in doing so—these engagements are very different in character from initiatives such as the Norwegian tax assistance in Zambia, which tend to proceed according to donor priorities. Added to this, of course, a lack of historical aid dependence in Angola has left little in the way of a neoliberal imprint on the local bureaucracy, whether in terms of administrative structures or ideological norms. Any potential departure from neoliberal policy orientation in the DDO cases thus faces greater obstacles, as is evidenced by the struggles of both Mongolia and Zambia to complete even the first necessary stage of this process—leveraging the conditions of the commodity boom toward significantly increased resource revenues.

Zambia

In September 2011, Michael Sata and his Patriotic Front swept to power in the Zambian general election, ending two decades of neoliberal MMD rule. After twenty-five years of decline, Zambia had returned to strong growth as the price of copper, its major export, surged, on the back of ever-increasing demand from China and others. Sata seemed to articulate the politics of the Zambian urban poor, who had largely missed out on the fruits of the new boom.

After more than seven years of PF government, however, under Sata and his successor, Edgar Lungu, there is no sign of any comprehensive reversal of neoliberalism in Zambia. Sata's government did marginally increase its take from the copper industry and demonstrated a capacity to break with neoliberal orthodoxy by reversing privatizations of the national telecommunications and rail industries, among other moves. Despite these piecemeal changes, though, Sata showed little desire to alter Zambia's relationship with the global copper industry or to offer a coherent alternative vision of national development. Lungu, coming to power in 2015 following Sata's death, has offered even less of a clear economic orientation, raising and then lowering copper royalties while turning increasingly authoritarian in the face of a postboom debt crisis.

I will briefly sketch Zambian postcolonial history as a means of illustrating the connections between the copper industry, the limited process of class formation that has sprouted around mining, and political change.

While the strength and unity of the mineworkers has varied over the years, they have remained the one group able to mobilize a coalition of sufficient force to push for political change. On two occasions (in 1991 and 2011) they contributed to the downfall of the government of the time, but they failed to advance an agenda favorable to their interests. Understanding the nature of their complex coalition, based on overlapping networks of both urban-class and rural-kinship ties, is vital to grasping the reasons for the PF's failure to develop a more thoroughgoing development strategy or to move more decisively to break with the neoliberal status quo.

The circumstances of Zambia's insertion into the world economy have been connected to the state of global copper markets since large-scale mining began, during the colonial era. Development of the mines brought industrialization and migration to the Copperbelt in the early twentieth century, giving rise to one of the very few substantial urban working classes in sub-Saharan Africa. When independence, in 1964, ushered in one-party rule under Kenneth Kaunda's United National Independence Party (UNIP), copper revenues were seen as a cornerstone of a nationalist-developmentalist agenda (Fraser 2010, 5–6).

Given the extent of Zambian industrialization and resource wealth, Kaunda's "humanism" initially appeared to be one of the most promising development projects to emerge from African decolonization. At the peak of copper production, in 1969, Zambia boasted a per capita GDP twice that of Egypt, and higher than even the likes of Brazil or Turkey (Lungu 2008b). Though the early postindependence years did bring some advancements in health and infrastructure provision (Shaw 1976), Zambia's overall economic fortunes have since mirrored changes in global copper markets, meaning a long decline since the mid-1970s, which has only been arrested by the commodity price boom of the past decade (Jepson and Henderson 2016).

As in many postcolonial experiences, a lack of domestic private capital left the Zambian state as the locus of economic power in the country. A tiny "true" capitalist class of white settlers and emergent black farmers and traders was present at independence, though, by the 1970s, the incorporation of many enterprises as parastatals stunted already weak private capital and strengthened the state capitalist model as the centerpiece of Kaunda's humanism (Scaritt 1983). Thus, political power meant access to economic power, and a dominant elite, comprising the upper levels of government/ UNIP structures plus the security forces and the managers of parastatals, cemented its position (Ollawa 1979, 55–56).[15] Nationalizations (including of the copper sector) increased the resources that flowed through the party/state and allowed the state elite to strengthen networks of patronage (Szeftel 2000), prompting the entirely unironic slogan "It pays to belong to UNIP."[16]

Though the presence of an elite whose rule depends substantially on vertical networks of patronage is feature common to all the states of both the DDO and EO types, Zambia is unique among these states in also possessing an organized and often militant formal labor sector centered on the copper mining unions. During one-party rule, the Zambian Congress of Trade Unions essentially functioned as the de facto opposition to Kaunda. Mining labor formed the organizational core as this opposition became more open and morphed into the MMD during the 1980s, involving Catholic churches and civil society organizations with ties to the miners but also including prominent support from the small private capitalist sector, which was moving toward a neoliberal orientation (Handley 2008, 221–23). As the MMD won its campaign for the restoration of democracy and reconfigured itself into a political party in order to contest elections in 1991, these neoliberal ideas formed a key plank of the MMD manifesto. Since mineworkers and the broader urban population around which the campaign had revolved tended to identify the state capitalist apparatus as the main enemy (rather than transnational capital or the global economic system), a program of economic reform that would apparently undermine the dominant class power base was certainly acceptable to this core base of MMD support.

With MMD victory in 1991, the ensuing neoliberal program attacked the unions through privatization, widespread layoffs, and casualization, driving down membership.[17] Those who remained were left understandably divided between continued loyalty to "their" government and resistance to its policies. Meanwhile, in the context of the collapse of state socialism in Europe, Zambia acquired new importance as a purported African example of dual transition to both liberal democracy and a free market economy. Multilateral support aimed at buying the MMD an extended honeymoon poured into Zambia and, with no revival in the copper sector, IFIs and donors became the most powerful political actors on the domestic political scene. As in Eastern Europe, these agencies were mostly interested in the broad outlines of a swift political-economic transformation, with relatively little attention paid to the details of how this was to be implemented.[18] Who became owners of newly privatized companies, and how, was of far less concern to IFIs than the fact of privatization.

When it came to implementation, the levers of power provided by access to the domestic state proved more than a match for the private business sector, which was in any case weak and now found itself internally divided over its approach to reform.[19] Individual businesspeople certainly benefited greatly from the liberalization program, but those who did so relied upon their entanglement with and access to state patronage rather than upon the institutional strength of a private capitalist class in general. As Handley (2008, 237) argues, a core of genuine support for neoliberal ideals was, in the end, outweighed by influential figures who saw in the reform process little more than a variety of new opportunities for personal enrichment— through asset stripping, privatization, and government procurement, for instance.

Another important source of funding was the flow of aid and loans, which were used to support the MMD government and were tied to Northern governments' fervent wish that the political-economic transformation of Zambia register as a success. There have been points, such as in 1996, when significant aid to Zambia has been temporarily suspended, owing to donor worries over corruption. Nevertheless, aid flows to Zambia have generally tended to "nourish" the informal patronage system in recent decades (Rakner 2012). Thus, the capacity for state elites to use access to an externally oriented copper sector as the linchpin of clientelism may have diminished with the industry's decline (and finally privatization), but, after 1991, new avenues opened up that were no less dependent upon access to different networks of foreign financing.

The privatization and liberalization process, therefore, did little to change structures of power and control in the Zambian economy, which continued to rely substantially upon a web of patronage ultimately emanating from the state. Handley (2008, 207), for instance, quotes former MMD agriculture minister (later PF vice president and briefly acting president after Sata's death) Guy Scott, speaking in 2000, as describing private business in Zambia as being "quasi-parastatal," both supplying and borrowing money from the government. Undoubtedly, some of the personnel making up the state and business elite changed between the UNIP and MMD eras, though, even here, Szeftel (2000) notes the continuities—a significant number of the MMD leadership during the 1991 election were former members of UNIP, having been cast out at some point in the past, with more switching sides over the following years.[20] The turnover that did occur, then, simply served to promote individual businesspeople to the ranks of the elite, to bind them more closely to it, or to return marginalized fractions of the dominant elite back to central positions—a shuffling of the pack which left the rules of the game unchanged, as Szeftel puts it (paraphrasing Upton Sinclair).

The continued dominance of a state elite dependent on its ties to transnational capital (whether extractive, financial, or donor) is also evident in the eventual sale of the copper industry. The government had resisted privatization of the copper industry for as long as it could, but in the end it was persuaded by the prospect of large-scale debt relief under the World Bank/IMF Heavily Indebted Poor Country Initiative, first presented in 1996. Previously, conditionality had involved debtor government commitments to reform before the release of funding. Now, the implementation of a program of reforms over several years *prior* to securing debt relief was demanded.

At this point, the MMD government gave up trying to promote the neoliberalization agenda to a domestic audience as good policy and simply presented it as a series of sacrifices demanded by the IFIs, which would result in the lifting of most of Zambia's onerous debt burden and therefore offer a chance to finally put the economy back on track (Fraser 2007). Portions of the industry were sold individually, between 1997 and 2000, under a process that was far from transparent, was almost definitely corrupt (Larmer 2005a), and involved the signing of secretive "development agreements" between the government and new investors, which resulted in the investors often paying effective tax rates of zero percent (Lungu 2008a). The sales themselves also failed to generate any great revenue. Privatization did help to recapitalize and refurbish aging mines, though at the expense of practically all resource rents, which now flowed overseas. The timing of the change was extraordinarily unfortunate, as well, coming just before the new copper boom, which began around 2003, mirroring the nationalization, which had occurred on the cusp of the long decline.

By the early 2000s, the diminished union movement had recovered much of its unity, which it directed against the MMD government, generally, and specifically against further casualization and loss of benefits and the handling of the eventual privatization of the mines. This sowed the seeds for a new mass movement against the government, with the mining unions at its heart. In 2011, this movement succeeded in removing the party that had been itself installed on the back of the same networks and resources, two decades previously. Grasping the workings of these networks is the key to understanding both the power of labor-centered social movements in contemporary Zambia and their inability to represent and advance the cause of popular classes on a national scale, in contrast to contemporary movements in Bolivia.

A complex social structure, spanning rural and urban zones,[21] has given rise to an enduring postindependence political coalition comprising three concentric layers. At the center are the mineworkers themselves, along with other formal sector workers, who often are also unionized.[22] This group, especially the mining sector, is well organized and has historically displayed an ability to agitate successfully for higher wages and improved conditions (Burawoy 1972), even though its power (and size) certainly waned during the neoliberal period (Heidenreich 2007).

The next layer is made up of the wider urban community—principally dependents and informal workers, such as street vendors, casual laborers, or domestic workers. As Larmer (2005b) points out, relatively high wages in the formal sector often have been used to support urban relatives through education or to finance informal ventures.[23] Furthermore, the state of the mining industry in general helps to determine opportunities in the informal sector. The urban investment that accompanied the latest commodity boom prompted a reversal of the large-scale migration from the Copperbelt to the countryside that had occurred over the course of the lean 1990s (Resnick and Thurlow 2014).

The outer circle consists of the rural Bemba speakers in Northern and Luapula Provinces.[24] Though colonial-era mass migrations to the Copperbelt drew from several areas, more came from these two Bembaphone areas than from elsewhere (Cheeseman and Hinfelaar 2010), evident in the enduring use of Bemba as a lingua franca in the Copperbelt today. There are extensive ties of kinship, cyclical migration, and remittances between the Copperbelt and the original two Bembaphone provinces, melding the economic interests of all three and promoting the spread of political ideas to the countryside.

Of course, movement among all three groups is likely—as miners retire to their home village, for example—and it is probable that this has intensified during the past two decades, with large population movements out of and then back into the Copperbelt as a result of neoliberalization and then the recent boom. The politics of these three groups and of the three provinces are thus intertwined, evidenced by the fact that these areas have a history of shared voting patterns. Despite Posner's (2005, 87–88) claim that, in the absence of class consciousness outside the Copperbelt, tribal and linguistic affiliations constitute the only basis for political coalition, this clearly is not simply a Bembaphone voting bloc. Since the Copperbelt, like all urban areas of Zambia, is ethnically heterogeneous, political strategies based on appeals to ethnicity have little salience there, and, in this sense, the province cannot be considered a "Bemba" region.

If Copperbelt voters cannot be mobilized around ethnicity and yet tend to vote in a bloc with the other two provinces, then the reason for the existence of this bloc surely cannot relate to ethnic solidarity.[25] Instead, shared economic interests seem to offer a more plausible explanation. Importantly, the two postindependence changes of ruling party in Zambia, in 1991 and 2011, came about through campaigns that were rooted in the structures of organized labor and expressed the concerns of the urban poor. With so many in Northern and Luapula Provinces being onetime—or sometime—Copperbelt residents or recipients of remittances from the cities, urban-focused economic appeals possessed an extended reach into the Bembaphone heartlands, which saw these provinces line up in support of the Copperbelt.

In 1991, for instance, the MMD relied heavily on mining union branch structures but was also backed in both Northern and Luapula Provinces. By the 2006 election, these same union branches had been taken over by the Patriotic Front and were the basis for their victories in these areas, once MMD heartlands, with the role played by retired miners in the two rural provinces apparently being of great importance (Cheeseman and Larmer 2015). Though the PF narrowly lost both the 2006 and 2008 elections, a larger majority in the three Bembaphone provinces, combined with winning Lusaka (still amounting to a minority of the nine provinces), was enough to lead them to victory in 2011.[26]

Nevertheless, the majority of Zambians are to a large extent reliant upon subsistence farming (Resnick and Thurlow 2014), most of which exists outside of the urban–rural network. This segmentation of Zambia produces a dual political logic—an urban Bemba group responsive to class-based (or populist-based) appeals, contrasted with the rest of the countryside, in which clientelism and patronage generally hold sway. The enduring result in Zambian politics has been a lack of push, on the part of the urban Bemba grouping, for a truly national developmentalist or redistributive agenda, combined with an absence of alternative coalitions with the requisite organization or consciousness to make these demands.

This, in my view, fundamentally explains the lack of any significant break with neoliberalism on the part of the PF government after 2011, despite an international environment that would seem to have permitted such a course, at least in its first few years. These points are best understood by tracing the rise of the PF as the populist fulcrum of a renewed politicization among mineworkers. Here, the intention is to highlight the urban Bemba coalition's contradictory centrality in Zambian politics; it is a force with sufficient power to topple governments but apparently not to advance the kind of coherent policy program that might otherwise have led Zambia to break with neoliberalism during the boom.

The Patriotic Front in Opposition

The PF came of age as a political force in the 2006 election, the first in which it attempted to plug into the coalition outlined here, by utilizing both the mineworkers' organizational networks and a populist discourse attuned to the urban poor, in the context of rising copper prices. The door had been opened to some extent by the actions of the MMD, which, worried about the solidity of its base in Copperbelt, Northern, and Luapula Provinces, even before the PF challenge emerged, had begun to concentrate on building an alternative rural political alliance with links to areas in all nine provinces. This is revealing, in that the resources used to build this support network—fertilizer distribution, authority over traditional chiefs, and the shift of patronage toward the co-opting of local leaders who would be able to deliver the loyalty of rural constituencies (Cheeseman and Hinfelaar 2010)—suggest an entirely different form of politics at work than that which is required to activate the support of the organized labor/urban/ Bembaphone coalition.

The 2011 election brought this contrast into focus. Although the PF itself doubtless offered various giveaways at rallies, it also campaigned on the slogan of "Donchi kubeba" (Don't tell), an attempt to undermine the government's efforts to secure votes through patronage. *Donchi kubeba*, which also became the title of an extremely popular song, encouraged Zambians to accept any gifts proffered by the MMD, without revealing their intention to vote for the PF.[27] This move seems to have been viewed with outrage by

MMD and other party leaders, seen as a dishonorable repudiation of the quid pro quo inherent to patron–client arrangements.[28] The centrality to the PF campaign of the rejection of patronage politics, in spirit if not always in deed, is illustrative of the divide between the vertical clientelistic networks used to mobilize votes in most of rural Zambia and the populist class politics that found far greater purchase among PF supporters. In turn, this schism reflects highly uneven levels of class formation and consciousness between, on the one hand, urban areas—and, indirectly and by extension, the rural Bemba hinterland—and, on the other hand, the countryside in general.

The PF finished a surprise second in the 2006 election, before losing by fewer than forty thousand votes in 2008, amid allegations of fraud and vote buying on both sides.[29] It seems clear that, as the incumbent, the MMD had considerable advantages (Rakner 2012), including influence over the electoral commission, which, in refusing to update the electoral roll between elections, deprived the PF of much of the urban youth vote, which was overwhelmingly in favor of the PF. Sata's initial rise to prominence before the 2006 election had hinged partly on strong and attention-grabbing rhetoric that especially targeted foreign investors ("infesters"), particularly the Chinese,[30] as well as growing competition from Chinese immigrants in local markets and informal trade (Fraser 2007).[31] This struck a chord among the urban poor in the context of an apparent boom in which the benefits seemed to be flowing largely upward and outward.[32]

There certainly was a large element of classically vague anti-elite (and nationalist) populism to Sata's campaign, but the PF did target substantive issues that were of importance to workers and the informal sector. For example, in addition to a focus on wages, conditions in the mines, and the creation of new formal job opportunities, the PF also stressed housing. Schemes relating to urban housing were included in the MMD government's Fifth National Development Plan in 2006. The development plan was a replacement for the previous Poverty Reduction Strategy Paper, reflecting a move on the part of the World Bank to stress "ownership" by encouraging governments to name their own development plans. In this case, the title of the document connected it with the four successive five-year plans instituted during the UNIP era, giving it a developmentalist sheen. In practice, the plan became a wish list of initiatives from which donors picked priority areas to fund, leaving the rest as commitments in name only (Kragelund 2014).

The development plan identified housing as "a pre-requisite to national development" and a "basic social need after food and clothing" (Government of Zambia 2006, 197, cited in Kragelund 2014) and promised house-building programs and the upgrading of urban compounds (slums). Since no donors chose to fund these efforts, however, they were not implemented, and indeed the MMD continued its policy of demolishing slum housing. Meanwhile, PF members of parliament came out in support of those dispossessed by the demolitions and pressed the issue of service access for the compounds, first in Parliament and then on the campaign trail (Resnick 2012).

In 2008, while maintaining the anti-elite discourse and stressing his concern for the conditions of labor, Sata sounded a more conciliatory note on foreign investment. This appears to have gained him the support of elements of a nervous urban middle-class constituency benefiting from the knock-on effects of the copper boom (Cheeseman and Hinfelaar 2010). Combining this approach with a redoubled focus on mobilizing his base after a low turnout in 2008 was enough for a PF victory in 2011, despite the MMD winning most rural seats. The question now was whether the PF government would follow through with a comprehensive program that was independent of donor priorities.

The Patriotic Front in Power

Early on, Larmer and Fraser (2007) noted parallels (as well as differences) between the PF and various populist Latin American parties that had come to power in, for instance, Venezuela, Ecuador, and Bolivia.[33] In each case, these governments, whose core support was similar to that of the PF, leveraged rising commodity rents in support of substantial policy departures from the neoliberal orthodoxy promoted by IFIs and donors. Facing a similarly favorable international environment, and with a new populist government, would Zambia demonstrate a similar deviation from the path of neoliberalization? My view is that the Patriotic Front did enough to demonstrate, during Sata's presidency at least, that they were capable of such, though change was not widespread and does not seem to have been grounded in any overarching strategy. Those policy changes that did occur suggest a rather different direction from those taken in the Latin American cases, which in turn reflects the significantly different makeup of the political and economic forces in Zambia.

Two years into Sata's administration, donor representatives expressed nostalgia for the days of the MMD and complained that the PF government paid them little attention.[34] As one interviewee acknowledged, this is significant, given the widespread complaints about corruption during the final years of MMD government, which led to donors such as Canada and the Netherlands pulling out of Zambia completely. With aid accounting for 5 percent of the budget in 2013 and 6 percent in 2014, down from 53 percent in 2001 (Kragelund 2014), it is not surprising that the government began to exercise more independence in setting policy priorities.

One example is the trend toward limited renationalizations. Though most Zambian privatizations occurred in the 1990s, further state divestment continued to be part of the donor agenda much later, as with the reluctant sale of national telecom company Zamtel to a Libyan consortium, in 2010. Alleging corruption, the new PF government unilaterally reversed this deal. Zambia Railways (principally a freight railway that carries copper out of the country) was also nationalized and has received heavy investment. Additionally, a large-scale road-building scheme was embarked upon.

In the key mining sector, reforms were timid overall. After the PF's surprise showing in 2006, which was significantly boosted by public revelations about the secretive development agreements that offered mining concessions with little or no tax liabilities, the MMD government of Levy Mwanawasa responded to the new threat by unveiling a populist measure of its own—a windfall tax on copper mining firms. This was a variable tax, to be applied at a rate of between 25 and 75 percent of revenues, but only when the global price of copper hit certain price thresholds (Lungu 2008a).[35]

Once again, though, as with both the nationalization and the privatization of the mining industry, the timing of change was unfortunate for the Zambian Copperbelt. In 2008, the effects of the global financial crisis began to be felt and the price of copper fell precipitously (though temporarily, as it turned out). Several investors suspended production or pulled out of the copper sector,[36] and the government, perhaps scarred by an earlier generation's experience—when a dip that was assumed to be temporary became a twenty-five-year slump—backed off. With the huge investment stimulus package in China that followed, copper prices rebounded, and though the proposed increase of royalty rates from 0.6 percent to 3 percent was retained from the tax reform plan, it seemed as though Zambia had missed an opportunity.

Mining taxes and royalties have continued to be a controversial topic since 2009, with "so many changes in taxation that Zambia had acquired an unofficial world record in mining tax instability" (Lundstøl and Isaksen 2018), partly in response to copper price movements and partly reflecting a split within PF ranks on the issue. Nevertheless, there were no further attempts to impose a windfall tax or to up the state's take to the extent seen in some other resource-exporting states over these years.[37] Though this is a systemic issue rather than one of individual corruption, it is interesting to note that a U.S. diplomatic cable made public by Wikileaks reports that an unnamed mining company had established "strong ties" with Sata and had begun writing his public statements on foreign investment (U.S. Embassy Lusaka 2008).[38] This was during the run-up to the 2008 election, when Sata indeed significantly toned down his anti–foreign investor rhetoric.

While higher prices, increasing production, and somewhat higher taxes helped the cause of budgetary independence in Zambia, they did not allow the fiscal space for a Latin America–style redistributive agenda.[39] PF policy, nevertheless, did seem to be following its election slogan of "More jobs, lower taxes, and more money in your pocket," which, at least to some extent, was directed principally at the urban poor. The income tax threshold was increased, to the frustration of donors who had recommended reducing this in order to broaden the tax base.[40] Formal sector minimum wages also were substantially hiked, especially for civil servants, but there were problems with enforcing the new rates.[41] With the economy growing at 6.8 percent in 2011 and 7.2 percent in 2012 (International Monetary Fund n.d.), jobs were undoubtedly created in both the formal and informal sectors under Sata, some directly by the government's road-building schemes.[42]

The government also intervened more forcefully at times, though in a somewhat piecemeal manner. In 2013, the state took control of Collum Coal Mine in Southern Province, citing a poor record of environmental, safety, and labor conditions and the nonpayment of royalties. This mine had become infamous, both domestically and internationally, for incidents in 2010, when Chinese supervisors opened fire on protesting miners, and in 2012, when one manager was killed and another injured during another protest (*Lusaka Times* 2012; Okeowo 2013). Also in 2013, the London-listed but predominantly India-based company Vedanta Resources announced plans to mechanize its Konkola Copper Mines, involving the dismissal of 1,500 workers. This met with a furious reaction from the government, which threatened to suspend Vedanta's operating license and canceled the work permit of the CEO while he was out of the country, prompting an apology from the company (Mfula 2013).

Throughout Sata's presidency and certainly now under Lungu, Zambia has never appeared likely to return to a state capitalist economy. PF governments have no longer seemed so beholden to donors but have been ideologically rudderless, channeling the interests of political elites while also responding in an ad hoc fashion to the demands of the urban constituency that had been key to their electoral success. Recently, and following the end of the boom, Lungu has in some ways mirrored the earlier shift of the MMD away from its urban base, with the PF incorporating key former MMD figures such as former president Rupiah Banda (Ismail 2017). In some senses, these maneuvers all look very similar to those seen under Kaunda: efforts to stabilize and maximize the potential for accumulation and consumption among the dominant elite while outflanking, co-opting, or repressing potential threats from organized labor and the cities.

Viewed from one angle, the ascendancy of the current government is simply another shuffling of the cards, the triumph of a formerly marginalized faction of the political elite.[43] The continuation of patronage politics is not hidden; in various by-elections since 2011,[44] Sata more or less explicitly offered voters a choice between impoverishment with the opposition or access to development funds if they were to install a government candidate.[45] Patronage politics has become even more obvious under Lungu (*Africa Confidential* 2016).

Meanwhile, mineworkers themselves have continued to show an impressive capacity to organize and demand improved pay and conditions. Lee's (2009) important paper demonstrates that workers in the Chambishi mine, owned by China Nonferrous Metal Mining, were aware of both the high price of copper and their relatively low wages in comparison with other Zambian miners during the first years of the boom. This led to successful industrial action, resulting in a 23 percent pay increase and a reversal of the casualization of the workforce. In a postscript to a later version of the paper, Lee (2010) discusses China Nonferrous's acquisition of the Luanshya mine, which had been shut down in 2009 as a result of the temporary drop in copper prices.[46] As with Chambishi, there were concerns about the

Chinese approach to labor relations, but workers were again able to negotiate a blanket adoption of permanent, pensionable contracts and wage increases.

However, these struggles, along with the minimum wage increases instituted by the government, had little resonance for the huge numbers of Zambians who were subsistence farmers. For these sections of the populace, the major result of the PF in power has been a recalibration of vertical patronage networks. In this sense, the PF's coming to power on the back of the urban-Bemba coalition has not resulted in the kind of national project seen in a case like Bolivia, where frustration among the urban poor over the inequitable distribution of the proceeds from natural resources produced a nationwide movement, leading eventually to the election of Evo Morales.[47]

Cox and Negi (2010) draw on a number of authors who discuss rural Africa in general, and they conclude that a limited process of peasant differentiation is under way as wages are reinvested in small-scale agricultural production for market and the informal purchase or rental of customary land. Nevertheless, in their classical Marxist version, they assert that the lack of separation of the rural population from the means of production in most of Africa means that the accumulation process and thus class formation cannot begin in earnest, leaving noncapitalist social relations intact.[48] In the Zambian case, the persistence of these social relations means that most rural areas continue to be dominated by vertical structures of authority interwoven with patronage networks flowing down from the central state, and those networks, in turn, are dependent upon the access of the central state to international networks of capital. Such structures contrast sharply with the more horizontal though complex linkages between organized labor and the urban poor, extending to some degree to the rural Bembaphone provinces.[49] These differences make the construction of the kind of national popular coalition that is seen in Bolivia exceedingly difficult, since the politics of the urban poor has little resonance in most of the Zambian countryside.[50] Even if mining labor, as the organizational core of the urban constituencies of Zambia, has proved its strength time and again, it most probably lacks both the numerical and geographic potential to lead and define, rather than simply participate in, a national movement along the lines of the MAS in Bolivia.

The occasional adoption of measures contrary to the views of donors illustrates that the PF was operating in an environment where a broader assertion of policy independence was possible, as the economy grew and donor dependence declined. The first obvious step here would have been a thorough reassessment of the mining tax and royalty regime, which in turn could have provided sufficient revenue to finance a more ambitious vision of development. Given that the previous attempt to impose a mining windfall tax, in 2008, had been overtaken by volatile copper markets, however, caution on the part of PF governments is perhaps understandable here. Such caution, however, is reinforced through the immediate interests of state elites. Having won the 2011 election on the back of a popular movement calling for a more equitable share of the mining bonanza, the PF found itself inheriting and slotting into a system that afforded them control of the reins of power sufficient for personal gain and relative political stability. Lacking any strong policy agenda or vision of development, there was little chance of a concerted effort to shift the neoliberal status quo emanating from within the state under Sata, and likely no social forces with the requisite strength and reach to force the issue.

Following Sata's death (and then a brief interregnum under Guy Scott), Edgar Lungu has maintained PF rule in the context of falling copper prices via a creeping authoritarianism, including the temporary jailing of his main political rival on trumped-up treason charges (Mfula 2017). While GDP growth has recently rebounded somewhat, the government has begun struggling to cover debt repayments, after both raising funds on capital markets and increasing its loans from Chinese state-owned banks during the boom (*Africa Confidential* 2019). In a situation that may well be come to be repeated in many other countries, it seems that the IMF (as of mid-2019) has refused to agree to a loan package because of concerns over the scale of debts and the lack of transparency around Zambia's Chinese loans. Some (disputed) reports have even suggested that the debt owed to China is much greater than official figures suggest and that these loans are secured against the state electricity company, ZESCO (*Africa Confidential* 2018; Beardsworth 2018).

Laos

In some senses, Laos seems an unlikely candidate for inclusion in the DDO type, given that it is still governed by the Lao People's Revolutionary Party (LPRP) and is still, at least officially, committed to state socialism. In contrast to the high degree of neoliberalization seen in states such as Zambia or Mongolia, liberal reform in Laos has tended to be slow and reluctant—private ownership of land was only made legal in 2003, for example. Liberalization, however, at least began relatively early, with the New Economic Mechanism, a program meant to institute a market economy, in 1986.

Rather than a process mandated by IFIs and Northern donors, the New Economic Mechanism constituted a domestic response to the end of aid flows from the Soviet Union. It was drawn up under the influence of Vietnamese and Soviet advisers, though no doubt with some attention also paid to contemporary events in China. From the perspective of the LPRP, and based on the experiences of Laos's larger neighbors, liberalization was seen as a means through which economic growth might be achieved, not as an end in itself but as a way of enhancing the legitimacy and prolonging the rule of the governing party (Stuart-Fox 2005).

Following the 1997–1998 Asian financial crisis, attitudes toward liberalization among the upper echelons of the party cooled. Nevertheless, the combination of a narrow tax base (even by least developed country standards), large debt obligations from the Soviet period, and persistent trade deficits have made Laos increasingly aid dependent, with ODA making up an average 39 percent of government revenue in the 2000–2010 decade (Bird and Hill 2010). This meant that neoliberalization continued, albeit more slowly and in the face of greater government intransigence, than prior to 1997. Externally, accepting donor conditionality was the price to be paid for the continuing budget support that underwrote both short-term stability and access to patronage resources.[51] Internally, demands from younger midlevel bureaucrats for neoliberal reform were balanced by a fear that marketization may, as in 1997, engender instability or create new groups powerful enough to challenge LPRP rule.

Large-scale copper and gold production began in 2003 and was expected to contribute 110 percent of 2007 GDP over the period 2007 to 2020 (Bird and Hill 2010). New mining investment, however, did little to shake up the political equation. Resource revenues and associated growth certainly were a significant factor in the substantial decline seen in aid as a percentage of GNI since the beginning of the boom. However, extremely low levels of state capacity mean that the prospect of Laos completing what in other cases was a necessary condition for a departure from neoliberalization—a favorable renegotiation of the state take from extraction—seemed out of reach over the boom years. Goldman (2006, 176), in his study of the

World Bank's participatory process relating to the Nam Theun 2 dam project, noted that most governmental departments with responsibility for natural resources were funded by the donors themselves, with donors also managing training of staff. Stuart-Fox (2005) mentions that many Laotian laws are drafted in English and French and may remain untranslated into local languages even several years after coming into force. Given this environment, it is hardly surprising that both the will and the capacity to strike a better bargain with extractive capital, let alone to formulate any comprehensive alternative vision of national development, was lacking.

Mongolia

Mongolia, like Laos, is a postsocialist state profoundly affected by the decline and collapse of the Soviet Union. Unlike Laos, though, Mongolia's political and economic transition was relatively rapid and extensive. In 1990, following the withdrawal of Soviet troops and officials from Ulaanbaatar, the new Mongolian authorities regarded the United States and European countries as the best potential defense against feared Chinese intervention.[52] This factor, combined with support and training for the most free market–oriented among the emerging political elite by the German Konrad Adenauer Foundation and the U.S. International Republican Institute (Rossabi 2005, 37–39), led to an early adoption of shock therapy, following World Bank, IMF, and Asian Development Bank recommendations.[53] Unfortunately, the reforms had rather disastrous effects across a range of social indicators (Wade 2004), with the decline of urban industry prompting a return to traditional pastoralism among large numbers of the newly unemployed[54] and the collapse of government revenues leading to an increasing dependence on foreign aid. With a relatively vibrant democracy, Mongolia has seen several changes of government since 1990, though, in terms of neoliberalization, the only difference among incumbents has been in the degree of enthusiasm with which conditionalities from donors and IFIs have been accepted.

Economic circumstances in Mongolia, however, changed rapidly during the boom, with an average annual GDP growth rate of 8.7 percent from 2004 to 2013 (International Monetary Fund n.d.), coinciding with a rush to exploit largely untapped reserves of copper, gold, and coal. The largest extractive project is Oyu Tolgoi, a huge copper mine close to the Chinese border, which at peak production will be the world's third largest and was predicted, prior to delays in a planned expansion, to account for one-third of Mongolia's GDP by 2020 (Hill 2011). The mine is jointly owned by Turquoise Hill Resources (in which the Anglo-Australian firm Rio Tinto holds a majority share) and the Mongolian state, with the government borrowing from Rio Tinto the capital for its 34 percent stake, which would then be repaid out of subsequent dividends. As costs exceeded original estimates, government liabilities correspondingly increased, leading to budget shortfalls in the face of rising public expectations from the boom, while successive governments have been through multiple rounds of disputes with Rio Tinto over Oyu Tolgoi terms and taxation (Zand 2013; Readhead and Mihalyi 2018). More broadly, mining's huge economic importance has made it a highly salient political issue in Mongolia, tied to questions of development, environmentalism, nationalism, and fear of foreign—especially Chinese—domination (Jackson 2015; Jackson and Dear 2016). Understandably, then, mining often dominates Mongolian politics.

Given Mongolia's small size, even the low proportion of the extractive surplus that the state recoups is significant. It is in the management of these flows that the first evidence of the Mongolian state's ability to make decisions independently of donor conditionality may be glimpsed. In line with donor recommendations, in 2008 Mongolia created a Human Development Fund, based partly on the Chilean model, that would save a proportion of resource revenues during times of high prices and then release them during commodity depressions (Isakova, Plekhanov, and Zettelmeyer 2012). The Human Development Fund was to be used to fund social spending, but it also was to be employed for the direct distribution of commodity revenues to all adult citizens. This second aspect of the plan had been inspired by the Alaska Permanent Fund, set up by Republicans to provide an incentive to the local population to resist any future government attempts to appropriate or direct the state's oil surplus.[55]

In the Mongolian case, however, the amount drawn from the fund was not mandated as a percentage of revenues but was left open as a value to be set by Parliament each year. The result was that directly distributed funds became the source of a bidding war between the government and the opposition during the 2009 presidential election campaign. Though the transfer that actually occurred was around one-tenth of the promised $1,000, this and continuing transfers of $15 per month were condemned by the World Bank as inflationary. Though no government in Mongolia over the boom years articulated a desire to break with a neoliberal development model, the persistence of direct distribution of cash from the Human Development Fund is evidence that a revenue base independent of donor and IFI flows presented a basis for at least some tentative steps toward such a departure.

Conclusion

It is clear that, during the commodity boom, DDO states largely continued to follow the donor-driven agenda, which constitutes a particular form of neoliberalization that had been adopted as a means of addressing some of the more obvious contradictions of the early structural adjustment programs. This is perhaps surprising, given that the potential for domestically derived changes in political-economic direction did open up during the boom. Export prices rocketed, aid dependence declined, and DDO states' natural resource endowments came to seem ever more attractive to transnational extractive firms. As with the other types, it is the nature of state–society relations in Zambia, Laos, and Mongolia that best explains this otherwise puzzling inertia on the part of their governments.

The typology of extractive regimes is premised on the overall argument that, with the path largely cleared of neoliberalizing pressures by China-driven changes in resource export markets, the approach taken by each state depended upon the nature of the particular social coalition that was able to gain control over the state and to set policy in a manner that favored its interests. In two senses, the DDO type may be said to stand as a variation upon this basic theme. First, as with the EO type discussed in chapter 7, in the absence of widespread class formation, it was the state managers themselves, along with allied elites, who constituted the dominant social sector. Although they were not, for the most part, engaged in large-scale accumulation, their position at the pinnacle of the state allowed them access to distributional resources that far outweighed any private sources of capital within the domestic sphere. In the (relative) absence of local capitalists or organized popular classes, political elites (though sometimes internally fractious) lacked serious challengers to their rule and were able to co-opt and absorb any nascent threats through control of patronage networks—as, for instance, in the regular defection of Zambian political figures to the current party of government.

Since rising extractive prices would seem to constitute an obvious source of increased resources for patronage, though, a turn to increase the state's take in these sectors might be expected, even if this were unaccompanied by any coherent political-economic agenda, as is arguably the case in a state like Angola. In fact, to some extent, this did occur, with Zambia and Mongolia both experiencing wrangles over extractive ownership and taxation regimes. That these efforts tended to be rather ad hoc and unsystematic, though, points to a second key variation seen in the DDO type that sets it apart from its EO counterpart. This is the legacy of aid dependence, which, in addition to effects on independent state capacity and bureaucracy, meant that DDO states, unlike those of EO cases, entered the commodity boom with a significant preexisting source of allocative resources, in the form of official development assistance. As aid levels dropped, there was clearly has been more room to challenge donor priorities; this was most obviously seen in Zambia under the PF. With ODA totals still relatively substantial, though, it is not surprising that state elites in DDO cases were generally reluctant to rock this particular boat, lacking pressure from other social groups to do so and in the apparent absence of any coherently articulated opposition to neoliberalism from within their own ranks.

CHAPTER IX

Homegrown Orthodoxy Type

Jamaica, Peru, South Africa, Colombia, and Indonesia

I apply the name homegrown orthodoxy to this type because its associated ideotypical trajectory during the commodity boom years essentially embodied the continuation of an orthodox neoliberal approach to policy. Much the same may be said, in broad terms, of the donor-dependent orthodoxy type discussed in chapter 8, though the HO formation lacks the distinctive variety of donor-driven continuity seen in the DDO cases. Instead, the persistent neoliberalization observed in Peru, Colombia, South Africa, and Indonesia (though not in the special case of Jamaica), while heavily influenced by engagement with international financial institutions, is essentially domestically derived and homegrown, eschewing the need to demonstrate "ownership" of the program in the manner of the DDO type.

As with the other types we have considered, I ascribe the course steered by HO cases since 2003 to the relative strength of particular social forces on the domestic scene. Rather than the inertia encountered among DDO governments whose interests tended to lie in acquiescence to donor priorities, relatively strong, externally oriented local capitalist fractions themselves ensured the survival and extension of neoliberalism in HO states. Peru, South Africa, Colombia, and Indonesia experienced the same takeoff in prices for their major exports as were seen across resource-rich states in the global South, and they were thereby presented with the same opportunities to draw upon favorable global circumstances as a material base for a change of political-economic direction. These states, therefore, possessed similar levels of potential policy autonomy as others but chose to maintain their neoliberalizing course.

Jamaica stands as an exception to this schema but is nevertheless included as part of the HO type due to the shared features of its continuing neoliberalization. Jamaica serves as an extremely useful counterfactual illustration of a central argument of the book—that a high export concentration in those natural resources subject to rapidly rising Chinese demand during the boom was a necessary condition for departure from neoliberalization—because the Caribbean island is unique among all typology cases in being dependent upon a natural resource export sector (bauxite/alumina) in which Chinese import demand growth was comparatively slow over the boom years. As we will discuss, without the demand pull from the People's Republic of China, prices for aluminum (for which bauxite/alumina constitutes the raw material), unlike those for other metals, were relatively flat over the course of the commodity boom.

As a result, the case of Jamaica presents an opportunity to examine a resource-rich, highly indebted Southern state whose major export markets were not subject to the China effect. In many senses, global market conditions for Jamaica continued as though the rise of China had never occurred.[1] It is therefore particularly significant that, in the absence of any China effect on bauxite/aluminum exports, Jamaica continued to struggle under one of the heaviest debt burdens in the world and subsequently committed to an International Monetary Fund program that demanded annual budget surpluses equivalent to 7.5 percent of gross domestic product (Johnston 2015).

While Jamaica is a crucial case in this respect, its neoliberal orientation is still shaped primarily by external forces and constraints, with little likely hope of any alternative political-economic program emerging while this remains the case. For this reason, I also provide a longer treatment of Peru in this chapter as a more appropriate exemplar case of the HO type. One important characteristic of the HO type is continuing neoliberalization under the direction of transnationally oriented domestic groups, despite conditions in resource export markets offering the potential to set a different, non-neoliberal developmental agenda.

After this introduction, I will explore in more detail the rationale for the use of Jamaica as a counterfactual case, examining the differences between bauxite/alumina/aluminum markets and those for comparable metals, particularly copper, during the commodity boom. I will then demonstrate how these divergent market conditions have translated into a lack of opportunity for Jamaica to break with externally imposed neoliberal discipline, whereas HO cases have been presented with this opportunity as a result of their hugely positive export performance. After looking at the circumstances of these countries' insertion into the world economy, I then turn to the course of domestic politics. I discuss postindependence developmentalism in Jamaica, Michael Manley's attempt to install a form of democratic socialism, and then the impact of the debt crisis and pressures to neoliberalize. Next, I provide an account of Jamaica's struggles with debt in recent years and the rather desperate level of dependence upon multilateral creditors that resulted. I pay particular attention to the bauxite industry here.

Thereafter, I move to a somewhat lengthy account of the Peruvian case. This level of depth is provided for two reasons. First, Peru is presented here as the exemplar case of the HO type. Second, the trajectory of Peru, unusually among the typology cases, includes an attempt by a (purportedly) radical leader to capture the state and to apparently lead Peru along a distinctly non-neoliberal direction of travel, perhaps akin to that of Chavez's Venezuela or Morales's Bolivia, though this did not materialize in practice. The narrow loss by Ollanta Humala in the 2006 Peruvian presidential election was then followed by a successful presidential bid in 2011, by which point Humala had shed much of his *chavista* rhetoric and policies. In office, his administration did little to slow Peru's neoliberalization. Peru, therefore, provides an opportunity to analyze a "near miss" in terms of post-neoliberal turns among commodity exporters.

Finally, I summarize the political-economic trajectories of South Africa, Colombia, and Indonesia. In the case of South Africa, democratization, in 1994, was secured on terms favorable to large white capital, which had steadily shifted toward (often illicit) externalization during the period prior to the end of apartheid. Under African National Congress (ANC) rule, and with the gradual lifting of capital controls, the integration of the old bourgeoisie with its transnational counterparts accelerated, together with an acceptance of black capital into the fold. In spite of the socialist roots of the ANC and continued rumblings from its leftist elements (and allies), postapartheid South Africa followed an overall process of neoliberalization that favored a dominant and increasingly financialized fraction of capital. Price increases in South Africa's export commodities prompted calls in some quarters for the nationalization of mines, but despite the increasing use of the developmental state trope on the part of the Zuma administration, the commodity boom did little to disturb the South African trajectory of liberalization.

The history of Colombia in recent decades, sadly, has been dominated by conflict between guerrillas, paramilitaries, and state forces, which adds a heavily securitized spin to Colombia's neoliberalism. Colombia is a relatively late liberalizer, and support for the neoliberal program has been bound up in the ongoing conflict and the consequences of the cocaine trade. Most domestic capitalists are enthusiastic supporters of liberalization, and even initially resistant traditional landowners have come on board, convinced, in the context of the internal conflict, of the need to maximize foreign investment—particularly in extraction—as a means of funding huge security expenditures.

Indonesia entered the commodity boom only a few years after the Asian financial crisis of 1997–1998, which had brought a $40 billion IMF agreement and the fall of the thirty-one-year New Order dictatorship under Suharto. A state-incubated capitalist class, comprising mainly ethnic Chinese–owned conglomerates and their allies in the bureaucracy, had begun to externalize and to become increasingly integrated with multinational capital during a period of selective liberalization in the 1980s and 1990s. Most of these business groups were able to rely on their connections to the state to ride out the late 1990s crisis with their economic and political power intact, with networks of influence now reconfigured around the new democratic landscape. A continuing, if ambivalent agenda of neoliberalization over the period broadly suited leading sectors of capital (particularly, though not exclusively, ethnic Chinese), especially when contrasted with occasional calls for an economic nationalism framed in terms of redistribution toward *pribumi* (indigenous) business.

External Market Conditions

In an important sense, the case of Jamaica does not properly merit inclusion in the typology of extractive regimes presented here. Indeed, the country stands as an important exception to the observed trend of markedly improved circumstances of insertion into the global economy for resource exporters during the commodity boom, which is extremely useful in demonstrating the centrality of Chinese demand to this effect. Bauxite, the ore from which aluminum is produced, has been a major Jamaican export since before independence, in 1962, and Jamaica today certainly meets the criteria for resource dependence in terms of export concentration, with bauxite and alumina together accounting for more than half of exports, from 2002 to 2008, before dipping but remaining above 40 percent throughout the boom years (Observatory of Economic Complexity n.d.).

However, though Chinese aluminum consumption has risen, broadly in step with other metals, the PRC's continued ability to mostly meet this demand through domestic sources meant that its total imports of bauxite/alumina, compared to most other hard commodities, were relatively small for most of the period.[2] This can be seen in figures 9.1 and 9.2. Figure 9.1 shows the value of the PRC's total annual imports of copper and aluminum (including bauxite and alumina) ores and concentrates.[3] The overall shape of import demand in aluminum ores and concentrates broadly matches what would be expected during the commodity boom—an upward trend begins in 2002, with a dip in 2008, followed by a recovery beginning a year later, as China's stimulus program began to kick in. It is clear, however, that, when compared with copper ores, aluminum import demand growth was proportionately small over the course of the commodity boom. Figure 9.2 compares finished copper and aluminum; although Jamaica does

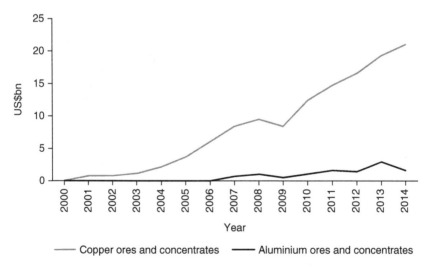

Figure 9.1 China copper and aluminum ores and concentrates imports (in billions of dollars), 2000–2014. Calculated from Chatham House Resourcetrade.earth database.

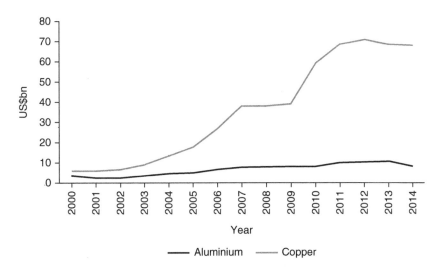

Figure 9.2 China copper and aluminum imports (in billions of dollars), 2000–2014. Calculated from Chatham House Resourcetrade.earth database.

not produce finished aluminum, a link between demand for processed aluminum and its raw materials would be expected.[4] Here, the difference in growth of Chinese import demand between the two commodities is even more stark.

That these contrasting trends in Chinese imports should have a large differential impact upon global markets for the respective metals is unsurprising. From 1997 to 2017, China accounted for 80 percent of global demand growth for metals (World Bank Group 2018b), and by 2014 the country's share of world consumption was around half for both copper and aluminum (International Monetary Fund 2015). Importantly, however, a much greater share of China's increasing consumption of aluminum could be met with domestic sources—indeed, the country was actually a net exporter of aluminum until 2007 (Farchy 2011). Figure 9.3, showing movements in both copper and aluminum prices on the London Metal Exchange, provides a picture that is entirely expected, given the combination of differential import demand from the PRC and the weight of China within the global market.

The relatively moderate price movements seen in aluminum markets over the commodity boom are helpful in demonstrating the counterfactual scenario of how prices in other metal markets might have changed over the commodity boom years in the absence of high levels of Chinese import

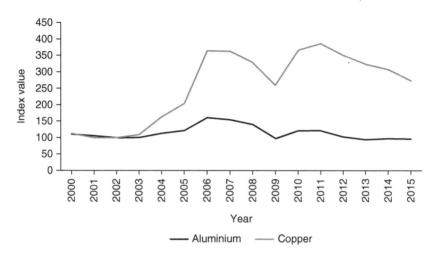

Figure 9.3 Aluminum and copper price indexes, 2000–2015. Calculated from World Bank, Commodity Price Data—Pink Sheet Data.

demand. Without the demand pull from the PRC, bauxite/alumina, and by extension Jamaica, has undergone a commodity "boom" that is a pale shadow of that experienced in other markets and countries.

Jamaica, then, presents an opportunity to examine a contemporary resource-exporting state in which the China effect has occurred only weakly, if at all. As would be predicted, the result was a continuation of pre–commodity boom conditions and therefore little change in the neo-liberalizing trend. In the absence of increased state bargaining power over the natural resource sector, the buildup of fiscal resources that in other states provided the key to (relative) policy independence from IFIs, capital markets, and donors was not possible. With a debt-to-GDP ratio of some 140 percent in 2013 (International Monetary Fund n.d.), contemporary Jamaica is certainly more dependent on the IFIs than any of the other states considered in this typology—perhaps more so than any other state in the world.

The other cases considered in this chapter also mostly continued in the neoliberal mold, in spite of their benefiting from largely China-driven demand and price hikes for their resource exports. Why, then, is there any reason to believe that differences between the bauxite market and those for other commodities prevented Jamaica from taking an alternative course, when others without this apparent constraint also failed to do so?

Juxtaposing Jamaica's trajectory with those of the HO states should help to answer this question by illustrating that, in the Jamaican case, the relevant constraint continued to be located in the transnational—in the circumstances of insertion into the global economy. In Peru, Colombia, and South Africa, however, external circumstances presented no such barrier. While the road away from neoliberalization was thus ostensibly open in these cases, internal drivers, particularly the relative strength of transnationally oriented domestic capital, were the main factors in explaining the persistence of their neoliberal trajectories.

This differentiation between Jamaica and the other HO cases, in terms of external constraints resulting from wildly divergent conditions in their export markets, is relatively easy to demonstrate through, for instance, changes in the purchasing power of exports from South Africa, Peru, and Jamaica, as shown in figure 9.4. From 2000 to 2002, Jamaica's export purchasing power declined, though not precipitously, and indeed was higher, in proportional terms, than that of South Africa in 2002. With the beginning of the commodity boom, however, strong trends of increasing export purchasing power in South Africa and Peru were not matched in the

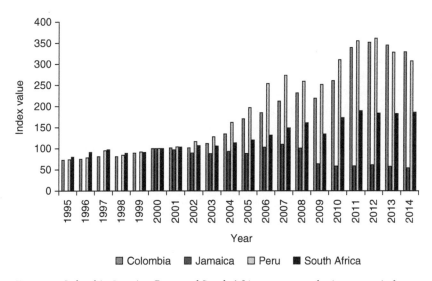

Figure 9.4 Colombia, Jamaica, Peru, and South Africa export purchasing power indexes.
Note: Jamaica data is not available for the years 1995 to 1999.
Source: United Nations Conference on Trade and Development, UNCTADStat data center.

Jamaican case. Some pickup occurred for Jamaica by 2007, but the 2008 crash coincided with a rapid falloff between 2008 and 2009, subsequent to which, with several mining operations shuttered (as we will discuss), there was little in the way of recovery.

South Africa and Peru, by contrast, followed the more expected commodity-boom path of rapid improvement after 2003, with a dip after 2008 and then strong recovery to 2011. In line with prices in most hard and energy commodity markets, the two states' export purchasing power then declined somewhat but, until 2013, nevertheless remained above levels seen prior to the global financial crisis. Peru, in particular, saw huge gains in its export sectors, caused not only by price increases in its main natural resource sectors of copper, oil, and various other base metals (as well as gold) but also by a 2,700 percent increase in mining investment from 2002 to 2012 (PriceWaterhouseCoopers 2013). The opening of Peru as a major resource frontier appears to have continued apace through the whole period, with an estimated \$57.4 billion of projects either under construction or awaiting approval in 2013 (Gacs 2014). One-quarter of this total was made up of ventures by Chinese firms, particularly in copper, and the PRC accounted for 17 percent of Peruvian trade in 2012.

Jamaica

In contrast to the other HO states, an exploration of Jamaica's path of persistent neoliberalization through the boom years depends principally upon a mapping of those external constraints that have done the most to determine this trajectory. As is typical for states considered in this book, these constraints primarily consist in the relationship between commodity prices, indebtedness, and the ability of creditors and investors to impose policy discipline. In common with most other cases included in the typology, the origins of neoliberal constraints lie in negative trends in the first two of these factors, from the 1970s on. The fundamental difference between Jamaica and any other case is the lack of sufficient positive change in commodity prices (in Jamaica's case, in bauxite prices) during the commodity boom years. Without the bargaining power that this afforded other governments, the Jamaican state was unable to extract better terms from investors in the mineral sector, leaving it with no capacity to build the fiscal base that, in other states, greatly diminished their reliance upon creditors.

As with many commodity exporters, the roots of Jamaican indebtedness lie in the 1970s. Following—and even prior to—independence in 1962, Jamaican developmentalism had, in Lewisian fashion, concentrated on promoting labor-absorbing basic manufacturing while encouraging foreign investments (Findlay 1980).[5] Ensuing growth brought with it both increasing inequality and a much larger constituency of urban poor, setting the scene for the 1972 election victory of Michael Manley's People's National Party (PNP). Though the PNP, much like the opposition Jamaica Labour Party (JLP), had stood on a classically vague populist platform, once in office, Manley declared a democratic socialist approach that became more radical in rhetoric (and, to some extent, in policy) over the following years (Huber and Stephens 1992).[6]

Initially, Manley's appeal to economic nationalism, arguing for greater state intervention in pursuit of self-reliance, was able to win the approval of domestic capital, in spite of the imposition of property taxes to pay for social spending and redistribution. A new levy on bauxite exports was also key, upping the government's take from $27 million in 1973 to $180 million the following year (Davies 1986). In this context, the 1973 oil shock had ambiguous consequences, raising the price for Jamaica's ore exports, though by proportionately less than for the country's energy imports.

An increasingly friendly relationship between Manley and Fidel Castro served to alienate both the United States (for which Jamaica was a major source of bauxite) and Jamaican business. This, coupled with rising taxes, drove a first round of emigration and capital flight as well as resulting in a suspension of U.S. aid and a drop in tourist revenues from North America. As in many Southern states, easily available loans were used to compensate for these problems and to finance the continued rollout of social programs and support for local industry, with the capital requirements of such spending itself being a net drain on foreign exchange.

In an increasingly polarized political scene, Manley was able to convincingly win the 1976 election by mobilizing the PNP's urban base on a more radicalized platform. By this point, however, and with falling bauxite prices, the IMF was called in to cover the deficit problems, resulting in loan agreements signed in 1977 and 1978. Though the first of these was relatively benign, the second agreement demanded severe austerity measures, combined with the stipulation that further disbursements would be predicated upon Jamaica meeting stringent performance targets. It seems very likely, as has been argued, that, given both poor relations between the fund and

Manley and U.S. concern over the government's leftward drift, these targets were made purposely unrealistic, both as a punishment and with the goal of weakening the Jamaican position during negotiations over further agreements (Bernal 1984; Bissessar 2014).[7]

In early 1980, the Jamaican government gave up on negotiating with the IMF. By this point, though, precipitously declining standards of living—due in great measure to the combination of imported inflation and repeated currency devaluations—had undermined support for the PNP, giving Edward Seaga's JLP an easy path to a landslide victory in the 1980 election. Seaga had cultivated relations with the United States and the IMF even while in opposition, and the fund certainly dealt more leniently with the new JLP government in an effort to make Jamaica a "showcase of capitalist development in the Caribbean" (Stone 1985) at a time of reescalating Cold War tensions in the region.

Seaga's own preference seems to have been for a brand of economic nationalism not entirely removed from that of Manley's early years. As Huber and Stephens (1992) detail, the state's participation in the economy actually increased over the 1980s, though this was combined with a thorough opening of domestic markets to imports, with the ensuing deficits being covered by further rounds of debt. The IMF, in turn, gradually upped the levels of conditionality, with more devaluations placing Jamaica firmly onto a debt-dependent path by the 1990s. Increasing neoliberalization prompted a general strike in 1985, but its defeat, combined with increasing unemployment, weakened the trade union movement significantly, along with the left wing of the PNP.

When the PNP eventually returned to government, in 1989,[8] the scale of the debt burden was such that there appeared to be little alternative to continuing austerity and neoliberalization, even if a path independent of the IFIs was forged. Jamaica, in fact, gives a rare and important illustration of the sheer extent of policy constraints faced by a highly indebted middle-income state in the 1990s, even for a government ill-disposed to working with IFIs. The long-standing rancor between the PNP and the IMF led P. J. Patterson's government to make a decisive break with the fund in 1996, though from 1992 onward there had been efforts made to shift the debt burden toward domestic bondholders (Johnston and Montecino 2011).[9] These moves allowed the government to set policy free of direct conditionalities, and the 1990s did see an increase in infrastructure spending, and some attempts to alleviate poverty, coinciding with a period of increased foreign direct investment. Nevertheless, even shorn of any direct policy impositions, Patterson's program essentially mirrored contemporary instances of so-called adjustment with a human face (Cornia, Jolly, and Stewart 1989) carried out elsewhere under IFI supervision.[10]

A second leg of the PNP strategy was the creation of a new domestic black business class (Robotham 2000).[11] This is somewhat comparable to the approach taken by the ANC governments in South Africa. In the absence of any feasible options for significant redistribution to the poor,[12] who formed the base of PNP support, the PNP attempted to create a new bourgeoisie from the majority ethnic group, thus appealing to a cultural politics of aspiration. Though the vast majority of Jamaica's population identifies as black, political and economic power have, since independence, tended to lie with a "brown" (multiracial) elite.[13] Many members of this multiracial group, however, had emigrated during the 1970s and 1980s. As the state payroll contracted over the same period, large numbers of black public sector professionals began to take on management—and then, increasingly, ownership—positions in the private economy.

At the same time, the further round of liberalization that occurred after 1989, which Robotham (2000) connects explicitly with the rise of the upwardly mobile black middle classes within the PNP, had the contradictory effect of concentrating capital in the hands of the remaining brown elite, who still controlled greater sums of capital and were therefore best placed to benefit from initial privatizations. When Patterson replaced Manley in 1992, loose monetary—and, to a point, fiscal—policy was implemented, with one goal being to promote the nascent black capitalist class. New black-owned financial institutions grew rapidly, combined with a redirection of government contracts and privatization deals away from the "brown" bourgeoisie.

High levels of inflation prompted the government to hike interest rates by 1994. Though the period of monetary stimulus had ended, a highly deregulated financial sector continued to grow—largely, it appears, feeding on the government's preference for domestic borrowing, which would then be recycled through linked instruments offered to private investors. With banks competing to offer better—and increasingly unrealistic—returns to depositors, the sector had unsurprisingly tipped into crisis by 1998, leading to a government bailout, which was responsible for the majority of the 71 percent increase in debt-to-GDP ratio seen between 1996 and 2003 (King and Richards 2008). The nationalized financial firms were then sold off, overwhelmingly to investors from the United States, Canada, and other Caribbean states.

With a return to the IMF being politically difficult, given the strength with which Patterson had repeatedly denounced the fund, the government attempted to meet its now much larger interest payments by upping consumption taxes, which was met with widespread rioting in 1999 and sealed the PNP's fate at the next election, in 2002. With the black embourgeoisement project thus derailed, JLP governments of the 2000s continued to pursue a homegrown neoliberalization under the weight of debt and a lack of other viable options.[14]

The attempt to forge a path independent of the IMF and to establish a black capitalist class had, if anything, ended in massive levels of indebtedness to a foreign-owned financial sector and a bondholder elite whose priorities were squarely in line with those of the IFIs.[15] From 2000 to 2010, in spite of running primary surpluses in excess of 5 percent of GDP every year, Jamaica posted a net fiscal deficit and saw its annual interest payments rise to as high as 17 percent of GDP (Johnston and Montecino 2011). The result, in effect, was a continuing and substantial redistribution upward, strengthening the bondholders at the expense of any real hope for economic recovery.

The fallout from the 1990s financial crisis heaped a further round of fiscal obligations onto Jamaica, above and beyond the levels of indebtedness seen in any other cases examined in this book. Since this occurred prior to the onset of the commodity boom, it is difficult, counterfactually speaking, to establish whether, had the boom in bauxite prices matched those seen in other minerals, conditions in Jamaica may have been propitious for a commodity-bankrolled break from neoliberalization, in the 2000s. Quite apart from the exceptionally high debt burden, the relative weight of domestic compared to foreign debt surely is significant in this regard.[16] It is certainly plausible to suggest that a plan to increase natural resource revenues under boom conditions might appeal to creditors' desire for a fiscally solvent state.

Mirroring the economy as a whole, however, the trajectory of the bauxite industry over the boom years was disappointing when compared to equivalent mineral sectors elsewhere.[17] As with Zambia's copper (discussed in chapter 8), state holdings in bauxite—a major source of foreign exchange, even under unprofitable conditions—had been privatized only reluctantly. Indeed, perhaps one legacy of Jamaica's non–IMF-path neoliberalism was the persistence of public stakes in several of the island's bauxite and alumina ventures. The state continues to own 51 percent of the Noranda bauxite mine, plus a 45 percent share of Jamalco (through the parastatal Clarendon Alumina Production), as well as holding a 7 percent interest in Windalco up to 2014. Until 2007, 93 percent of Windalco was owned by the British-Swiss firm Glencore, before Glencore's aluminum interests were split off and merged with those of Russian firms Siberian-Urals Aluminum Company and RUSAL to create the Russian-headquartered UC RUSAL, which became the world's largest aluminum company. UC RUSAL was also the sole owner of Alpart, formerly the biggest alumina producer in Jamaica, until it was sold to the Chinese firm Jiuquan Iron and Steel (JISCO) in 2016 (Drakapoulos 2018).

UC RUSAL shuttered the Alpart and Windalco alumina refineries in 2009, citing low demand and high production costs. There is some merit in these claims, insofar as the long history of bauxite mining in Jamaica means that the remaining deposits are relatively deep and difficult to extract, and this is coupled with the high cost of energy in Jamaica, as a function of its almost total reliance upon imported oil.[18]

Even so, one sectoral expert was certain in their belief that UC RUSAL was using its increasing power within the Jamaican bauxite sector to influence the government in several ways. [19] In the first place, and in the short term, negotiations were begun with the government over reopening the Windalco facilities, with one of the refineries being restarted in 2010, after the government agreed to a halving of the bauxite levy. The Alpart refinery, meanwhile, seems to have been used as a bargaining chip in a dispute between UC RUSAL and the government over the public stake in Jamalco.[20]

With three out of four of Jamaica's refineries remaining closed for several years, it is very evident that the Jamaican government was negotiating from a position of weakness, making concessions in order to try to guarantee the survival of as much of the sector as possible. In addition to supplying foreign exchange, and although the bauxite/alumina sector is not a large employer, the mines often are the main economic locus in their rural locations, with small businesses depending upon sales to miners.[21]

There is a marked contrast here with extractive industries in almost all the states surveyed in the typology over the boom years. Even under neoliberal governments in Peru, for example, royalties on mineral exports were raised, with few concerns apparently expressed on behalf of the mining firms, given continuing profitable operating conditions (Reuters 2011). In Zambia, which is perhaps an appropriate comparator for Jamaica here, given that it, too, is a high-cost mineral producer, several mines were shuttered following the global financial crisis. When copper prices rebounded to above precrisis levels, however, these mines were quickly reopened, with Chinese firms purchasing some of the ventures during the lull. In Zambia, the government did not need to offer extra concessions to firms—in fact, though a proposed windfall tax was never pursued, royalty rates on copper were later raised.[22] It seems reasonable to suggest, therefore, that if Jamaica had been a copper producer, or if China were a major importer of bauxite, the sector would have been a point of strength rather than weakness for the Jamaican government, especially given the state's direct control of parts of the industry. It is, of course, much harder to ascertain whether this would have been a tool of sufficient leverage to escape the exceptional and unusual circumstances of indebtedness seen in Jamaica since the late 1990s.

Recent Jamaican governments have attempted to mitigate the short-term domestic debt problem with two rounds of restructuring, in 2010 and 2013, which lengthened maturities and so lowered interest payments, but left the principal untouched for fear of undermining local financial institutions (Johnston 2013). In both cases, these processes were meant to allow for a reengagement with the IMF, after an absence of fourteen years. The initial agreement, signed in 2010 and requiring a new round of expenditure cuts, was suspended after a Jamaican court ruled in favor of a group of public sector employees who were demanding back pay, leading to a suspension of multilateral funding and new concerns over even short-term fiscal sustainability (*Gleaner* 2010).

The extent of Jamaican political change over the past two decades, as well as of the public's sheer desperation, is rather revealed by the fact that the 2011 election was largely fought over which party would be able to secure a renewed deal with the IMF.[23] Portia Simpson-Miller's opposition PNP proved victorious and, indeed, has negotiated access to some $2 billion of IMF, World Bank, and Inter-American Development Bank funds. This came with the requirement to run a 7.5 percent primary surplus in 2013, which, as Johnston (2013) points out, in citing the IMF's World Economic Outlook of that year, would be the highest in the world, outside of oil exporting states.[24] Even after three years of hitting these targets, Jamaica's debt-to-GDP ratio was still 122 percent for the fiscal year 2016/17 (International Monetary Fund n.d.).

Peru

Peru's major exports include copper, hydrocarbons, lead, and zinc, all commodities which have been subject to the China effect on price movements since 2003.[25] With regard to Peru, as with Colombia, South Africa, and Indonesia (but unlike Jamaica), I make the claim that (similar to the conditions under the neodevelopmentalist type, discussed in chapter 5) the political-economic agenda is shaped most significantly by a domestic capitalist class, which is relatively strong and unified and thus is able to exert a greater influence than competing (though sometimes co-opted) popular class movements. Unlike in Argentina or, to a lesser extent, in Brazil, though, the dominant segment of capital in Peru comprises externally oriented interests in finance, mining, and other export industries. The commodity boom, when it came, tended to further strengthen this fraction of capital, which already exerted a considerable influence at the heart of the state.[26] Combined with a relative fragmentation of popular protest into various localisms, the result has been one of continuing neoliberalism in Peru, despite greatly expanding resource exports, which might well have financed a change of direction.

At one point, however, a post-neoliberal turn appeared plausible. A strong electoral challenge by an ostensibly radical leftist, Ollanta Humala, was ultimately unsuccessful in 2006, before he returned to win, in 2011, on a significantly moderated platform. The fact that Peru apparently almost selected a president committed to breaking with neoliberalism in 2006, but then backed the same candidate in 2011, who subsequently governed as a neoliberal, is something of a puzzle that requires rather detailed examination in order to solve.

The Stalled Rise of Ollanta Humala

Reminiscent of Hugo Chavez in Venezuela, Humala was an army officer who first came to national prominence after leading an abortive rebellion—in his case, during the last days of the Alberto Fujimori regime, in 2000.[27] He first organized a political party in 2005, building a base through a network of army reservists and veterans, particularly in the Southern and Central Andes (the former epicenter of conflict with *Sendero Luminoso*, the

Shining Path) and the Amazon (where the military had long played a developmental role). Though he was privately educated in Lima, Humala's mestizo ethnicity (and indigenous surname), along with a nationalist, anti-elite, and anti-neoliberal discourse, gained him a good deal of support among low-income and indigenous voters, especially in his areas of organizational strength, which correspond to a significant degree with the poorest and historically most marginalized regions of the country (Burron 2011; Cameron 2008).

Humala, evoking Peru's 1970s leftist military regime of General Juan Velasco as well as Chavez, advocated the repudiation of a free trade agreement with the United States, the nationalization of strategic national resources, and the election of a constituent assembly tasked with writing a new constitution. In spite of the fact that incumbent Alejandro Toledo had himself been elected on a populist outsider platform, Humala managed to portray himself as an antidote to an ossified Lima elite, referring to the government as a "dictatorship" of "traditional politicians" and even proposing the introduction of the death penalty for political corruption (McClintock 2006; Levitsky 2011).

Although it is impossible to know how Humala would have governed if elected in 2006, the political style and policy positions of his later government suggest an intention to follow a path lying squarely within the extractivist-redistributive type explored in chapter 6. The political dynamics that produced Humala's core base of support in the marginalized southern highlands and Amazonia also bear a striking resemblance to those that propelled Evo Morales to electoral success in neighboring Bolivia. Local protests over dispossession, environmental damage from mining, and neoliberalization of public services were widespread in both cases, with the emblematic 2002 struggle against electricity privatization in Peru's southern city of Arequipa appearing to mirror the Bolivian "water war" in Cochabamba, two years previously. The water war is widely seen as a key moment in the mobilization of social movements, which would eventually culminate in Morales's victory in 2006 (Webber 2010).

During the same year, it appeared that Peru was moving in a similar political direction, as Humala won the first round of presidential elections, mainly on the basis of strong support in the south, the center, and Amazonia. Humala, however, then lost the runoff election to Alan García—who had promised to continue the neoliberal policies of the incumbent Alejandro

Toledo—largely because of Humala's failure to attract sufficient support from the populous slum districts of Lima.[28]

The failure of the protests in Arequipa, among others, to coalesce toward the kind of national momentum seen in Bolivia is most often attributed to a series of decentralization measures instituted during the early 2000s (Balbi 2008; Eaton 2011). These measures effectively shifted the locus of protest to the local level, while leaving most crucial decision-making (such as in matters relating to mining) in the hands of the central government. A handful of somewhat radical regional leaders appeared, though with few connections and little presence at the national level. Adding to this, decentralization encouraged subnational governments at various strata to compete for investment and public funds. While this system no doubt encouraged atomization, a similar structure had been in place in Bolivia since 1994, and a comparable shift toward local-level political contestation occurred there too (Kaup 2013b, 85).[29] Appeals to ethnicity may well have helped overcome these obstacles in Bolivia, in contrast to Peru, which lacks both an indigenous majority and a national indigenous political party. Nevertheless, Humala's base, drawing particularly upon the south, the center, and Amazonia, represented a constituency of marginalized indigenous and mestizo voters—analogous, if not identical, to that which underpinned Morales's electoral success (Madrid 2011).[30]

Divergent electoral fortunes for the candidates spearheading these forces' electoral bids seem to be grounded in differences in the relative strength of domestic class groups in the two Andean neighbors, and in demographic and geographic factors. In first place, the structure of Peru's capitalist class differs from its neighbors Ecuador and Bolivia in that it is relatively unified and concentrated on the coastal lowlands, around Lima and the nearby port of Callao. Partially, this is a legacy of the long-standing political and economic primacy of Lima, in contrast to Ecuador's rival centers of Guayaquil and Quito or Bolivia's analogous highland–lowland fracture. The dominance of Lima, however, was further reinforced under General Velasco (1968–1974), who instituted a land reform program that, though rather botched, effectively destroyed the traditional agrarian oligarchy concentrated in the highlands.[31] A powerful capitalist class concentrated on the coast emerged during the import substitution industrialization of the late Velasco years, as a result of deliberate efforts to construct a new national (and nationalist) bourgeoisie (Figueroa 2012). The fortunes of this group were then substantially bolstered during the "soft," IMF-friendly second phase of dictatorship, in the late 1970s.

With the return of democracy, the civilian government of Fernando Belaunde-Terry (1980–1985) was primarily externally oriented, toward accommodation with the IMF and the World Bank, but the subsequent influx of foreign capital allowed a strengthening of exporters, especially the midsize mining sector, or *mediana minería*, who became junior partners to foreign investors and provided ancillary services at the time of the brief surge in mineral prices during the early 1980s. By now, the center of gravity for the domestic capitalist class resided in a small number of coastal-based and primarily externally oriented *grupos economicos* with interests in finance, mining, commerce, and agro-exports. This geographic concentration, combined with cross-sectoral spread, meant that, while the dismantling of ISI-era protections did split the bourgeoisie, with impacts felt until the 1990s, this never produced the kind of fracture that occurred in Bolivia and resulted in split party loyalties among sectors (Conaghan and Espinal 1990; Conaghan, Malloy, and Abugattas 1990).[32]

A radical-populist interregnum under a first presidency for Alan García, during the late 1980s, saw a serious political and economic crisis that represented the death rattle of Velasco-era national industry but also exposed an overall capitalist weakness. A concurrent collapse of the left opened space for the election of outsider candidate, Alberto Fujimori, in 1990. With an economic team heavily reliant upon technocrats with few domestic ties, the autocratic Fujimori was able to push through a radical neoliberalization that, though broadly supported by domestic business leaders, tended to favor international investors in a manner that may not have been possible under a less autonomous government.[33] By the middle of the 1990s, a restructured Peruvian capitalist class, ever more tightly integrated with external capital and markets, itself began to take up the mantle of neoliberal reform through the growing weight of the umbrella trade group Confederación Nacional de Instituciones Empresariales Privadas (National Confederation of Private Enterprise Institutions, CONFIEP), several members of which served in later Fujimori cabinets (Arce 2006).

On the other side of the ledger, the neoliberal era in Bolivia effectively laid the groundwork for the worker–peasant (or, more accurately, informal sector–peasant) alliance that would eventually prove decisive for Morales's electoral fortunes, while events in Peru during the 1980s and 1990s moved in a very different direction. The decline of the tin mining sector and the liberalization of agricultural imports in Bolivia from the early 1980s onward sparked the large-scale migration of miners and campesinos into the three main urban centers of La Paz, Cochabamba, and Santa Cruz. An ensuing growth of neighborhood organizations in urban zones such as El Alto (now considered a separate city, perched on a plateau overlooking La Paz) provided the beginnings of the structures upon which the Movimiento al Socialismo would later build.

Meanwhile, because the rapidly growing cities hardly offered much in the way of economic opportunities, a secondary migration of dispossessed peasants and miners toward coca-growing regions began (with Morales himself emerging as a leader of the *cocaleros'* union) (Kaup 2013a). Concurrent local struggles against dispossession and marginalization began to snowball—against coca eradication in the Yungas and the Chapare and for provision of services in the swelling peri-urban areas. The circulation of people and continuing ties among old mining areas, informal urban settlements, and coca-growing regions, together with the organizational potential provided by both former unionized miners and appeals to shared ethnicity, allowed for initially local movements to knit together into a loose but politically powerful national movement. The issue of natural gas revenues then happened to provide a national issue, which acted to galvanize this nascent coalition toward an eventual capture of state power.[34]

In Bolivia, the strongest contestation of the MAS has come from the lowland Media Luna provinces, where the agro-industrialist capitalist fraction continues to wield considerable influence. This has been most notably manifested in regional autonomy movements (Eaton 2011), which, though primarily drawn from elites and the middle classes, were able to rally a degree of support from the urban poor, particularly in Tarija and Santa Cruz. To a limited degree, these developments exposed and exploited something of a split in the MAS coalition; lowland indigenous groups have been less enthusiastic followers of Morales than have their Andean counterparts.[35] Nevertheless, lowland capitalists' ability to sway poor voters during elections appears not to extend beyond these heartlands.

In Peru, mass rural–urban migration during the 1980s and 1990s had somewhat different drivers than was seen in Bolivia, but initially, at least, also showed notable parallels. The land reforms of the 1970s had created a large surplus of rural labor, now free to move in search of economic opportunity. The process of stitching together the political aspirations of the resultant new wave of urban residents and those remaining in the countryside advanced considerably faster than in the Bolivian case, given existing popular rural and urban popular organizations, which had been at least tolerated by the military governments (Roberts 1996). Indeed, as a consequence, by the early 1980s, Peru had the strongest leftist opposition in the region, with Alfonso Barrantes's Izquierda Unida (United Left) peaking at just under 25 percent of the vote in the 1985 presidential election. Support for the United Left rested principally upon the solid dual bases of the Lima slums and the southern and central highlands. However, a combination of worsening economic crisis and the rise of the Shining Path insurgency acted to fatally undermine the United Left's electoral prospects by the end of the decade.

The economic implosion of the late 1980s served to concentrate domestic capital and bind it more tightly to its external counterparts, although this process did not instill an internal cohesion among Peruvian capital until the coming of Fujimori's brand of Bonapartism, in the 1990s. Conversely, the relatively large industrial workforce, which had grown during military rule, was significantly reduced in size during the 1980s, with urban popular classes being segmented into permanent, temporary, and informal sectors all possessing conflicting interests, at least in terms of the defensive, short-term strategies encouraged by the crisis (Chavez O'Brien 1992).[36]

Also highly significant was the advance of the Shining Path, from the early 1980s on. In addition to setting up organizational structures that competed with those of the United Left and independent popular groups, the Shining Path infiltrated rival organizations and assassinated their activists and leaders. The movement's violence prompted widespread fear and revulsion across Peruvian society and, particularly in urban areas, has acted as a drag on the credibility of leftist politics to the present day, a factor clearly evident in the panicked reaction, among Lima's elite and middle classes, to Humala's candidacy in 2006.[37]

Given the mass killings and displacement of the 1980s, combined with the disintegration of both the structures and base of the legal left, it is hardly surprising, in hindsight, that Fujimori's authoritarian and "antipolitics" outsider presidential bid was able to prevail in the 1990 election, setting the scene for a decade of antidemocratic retrenchment and neoliberal transformation.[38] Though Fujimori's government was able to neutralize the Shining Path threat, one important consequence of the internal conflict was a further disintegration of peasant and labor movements, caught between the pincers of insurgent violence and government repression (Kay 2007).

With a return to democracy, in 2001, Alejandro Toledo's government essentially picked up where Fujimori had left off, drawing upon antisystem appeals to attract a similar tranche of support from Lima's poorer districts, as well as from the Southern and Central Andes and the Amazon. As a mestizo former World Bank official with no previous ties to Peruvian politics, Toledo was the ideal candidate to navigate the contradictions of neoliberal populism, at least to the point of securing election. Toledo's period in power, though, coincided with the beginnings of the commodity boom and a related surge in economic growth, the benefits of which accrued mainly to the coastal regions while prompting a surge of protests around both mining and broader marginalization in the south and center of the country. Though Toledo himself was almost universally unpopular by the end of his constitutionally mandated one term in 2006, the diverging fortunes of coast and hinterland set the scene for a splitting of the political preferences of these zones, which had tended to vote together since the 1980s.[39]

It is therefore unsurprising that, in the 2006 election, Humala was able to plug into the simmering discontent of ever more marginalized regions and win the first round, particularly with the pro-system vote split between several candidates. However, emerging from the assaults of the 1990s, popular movements hardly had time to coalesce into a national coalition in the manner seen in Bolivia, where the coalition-building process began in the 1980s. A national Peruvian popular movement was made even more unlikely by the growing rift between the economic circumstances of the poor of the coastal slums and their counterparts inland.[40] The military reservist network, which represented the backbone of Humala's organization, was a poor substitute, since it did not reach into the urban littoral— nor, indeed, into the northern highlands. The highlands supplied the historic base of strength for Alan García's American Popular Revolutionary Alliance (APRA), providing a springboard for García to qualify for the runoff.

Though much of the Peruvian elite had uncomfortable memories of García's first presidency, during the late 1980s, which had seen hyperinflation, attempts to nationalize banks, and the growth of the Shining Path, once into the second round of this election, he presented an orthodox platform that attracted most of the votes given to the pro-system candidates in the previous round. Some observers (for example, McClintock 2006; Madrid 2011) make perhaps too much of the coastal poor's enthusiasm for such policies, given that the majority of the benefits of the boom, even here, tended to bypass these voters. Nevertheless, García's professed belief in "moderate change" was easier to sell in the coastal slums than in Humala's heartlands, particularly once the Lima elite and media began to swing behind APRA as, at least, the lesser of two evils (Cameron 2008).[41] In this sense, García's victory allowed for the release of popular resentment toward the political order through the election of a populist able to present himself as an outsider, while in fact he preserved this status quo, at least in terms of political-economic continuity with the Toledo era.

In a somewhat bizarre turn of events, when Humala returned to win the presidency, in 2011, his candidacy—to an extent—fulfilled a role similar to that of García in 2006, by embodying a less unpalatable choice for the coastal middle classes than the second-round alternative. In 2011, this was Keiko Fujimori, daughter of the former autocrat. Fujimori's father, by this point, had become the only former head of state to be jailed for human rights abuses and corruption committed while in office. The level of distaste felt by much of the Peruvian elite toward both candidates is summed up by the widely repeated comments of Mario Vargas Llosa—a Nobel laureate and himself a former presidential candidate—that the decision was akin to choosing between "AIDS and terminal cancer" (quoted in Levitsky 2011, 85). Humala did not assume the mantle of second-round pro-system candidate to the extent seen with García in 2006, since the Lima media, surely reflective of at least a degree of elite sentiment, certainly preferred Fujimori.[42] Nevertheless, with pro-system elements split, Humala's antisystem coalition drawn from marginalized areas proved sufficient for a second-round majority.

Before the first round, a Fujimori–Humala runoff seemed a remote possibility. Given the one term limit, though, García was barred from running for reelection, and internal wrangles meant that the incumbent APRA failed to present a presidential candidate. This left three potential claimants for the continuity vote—Toledo, Pablo Kuczynski, and Luis Castañeda—who between them garnered 44 percent of the first-round tally. Had one of these figures successfully navigated the first round of voting, it seems likely that he would have attracted the endorsement of the two losers, as well as the vast majority of support from Peruvian business and the Lima media. Instead, the fragmentation of the center and center right allowed for a second round contested by Humala and Fujimori.

Many authors (Burron 2011; Lupu 2012; Levitsky 2011) ascribe the success of Humala's comeback, in large measure, to a notable overhaul of political style. Gone was the 2006 candidate, wearing a red shirt and professing his admiration for Chavez and Velasco. Instead, the 2011 Humala hired several of Lula's campaign team, wore a suit, and swore on the Bible to respect the Peruvian constitution and private property. Nevertheless, as Madrid (2012, 143) points out, though Humala's message and presentation may have been moderated, the broad themes of his 2011 campaign were similar to those seen in 2006. His manifesto, entitled "The Great Transformation," explicitly criticized the neoliberalism of past governments, argued for redistribution, and made specific appeals to the Amazon and the Andean regions.

In the first round of voting, Humala again finished first, thanks to support from his base in these areas. Given an apparent inability to make inroads in other areas of the country, however, it was at this point that Humala's policy stance was significantly moderated. After an agreement was reached with Toledo, who had been eliminated in the first round, several of Toledo's economic advisers joined Humala's team and produced a "road map" for policy, which, while committing to expanded social programs, emphasized the importance of foreign investment and fiscal prudence.

Toledo's endorsement of Humala was, in some senses, remarkable, given the level of distrust with which Humala tended to be regarded by the majority of the Lima elite. Undoubtedly, in common with many Latin American political contexts, the coastal elite viewed the prospect of a Humala victory, both in 2006 and in 2011, through both class- and race-tinged lenses, something very much reflected in media coverage of the campaign. Fujimori, seen as running on a platform that echoed her father's aggressive neoliberalism and hard-line security policies, attracted strong support from some sections of the urban poor, who had been the recipients of significant patronage spending during Alberto Fujimori's tenure. Meanwhile, heightened social conflict, particularly around mining, allowed Keiko Fujimori to mobilize a degree of reactionary sentiment in a country where memories of the Shining Path insurgency still held resonance and motivated a good deal of the suspicion around Humala.[43] In the second round, however, the combination of a particularly divisive opponent and concessions to the center meant that Humala was placed in the unexpected position of being the more moderate candidate, leading to a narrow victory.

In this light, the fact of Humala's 2011 victory appears relatively unremarkable. The real surprise, or at least the phenomenon that appears to merit greater attention, is the question of why Humala, in office, governed with such a high degree of neoliberal policy continuity with his predecessors. In fact, Levitsky (2011, 91), in discussing his (accurate) prediction that Humala would not govern as a radical, largely concurs with my arguments, citing opposition from a "robust private sector . . . considerably stronger than in previous decades," along with foreign investors, the media, and the Church.

Neoliberalization

A first attempt at neoliberalization had collapsed under the Belaunde-Terry administration, in the early 1980s (Conaghan, Malloy, and Abugattas 1990). By the 1990s, however, a confluence of economic crisis, widespread contempt for democratic institutions, and fear of the Shining Path insurgency created an environment conducive to Alberto Fujimori's authoritarian neoliberal "Fujishock" program (Conaghan 1996). Since Fujimori had been both an outsider candidate and a post-electoral-victory convert to neoliberalism, he owed few political favors to any fraction of domestic capital, which was reflected in his appointment to key positions of neoclassical economists educated in the United States and with little in the way of political or business records within Peru. When initial reform efforts became bogged down in Congress, public antipathy for legislators was such that Fujimori's move to dismiss them, in his 1992 *autogolpe* (self-coup), gained broad approval.

From this point, the government's economic team, operating from a position of autonomy, was able organize a rapid reconfiguration of state and capital, divesting the state of the tattered remains of Velasco's state-owned industry and favoring its sale to foreign over domestic investors (Arce 2006). Many domestic *grupos*, however, then thrived as junior partners to Chilean, Spanish, and U.S. investors. Initially lukewarm domestic business support for Fujimori's program morphed into greater enthusiasm by the mid-1990s, and government from this point became increasingly embedded with these interests, with many later cabinet appointees being drawn from their ranks and regularized ministerial access established.

The subsequent administrations of Toledo and García, for their part, reflected a changing emphasis, championed by the IFIs but supported by most domestic capital, toward second-generation neoliberal institutional reforms, which were probably incompatible with Fujimori's authoritarian personalism.[44] Toledo's policies, in particular, reflected his sympathy with the principles embodied in the IFI turn toward the "participatory" agenda examined in chapter 8. The internal Peruvian version involved the establishment of policy roundtables drawing upon business, nongovernmental organizations, donors, and the Catholic Church (Burron 2011). Though Toledo was forced by the 2002 Arequipa protests to back down on public utility privatization, both he and García advanced an administrative decentralization that inhibited the formation of nationwide protest movements, as discussed previously.

Nevertheless, especially in relation to the rapidly expanding mining frontier, decision-making continued to reside with the central government, seen most strikingly in García's use of presidential decrees to implement legislation compliant with the 2006 Free Trade Agreement with the United States. Localized protests and violent conflicts over extraction mounted, culminating, in 2009, with the death of thirty-one protesters and police at a demonstration against oil development at Bagua in the Amazon (Aiello 2010).

Though many protests were primarily opposed to the expansion of extraction itself, rather than the distribution of the ensuing revenues, the obviously inequitable impact of the commodity boom, combined with resurgence of state involvement in mining and hydrocarbons in neighboring countries, certainly focused attention on the neoliberal extractive regime (Arce 2008). As in other states, bilateral and multilateral investment agreements and tax stability contracts signed in the 1990s meant that the vast majority of the extractive surplus flowed abroad, something which became less politically tenable as prices continued to rise throughout the 2000s. While campaigning, García had promised to review mining contracts, but once he was in office, this exercise was radically diluted into a scheme that asked for a voluntary contribution of 3.75 percent of mining firms' total profits while prices remained high (Eaton 2015). It is difficult to argue with Arellano-Yanguas (2011, 621) that the "mining alms" that resulted from these negotiations "clearly [signaled] the subordination of the government to mining interests." Perhaps more importantly, the establishment of this system itself represented a growing penetration of neoliberal norms into rural service provision. Payments were to be made into trusts managed by the firms themselves, with wide discretion over the projects that they would then choose to finance.

Upon assuming office, Humala did quickly institute a promised windfall tax on mining profits, as well as a negotiating an additional "duty" for those companies covered by previous tax stability contracts (reminiscent of similar moves in neighboring Chile). However, extra revenue collection was substantially reduced by a provision that allowed firms to deduct operating costs from any taxes due. García's voluntary contribution scheme, meanwhile, was overhauled and replaced by the Obras por Impuestos (Works for Taxes) program. The new arrangement allowed all companies (not limited to the mining sector) to directly fund local social projects of their own choosing, paying construction, operation, and maintenance costs in lieu of up to half their overall tax burden (Eaton 2015). There is an efficiency argument here, given Peruvian regional governments' notorious lack of administrative capacity in allocating decentralized mining revenues (Eaton 2011), though it is difficult to see how this mix of private and publicly funded projects could produce anything approaching a coherent program for service or infrastructure provision. For a government better disposed to and more closely integrated with mining and other industries than often obstructive local governments, though, there was an obvious political expediency to taking some degree of these responsibilities away from localities and placing them under the control of business.

In this sense, Humala actually presided over a rather radical extension of neoliberal governance in this sector. In most other ways, however, the Humala government looks strikingly similar to its two predecessors in both policy and (to some extent) personnel. As with Toledo and García, Humala began with the appointment of orthodox, North American–educated economists to senior cabinet positions. Miguel Castilla, deputy minister of finance under García, was promoted to head the Ministry of Economy and Finance, with central bank governor Julio Verlarde retained in his post. The new government did, of course, to some limited degree, reflect its coalition of electoral support, with left-leaning intellectuals given jobs in ministries relating to social policy (Achtenberg 2011). With a bureaucratic structure largely unchanged from the Fujimori era, though, these positions had little influence in a system where the Ministry of Economy and Finance continued to play a dominant role in decision-making, as per the neoliberal norm (Phillips et al. 2006).

Another legacy of Fujimori has been the continuing ability of CONFIEP and other private sector associations, especially the Sociedad Nacional de Minería, Petróleo y Energía (National Society of Mining, Petroleum, and Energy, or SNMPE) to access and influence both line ministries and the presidency, with "government [making] policy at the behest of a small group of corporate interests, arguing that such policies are—in the long run at least—identical with the interests of the nation as a whole" (Peru Support Group 2014).

Such state capture was especially evident in the Ministry of Energy and Mines. Not only had most ministers previously worked in the mining sector, under Toledo, García, and Humala, but also the ministry itself embodied a fundamental conflict of interest in that it was responsible for both promoting investment and conducting the environmental impact studies that might serve to constrain this. Humala, under pressure from escalating protests, did move the assessment function to the Ministry of Environment, in 2012. However, not only was this ministry generally considered to be weak in terms of bureaucratic capacity (Eaton 2015) but also the directors of the certification authority, while nominally under the auspices of the ministry, were drawn from elsewhere (de Echave 2013). Under pressure from the SNMPE, which argued against procedural delay, the process for certification assessment was limited to a maximum of one hundred days, which José de Echave, himself a former environment minister, argues is insufficient for any rigorous examination, given the lack of capacity within the institutions involved.

These kinds of internal conflicts were an ongoing feature of the Humala government, resulting in multiple cabinet reshuffles as the government repeatedly changed political tack, at least in terms of line ministry appointments.[45] Turnover of personnel tended to come in the wake of various scandals—including corruption and spying accusations—though also in response to a seemingly ever-growing tide of protests. Fallout from sometimes deadly anti-extractive conflicts, together with a rising crime rate, claimed a slew of justice and interior ministers' jobs. Even the position of prime minister was held by seven different individuals over Hulama's term (Kozak 2015). Only one of these, Ana Jara, came from the ranks of the Gana Perú (Peru Wins) alliance, which had won the 2011 election. That Gana

Perú itself dissolved in 2012 and Humala's own Partido Nacionalista Peruano (Peruvian Nationalist Party) fielded no candidates in the 2016 presidential and legislative elections is undoubtedly reflective of a weakly institutionalized party system.

However, far from the absence of a strong governing party allowing Humala the chance to advance a radical personalist vision, his chaotic term serves as evidence that party weakness also can act as a brake on the emergence of any coherent trajectory or vision on the part of a government. The one area in which such coherence and consistency was visible was in a more-or-less strict adherence to an "inclusive" neoliberal political economy model, centered on and directed from the Ministry of Economy and Finance, a bastion of relative technocratic stability. Castilla, at its head from 2011 to 2014, was one of Humala's longest-serving cabinet appointments. Though he was eventually forced to resign, Castilla was immediately replaced from within the ministry by Alonso Segura Vasi, yet another former IMF official (Schiipani and Rodrigues 2014).[46]

To some extent, the inability or unwillingness of the Humala government to venture into more heterodox economic territory, whether in personnel or policy, may be explained by its reliance upon votes from Toledo's Perú Posible (Possible Peru) party in the legislature. Nevertheless, looking at the few initiatives that did depart from neoliberal orthodoxy, it is possible to see that the fundamental policy constraints that Humala faced emanated, at their base, not from political fragmentation but from CONFIEP as the powerful voice of capitalist interests. For example, when the Spanish oil company Repsol announced plans to sell off its Peruvian holdings, including a refinery and a chain of filling stations, the government proposed that the state should acquire them under the auspices of the state-owned enterprise Petroperu. The Lima media presented the move as confirmation of their worst fears around Humala, painting the proposal as the first step toward a Peruvian *chavismo* (Peru Support Group 2013). The furor generated by these attacks, combined with a CONFIEP "ultimatum" to the government, was enough to not only scupper the purchase but also actually move the government toward the sell-off of 49 percent of Petroperu by the end of the year (Economist Intelligence Unit 2013).

In many senses, the Latin American leader whom Humala most closely resembled is not Chavez, Morales, or even Lula but ill-fated Ecuadorian president Lucio Gutiérrez. Both were former army officers elected on a moderately anti-neoliberal and antisystem platform, with a base of support in indigenous and marginalized areas. The political record of both is perhaps evidence that neither was especially committed, on a personal level, to an anti-neoliberal agenda. Despite this, their diverging fates reveal the significance of very different respective balances of domestic social forces in determining the continuing viability of the neoliberalization that they both, as candidates, professed to oppose.

Gutiérrez was forced to tack right even before assuming office, partly as a result of alliances with center-right parties and partly because of a pressing need to maintain credit lines with the IFIs (see chapter 6). In the context of Peru's mineral boom (even given relatively meager tax revenues), and with Peruvian public debt at 22 percent of GDP in 2011 (World Bank n.d.), Humala did not face the external constraint of heavy dependence on the IFIs. As with Gutiérrez, though, Humala did require political alliances with parties wedded to a continuing neoliberalization. In an Ecuadorian context in which mass mobilization had previously removed the Jamil Mahuad government and set the scene for Gutiérrez's ascendancy, a failure to depart from neoliberalization led to a renewed mobilization, in turn clearing a path for the rise of Rafael Correa. Correa, as with Chavez and Morales, but in contrast to Humala, was able to harness this mobilizational power to override neoliberal opposition in the legislature.

The level of disappointment felt by Humala at his failure to advance his relatively radical platform of 2006, or even its moderated form of 2011, remains an open, though rather moot, question. A strong domestic business elite able to articulate its interests widely, through the media, and deeply, in terms of ministerial access and influence, presents a hurdle that would appear impossible to surmount without the kind of popular mobilizational capacity that neighboring leaders were able to call upon. Though there was clearly anger, disappointment, and a rising tide of protest in the areas that composed Humala's political base, the continuing segmentation of Peruvian popular movements effectively prevented such sentiments from spilling into coastal areas and threatening the government directly. Perhaps more accurately, violence arising from protests may well have posed a threat to individual ministers (and even prime ministers), but it could not shake the technocratic core of the Peruvian state established by Fujimori, extended by Toledo and García, and buttressed by its pervasive integration with key elements of domestic capital. Humala, in this sense, may have occupied the presidency, but he was little more than a passenger when it came to Peru's trajectory of persistent neoliberalization.

South Africa

The South African political-economic terrain has been usefully illuminated with the development of the minerals-energy complex (MEC) concept by Ben Fine and colleagues (Fine and Rustomjee 1996; Fine 2010). The MEC is meant to denote a system of accumulation stemming from the particular history of capital and labor relations in South Africa. Briefly, the economic primacy of mining following the discovery of diamonds and then gold in the second half of the nineteenth century encouraged the consolidation and then dominance of English conglomerates whose interests spread beyond extraction to linked sectors such as chemical manufacturing.[47]

With the rise of Afrikaner nationalism over the first half of the twentieth century, a clear tension developed between the economic power of large English capital and the political power of the more numerous Afrikaans speakers. Particularly after the election of the National Party, in 1948, state involvement in mining-related sectors such as steel and electricity, together with the nurturing of private Afrikaner capital, allowed for a growing interpenetration of English and Afrikaner capital (Ashman, Fine, and Newman 2011), concentrated on heavy industry either feeding or fed by the mines.[48]

The combination of high gold prices in the 1970s and a gathering crisis of the apartheid system in the 1980s led to a disinclination, and then an inability, to break out of the core MEC industries into the development of a broader manufacturing sector. As international sanctions began to bite during this era, most South African capital accumulation was trapped within the domestic sphere, engendering a concentration of capital and the growth of an increasingly sophisticated financial sector. Though South Africa may have been globally isolated in many respects, changes to its economic structure in some ways thus reflected trends elsewhere, as did South African investors' preferences for diverting an increasing share of capital into short-term financial rather than long-term productive uses.

It now seems clear that influential figures within the ANC had also moved some way toward neoliberal orthodoxy by the late 1980s (Freund 2013; Pons-Vignon and Segatti 2013). Unsurprisingly, this subject has attracted a great deal of attention (see, among others, Peet 2002; Bond 2000; Williams and Taylor 2000; Hart 2003), given the disjuncture between the relatively radical aspirations of the ANC in opposition—encapsulated in the 1955 Freedom Charter—and the persistent neoliberalization that ANC governments have overseen since 1994. The usual suspects—international financial institutions—certainly played a role in the initial postapartheid trajectory, though their role was less crucial than in many other cases.[49] More broadly, during the early 1990s, international actors in the shape of the U.S. and British embassies, as well as domestic business representatives, pursued a campaign to persuade ANC leaders—including Nelson Mandela—of the importance of a neoliberal approach. According to Hirsch (2005, 28–30, cited in Freund 2013), Mandela's attendance at the World Economic Forum in 1991 was a key moment in convincing the future president of the importance of foreign investment and the abandonment of a former commitment to nationalizations.

Nevertheless, there is a definite homegrown quality to South African neoliberalization, which helps to explain its persistence over the commodity boom era. A central component of this was the stance of domestic capital—as well as liberal economists—prior to political transition, which presented the ANC leadership with "the sugar cube of understanding chat about the evils of racism and the need for change, but also . . . the stick of what might happen if they tried to defy business consensus, both nationally and internationally" (Freund 2013, 528). A major fear, and indeed one which has come to be partially realized, was of massive capital flight in the wake of the removal of sanctions (Ashman, Fine, and Newman 2011).

Initial neoliberalization since 1994, therefore, might easily be viewed as pragmatism in pursuit of more fundamental goals of deracialization and consolidation of majority rule. There can be little doubt, however, that key ANC figures, such as long-serving finance minister Trevor Manuel and Mandela's successor as president, Thabo Mbeki, were personally convinced of the desirability of a neoliberal macroeconomic approach. Mbeki, especially, seems to have played a crucial role in the reorientation of the ANC government toward liberalization, signaled most clearly by the adoption of the misnamed Growth, Employment, and Redistribution plan in 1996.

For all that particular ANC leaders may be seen to have influenced the course of South African political economy after apartheid, the role of domestic capital in prompting the ruling party as a whole to move toward a neoliberal macro framework points toward more basic structural causes at work. The sanctions and divestment of the late apartheid period had produced an unusually large financial sector tightly integrated with the core MEC in a small number of dominant conglomerates. The main prize for

South African capital in ending apartheid, therefore, lay in the prospect of escaping its domestic confinement and allowing its internationalization.

Given this, postapartheid macroeconomic policy, in both its overall neoliberal orthodoxy and its exceptional features, can be seen as defensive, from the point of view of the state, but also as fundamentally acting in the generalized interests of MEC conglomerate capital. Despite a persistent current account deficit in recent years, capital controls, gradually eased, have prevented a stampede, which might have brought balance of payments and currency crises, either of which would have been disastrous for firms trying to off-load their rand-denominated assets (Fine 2012). The necessary complement here has been the maintenance of a high interest rate in order to attract compensatory inward investment, which, unsurprisingly, has come mainly in the form of short-term flows. As Fine points out, this creates a vicious circle, through which the economy becomes more vulnerable to speculative attack as the process advances, making the strict maintenance of sound orthodox macro policy ever more central. Meanwhile, the growing integration of South African capital with its transnational counterparts—with many of the largest firms relisting on the London Stock Exchange—has strengthened its neoliberal orientation while affording it greater disciplinary power over its "home" state.

The very fact of the end of apartheid does, of course, show that popular class movements have been a significant countervailing force in South Africa in recent decades. This explains some of the deviations of the South African homegrown neoliberal trajectory from the IFI-endorsed template. Clearly, even if the ANC was shifted rightward in the 1990s on issues relating to economic restructuring, any broadly acceptable postapartheid settlement would need to involve some efforts to redress the country's racialized inequalities. Social spending, expanded from the apartheid era whites-only system, includes pensions for those over sixty years old, child support payments, and grants for the disabled, foster parents, and caregivers. Taken together, these schemes covered 14 million people by 2010, out of a population of almost 50 million (Woolard and Leibbrandt 2013, 365). In the context of overall increasing inequality since 1994, however, welfare payments have done little more than compensate for declining household incomes among the poorest 50 percent of the population (Leibbrandt et al. 2010).

One signature policy of the ANC has been to engineer the creation of a new black bourgeoisie through the Black Economic Empowerment (BEE) program. Interestingly, this scheme is in many respects reminiscent of the black embourgeoisement plans of the PNP in 1990s Jamaica. There, similarly, a nominally leftist government with a core support base in a historically disadvantaged majority black population, but without the structural capacity (or perhaps political will) for any thoroughgoing redistribution, attempted instead to create a new black capitalist class. In South Africa, this involved a more overt set of state interventions, including minimum black ownership thresholds for most firms, the favoring of black-owned businesses in government procurement, and the commercialization of parastatals, often as public–private partnerships (Freund 2007; Ponte, Roberts, and van Sittert 2007). The ANC government has generally been cautious in deploying BEE in any manner that might provoke fear in domestic and foreign capital (Tangri and Southall 2008), though clearly a new, if narrow, group of black capitalists with significant asset holdings, including in core MEC sectors, has been produced. This "BEE elite" (Freund 2007) is both loyal to the ANC (indeed, most of the new owners are former and current government figures or their relatives) and highly integrated with the white capital of the MEC, stitching together more tightly the interests of state and dominant capital in maintaining a neoliberal course.

Clearly, the persistence of neoliberalism in South Africa, initially justified as necessary in terms of stabilization of the new democratic government (Segatti and Pons-Vignon 2013), has been a major disappointment to many, particularly the leftist sectors of the tripartite alliance (the ANC, the Congress of South African Trade Unions, and the South African Communist Party) that officially supports the government. In response to the rumblings of discontent, the government has, since the mid-2000s, been officially focused on South Africa becoming a democratic developmental state (Marais 2011, chap. 11; Ashman, Fine, and Newman 2010). Partially, of course, this has drawn on the growing attention devoted to the experiences of the East Asian developmental states and, latterly, has been associated with South Africa's status as the newest of the BRICS countries. The concept as deployed by the South African government, though, has been strangely devoid of specific content, accompanying, at various times, a range of different policy proposals from opposing factions within the state. The Congress of South African Trade Unions and the South African Communist Party—who have taken the developmental state to mean a model sharing some features with the newly industrialized countries and some with contemporary Brazil—hoped to advance their cause by successfully backing Jacob Zuma as the new ANC president, in 2007, and as national president, in 2009 (Botiveau 2013). Zuma made some concessions to these interests, such as creating a new Department of Economic Development, though this office remained underresourced and a minor voice in policy formation, particularly when compared with a dominant national Treasury. Rather than a policy realignment, Zuma's presidency (2009–2018) was defined by the Marikana massacre (where police killed thirty-four striking miners) and a number of corruption scandals involving the powerful Gupta business family (Fogel and Jacobs 2018).

Colombia

External pressure for neoliberalization in Colombia was, at least at first, relatively moderate. The country was the only Latin American state to register positive growth in every year of the 1980s (Aviles 2006, 44), and it faced debt and balance of payments problems which, while hardly trivial, were manageable in comparison to the regional norm. Nevertheless, access to international credit in the wake of the 1982 Mexican debt crisis was difficult for any Latin American state, leading Colombian governments to seek IFI approval in a series of agreements, beginning in the mid-1980s, initially focusing on austerity measures before moving to trade liberalization, labor deregulation, and then a raft of privatizations during the 1990s (McKeown 2011).

Neoliberalization has increasingly come to be viewed as a necessary means through which foreign capital, particularly in extractive sectors, might be attracted to Colombia in spite of the risks posed to investors by more than a half century of internal conflict. Most of the dominant sectors of Colombian capital—which has little of the history of fractiousness seen in most other Latin American cases (Schneider 2004, 151)—have interests compatible with neoliberal policy. Those that might seem to be less likely supporters of liberalization, such as traditional large landowners, have tended to favor a more aggressive and militarized approach to the conflict. Since such an approach has meant an ever-rising defense budget, encouraging investment with which to fund the war against guerrilla groups has become something of preoccupation for agrarian elites, leading to a near consensus among Colombia's capitalist class as to the desirability of continuing neoliberalization.

The emergence and persistence of this neoliberalization in Colombia clearly was bound up with the effects of the internal conflict. As in Peru, the twin pressures of a guerrilla insurgency and state (plus paramilitary) repression effectively removed the possibility of an electoral victory for any party connected to popular class movements.[50]

In fact, Colombia has been described as the worst place in the world to be a trade unionist, with four thousand murdered between 1986 and 2003 (Solidarity Center 2006, 11).[51] These crimes are mostly attributed to paramilitary groups such as the Autodefensas Unidas de Colombia (United Self-Defense Forces of Colombia) and their successors, many of whom have ties to large landowners, the military, and government (Gill 2015, 89–92; on the Álvaro Uribe government, in particular, see Aviles 2006, 135–36). The Fuerzas Armadas Revolucionarias de Colombia (Revolutionary Armed Forces of Colombia, or FARC), along with the Maoist Ejército de Liberación Nacional (National Liberation Army, or ELN), have also been responsible for the deaths of figures from the legal left, at various points.

The cocaine trade is, of course, a well-known aspect of the Colombian conflict, as is the involvement of both paramilitaries and guerrillas in production of the drug.[52] Cocaine's impact on social structure, and thence on neoliberalization, has been less widely discussed. Colombian drug traffickers initially became internationally important during the *bonanza marimbera*, a boom in cannabis production and export during the 1970s. This experience left Colombian cartels in a position to dominate the international cocaine trade when it began to boom in the 1980s, making traffickers far more significant in the Colombian context than their counterparts were in Peru and Bolivia (Thoumi 2002). Thoumi estimates the value added generated by illegal drug industries in Colombia at 7 to 10 percent of gross national product in the early 1980s.

A rising "narco-bourgeoisie" found land acquisition to be the easiest way to invest and launder money, leading to an eventual legitimization of the *narcos* as large agrarian landowners. A more immediate impact was a rising tide of speculation on land values as other sections of the capitalist class joined in (Richani 2010). In turn, peasant dispossession, usually at the hands of paramilitary groups who had begun as private security for landowners, became an increasingly important aspect of the internal conflict, more deeply implicating a bourgeoisie for whom land was becoming more central. The rise of the narco-bourgeoisie—who are generally in favor of neoliberalization as providing avenues for greater legitimization (McKeown

2011)—has thus helped to tie conservative agrarian elites to more outwardly oriented fractions.

At various points in recent decades, ascendancy within the dominant bloc has alternated between these two groups. This has been mirrored in the approach to the FARC, with more transnationalized sectors favoring negotiation and the eventual peace accords ratified in 2017. Traditional landowners, most obviously represented by Álvaro Uribe, who was president from 2002 to 2010 (and now by President Ivan Duque), have tended to be more vociferous in their condemnation of the guerrillas, have stronger links to paramilitary forces, and rejected the peace deal (Aviles 2006, 90–93; Richani 2010).[53] While this group may, under other circumstances, have been less inclined to support continuing neoliberalization, the needs occasioned by their approach to the internal conflict have driven them to champion such an agenda. In part, this has been a consequence of Colombia's heavy reliance on U.S. military aid (Stokes 2006), a precondition of which, since the Bill Clinton administration, has been the adoption of "sound" neoliberal economic policies.

More important, though, has been a desire to attract foreign investment, particularly in extractive industries, as a means to pay for increasing military spending, which moved from 2.2 percent of GDP in 1990 to 5.6 percent by 2008 (Richani 2010). Unusually for Latin America, because of long-running conflict and instability, Colombia's potential for natural resource extraction was relatively undeveloped (and underexplored) prior to the global push for new extractive frontiers that was prompted by the commodity boom. The guerrilla struggle, which saw the FARC and the ELN launch at least a thousand attacks on oil pipelines during the 1980s and 1990s (Aviles 2006, 79), hardly afford Colombian governments the strong bargaining position that the commodity boom has brought elsewhere.[54] This has meant that high levels of investment in extractives have only been secured through linked processes of liberalization and militarization. As a result, Colombia saw FDI flows balloon from $2.34 billion in 2000 to $16.2 billion in 2012, much of this in oil and coal (World Bank n.d.).

The link between a need to please foreign investors and the internal conflict is made obvious by the role that campaign contributions and lobbying efforts on the part of U.S. firms active in Colombia have played in securing U.S. military and development aid (Aviles 2008, chap. 7). Often, this aid has been directly used to protect investors, as with the $100 million of U.S. government funding for a special Colombian brigade to guard

Occidental Petroleum's pipeline in Arauca (Aviles 2006, 132). It was the Uribe administration's Democratic Security and Defence Policy, though, which most explicitly expressed the symbiosis of further militarization and a neoliberal conception of development. McKeown (2011, 82) cites the U.S. Colombian Embassy's formula, which succinctly sums this up: "Democratic security = [Foreign investor] confidence = Investment = Growth."

Indonesia

Indonesia's economic orientation during the Suharto years (1965–1998) can be divided into three broad periods (Winters 1996), of interest because they illustrate a swing in the country's policy autonomy that presents a parallel to that described in this book in relation to resource exporters during the 2003–2013 period. The first period, from the mid-1960s to 1973, saw great efforts to attract foreign capital to the country in the aftermath of the mass killings and upheaval that marked the transition from Sukarno's Guided Democracy to the New Order regime. The IMF was welcomed into the country, Western-educated technocrats were appointed to key positions in the bureaucracy, and the inward investment regime was liberalized. The second period coincided with the 1970s oil boom, revenues from which made Indonesia less reliant upon what Winters (1996, 41–42) terms "mobile capital," including both foreign investors and elements of domestic business, especially ethnic Chinese capital (see also Rosser 2002, 26–32). This phase, especially in the aftermath of the second oil price spike, in 1979, saw a shift toward more dirigiste policies and the channeling of resources from the state to emerging *pribumi* (indigenous) firms. Declining oil prices across the 1980s then brought a third phase, with partial moves toward liberalization, including in capital markets, allowing for both an influx of foreign investment and a growing internationalization and financialization of large Indonesian capital over the next two decades (Robison and Hadiz 2004).

Over all three periods, however, the New Order state held the reins of an extensive system of patronage, exercised via control over credit, mining, and timber concessions; import licensing and procurement; and important SOEs in sectors such as oil, mining, power generation, banking, and trade (Hadiz and Robison 2013).[55] As Robison (1986, 26–27) shows, over the first two decades of Suharto's rule, this apparatus served as midwife to a domestic class of capitalists drawn especially (though not exclusively) from the ranks of Indonesia's ethnic Chinese minority. Ethnic Chinese business figures were limited in their ability to participate directly in domestic politics, and so, even as their conglomerates grew in economic importance, they continued to depend upon alliances with military and bureaucratic patrons, who could function as rentiers through their discretionary power to award contracts and licenses to favored clients. By the 1980s, bureaucratic elites began to outgrow their role as fixers and increasingly moved into business for themselves, either directly or via family members. Economic reform during this period included moves such as the ending of state monopolies in key sectors that ostensibly might have served to weaken the nexus of patronage—but in reality saw the persistence of such activities, now shifted into the private sector (Hadiz and Robison 2013).

In 1997, the Asian financial crisis hit with speculative attacks on the rupiah. By this point, Indonesian businesses were heavily exposed to the crisis through the accumulation of short-term foreign debt. A collapsing currency then led to bankruptcy for many of the most prominent conglomerates, implosion of the country's deregulated banking sector, racing inflation, a severe fiscal crisis, and growing political unrest (Rosser 2002, 171–72). Though the government dragged its heels, it had little choice but to eventually accept a $41.5 billion IMF loan, which the fund saw as a lever for the transformation of Indonesian capitalism (Robison and Hadiz 2004, 259) through thoroughgoing neoliberalization. Meanwhile, the crisis had fatally undermined Suharto's political and economic base among the wealthy and the middle classes. Widespread rioting, the occupation of Parliament by students, and abandonment by key regime figures would trigger Suharto's resignation in May 1998 (Robison and Hadiz 2004, 6).

Under Suharto's successors B. J. Habibie and Abdurrahman Wahid, much of the IMF's package of reforms was implemented, including a reduction of subsidies, liberalization of trade and capital markets, and privatization or ending of monopolies for SOEs. Nevertheless, the severely weakened alliances of crony capitalist and state officials that continued to undergird economic and political power in Indonesia were largely able to survive the crisis and to emerge in a reconfigured form adapted to the introduction of democracy. As Robison and Hadiz (2004, 187–222) detail, IFI-sponsored initiatives aimed to rein in the old predatory networks and introduce transparent governance mechanisms. But the process remained largely in the hands of political interests, which worked to maintain and restore the essence of the old system under the carapace of new institutional forms. Bank and debt restructuring programs, for example, often resulted in the state propping up unviable banks and shouldering the debt burdens of distressed conglomerates, while effectively allowing the such conglomerates to retain their assets. A relatively swift return to economic growth, in the early 2000s, then provided a renewed base of accumulation for domestic capital while reducing the structural leverage of the IFIs, leaving many of the liberalization programs only partially completed.

The absence of an anticipated influx of foreign investment in the initial post-Suharto years amplified the need to entice the substantial sums of Chinese Indonesian capital (estimates vary widely, from $5 billion to $165 billion), which had fled the country in the wake of the crisis (Chua 2008, 88). This is one indication that, while the alliance of capital and bureaucracy persisted, new conditions began to tip the balance of power within these networks toward capital. Though authors disagree on the degree to which this process has advanced since that time (Choi 2014; Aspinall 2013), democracy has opened new channels of political influence for capitalists, through the opportunity for media ownership and through aspiring politicians' need for campaign finance. In some cases, wealth has become the basis for securing political office, rather than the reverse, with prominent business figures—including a smattering of Chinese Indonesians—entering politics for themselves.

Chinese Indonesian capital, which continued to account for ownership of most large conglomerates, tended to ambivalently but broadly favor a continuance of liberalizing policies (Chua 2008). This was in part a defensive strategy, since currents of economic nationalism that have periodically surfaced in Indonesia (and that ebbed and flowed over the commodity boom years) are associated with state support for *pribumi* capital and perhaps redistribution along ethnic lines. In this sense, it is hardly surprising that the administrations of Megawati Sukarnoputri (2001–2004) and Susilo Bambang Yudhoyono (2004–2014), both enmeshed within familiar elite networks of patronage and money politics, oversaw an overall continuity of policy that won (sometimes equivocal) praise from IFIs and investors at home and abroad (World Bank 2009; Sidel 2015). The overall trend of neoliberalization, however, seems more reflective of the search for particularistic advantage among the most influential segments of capital and their political allies than of any strong ideological commitment. In the post-Suharto era, corporate control of Indonesia's largest firms continued to lie, to a large extent, in the hands of powerful families (many ethnic Chinese and some *pribumi*) with extensive formal and informal political ties, while these groups had simultaneously become increasingly powerful in relation to the state and increasingly interpenetrated with foreign investment (Aspinall 2013; Leuz and Oberholzer-Gee 2006).

Shifts in some mining sectors, beginning during Yudhoyono's second term, seem indicative of both Indonesian capital's political influence and its ambivalent attitude toward neoliberalism. A 2009 mining law increased royalty rates, mandated that foreign firms divest 20 percent ownership of mines within five years of operation, and banned the export of some unprocessed ores while heavily taxing others.[56] Warburton (2017, 299) argues that this legislation reveals "the ambitions of politically connected domestic capitalists . . . driving policy." More interventionist and nationalist policies have been adopted in mining because this is one area of the economy where foreign and domestic capital are highly differentiated; that is, most firms are clearly either domestic or foreign owned, with foreign ownership mostly concentrated in copper and gold. This has left these firms subject to aspiring domestic capitalists looking for legislative help to acquire assets in these subsectors. In Warburton's counterexample of palm oil, ownership structures are much more complex and blended between domestic and international capital, providing a strong incentive for political-economic elites to reject moves toward capping foreign investment in the sector.

Popular opposition to elite predation and corruption has been prevalent throughout Indonesia's years of democracy, as inequality rose—the Gini coefficient climbed from 30 in 2000 to 41 in 2013 (World Bank 2015)—and social spending stagnated. Nevertheless, public sentiment did not coalesce into a coherent movement for substantive change. Successive presidential candidates won on antigraft platforms despite being enmeshed in familiar networks of patronage and money politics themselves. By the 2009 election, politicians were pejoratively using the term "neoliberal" to accuse opponents of alignment with big business and foreign interests, though this hardly amounted to a comprehensive critique or alternative economic program (Kuncoro, Widodo, and McLeod 2009).

Interestingly, and somewhat out of sync with other cases, populism emerged as an electoral force in Indonesia at the end of the commodity boom, with the 2014 election of Joko Widodo (known as Jokowi), a figure who had emerged from local politics and was initially relatively unencumbered by ties to existing elites. However, without a strong party or mass movement base of the type encountered in many other cases of electoral populism, Jokowi in office has had to rely on alliances with forces from within the existing system—the Indonesian Democratic Party of Struggle as well as prominent business figures and generals. Jokowi's economic agenda has been an ideological "mash-up" (Baker 2016), combining elements of redistribution, such as efforts to widen access to health care; liberalization, such as removal of subsidies on fuel, deregulation of business, and investment and trade in some areas; and more statist and nationalist policies, such as implementation of export bans in mining, new consumer subsidies, and a revitalization of the SOE sector (Busch 2015). The totality has been described in some quarters as developmentalism (Warburton 2016; Baker 2016). It is probably more accurate to characterize this somewhat ad hoc series of measures as a part of a strategy aimed at meeting the varied demands of Indonesian capital—never as strongly or broadly committed to liberalization as in other HO cases—and, under the pressure of declining commodity prices and foreign investment, seeking new avenues for rent and accumulation via the state (Hadiz and Robison 2017).

Conclusion

The HO type, much like all the others, displays a trajectory under commodity boom conditions that can be accounted for by a particular pattern of domestic social configuration, with the decisive element for the HO type being a strong, externally facing fraction of capital with extensive ties to its transnational counterparts. As with the DDO cases, the observed trend over the boom was one of continuing neoliberalism. However, compared to those states, the HO type is distinctive in that the persistence of a liberalizing policy agenda was driven by its dominant domestic fraction of capital, which perceived its interests to be served through the maintenance and extension of the neoliberal settlement.

In the extractivist-redistributive and neodevelopmentalist (ND) types, the lifting of external neoliberal discipline brought about by the China effect on commodity markets allowed previously circumscribed groups of productive capital and popular classes to mount successful challenges to neoliberally inclined domestic elements for control of the state. In the HO cases of Peru, South Africa, Colombia, and Indonesia, the similar easing of external constraints also left the way open for possible post-neoliberal turns. In this sense, HO states during the commodity boom (unlike Jamaica) have potentially possessed just as much freedom of action to set policy and define national development projects as those of the ND or ER types.

That state managers in HO cases chose not to pursue breaks with neoliberalism was not due to any lack of material base from which do so—resource exports have boomed, bringing the potential for significant increases in state revenues. Instead, the continuity of neoliberalism was the result of independent, domestically driven policy setting in the HO type. The force of IFI demands may have been greatly diminished under the new conjuncture, but it was then that the voice of externally oriented domestic capital came to speak loudest, sounding remarkably similar to its previously dominant IFI allies.

In Jamaica, of course, the story is somewhat different. The Caribbean country serves as an illustration of the dire circumstances (and tight neoliberal conditionality) that other resource-rich states might have faced over the same period, absent of the rise of China. It also provides a demonstration of why it is significant that China drove this commodity boom and thus shaped it in ways that mirror the structure of its own economy. Because Jamaica missed out on the major part of the China effect, external voices continued to paramaterize the country's domestic agenda. Despite a fractious history of engagement and breaks with the IMF itself, the island has never been able to chart a course away from the neoliberal demands of the IFIs. A particularly heavy debt burden, much of which stems from a disastrous effort to liberalize the financial industry, has become so debilitating that the IMF called for a primary budget surplus that, proportionally, is more than double what the troika asked of Greece. For now, Jamaican governments seem to have little choice but to accept the IMF's conditions and acquiesce to this debilitating demand.

CHAPTER X

China and Global Transformation

The purpose of this book has been to show the scale of disruption to commodity markets caused by the rise of China since the early 2000s, and, in turn, to illustrate the opportunity that this process presented for Southern resource-exporting states to break with the disciplinary constraints of global neoliberalism and autonomously define their own development strategies, for better or for worse. Though the theoretical bedrock for these explorations has been provided principally by Giovanni Arrighi's secular cycles of accumulation model, my goal has not been to suggest that the changes seen in resource-exporting states amount to a new global regime of accumulation, replacing neoliberalism, or to advance a case for China as the coming hegemon. Such predictions are at best highly premature.

China's economy has been expanding at pace for so long that it is easy to take this for granted and to extrapolate high gross domestic product growth figures for decades to come. In fact, it appears that it is extremely rare for any state to sustain growth of 6 percent or more (which is well below China's average in the postreform era) for any period longer than fifteen years (Pritchett and Summers 2013). While it must, then, be remembered that China's record is exceptional—if not entirely without precedent—it remains an open question whether we should therefore expect the People's Republic of China to continue bucking the historical trend, or whether either regression to the late-developer mean or perhaps a major forthcoming crisis are likely (see, for example, Babones 2011; Gulick 2011; Fischer 2015; Hung 2016; Li 2016).

As of 2019, China's economy certainly has decelerated from its previous breakneck speed, averaging 6.75 percent from 2015 to 2018 and currently projected to slow further over the coming years (International Monetary Fund n.d.). World prices for natural resources began to fall around 2013, as Chinese demand growth slowed and the prior wave of investment in new production, triggered by the boom, resulted in supply surpluses. These price drops have had debilitating impacts on the economies of many of the countries surveyed in the previous chapters. An array of looming political-economic problems in several of the largest Southern economies seems, if anything, to signal a reversal of many of the trends of the previous decade, around which the arguments advanced in this book are built.

Perhaps surprisingly, though, there has been considerable variety across resource exporters, both in how well they have weathered the storm and in the strategies they have pursued in reaction to it. Venezuela, for example, has descended into severe economic and political crisis—in part due to shortfalls in oil revenue but partly, too, because of damaging policy decisions by the Nicolas Maduro government (Weisbrot 2014a; Buxton 2016) and because of U.S. sanctions (Rathbone and Pan 2018). Argentina and (especially) Brazil also have seen their share of turmoil and have recently experienced swings back toward neoliberalism. In Argentina, Mauricio Macri's government inherited a troubled economy but began with measures—cutting taxes and devaluing the peso while maintaining public spending—that only deepened the problems, before eventually agreeing to a return to the International Monetary Fund, with a $57 billion bailout, in 2018 (Gillespie and Oliveira Doll 2018). The *lava jato* scandal combined with recession to upend Brazilian politics, first presenting an opening for the removal of Dilma Rousseff by impeachment and then undermining all the other established parties in the 2018 vote, which culminated in the election of far-right outsider Jair Bolsonaro (Anderson 2019). Angola, too, looks to be moving toward a somewhat more orthodox path for now.

On the other side of the ledger, Bolivia has so far endured in relative stability, even if negative reaction to Evo Morales's decision to run for president again in 2019, ignoring a referendum result on term limits, means that he is by no means certain to win. In Kazakhstan protests greeted the retirement of longtime president Nursultan Nazarbayev and the apparently stage-managed election of his handpicked successor Kassym-Jomart Tokayev (Al Jazeera 2019). Meanwhile, the government has actively pushed back against negative external conditions by pursuing a significant countercyclical spending program (Brown 2018).

All this suggests that, should prices decline or stagnate in the longer term, the consequences for the states examined in this book are unlikely to be simple or unidirectional, just as they were not during the boom years. Because many resource exporters increased their borrowing during the recent period of high global liquidity, any significant hike in U.S. interest rates may well tip many more commodity producers into crisis. Such a course of events would seem, in many senses, to echo the sequence of the 1970s, whereby assertions of political-economic independence on the part of several Southern resource exporters were bound up with a commodity price boom that was brought to a decisive end (following a second, temporary peak, in 1979) by the Volcker shock, the debt crisis, and the rollout of structural adjustment programs.

From here, a rather similar trajectory is possible, though by no means inevitable. There has been much talk that, following the financial and then European debt crises, a third phase of reverberations from the 2008 crash may be coming to a head. This time, the epicenter lies in the South and the emerging markets, which, to this point, had seemed to offer something of a crutch for the wounded global economy in the face of instability and then stagnation in the North (Cameron and Stanley 2017; *Economist* 2015). If growth in China proves no longer able to prop up commodity markets, and should the costs of debt financing suddenly rise, the situation would quickly become critical for many resource producers.

With Chinese state-owned banks playing an ever-increasing role in development finance, concern has been raised in some quarters that Chinese lending associated with the Belt and Road Initiative may be pushing some states' debt burdens to dangerous levels (Hurley, Morris, and Portelance 2018), though in many cases the proportion owed to Chinese creditors appears relatively low (Eom, Brautigam, and Benabdallah 2018). A novel and unwelcome element in the current conjuncture is a brewing U.S.–China trade war, which might do major damage to the global economy, should it continue to escalate. Finally, there has been speculation for decades now about the possibility of a Chinese "hard landing"—and a major crisis certainly seems possible at some point, given the buildup of bad debts and a still-inflating asset bubble.

The turn toward austerity as postcrash "common sense" across much of Europe (Arestis and Pelagidis 2010; Blyth 2013) foreshadows the potential consequences for resource exporters should their ability to service debts begin to falter. As events in Greece have shown, the imposition of severe austerity programs has proceeded even in cases where public opinion, and the country's government, were clearly opposed. If unsustainable levels of debt mean that resource-exporting states feel the need to once again turn to international financial institutions for assistance (as has already happened in the case of Argentina), it seems extremely likely that such help would come with renewed conditionalities that would threaten any post-neoliberal programs developed over the previous decade. In some cases, of course, domestically led reliberalization has already started to occur, without the need for IFI insistence.

A different trajectory is at least possible, however. First, prices for metals and minerals are still above their preboom levels, and in most cases are higher than any time before that, back to the 1980s. Indeed, for a number of commodities, prices have strengthened in the past two years, with some (very tentative) indications that they may continue to do so, as demand fundamentals remain reasonably strong (Baffes et al. 2018). If China's prospective shift toward greater domestic consumption is managed successfully, this is likely to lead to a less resource-intensive path of growth overall, but in all probability it also will have a differential impact on commodity markets—as demand is likely to shift away from coal and toward natural gas and oil, for example. Currently marginal commodities such as lithium might well experience a boom as demand for electronic vehicles and storage for renewables-produced energy increases over time.

Recent stimulus measures in China also signal that the investment-led growth path, which many assume to be a dead end, may not be quite finished just yet, whatever further economic imbalances it continues to pile up (Reuters 2019). Externalization of China's capital-intensive investment model via the BRI (Chin and Gallagher 2019), as well as the rollout of various other large transnational infrastructure initiatives (Kanai and Schindler 2018), also may play some role in future commodity demand.

Even should prices crash and debt levels become unsustainable, however, and a new wave of liberalizations roll across the resource exporters surveyed in this book, the post-neoliberal turns of the commodity boom era will remain significant phenomena in their own right, for two main reasons. First, the social structures that have underpinned these divergent political-economic trajectories—and which, in turn, are both reproduced and transformed by them—will provide distinct and in many respects novel contexts within which any forthcoming turbulence, crisis, or other changes to the global dynamic will manifest and play out in these states. We can already see nascent patterns emerging as states and societies have begun to confront harder times during the past five years.

Second, as the embodiment of a world-historical moment in which prevailing global dynamics were challenged from the South, the commodity-based post-neoliberalism of the first decade and a half of the twenty-first century is, as noted in the introduction, of at least comparable significance to the period of the New International Economic Order. Both involved (rather different) attempts on the part of formerly weak Southern states to parlay favorable external market conditions into new political-economic settlements, and both are illustrative of the possibilities for social and economic change that arise at moments of global structural shift.

It is entirely possible that the material factors that acted as midwife to resource-based post-neoliberalism in the South are now fully played out. Nevertheless, the circumstances of the current conjuncture imply coming global turbulence of one sort or another, whether this is produced by, for instance, a deceleration or perhaps crisis in the PRC's economy; a longer-term rebound, and perhaps reorientation, of Chinese growth; continuing growth and increasing resource needs of India, Indonesia, Nigeria, and others; the escalation of impacts from climate change; a reassertion of U.S. power; or some as yet unforeseen vector of transformation. With all this in mind, it is hoped that the dialectic of global and local structural change traced in this book may serve as a departure point from which some possible future trajectories may perhaps be anticipated, though not predicted.

For now, I aim to accomplish two tasks. The first of these is to restate the book's principal arguments in making the case for the 2000s commodities boom as a demonstration of the global and national political-economic possibilities that can open up when structural change occurs within the capitalist world-system. Second, I will draw upon the dynamics of interaction between China and the global South—which the book has explored over the period 2002 to 2013—in an effort to suggest possible scenarios for the medium- and long-term outlook for commodity markets, and with it the prospects for the maintenance, elaboration, and emergence of new, resource-grounded breaks with neoliberalization. I also will look at the challenges faced by the Chinese economy, and the likely implications for commodity markets, as the PRC grapples with the growing but perhaps not insurmountable contradictions in its development.

The foundation of this book's argument is the claim (detailed in chapter 1) that the 2002–2013 commodity boom was to a substantial degree driven by industrialization in the PRC and China's consequent demand for imported raw materials. There are, of course, other elements to this story. Constrained global supplies of many extractive commodities, following an era of low prices and thus low investment levels, provided a context within which Chinese demand began to make itself felt, in the early 2000s. Commodity speculation, linked to larger trends of financialization, seems to have amplified the extent and volatility of price movements, but such speculation essentially responded to, rather than created, an underlying upward trend in fundamentals (Farooki and Kaplinsky 2013, 161–62).

By far the most significant of these fundamentals was the rapidity, scale, and persistence of Chinese economic expansion, which was highly resource intensive. Of course, the Chinese economy had been growing swiftly since well before the early 2000s. However, as chapter 1 demonstrated, the beginning of the commodity boom coincided with the point at which the PRC—despite itself being a major producer of oil, coal, copper, iron ore, and other resources—began to outstrip domestic supplies and depend upon world markets for key energy and hard commodities. As tables 10.1 and

TABLE 10.1

China's share of global consumption, 2012

Copper	Nickel	Aluminum	Oil	Soybeans
43%	48%	45%	12%	30%

Source: Calculated from United Nations Conference on Trade and Development, UNCTADStat data center.

TABLE 10.2

China's contribution to global consumption growth, 2002–2012

Copper	Nickel	Aluminum	Oil	Soybeans
113%	132%	81%	48%	60%

Source: Calculated from International Monetary Fund, World Economic Outlook Database; United Nations Conference on Trade and Development, UNCTADStat data center.

10.2 show, at the peak of the boom, in 2012, China accounted for more than 40 percent of global consumption of copper, nickel, and aluminum and 30 percent of soybeans. Even in oil, where China's global weight is less significant, the impact of Chinese industrialization on global markets is clear, with the demand from the PRC accounting for almost half of total consumption growth in the decade beginning in 2002.[1]

At this point, it is worth briefly retracing the course of price movements since the beginning of the boom, around 2002, to emphasize the magnitude of this China-led, decadelong transformation in commodity markets. Figure 10.1 shows real annual prices for the two most important commodity groups—energy and metals. Despite some volatility, metals prices remained stagnant through the 1980s and 1990s (and much lower, on average, than during the 1970s), until the boom commenced in 2003. Prices peaked in 2007, before falling sharply with the global financial crisis. Following this dip, however, a strong rebound in 2010 and 2011 coincided with the Chinese investment stimulus and indicates that metals prices were not, by this point, primarily driven by demand in the still-struggling North. Prices then began to fall again, beginning in 2012, seemingly influenced by moderating import demand from China and the commencement of

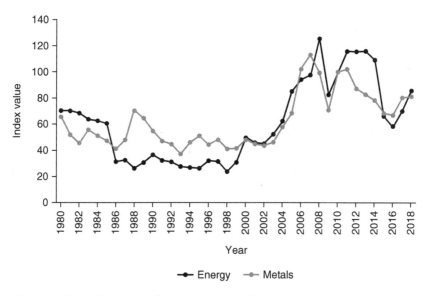

Figure 10.1 Real price indexes for energy and metals, 1980–2018.
Source: World Bank, Commodity Price Data—Pink Sheet Data.

production from several large extractive projects whose development had been prompted by the high prices of the mid-2000s (International Monetary Fund 2014, 36; World Bank 2014, 8).

In energy, following the falloff in oil prices during the mid-1980s, which was brought about by OPEC's decision to ease supply constraints, price movements have, for the most part, mirrored those of metals, though without the 2012–2014 decline. Empirical data relating to the typology cases, presented in chapters 5 through 9, reveals the scale of the 2002–2013 boom's impact on the revenue, export purchasing power, and GDP growth of resource-exporting states. Principally because of the China effect, previously stagnant export sectors would now provide the material basis for states to end dependence on IFIs and donors and to break free of their neoliberal constraints.

Over the period 2002 to 2013, then, China's rise and consequent impact on commodity markets shifted the circumstances of insertion into the world economy for those Southern states reliant upon exports of natural resources. There are two main component parts to this effect. One of these, all things being equal, occurred in every resource-exporting state regardless of policy, whereas the second has required governments to act in order to reap the benefits.

First and most obviously, rising demand in a context of relatively inelastic supply meant an increase in prices and thus in revenue for the state in absolute terms. Of more significance than this largely automatic effect, though, was the growing attractiveness of resource sectors as destinations for investment. As prices rose, extraction still could be profitable for multinationals, even with the imposition of new taxes. These new operating conditions, coupled with the risk, delay, and expense involved in developing new mining ventures elsewhere, meant that states acting as the landlords of their subsoil resources now possessed greater power to bargain with extractive capital and were able to secure a larger slice of the expanding pie. Thus, where state managers were politically disposed to exploit this opening, gains in the relative share of extractive revenue could often be highly significant.

In most of the cases presented as part of the typology in chapters 5 through 9, governments did act to raise tax or royalty rates on their natural resource exports. In Zambia, for instance, the commodity boom prompted a reexamination of secretive development agreements, which provided concessions to private copper miners within the country and, in some cases, allowed these firms to operate at an effective tax rate of zero percent. Other governments, however, went much further in pressing their claim to resource revenues, in ways that would have been inconceivable during the previous era of low prices. Both Northern and Chinese oil firms, for example, continued to operate profitably in Ecuador under the government of Rafael Correa, despite a step change in the state's take of revenues from a new per-barrel flat fee. States like Ecuador sought to overhaul the balance of public and private gains from extraction, while others were able to reap the full benefits of the boom via control of existing, often revitalized state-owned mining and energy enterprises. In such cases, the growth of revenues was sufficient to provide a potential fiscal basis for a break with neoliberal policy constraints, opening the way for the formulation and implementation of new, nationally defined development strategies.

Chapter 2 outlined the conceptualization of neoliberalism employed throughout the book: as a (contradictory and uneven) global regime of accumulation, identified with the financial phase of a U.S.-led cycle of the capitalist world-system and observable in national policy orientations across the world. As has been well rehearsed in the literature, the rise of the neoclassical paradigm as economic orthodoxy, the faltering of the Fordist–developmentalist project, the increasing ascendancy of finance capital, and the post–Volcker shock Southern debt crisis all combined to set the scene for the globalization of neoliberalism. Despite variations in form, extent, and process, a standard laundry list of policies flowing from the watchwords of liberalization, privatization, and deregulation was widely implemented across most regions of the global South during the 1980s and 1990s, with notable exceptions.

These policies were not simply imposed upon an unwilling South by the North. In many cases, Southern elites trained in Northern economics departments enthusiastically jumped on the neoliberal bandwagon. Nevertheless, state managers in the large proportion of Southern countries struggling under the weight of severe indebtedness had little choice but to accept neoliberalization, no matter how grudgingly. Most obviously, chronic dependence upon IFI loans meant acquiescing to the conditionalities demanded as part of each structural adjustment program.[2] Where highly indebted states attempted to carve a path independent of IFIs, experiments with heterodox policy approaches resulted in severe punishments from creditors, triggering economic chaos, as in Argentina and Peru during the 1980s. A case like Jamaica, with its fractious history of relations with the IMF, could still, at times, reject engagement with the fund, though only while assiduously cultivating creditors' trust via a homegrown neo-liberalization program.

In this environment of indebtedness, the requirement to secure constant fiscal inflows from abroad, whether from IFIs, capital markets, or donors, therefore functioned as a powerful disciplinary force which mandated the adoption of a neoliberalizing political-economic orientation, whether will-ingly or via the lever of conditionality. As often occurred, governments might find ways to resist or stall implementation; the removal of subsidies or axing of public sector jobs might prompt protest and riots. What could not and did not occur, however, was any thoroughgoing reversal of the underlying neoliberal policy trajectory—not without almost complete dis-location from the global economy as the consequence. In this sense, and in the context of highly indebted states of the global South during the 1980s and 1990s, there really was little, if any, alternative.

In these cases, the emergence of any plausible alternative would clearly have to involve an end to chronic dependence upon IFI loans and Devel-opment Assistance Committee aid and thus an escape from neoliberaliz-ing conditionality (barring a sea change in economic thinking among cred-itor and donor nations). By allowing for huge increases in state revenues from resource exports (in both absolute and relative terms), the China-led commodity boom of 2002 to 2013 provided the building blocks for such alternatives. For the first time in decades, resource-rich highly indebted states in the South had access to a fiscal resource independent of IFIs, donors, and finance capital, and of sufficient weight to negate or at least mitigate the need for help from these external sources. Brazil's early payoff of IMF debts in 2005, Argentina's break with the fund following the 2002 collapse, and Angola's refusal to enter the Poverty Reduction Strategy Paper pro-cess after the civil war all are manifestations of a declining need for IFI assistance on the part of natural resource exporters. Less assistance, of course, meant less in the way of conditionality and supervision, paving the way for deviations from political-economic orthodoxy, while commodity revenues helped to pay for the emergent heterodoxies.

Just as maximizing the state's share of revenue from resource exports required conscious policy change on the part of governments, so too did the formulation and implementation of any policy program attempting to move away from the neoliberal status quo. It is for this reason that the first major claim of this research is framed in terms of necessity but not suffi-ciency. That is, a high export concentration in natural resources subject to increasing Chinese import demand is a necessary but not sufficient condition for a break with neoliberalism on the part of a given Southern state. The rise of China has not compelled states to follow post-neoliberal trajectories, but it did open the door—previously sealed shut by debt and conditionality—for them to do so.

Chapter 3 tested this proposition, using qualitative comparative analysis on a set of eighteen country cases from the global South during the 2002–2013 period. Within the specified scoping conditions (the most important being a high level of indebtedness), the findings give strong support for the proposition that post-neoliberal turns were possible only in those states affected by Chinese-driven shifts in the markets for energy commodities, metals, and soybeans. They further suggest that a lack of dependence on official development assistance was also a necessary condition for a break with neoliberalism to take place—a finding which I picked up again in chapter 8.

If a high degree of reliance upon these China-disrupted markets is a necessary but not sufficient condition for a state to break with neoliberalism, this raises the question of why such breaks occurred in some but not all states subject to this China effect. The second half of the book is concerned with this topic. In chapters 5 through 9, I presented a typology of resource-dependent Southern states whose export markets have been heavily affected by Chinese demand and where, therefore, according to the qualitative comparative analysis, the necessary condition for a break with neoliberalism was present during the 2002–2013 period.[3] From a subsequent detailed survey of fifteen such cases, I conclude that whether a post-neoliberal turn occurred or not in each case depends primarily upon the nature of state–society relations, particularly the balance of domestic social forces.

Building on transnational capitalist class theories and the work of Brent Kaup, I conceptualize neoliberal-era dependence upon external flows from IFIs and donors as corresponding to the ascendancy of transnational capital within the domestic sphere. The degree to which such dominance was directly exercised by external forces varied, though, and always involved partnership with transnationally oriented domestic capital whose interests lay broadly in tune with the neoliberal agenda demanded by the IFIs. Any significant deviance from the neoliberalizing path would prompt a withdrawal of external flows, with the ensuing economic meltdown making such maneuvers politically impossible, even for governments that had proposed breaking with neoliberalism while in opposition (as happened in much of Latin America). The political necessity for governments to maintain creditors' and donors' trust thus narrowed the bounds of the possible in terms of economic policy, even where constraints were not directly imposed via SAPs. In this way, the hegemony of transnationally oriented fractions of capital, both domestic and foreign, was maintained, placing the state out of bounds as a site of contention for possible rival fractions.

Seen in these terms, the impact of the commodity boom on resource-rich but indebted countries was to reignite competition for the state among the various arms of domestic society. The boom presented the potential for those in control of the state to capture new revenue flows independent of IFI and donor control. These new revenue potential streams were of sufficient size that, if tapped, they generally obviated the need to secure further IFI loans, while also reducing aid dependence in the poorest states. Control of the state under the new conditions, therefore, meant the possibility of policy change within a now far expanded spectrum, since creditors and donors no longer had the power to trigger a disastrous withdrawal of funds in response to departure from orthodoxy. With the capacity of their external allies to influence the domestic sphere drastically reduced, domestic transnationally oriented capital could no longer guarantee that the tools of the state would be deployed in the service of their interests. Instead, any social force or coalition capable of securing control of the state might plausibly use its new freedom of action to institute a new, and likely non-neoliberal, project of accumulation attuned to its needs above others.

On this theoretical grounding, I divided the fifteen cases of Southern resource-exporting states into five groupings, based on degree of family resemblance to five ideal types. These types consist of two major elements: the configuration of domestic social relations and a corresponding political-economic orientation, expressed via a set of policies that, for the most part, act to advance the interests of dominant classes and class fractions. For the purposes of the typology, I consider a break with neoliberalism to be the formulation and pursuit of a set of political and economic policies that conflict in substantive ways with orthodox goals of deregulation, privatization, and liberalization. While I judge it unnecessary for these programs to amount to a coherent, competently implemented, and theoretically informed vision in order to meet the definition of a post-neoliberal break, I did not include cases where only ad hoc reversals of neoliberal policies have occurred. My contention, essentially, is that a government's policy program should be considered post-neoliberal if it would have been infeasible under IFI supervision during the pre–commodity boom era.

Of the five types, three are identified as representing this kind of break: the neodevelopmentalist, extractivist-redistributive, and extractivist-oligarchic types. In ideotypical terms, the ND type denotes a state in which the receding power of transnationally oriented fractions of capital has allowed industrial capital to move back to the fore, in a coalition with popular class groups. It is no surprise that the two cases I include within the type, Argentina and Brazil, are two of the Latin American states that saw the most extensive industrialization and growth of urban classes under import substitution industrialization programs during the mid-twentieth century. Though diminished by the withdrawal of state support and the opening of markets during the neoliberal era, a sufficiently large industrial sector endured in these countries to provide the basis for an alternative, post-neoliberal accumulation project under commodity boom conditions. These programs built upon neodevelopmentalist thought developed in Brazil and, to a lesser extent, in Argentina, which sought to adapt the lessons of successful East Asian industrialization to the realities of a globalized economy. Following its decisive break with the IMF in 2002, Argentina was able move more quickly and decisively in implementing its version of neodevelopmentalism, compared to the gradualism seen in Brazil, and so Argentina was used in chapter 5 as the exemplar case for the type.

In many senses, the governments of both Nestor and Cristina Kirchner represented a return to the original Peronist program. State revenues, significantly aided by increasing taxes on booming soybean exports, were redistributed to domestic productive capital via a range of production and consumption subsidies, with some gains also for largely co-opted forces of industrial labor and the unemployed. Devaluation of the peso after the 2002 abandonment of the dollar peg (the centerpiece of previous agreements with the IMF) meant that an already high-productivity soy sector was given a major boost just as Chinese demand for soybeans as feedstock began to take off. The story of Argentina's impressive economic rebound after 2003 cannot be accounted for, in direct terms, by soy alone, and producers of goods for the domestic market were certainly also aided by the devaluation, which made imports of many consumer goods uncompetitive. The ability of soy exporters to turn a profit even as export taxes rose to levels of 35 percent, however, meant that the government was able to treat the sector much like an extractive industry. The ensuing rents were employed to reduce producers' energy costs as well as to grow the domestic market via wage increases and transport subsidies.

The limits to this strategy were laid bare in 2008, when an agriculturalist-led mobilization in rural areas led to the defeat in Congress of further export tax increases. Cristina Fernandez de Kirchner's government then sought to maintain its bankrolling of industrial policy, using a variety of alternative measures, in an effort to avoid reengagement with the IFIs, an outcome which would almost certainly have necessitated abandonment of the neodevelopmentalist model. Direct Chinese involvement, in the form of loans for infrastructure and, latterly, currency swap lines, were undoubtedly of use here. With mounting economic turbulence during the final years of Cristina Fernandez de Kirchner's administration, however, it was the unorthodox move to use central bank reserves to bridge fiscal imbalances that allowed her government to see out its second term without recourse to the IFIs and, most likely, the renewal of neoliberal conditionality. Though the decision to rely on reserves for this purpose may have been born of desperation, even having this policy instrument available depended upon the swelling of central bank coffers effected by the boom in soy exports, which was caused, in turn, by surging Chinese demand.

The extractivist-redistributive type—which includes Ecuador, Venezuela, and Bolivia—comprises a state with a weak and divided domestic bourgeoisie juxtaposed with relatively strong, if heterogeneous, popular class groups centered on a populist leader. Infighting among local capitalists allowed these populist rulers to gain and maintain power during the commodity boom via nearly constant campaigns of referenda and elections, frequently renewing their mandates and using this legitimacy as a basis from which to undermine traditional elites. In policy terms, an aggressive renegotiation of the state share in extractive revenues or ownership provided the fiscal base for redistribution, infrastructure development, and increased social spending.

Given the leading role played by popular classes, some observers on the left have been disappointed by both the failure on the part of ER governments to move beyond capitalism and the fact that extraction and sale of natural resources on the world market remains the fundamental dynamic of these economies. Certainly, this resource export has brought contradictions, as in Bolivia and Ecuador, where an expanding extractive frontier placed governments in conflict with previously supportive social movements.

Nevertheless, capitalism in general should not be confused with its neoliberal form in particular, and labeling any of the ER cases as neoliberal in orientation seems to fall squarely into this trap.

In Ecuador, Rafael Correa's administration oversaw the funneling of much-expanded oil revenues toward the Human Development Bond payment, which provided $80 per month to the poorest 40 percent of the population. Major public sector initiatives in transport and energy generation, backed by Chinese financing, sparked a boom in construction. Correa was able to implement these plans—as well as measures to disempower unpopular domestic financial groups and a vociferously conservative media—while simultaneously achieving a highly favorable renegotiation of Ecuador's debts to international creditors. There is every reason to believe that a counterfactual Ecuador, which did not experience a surge in oil revenue, would have remained chronically dependent upon IFI loans. As such, an agenda such as Correa's would remain beyond the realm of possibility, since, in this scenario, the IMF would retain the ability to engender economic chaos via the withdrawal of credit—a tool which held little force under commodity boom conditions.

The third group that I judge to merit the label post-neoliberal, in terms of political-economic direction of travel, is the extractivist-oligarchic type, which includes Angola and Kazakhstan. In these states, an absence of powerful and autonomous domestic class fractions produced a situation in which the state managers themselves formed the dominant social force, via their control of the external rents that passed through the domestic sphere. Even prior to the commodity boom, state elites in such cases would tend to use their centralized control of rents as a means through which to distribute patronage to various tiers of supporters, thus cementing their rule. During the neoliberal era, a large proportion of the external flows on which this system rested were conditional upon acceptance of neoliberal reforms. With the onset of the commodity boom, however, this was no longer the case, with rising resource rents allowing for an expansion of patronage networks while obviating the need to follow IFI-mandated policy.

In Angola, the exemplar case for the type, decades of civil war meant that, unusually, the country had never fully experienced direct IFI or donor supervision, up to the end of hostilities in 2002. With a dire need to repair public finances in the aftermath of the war, it seemed likely that the government's resistance to donor demands for liberalization would soon falter and Angola would join almost every African state in agreeing to a PRSP process. The failure of this to occur is often ascribed to China's entrance onto the scene and the signing of several of the loans-for-oil deals that have become synonymous with Angola. However, as chapter 7 showed, the accelerating rise in oil revenues, which began during the same period, is almost certainly of greater causal significance in explaining the Popular Movement for the Liberation of Angola government's ability to turn its back on donors and IFIs.[4]

Without externally imposed policy constraints, Angola's postwar economic strategy, rhetorically at least, rested upon a pre-neoliberal developmentalist vision of state-led reconstruction and the creation of a national bourgeoisie. These plans mainly existed to justify a highly inequitable distribution of oil-derived patronage to an urban elite. A huge program of infrastructure reconstruction may, in reality, have had more to do with opportunities for predation than with any genuine developmental ambitions. Nevertheless, extensive new road and rail networks were created. Other projects, in agriculture, food distribution, and manufacturing, have apparently failed as developmental initiatives. However, the sheer quantity of oil rent passing through the Angolan economy had the potential to shift elite strategies from sheer plunder and patronage toward accumulation. Here, I draw on the sequence of historical growth of a domestic capitalist class in the Gulf states as a point of possible comparison.

The other two types identified are populated by states that have not moved to break with neoliberalism, despite possessing the natural resource sectors that would have allowed them to do so under boom conditions. I ascribe the three distinct post-neoliberal trajectories in the first three types discussed to differences in domestic social configurations; likewise, I argue that these factors largely explain the maintenance of the neoliberal status quo for the remaining two types. In terms of social forces, however, the first of these remaining types, donor-dependent orthodoxy, is similar to the EO type. I explain the divergence between EO and DDO cases since 2002 in terms of an additional factor: the experience of aid dependence.

In the DDO states of Zambia, Mongolia, and Laos, as in the EO cases, political rulers have long leveraged control of the state—and thus access to the entry point for externally derived revenue flows—in order to support clientelistic rule. Unlike the EO cases, however, in DDO states, aid made up a significant proportion of these patronage resources and was subject to approval by a donor community wedded to a vision of development that was fundamentally grounded in neoliberal principles. As prices for their resource exports rose, beginning in the early 2000s, aid dependence in DDO states correspondingly declined, opening the path for a possible break with the donors' agenda.

However, with much of the legitimacy of their rule having been cemented through patronage networks built on the distribution of aid flows, state managers in DDO states appeared hesitant to risk the loss of these rents, which continued to provide an important, if diminished, source of income. In contexts where no domestic class forces of sufficient size or organization existed to push state elites into action, there seemed little reason for elites to act to challenge the status quo. EO governments, by contrast, had little to lose from the assertion of policies running contrary to the wishes of donors, from whom they received very little.

The Zambian case is particularly important because, first, it demonstrates that a post-neoliberal turn was certainly possible in a DDO state during the boom years and, second, it shows the significance of organized social forces for pushing through any break that might occur. The Patriotic Front government in Zambia rose to power on the back of a populist campaign, which activated an alliance of mineworker unions, marginalized groups in the Copperbelt, and rural dwellers linked by kinship to the urban core. Although the Patriotic Front drew support with promises of redistribution to these groups, once in government, they declined to pursue any real challenge to the country's neoliberal direction of travel, despite some individual policy changes that demonstrated the ability to do so. In chapter 8, I contrasted the situation in Zambia with that seen in Bolivia, arguing that less extensive class formation in Zambia led to a failure of the movement behind the PF to encompass popular classes nationwide. As a result, while mineworkers and their Bemba relatives in the north of the country could secure a narrow electoral victory for the PF, they could not form a broad front capable of formulating a comprehensive political vision for the nation as a whole or of pressuring the new government into substantive change.

The final type, homegrown orthodoxy, denotes a domestically driven continuity in policy direction from the preboom years. Encompassing South Africa, Peru, Indonesia, and Colombia, these are states in which the transnationally oriented elements continued to make up the dominant domestic class fraction through the course of the boom. Thus, whereas in other types boom conditions acted to lift externally imposed neoliberal discipline, such conditions had little effect on the trajectories of HO states.

In these cases, neoliberalization had been and continued to be driven primarily by domestic forces. In Peru, for example, the government of Ollanta Humala was staffed with a revolving cast of ministers from across the political spectrum, but, subject to pressure from powerful domestic business interests, they maintained the neoliberalizing course that has remained the constant core of Peruvian governments since the shock therapy of Alberto Fujimori.

Turning toward an analysis of current and future scenarios, significant political-economic impacts flowing from commodity price movements are far more likely to be induced, sustained, or undermined by market trends over the medium to long term rather than by short-term fluctuations. This is evidenced by the relative lack of impact upon post-neoliberal turns of the 2008–2009 price "glitch" following the global financial crisis. It therefore seems of little value to examine in detail the kinds of short-run projections that are commonly published in the financial press.

It is worth remembering that price trends do not automatically follow the mechanics of the global economy. The centrality of oil (and, to a lesser extent, of other hydrocarbons) to industrialized production and consumption has made energy resources a major nexus of geopolitical competition, particularly since the heyday of the NIEO in the 1970s, meaning that political and security issues play a significant role in driving price trends. Though other extractives are less fundamental to the functioning of the global economy, it may be that, should sources become increasingly marginal, risky, and scarce, similar kinds of security issues might arise in, for example, copper or rare earth metals, as extraction becomes a "race for what's left" (Klare 2012). For slightly different reasons, a similar argument applies equally to agricultural sectors, given a rising global population, the threat to arable land posed by climate change, and the increasing use of land to produce biofuels (White et al. 2012; Cotula 2012).

Even if competition for resources does not reach the point at which its main contours become those of geopolitical struggle, some recent assessments agree that constrained supplies are likely to result in prices remaining at relatively high levels for most commodity categories over the longer term (United Nations Conference on Trade and Development 2014, 12; Canuto 2014). Malthusian predictions of the exhaustion of natural resource reserves have proven incorrect, or at least premature, more than once in the past (*Economist* 2013), as increasing prices have driven various combinations of conservation, substitution, exploration, and technological advancement.

Nevertheless, and especially with the looming threat of climate change, shifts in patterns of production and resource use may well see demand for some commodities diminish significantly (as with fossil fuels), while others (such as lithium or nickel, for example) may become much more important.

While all of these factors seem certain to factor into any future scenarios, the depletion of many of the most accessible reserves means expansions now involve the opening of new and expanding of older resource frontiers, giving rise to a pattern of cyclical swings. Essentially, new production takes time to come on line and meet expanding demand, making for a shortfall and increasing prices, before tending to overshoot with a supply glut, reducing prices and making investment less attractive (and thus sowing the seeds for an eventual new round of shortfall in supply). However, many of the deposits that are newly being exploited have very high operating costs for extractive capital, either owing to technical difficulty, as with shale gas and the deepwater pre-salt Brazilian oil reserves, or to political risk, as in, for example, the Chinese-owned Mes Aynak copper mine in Afghanistan (Loewenstein 2015). A 2013 McKinsey study, whose conclusions are broadly in line with recent work by the IMF and UNCTAD, concluded that long-term supply costs (and, indeed, the costs of locating new reserves) seem set to increase across most commodities, even given likely advances in technology and efficiency (Dobbs et al. 2013).[5]

Although global commodity supplies may become increasingly constrained, it seems likely, though not certain, that demand for many will continue to rise over the medium to long term, if perhaps not at the same rate as experienced during the commodity boom (International Energy Agency 2018). Moves toward renewable energy (especially hydropower and solar) are starting to ramp up, especially in China (Kong and Gallagher 2017). However, China's consumption of coal—still its most important fuel source—is shrinking slowly, if at all (Hao and Baxter 2019), and the country is still funding the development of coal plants in other countries, alongside financing for renewable energy under the Belt and Road Initiative (Shearer, Brown, and Buckley 2019). Despite a continued reliance on coal, various initiatives are under way in China to shift toward relatively less-polluting fuels, including natural gas (International Energy Agency 2018).

For metals, the IMF model gives a high current income elasticity of consumption, in a sector where China is clearly already the major driver of demand (see tables 10.1 and 10.2). Interestingly, however, there is a predicted divergence in income elasticity of demand among metals as incomes rise and consumption patterns change. If the PRC shifts toward lower relative levels of infrastructure development and more consumer durables consumption—as the IMF (2014b, 37–39) argues has already begun to happen—rising demand for copper and iron ore may level off in favor of higher-grade metals such as aluminum and zinc. Clearly, this may have important consequences in terms of relative gains for different types of commodity exporters and may offer some hope to bauxite/aluminum-producing states such as Jamaica, which to this point have largely missed out on the China-led boom.

Similar trends are already evident in agriculture. Part of the reason for including soy along with minerals and fuels in earlier chapters' analysis is the relatively larger price effects of Chinese demand here when compared to other agricultural commodities. Chinese soy consumption is linked to a move toward intensive livestock (particularly pig) farming in order to meet demand for meat as food preferences change with rising incomes (Hansen and Gale 2014). The notion that China has led a "land grab," buying up arable land in Africa and elsewhere for the purposes of domestic food security, seems to be overblown (Brautigam and Zhang 2013). Nevertheless, with major environmental problems in China, including desertification of fertile land, import demand for food commodities, particularly of protein sources, might well produce a level of impact for certain agricultural exports similar to that seen since 2003 in soy and hard commodities.

As was detailed in chapter 5, soy industries such as those in Argentina and Brazil are, from the point of view of a state, somewhat similar to natural resource sectors in terms of the potential for revenue capture. Even with a major boost to price levels, state retention of a large proportion of the surplus from most other kinds of agricultural exports may prove more difficult, given the greater prevalence in the global South of labor-intensive production dispersed among smallholders or relatively large numbers of individual farmers. It is certainly possible that the spread of industrialized agriculture may alter these variables significantly, though this would be difficult to manage without causing widespread dispossession and unemployment. Another possibility would be a return to something along the lines of the agricultural marketing boards seen in many Southern states during the developmentalist era, which acted as monopsony buyers for export commodities and used this position to save revenues toward development projects.[6]

Overall, in terms of future demand for commodities within the PRC, most of the IMF, International Energy Agency, World Bank, and UNCTAD projections have been based upon the assumption that Chinese GDP growth will continue broadly within its post-slowdown "new normal" (*South China Morning Post* 2016) range of perhaps 6 to 8 percent per year until 2030. The accompanying, rather breathless list of postulated implications—a jump from seventy-five to six hundred cars per thousand people by 2030 (Clemente 2015), 1 billion urban dwellers by 2030 (*Economist* 2014), two hundred new cities with populations between 1 million and 5 million—would perhaps seem highly dubious, had the record of Chinese development in past decades not produced change at a similarly implausible pace. Nevertheless, with the impact of a U.S.–China trade war and a generally slowing global economy, the IMF has revised down its growth projections for China, to around 5.5 percent per annum by the middle of the 2020s (International Monetary Fund n.d.). All of these efforts are necessarily somewhat speculative, but given China's present weight within the global economy, even a scenario of slower growth in the PRC would seem to suggest rather momentous future requirements in terms of infrastructure, transport, and household consumption, particularly when the Belt and Road Initiative is added to considerations.

In the most direct sense, BRI projects provide a way to absorb at least some of China's surplus production of steel, cement, and other inputs. But since the BRI is not a single blueprint but an umbrella term under which new projects may continually be proposed and added, it is extremely difficult to come up with reliable estimates of the total financing or the extent of infrastructure development that will eventually be involved (Cai 2017; Dollar 2018; Chin and Gallagher 2019). This is doubly the case when one considers political uncertainties, as there has been considerable controversy in some BRI states around the costs of agreed projects as well as fears of growing Chinese influence (Soeriaatmadja 2019; Mundy and Hille 2019).

Major BRI investments such as the China–Pakistan Economic Corridor (which connects the western Chinese city of Kashgar to the Arabian Sea and includes roads, rail, a gas pipeline, telecom links, dams, and coal power plants) are to a large extent designed to "crowd in" further investment from both Chinese and other sources. As such, the impact of BRI on commodity markets will depend to a significant degree on how far such planned megaprojects are able to stimulate overall development, both in the countries concerned and in more peripheral parts of China to which they are connected (Cai 2017). Related to that possibility, though not entirely dependent on it, is the question of whether rapidly growing economies other than China's, especially in South and Southeast Asia, might provide a new engine of growth for the global economy, particularly if the Chinese miracle should finally falter. While it seems clear that, as far as commodities go, there is no new China, robust demand from India and other large states, such as Indonesia, could help to ensure that commodity prices do not decline back toward preboom trends, at least (Humphreys 2018).

Nevertheless, as Hung (2008, 150) reminds us, "the experiences of Japan plunging into a decade-long crisis right at the peak of the 'Japan as No. 1' talk and the outbreak of the 1997/1998 Asian financial crisis in the middle of the widely envied 'Tigers miracle' do remind us of the plausibility of abrupt, unexpected turnabout of a booming economy." In China's case, perhaps such a turn of events would not be entirely surprising. Writing before the 2008 crash, Hung identified the factors that, to this day, leave China vulnerable to economic crisis: a disjuncture between high levels of investment and low levels of consumption, with excess capacity met only through the continued growth of export markets. Before 2008, a symbiotic though dysfunctional relationship between China and the United States powered both Chinese and global accumulation, as expanding production in the PRC was soaked up by a credit-fueled consumer boom in the United States. The other side of this huge trade imbalance was the continuing purchase of U.S. Treasury Bills on a massive scale, underwriting the dollar's hegemonic position and essentially allowing the U.S. government to continue operating without any serious balance of payments constraint (Hung 2013).

In the wake of the 2008 crisis, recession in the United States, and in the global North more generally, effectively meant that one half of this cycle temporarily ceased to function. The Chinese government's response was to plug the loss of export markets through a huge stimulus package of infrastructure development, cheap credit, and industry restructuring, equivalent to 12.5 percent of GDP (Naughton 2009). This led to a surge in resource imports, which was largely responsible for the quick rebound of global commodity prices following the crash. Annual Chinese GDP growth was duly maintained above 9 percent from 2008 to 2011, though at the cost of deepening the contradictions already evident in the growth model by further widening the tendential gap between overinvestment and under-consumption, with no guarantee of a return to business as usual in export markets (Breslin 2011a).

Much of the stimulus was earmarked for regional authorities' use on construction projects of various kinds (Naughton 2009). Unusual financing arrangements mean that Chinese regions tend to rely to a great extent upon the sale of long-term land leases to balance budgets, and they increasingly use an unregulated shadow banking sector (Breslin 2014). Some argue that the construction boom has not, overall, misallocated resources on the grand scale that is often alleged or created the apparently useless ghost cities that have often featured in Western media reports of recent years (Anderlini 2014; Reuters 2015). But, more broadly, there can be few doubts about the vulnerabilities inherent in China's extraordinary credit boom, which a 2018 IMF paper cited as one of the largest, and certainly the longest, on record (Chen and Kang 2018). According to the same article, it took three times as much credit in 2016 as it took in 2008 to achieve the same amount of growth, as new loans are used to repay existing debts and it becomes ever more difficult to find destinations for productive investment.

However, the PRC is less vulnerable to full-blown financial meltdown than many other states, principally because of its enormous currency reserves, capital controls, and state ownership of the banking sector. While this means that the government has ample capacity to prop up the financial system for the foreseeable future, the ability to keep "kicking the can down the road" in this way has drawn comparisons to Japan, where, after the bursting of a speculative bubble in 1989, the government continued to prop up "zombie" banks and firms, moves which are often seen as a major contributor to Japan's subsequent stagnation (Krugman 1998; Yao 2018).

Whether a crash occurs in China or not, the notion that comprehensive rebalancing away from exports and toward investment in domestic consumption is necessary to the long-term health of the PRC's economy has become a major theme of non-Chinese media coverage and is clearly also a preoccupation of the current leadership (Heydarian 2015). As Breslin (2013) points out, the crux of the problem has been understood in domestic policy circles for some time, first being raised after the late 1990s Asian financial crisis. Efforts to effect systemic change have been piecemeal, though they do point toward means by which the party leadership may be able to change course. For instance, in the mid-2000s, rural taxes were lifted and the government purchase price for agricultural products increased, easing the pressure on the countryside and, in turn, slowing the flow of rural–urban migration, which had been the foundation of the low-wage manufacturing economy (Zhan and Huang 2013). The result was a modest increase in wages, though any more ambitious plans toward rebalancing that may have existed at this point were shelved in the face of the 2008 crash.

Powerful coastal interests have, it seems, repeatedly acted to slow or stymie any reforms that might undermine the export industries from which they benefit (Breslin 2014; Hung 2008). More broadly, though, any significant reorientation is likely to be a slow and complex process (ten Brink 2014), and it risks unpicking the threads upon which China's impressive growth record (and, with it, a major source of legitimacy for the Communist Party) rests. Given reports of localized but persistent social unrest (Zhou and Banik 2014), the unemployment that may result from rebalancing is a serious concern for the leadership. Similarly, current high levels of household saving are induced by the lack of social provision on the part of the government. This is despite very low (and often negative) real interest rates, which have effectively meant a massive subsidy from households to the banking sector (Breslin 2014). Thus, it would seem that shifting to a consumption-based growth model would require major—and no doubt, in the short term, painful—structural change across the whole economy.

Switching focus once again to the *longue durée*, the major contradictions evident in China's accumulation path do not necessarily point toward its exhaustion, even should a major crash occur. It is worth remembering that, in Arrighi's schema, such crises, while by no means given, are likely to crop up in rising centers of accumulation that develop, to some extent, outside the full constraints of the prevailing regime of accumulation. In such cases, a period of breakneck, reckless growth terminates in crisis, but this does not significantly affect the rising economy's deeper-rooted positional advantages, which arose from the contradictions of the prior regime and made the original burst of accumulation possible (Arrighi 2010). On previous, similar occasions, such as the Wall Street crash in 1929, crises in ascending powers have tended to force a search for structures within which growth might be reestablished and stabilized.

It is of course obvious that today's global economy differs in very many respects from that seen on the eve of the Great Depression. For China, in particular, a closer analogue may well be with the position of the United States toward the close of the nineteenth century. It is a country in the midst of a period of rapid industrialization and on the verge of becoming the world's largest single economy, though still clearly struggling with apparently anachronistic institutional forms and occupying a subordinate position within global structures centered around an existing hegemon.

Among the many distinctions between today's China and the United States of the Gilded Age, perhaps one of the most consequential for the rest of the world is the different level of external political–economic linkages seen in the two rising powers. One of the foundations of the rise of the United States in the late nineteenth century lay in its large and relatively autonomous domestic market, fed by raw material inputs largely sourced within the United States or in neighboring countries (Wright and Czelusta 2004; Bonini 2012). The fortunes of a rising China, by contrast, have been intimately linked with the quest for export markets and, increasingly, by the need to source primary commodity inputs from all corners of the globe.

Given the scale of China's globalization, even while at still relatively low levels of per capita GDP, speculation about the prospects for Chinese hegemony, collapse, or deceleration is not required in order to demonstrate the profound disruption that the PRC has already produced in the structures of the world economy. This book has provided evidence of the scale of this phenomenon, which loosened previously solid transnational constraints and, through shifting the entrenched patterns of global commodity markets, afforded natural resource–exporting states of the South a level of freedom to define their own development strategies—a degree of freedom which most had not enjoyed in decades. Without the rise of China, such autonomy would have remained a distant mirage.

Research Design

Qualitative Comparative Analysis and Interviews

This book makes two key claims, which are summarized in the introduction as follows:

Claim A. For states in the global South with substantial levels of public debt, a high export concentration in point-source natural resources (particularly fuels and minerals), imported in large and growing quantities by China, was a necessary but not sufficient condition for a break with neoliberal policy orientation during the years 2002 to 2013.

Claim B. For each resource-exporting state, whether such a break occurred—as well as its form and direction—depended primarily upon the dynamics of its domestic state–society relations.

Qualitative comparative analysis is used to test claim A, and the results are summarized in chapter 3. This appendix provides a more detailed rundown of the research design pertaining to this aspect of the book. The use of Charles Ragin's (1989, 2008) qualitative comparative analysis approach means that some of the common methodological trade-offs in deciding between qualitative and comparative may be transcended, to some extent. Briefly, QCA mimics the thickness of qualitative case-based comparative studies but enables the comparison of a much larger number of cases than is typically possible with such methods. It does so by following case-based analysis with the reduction of each case to a configuration of conditions (the equivalent of variables in QCA nomenclature), which then may be easily compared.

I employ QCA in the first stage of this research in order to assess the credibility of the central hypothesis and to explore for other potentially causally important conditions, using a set of nineteen cases from the global South. Even though many of the conditions I set out here are based in quantitative indicators, it is still the case that their selection and operationalization are both theoretically informed and rely on an understanding of individual cases and their contexts.

QCA was also chosen because it is particularly suitable for testing causality in terms of necessary conditions, even if it is perhaps most commonly associated with for tests of sufficiency (see, for example, Rihoux et al. 2013; Kirchherr, Charles, and Walton 2016). The use of QCA as a first stage in a mixed-methods approach is well established (Liebermann 2005; Schneider and Rohlfing 2013). However, in much of the discussion on mixed methods, the goal is to combine two methods to generate and/or test the same hypothesis (or hypotheses), with, for example, a small number of case studies being used to establish a series of claims, which are then tested across a method like QCA, which allows for greater generalizability.

The research design here is different because the two methods used (QCA for claim A and case studies/typology formation for claim B) focus on testing and elaborating two different (but linked) hypotheses. The second stage, typology formation (the subject of chapters 4 through 9), involves a process of detailed case-based investigation, followed by the drawing out of sometimes quite complex dynamics and processes within the cases, and then finally an abstraction of these features into distinct types. QCA's basis in an operation of reducing cases to a series of discrete values indicating the presence or absence of fixed conditions means that it was not suitable for the second stage of research (though, with the typology now in hand, one potential way to extend the book's findings would be to test the claims that inform the typology, using QCA on a larger set of cases). Theoretical and methodological concerns relating to typology formation (and claim B) were dealt with in chapter 4. The rest of this appendix, therefore, is devoted to the QCA stage and the testing of claim A.

Making an empirical claim about the presence of one variable enabling, but not causing, a change in the value of another variable requires a different formulation than the probabilistic relationship assumed in most statistical models. QCA allows for this by considering outcomes and causes as subsets of one another. Cast in set-theoretic terms, my hypothesis may be restated as "instances of Southern states breaking with neoliberalism are a subset of instances of Southern states with high export concentrations in hard commodities demanded by China." Here, the outcome (break with neoliberalism) is presented as a subset of the cause (states with high export concentrations in resources). Expressed another way, the cause is a necessary but not sufficient condition for the occurrence of the outcome.

I define a break with neoliberalization as the adoption of an overall policy trajectory on the part of a given government that would not have been acceptable to international financial institutions or donors during the neoliberal era of the 1980s and 1990s and thus would have been impossible to enact without a highly damaging rupture with creditors or Development Assistance Committee members. Importantly, I conceptualize this as a question of direction of travel (i.e., whether a state's policies are oriented toward continuing neoliberalization or along a different trajectory), rather than of starting and ending points. So, for example, Venezuela is usually understood as having undergone less extensive neoliberal reform over the 1980s and 1990s than, say, Bolivia (Lora 2012), but nevertheless as having neoliberalized to some extent. I see Venezuela as having made a break with neoliberalism during the commodity boom period not because it was, so to speak, less neoliberalized than other cases at the end of the boom but because it shifted from an overall orientation of liberalization to a substantially different policy direction over the period (see chapter 6).

Since QCA demands relatively in-depth research on all cases used in the analysis, some initial selection to narrow down the number of cases to be considered is required, for reasons of practicality. The solution adopted here, in line with recommended practice within QCA (Rihoux and Lobe 2009), is to reduce the number of cases to a manageable level by identifying and selecting cases based on theoretically relevant background conditions. Though this may at times result in somewhat arbitrary cutoffs, a benefit is that such a method effectively controls for these conditions and therefore simplifies the identification of causality within each case. These scoping conditions do limit the applicability of the findings, in the first instance at least, to those cases considered. However, since the QCA (as well as the later empirical chapters) are concerned with the specification of causal mechanisms rather than simply correlation of cause and effect, the results, while not strictly generalizable outside the limits of the scoping conditions, should at least suggest whether similar mechanisms might apply, and in which cases.

First, all cases are drawn from the global South. The boundaries of the global South are somewhat subject to interpretation, but for the purposes of this analysis, I take it to include all states in Africa, Asia, Latin America, and the Pacific with a per capita gross domestic product lower than $20,000 in 2002 (World Bank n.d.).

Second, levels of indebtedness seem to have an important role to play both in neoliberalization and in putative breaks with it. High levels of public debt imply a lack of fiscal space with which to engage in discretionary spending, as well as a likely reliance upon IFI loans or aid, bringing the imposition of policy stipulations. A condition relating to debt levels thus does two things. First, it sets a higher bar for the hypothesis, in that the fiscal impact of China-driven export revenues (whether direct or indirect) must be significant enough to negate this strong prior debt constraint. Southern states with low levels of debt may find it much easier, should they wish, to adopt non-neoliberal policies without any help from hard commodity export revenues, given the weaker disciplinary strength of IFIs and financial markets that this implies. Second, all things being equal, highly indebted Southern states, through the extended reach of market discipline into their political economies, are likely to have experienced higher levels of neoliberalization than their less indebted counterparts. I therefore limit the case selection to states with external debt stocks equivalent to 40 percent or more of gross national income at the beginning of the commodity boom, using the average figure for 2001 and 2002 in order to smooth out any large temporary swings that may have occurred over these years (World Bank n.d.).

As a third scoping condition, it is assumed that any identifiable move away from neoliberalization requires a minimal level of political stability in order to successfully implement a chosen policy direction. For this reason, I rule out any states that experienced wars, revolutions, or sustained periods of widespread civil and political turmoil over the years 2002 to 2013.

Fourth, I exclude small states with populations under 10 million (as of 2016) (World Bank n.d.), which may be may be more easily influenced by external forces (Haggard and Kaufman 1989). Controlling for such conditions, even imperfectly, again enhances the comparability of cases. Further, a few states are omitted from consideration, owing to a lack of data on one or more of the conditions analyzed in the next section of this

TABLE A.1

Change in liberalization, 2001/2002–2013/2014

Angola	−0.64	Ghana	+0.54	Philippines	0.96
Argentina	−1.37	Indonesia	+0.49	Senegal	+0.60
Bolivia	−0.34	Kazakhstan	−0.51	Tanzania	+1.24
Brazil	−0.48	Malawi	+0.43	Uganda	+0.84
Ecuador	−1.13	Malaysia	+0.95	Venezuela	−0.41
Ethiopia	+0.19	Peru	+0.30	Zambia	+0.06

Source: Calculated from Fraser Institute, Economic Freedom dataset.

appendix. This leaves eighteen states from across the global South (including sub-Saharan Africa, Latin America, East Asia, and Central Asia) as cases for QCA analysis (see table A.1).

Analysis of Necessary Conditions

This section lists the conditions employed, for testing as to their possible necessity, and gives the theoretical rationale for their selection as potentially causally significant. Since I use the crisp set version of QCA, all conditions have only two possible (Boolean) values: 1, indicating the presence of the condition, or 0, indicating its absence. I explain how data has been operationalized and values of 1 or 0 have been specified in relation to each condition. Conditions are constructed by comparing the beginning of the boom with its end. The 2008–2009 crisis fell in the middle of this period and obviously had a major impact upon commodity markets, prompting interest in the ability of some resource exporters to use countercyclical policies in ways that had not been available to them during previous crises (Griffith-Jones and Ocampo 2009). I briefly discussed some of these moves in relation to particular cases in the book's later chapters. However, since this episode turned out to be a temporary pause rather than the end of the boom, here I look at changes that occurred over the whole length of the period.

• BRK: This is the outcome condition. A value of 1 indicates that the given state made a break with neoliberalism over the course of the commodity boom, whereas a value of 0 indicates that it did not. There have been several attempts over the years to put together inexes of liberalization across developing world economies. However, these tend to be limited in geographic coverage or in the indicators they survey (Lora 2012; Morley, Machado, and Pettinato 1999; Sachs and Warner 1995; Wacziarg and Welch 2008). Others seek to measure more expansive sets of indicators, such as institutional quality along with liberalization (as in the World Bank's Country Policy and Institutional Assessment scores). Two right-wing think tanks, the Heritage Foundation and the Fraser Institute, publish annual rankings of what they refer to as "economic freedom." On the face of it, neither of these is especially useful, because both conflate data on policy changes (such as rates of taxation or tariffs) with economic outcomes (such as the rate of inflation), as well as with broader issues beyond the realm of economic policy choice (as in the Fraser Institute giving a score for the impartiality of a country's court system). Naturally, putting these rather different categories together results in a ranking that tends to show those states with well-functioning institutions and good economic performance as the most economically free—precisely because all of these things are taken as indicators of economic freedom—lending a tautological character to these judgments.

However, the Fraser Institute's (n.d.) Economic Freedom dataset, in particular, is a useful source of data for my purposes. By selecting only indicators relating to core areas of economic liberalization, I construct an index that is used as the basis for scoring cases on the BRK condition. These indicators are size of government (based on share of government consumption in the economy, transfers and subsidies, state-owned enterprises and state investment, and top marginal tax rates); trade (tariff rates and nontariff barriers); and labor market regulations. Each of these three areas is scored from 0 (least liberalized) to 10 (most liberalized), on an annualized basis. I calculate overall scores for each case from a simple average across my three indicators.

Table A.2 shows the change in score between the average for 2001/2002 and the average for 2013/2014, for all eighteen cases. Positive scores indicate an overall increase in liberalization over the period and are assigned a 0 value on the BRK condition. Negative scores indicate a decrease in liberalization and thus are assigned a 1 value on the BRK condition (that is, as breaks with liberalization). Data for Angola, Ethiopia, and Kazakhstan only extends back to 2005, so for these cases, the change in liberalization

TABLE A.2

Qualitative comparative analysis truth table

Case	BRK	RES	CFF	POR	ODA	FDI	ENG
Angola	1	1	1	0	0	0	1
Argentina	1	1	0	0	0	0	0
Bolivia	1	1	1	0	0	1	1
Brazil	1	1	0	1	0	0	0
Ecuador	1	1	1	0	0	0	1
Ethiopia	0	0	1	0	1	0	0
Ghana	0	0	1	1	1	1	0
Indonesia	0	1	0	1	0	0	1
Kazakhstan	1	1	0	0	0	1	1
Malawi	0	0	1	0	1	0	0
Malaysia	0	0	0	1	0	1	0
Peru	0	1	0	1	0	1	0
Philippines	0	0	0	0	0	0	0
Senegal	0	0	0	1	0	0	0
Tanzania	0	0	1	0	1	1	0
Uganda	0	0	1	0	1	1	0
Venezuela	1	1	1	1	0	0	1
Zambia	0	1	1	1	1	1	0

shown in the table is calculated from the difference between the 2005 score and the 2013/2014 average.

• RES: This is the hypothesized necessary condition, indicating the absence or presence of a substantial export sector in energy commodities (crude petroleum, natural gas, and coking/metallurgical coal) and metals (including ores and refined metals, excluding gold and silver, and not including alloys or manufactures) subject to the China effect on prices and demand. As was explained in detail in chapter 5, this total also includes soybeans (and minimally processed soy products), because China's demand impact on the market for soybeans is comparable to that in metals and minerals, and because the particular structure of the soybean industry means that it has certain similarities with extractive sectors, uniquely among agricultural products that make up a substantial share of exports in any of the cases examined.

A score of 1 on this condition indicates a case for which total exports of commodities of this type averaged 25 percent or more of total merchandise exports during the 2002–2013 period. Data is drawn from the Chatham House Resourcetrade Database (Chatham House n.d.) and the UNCTADStat data center (United Nations Conference on Trade and Development n.d.). Alternative operationalizations are possible, using resource exports as a percentage of GDP or of government revenue. I deem the government revenue measure unsuitable because this partially depends upon government policy such as taxation and royalty levels, which themselves make up part of the outcome value (as a potential part of policy moves toward and away from a neoliberal trajectory). The 25 percent of exports threshold is adopted as being in line with conventions in much of the relevant academic and policy literature (see, for instance, Haglund 2011; Thomas et al. 2011) and on the basis of readily available data over the full period.

• ENG: Similar to the RES condition, but counting toward the 25 percent threshold export concentration exclusively in fuels (oil, natural gas, and coal) and excluding other natural resource commodities such as metals. This condition is included as a means of distinguishing between the causal impacts of natural resource export sectors in general and fossil fuels specifically. Data is again taken from the Chatham House Resourcetrade database.

• FDI: It is plausible that high levels of foreign direct investment may limit states' range of policy choices, in the sense that a market-friendly orientation may be required (or perceived to be required) on the part of a government to attract or sustain inward investment. Membership of this set covers those states whose average annual inward FDI flows as a percentage of GDP over the 2002–2013 period exceed the developing country average of 2.7 percent (calculated from UNCTADStat data center). This measure was adopted in preference to an indicator based on FDI stocks because FDI stocks may reflect legacies of investment undertaken before the period studied and therefore may have occurred under different global conditions (considering that extractive capital, in particular, tends to be relatively immobile). Also considered was inward FDI as a proportion of gross capital formation, though this was rejected on the grounds that gross capital formation appears to be correlated, to some degree, with level of development.

- ODA: The set of cases classified as being dependent on official development assistance, in the sense that the degree of reliance upon foreign aid to finance basic state functions means that donors control budgetary resources to an extent that may impose significant constraints on states' abilities to set policy independently. A standard measure of aid intensity is total aid flows per annum as a percentage of GDP, with a suggested threshold of 10 percent for aid-dependent status (Brautigam and Knack 2004). World Bank World Development Indicators give the slightly different but equivalent measure of net official development assistance (including concessional loans) as a percentage of gross national income. I use a threshold of 10 percent or more on this metric, averaged across 2002, for a case to score 1 on this condition. I reviewed the notion of aid dependence in chapter 8.

- CFF: Chinese financial flows. Tracking Chinese overseas finance is somewhat complicated by a lack of transparency in officially released numbers and by the fact that these flows do not always fit neatly into standard categories as per, for example, Organisation for Economic Co-operation and Development definitions of concessional finance (Brautigam 2011). This condition is meant to capture the totality of official Chinese financial flows, including aid (which is a relatively small component) as well as other official financing streams directed to governments and SOEs in each of the cases. In this sense, it is meant to represent a way to test for the causal impact of Chinese development finance, as analogous to the role of IFIs and established donors. The extent to which Chinese flows might differ in character, and the implications for recipient states in terms of policy autonomy, is a subject that has garnered considerable interest in the literature (Woods 2008; Gallagher, Irwin, and Koleski 2012; McEwan and Mawdsley 2012; Kragelund 2015).

I draw on AidData's Global Chinese Official Finance Dataset (Dreher et al. 2017) here, which covers the period 2000 to 2014. Earlier versions of this dataset have attracted some criticism (Brautigam 2013) for its reliance on media reports for data collection. However, newer versions appear to have addressed many of the earlier concerns. While the authors readily admit that this is a second-best source in the absence of reliable official data, it is nevertheless the only dataset of its type that spans all geographic regions of the South. I take note of the authors' advice by including only records marked "Recommended for research," these being projects at either the commitment, implementation, or completion stage (rather than those that have only been pledged). I score membership of this set based on total Chinese financial flows received as a percentage of 2014 GDP (International Monetary Fund n.d.), with a threshold of 4 percent. I come to this figure based on an appraisal of the significance of Chinese official finance in the various cases. Venezuela appears to have the lowest total (at 4.5 percent) among states where such financing has, on the face of it, played a major in the political-economic course of the period (Muchapondwa et al. 2016).

• POR: This condition measures changes in net portfolio investment in the balance of payments account for each case over the years 2002 to 2013. This is meant to give an indication of the behavior of external investors, in light of the possibility that their withdrawal of capital might serve to "punish" moves on the part of states to shift away from orthodoxy liberal policies (Campello 2007; compare with Block 1977). Here, I score cases as belonging to this set when they have an average annual net outflow of 0.5 percent of GDP or higher. Though movements in portfolio investment are likely to be affected by factors other than markets' judgments on policy choices, this nevertheless sets up a test of whether breaks from neoliberalism can take place in conditions of sustained capital flight over the period. What this condition does not test for is the impact of sudden capital stops.

Table A.2 gives the data used for the QCA in tabulated format (known as a truth table), showing the scores for each case across the range of conditions. Performing an analysis of necessary conditions for the outcome BRK (Using fsQCA software) gives the results shown in table A.3.

Table A.3 lists results of testing the presence or absence of each condition as a possible necessary condition for the outcome (BRK). The presence of a tilde (~) before a condition indicates a set negation—that is, testing for the absence of that condition. Consistency scores give a measure of the degree to which cases with a positive score on the outcome value are a subset of cases with a positive score for each particular condition. For instance, the consistency score of 1 for the condition RES, as shown in the table, means that cases where the outcome is present (that is, where a break with neoliberalism took place) are a subset of those where the condition RES is present (that is, those cases that are resource exporters). Thus, all

TABLE A.3

Analysis of necessary conditions

Condition tested	Consistency	Coverage
RES	1.000000	0.636364
ENG	0.714286	0.833333
CFF	0.571429	0.363636
POR	0.285714	0.222222
ODA	0.000000	0.000000
FDI	0.285714	0.222222
~RES	0.000000	0.000000
~CFF	0.428571	0.375000
~POR	0.714286	0.500000
~ODA	1.000000	0.538462
~FDI	0.714286	0.500000
~ENG	0.285714	0.153846

Outcome variable: BRK

cases where a break with neoliberalism took place are resource exporters—making the latter a necessary condition for the former. Significantly, ~ODA (that is, an absence of official development assistance dependence) is also a necessary condition for a break with neoliberalism to take place. I discussed this finding in more detail in the case study chapters, particularly chapter 8.

Some caution needs to be exercised here, particularly given the scoping conditions used to select cases (such as levels of indebtedness or population size), which limits the generalizability of the results, to some degree. Nevertheless, this finding is strong evidence in favor of my claim that a high concentration in resource exports demanded by China is indeed a necessary condition for a break with neoliberalism on the part of Southern states.

Coverage scores also are provided for each condition. These show the extent to which instances of a condition are a subset of those in which the outcome is present—essentially, the degree to which they are sufficient conditions for breaks with neoliberalism to take place. As can be seen, none of the conditions tested were alone sufficient for the outcome. However, ENG, the condition denoting a high export concentration in energy commodities, has a high coverage score—in fact, of the cases where ENG is present, only Indonesia did not break with neoliberalism.

The ten cases belonging to the set RES in the analysis make up the bulk of the cases explored in the typology chapters (chapters 4 through 9). I increase the set of typology cases to fifteen by relaxing the conditions on debt and population, in order to include Jamaica, Laos, Mongolia, South Africa, and Colombia in the comparison.

Interviews

Three of the cases included in the typology (Ecuador, Zambia, and Jamaica) are partly informed by short periods of fieldwork in each location over the course of 2013. Anonymous interviews are cited in relation to these cases in chapters 6, 8, and 9, corresponding to the lists of interviewees in tables A.4, A.5, and A.6.

TABLE A.4
Ecuador interviews

Interview Number	Organization	Position
1e	Universidad Andina Simón Bolívar	Academic
2e	Universidad San Francisco de Quito	Academic
3e	Opposition party	Politician
4e	Private Banking Association	Official
5e	West European Embassy	Official
6e	—	Former finance minister
7e	Patriotic Society Party	Politician
8e	Chamber of Commerce, Guayaquil	Official
9e ·	Chamber of Industry and Production, Quito	Official
10e	NGO (environment)	Official
11e	National Secretariat of Planning and Development (SENPLADES)	Official

TABLE A.5

Zambia interviews

Interview Number	Organization	Position
1z	Transnational mining firm	Official
2z	Norwegian embassy	Official
3z	British embassy	Official
4z	International financial institution	Official
5z	—	Former opposition party politician
6z	German Development Agency	Official
7z	University of Zambia	Academic
8z	United Party for National Development	Politician
9z	Patriotic Front	Local organizer

TABLE A.6

Jamaica interviews

Interview Number	Organization	Position
1j	University of West Indies	Academic
2j	Jamaica Labour Party	Former minister
3j	People's National Party	Politician
4j	Mining company	Bauxite mining expert
5j	Planning Institute of Jamaica	Official
6j	Nongovernmental organization	Official
7j	Private Sector Organisation of Jamaica	Official
8j	Jamaica Chamber of Commerce	Official
9j	—	Former senator

Notes

Introduction

1. There is also a connection between this kind of structuralist argument and several versions of the much-touted "resource curse" thesis, whereby resources are said to hinder attempts at development and growth. Most mainstream examinations of the resource curse rely on "internalist" accounts (Auty 1993; Sachs and Warner 1995; Pomfret 2012), which tend to argue for the uniquely distorting effects of resource-derived revenues on national institutions and political stability. Few of these accounts, however, consider the fact that natural resources appear to have been associated with relatively successful development in periods of more favorable terms of trade for raw material exports (Bonini 2012). The discussion of contemporary cases of resource-exporting states (chapters 5 through 9) suggests that a wide spectrum of institutional outcomes, ranging from developmental to predatory, are possible under commodity boom conditions. In any case, while the resource curse is one of the major lines of investigation on the connection between commodities and development, I do not devote a large amount of time to its consideration. My focus here is not on whether states can defy the supposed curse by adopting one or another of the various developmental programs that I identify as emerging since 2003 but on illustrating that it is the commodity boom (and, ultimately, the rise of China) that has made the pursuit of this range of options possible, whether successful or not.

2. I do not consider soft commodities—that is, food and agricultural inputs—as part of the analysis, for two reasons. First, while prices for these classes of goods rose over the period, these increases were proportionately smaller than those seen in energy and minerals. Second, the nature of the energy and minerals sectors as point source, nonrenewable, and capital intensive facilitates the ability of states to control access and extraction

(and thus revenue collection), unlike more diffuse and less capital-intensive sectors such as agriculture. One exception here is soybeans. The capital- and technology-intensive nature of production and high level of concentration in most producer countries' soy industries means that, in some respects, they approximate the features of an extractive rather than an agricultural sector. Price increases have also been substantial and have been driven by China. As I will discuss in chapter 5, these factors mean that soy industries were subject to changes similar to those seen in extractive sectors and thus potentially conferred similar advantages of policy autonomy (as occurred, especially, in Argentina).

3. I use the hyphenated term "Fordism–developmentalism" to denote the unified but variegated nature of global capitalism over the period from roughly the end of World War II to the onset of crisis, in the 1970s. As seen from the global North, this era is associated with the spread of Fordist mass production from North America to Europe and then to Japan, buttressed by high mass consumption and demand management grounded in welfare states and a broadly Keynesian approach to economic policy. Mass production was not extended to most of the global South and Northern consumption standards were achieved only by Southern elites. Nevertheless the principles of developmentalism (whether of the modernization or the structuralist variety) were largely of a piece with those informing policy in the North. Many institutional arrangements, meanwhile, were global in character (or at least in intent). These include the United Nations, the World Bank, and the International Monetary Fund but also the universalization of the nation-state.

4. My usage is borrowed from Harvey (2005, 11), who describes the separation of national spaces into relatively autonomous spheres during the developmentalist era as providing a force field, behind which domestic political struggle is isolated from the pressures of the world market.

1. World Markets in China's Wake

1. The first of these booms occurred at the height of the materials-intensive postwar reconstruction period (1951–1953), compounded by the effects of the Korean War, and the second was during the era of the first oil shock, 1973 to 1975. The latter episode is particularly interesting in that its structural conditions appear to be somewhat similar to those of today, with the United States apparently beginning to lose its hegemonic grip and with new challenges emerging in the global South, represented in the earlier period by the New International Economic Order. Though these attempts to present alternatives to the emerging shift between Fordism–developmentalism and neoliberalism failed for nonfuel commodity exporters and had a disappointing impact on a global scale, oil states did in fact manage to keep prices high for some time and often achieved rather impressive (albeit usually noninclusive) development in the wake of the oil shock. Many oil exporters, particularly in the Middle East, are still among the least neoliberalized states in the contemporary world, marking an interesting parallel with the claimed possibilities for other commodity exporters today.

2. The 1947–1975 period is sometimes identified as such a cycle (containing within it the two short-term booms mentioned in note 1), associated with reconstruction and industrialization in a range of economies and coinciding with the theoretical model discussed later, which posits this period as an era of material expansion within the U.S.-led secular cycle of accumulation that currently may be entering its final phases. The apparent stalling of the contemporary commodity boom from around 2014 may signal a somewhat premature end to the China-driven cycle or, alternatively, may represent a lull, should Chinese growth continue over the longer term or be replaced by expansion of other large economies in the South, such as India. (These and other scenarios will be considered in more detail in chapter 10.)

3. Demand for gold and diamonds is subject to rather different demand pressures, and China is not expected to become such a central driver here as for other commodities. Gold prices reached historic highs since the financial crisis as investors hedged against a weak dollar and other under-pressure currencies. This, though, along with the demand for diamonds, is not directly or substantially linked to the rise of China. For this reason, I do not include these commodities as part of the analysis.

4. In the wake of the financial crisis, many Western firms backed away from planned investments in extraction, discouraged by a short-term volatility associated with commodity speculation. Chinese firms (especially state-owned enterprises), however, tend to employ more patient capital and are less focused on short-term profit maximization (Lee 2014, 2017).

5. During the last period of sustained high copper prices in the 1970s, aluminum was used as a substitute for household wiring in the United States, a practice which stopped after a wave of fires resulted from the poorer quality connections.

6. Energy use per unit of gross domestic product tends to increase while an economy is industrializing, before declining at higher levels of GDP, when service sectors become progressively more important (though there is significant variation in the shape of this trajectory) (Humphreys 2018). South Korea is used as a comparator here because of its somewhat similar developmental path, which, like China's, included a heavy emphasis on investment and manufacturing.

7. The term "world-system" is most prominently associated with Immanuel Wallerstein and has been criticized from many angles, sometimes justly (Brenner 1977; Skocpol 1977; Wood 2002). I apply the label loosely here in recognition of the many elements that Arrighi's works share with the more Wallersteinian treatments of the world-system. A full survey of Arrighi's departures from Wallerstein's version lies beyond the scope of this book, though perhaps most important is the idea that the system is not a stable hierarchy but one that is subject to constant, open-ended, and qualitative transformation (Arrighi 1994; Arrighi and Silver 1999). Arrighi shares with Braudel (1982) the notion that each successive cycle of accumulation may, in many senses, be viewed as a separate world economy (or system) in its own right, making for a less deterministic structure than what has been termed Wallerstein's "orrery" (Pieterse 1988). This makes it easier, for instance, to incorporate the rise of China into the model, since the Wallersteinian alternative—that individual nations may well ascend in the world-system hierarchy but that this does nothing to alter the enduring structure—seems rather

far-fetched when considering a state that is home to around one-fifth of the global population and has averaged more than 9 percent annual GDP growth for more than three decades (Cheremukhin et al. 2015).

8. Perhaps one of the most significant interventions into the growing literature on China and development is Lee's (2017) *The Specter of Global China*, since it moves beyond the usual empirical analyses and offers a theorization of the nature of Chinese state capital as it appears in the global South. Lee's thesis is essentially that the Chinese state's "variety of capital" is driven by a distinct logic of accumulation (which incorporates political as well as profit-maximizing priorities) as compared with global private capital. As such—and as Lee shows with respect to Zambia—Chinese state capital potentially may be more flexible and accommodative of political demands on the part of states and social forces in host countries. This line of research holds a great deal of promise, though it is less applicable to the arguments of this book, which focus mainly on China-driven shifts in market conditions rather than on the direct impact of Chinese capital flows.

9. It is wise to be cautious in making predictions of this sort. For instance, a late nineteenth-century observer convinced of the merits of Arrighi's arguments might well have singled out Germany rather than the United States as the ascendant power more likely to replace Britain in the long run (see Arrighi 1994, 59–60).

10. Prices for many commodities began to rally in 2018, which has been variously ascribed to strong global GDP growth, the working through of a previous supply surplus, and production cuts in oil (OPEC) and in steel (China) (World Bank 2018; *Economist* 2018).

2. Natural Resources and Development Under Shifting Global Regimes

1. The use of natural resources, of course, long predates European arrival in most areas of the world, though colonialism, whether in the sixteenth-century Andes or in twentieth-century Southern Africa, tended to bring some combination of reorganization in production and exchange relations, extension of the extractive or agricultural frontier, and intensification of exploitation (see, for example, Bunker 1988). All of these changes fit the colonial notion of development detailed in this section.

2. Unless otherwise stated, in this chapter I use "European" to refer to European metropoles and their settler colony offshoots in what is now the global North.

3. Coercion and accumulation by dispossession often had a direct role to play in setting up this uneven playing field, most famously in the British destruction of the Indian textile industry.

4. For most of the book, I use the terms "core," "periphery," and "semiperiphery" in line with those understandings most commonly adopted in most world-systems literature (Wallerstein 1974; Hopkins and Wallerstein 1977; Arrighi and Drangel 1986; Goldfrank 2000), though at various points I discuss the problems that the rise of China may pose to this schema. When discussing structuralism, I employ "center" rather than "core," in line with this school's terminology.

5. There is a second strand of argument relating to declining commodities terms of trade, based on the concept of unequal bargaining power between center (scarce and organized) versus periphery (plentiful and atomized) labor. I do not explore this in greater detail here given my main focus on capital-intensive resource industries which require little labor to operate.

6. Notwithstanding Russian and then Soviet expansionism within Eurasia.

7. African socialist governments, for example, such as that of Julius Nyerere in Tanzania, often mixed European socialist concepts with a desire to restore what was often idealized as a classless precolonial society. Industrialization and developmentalism were still watchwords in these cases, however.

8. The greater endurance of higher oil prices can be ascribed to a combination of the Iranian Revolution in 1979 (bringing the second oil shock) and the comparative effectiveness of OPEC as a cartel, relative to similar bodies in, for example, copper. A scramble to develop new sources of oil created a dilemma for OPEC producers. One route was to ration production and thus keep prices afloat while seeing market share decline (and with it, eventually, OPEC's leverage as a cartel). The second was to abandon efforts to control market prices and instead to maximize production volumes, which, in the case of West Asian members, afforded an advantage based on low production costs (Al-Chalabi 1988). This latter course, eventually adopted in 1986, signaled a final shift of the global commodities regime, in line with the neoliberal order, as well as a return to principles of comparative advantage in trade policy.

9. As Babb (2013) points out, structural adjustment programs were somewhat marginal until they were backed by the United States following the Brady debt plan of the mid-1980s.

10. Harvey (2005, 45) notes that the template for the newly reoriented international financial institutions had its roots in the New York City debt crisis of the early 1970s, in which repayment of creditors became the overriding priority of settlement negotiations.

11. There are notable exceptions here, of course, not least in East Asia.

12. In fact, in cases with high levels of government debt, pressures toward neoliberalization have been extremely difficult to escape from, even when engagement with the IFIs has been rejected, as the experience of Jamaica in the 1990s illustrates (see chapter 9).

3. The Rise of China as a Necessary Condition for Post-Neoliberal Breaks

1. This chapter contains a summary of the qualitative comparative analysis process and findings. The appendix provides a more detailed discussion of issues such as case selection and operationalization of conditions (equivalent to variables in QCA nomenclature).

2. As noted, there clearly is a range of variation here. A number of East Asian economies were able to chart relatively independent policy courses and avoid excessive indebtedness, at least until the late 1990s crisis. Southern oil producers (such as Venezuela, Algeria, or Iran) often were able to hang on to statist features of their economies and liberalized at

a slower pace than many of their neighbors. And some of the largest Southern states (such as India and Brazil) also seemed to exercise more control over the pace and extent of reforms. But while processes of liberalization often were not fully implemented and experiences varied in terms of speed, scale, and scope, virtually no states in the global South have remained untouched by neoliberalization without suffering the severe consequences of dislocation from the global economy or earning political pariah status, as is the case with North Korea, for example.

3. Full details regarding methodological issues (for example, the decision to use crisp-set rather than fuzzy-set QCA), case selection, and operationalization of conditions can be found in the appendix.

4. The Organization for Economic Co-operation and Development's Development Assistance Committee is the primary coordinating body for the major sovereign foreign aid donors.

4. A Typology of Political-Economic Trajectories Under Commodity Boom Conditions

1. In the following discussion, the notion of political-economic orientation is framed primarily in terms of state–society relations and their expression in the form of state policy sets.

2. World-systems approaches have long been criticized for a failure to satisfactorily account for internal (especially class) dynamics (Brenner 1977; Skocpol 1977). Even world-systems scholars themselves are often pessimistic when it comes to bridging the analytical gap between global and the local scales (Bergesen 2015). My purposes here do not lie in resolving the many contradictions between globally and nationally framed accounts—much less controversies around the definitional nature of capitalism. Nevertheless, it seems perfectly possible, as in earlier literature (Cardoso and Faletto 1979; Paige 1978; O'Hearn 2001) to examine the inner relations of particular national societies and their states without giving up the notions of a larger (uneven) global parameterization of these workings or of an unequal world division of labor.

3. The results of these struggles also, in reciprocal fashion, feed back into redefining the global terrain, though, with a few important exceptions (not least China), most Southern states are far more shaped by than shaping of world economic conditions.

4. Perhaps the most prominent theoretical current on how to categorize states according to political-economic model or orientation is the varieties of capital school (Hall and Soskice 2001). Theoretically and empirically, I see the cornerstone of the typology I present here as the relationship between a given state's social dynamics and its policy orientation under the shifting conditions of insertion into the global political economy brought by the commodity boom. I therefore do not engage with varieties of capital models here, which tend to understand different types of capitalism primarily in terms of relatively enduring institutional complexes framed by national boundaries (Lee 2017, 163). There also is the problem that the majority of varieties of capital scholarship focuses on advanced economies—and that which looks at cases in the global South tends to

involve collapsing important variation among cases into expansive overarching categories (Nölke and Claar 2013). For example, most varieties of capital literature contends that all Latin American capitalisms belong to a single type of hierarchical market economy (Schneider and Soskice 2009).

5. I assign cases to one type or another based on shared characteristics, with the ideal type constructed according to the principle of family resemblance. This notion, first developed by Ludwig Wittgenstein, describes a means of placing cases into categories on the basis of shared overlapping features, without any one particular characteristic being required for category membership. Goertz (2006, 59–60) uses an example from Hicks, whose study of 1930s welfare states defined the latter as a system possessing at least three of five features (health insurance or pensions, for instance), without any one of the five being necessary. Such a conception is also widely used in medicine and psychology, with, say, the presence of any four of seven symptoms resulting in the diagnosis of a particular condition.

6. As Chibber (2003, 2005) has pointed out, the empirical record in many Southern states since World War II suggests that the existence of a separate, identifiable national bourgeoisie may be in doubt. In the main, Chibber's argument concerns the failure of any supposed domestically oriented capitalist fraction to fulfill the mission of national development, which has often been inferred from its apparent objective interests. Nevertheless, if an identifiable national bourgeoisie exists in a particular case, it may still be expected to press for policies generally associated with the developmentalist era—subsidies and protection of domestic markets, for instance—even if the intent here is more parasitic than developmental. This is what occurred in Chibber's main case of India.

7. Briefly and in ideotypical fashion, these two types of policy orientation are meant to signal a mixed economy, capital controls, selective trade barriers, import substitution industrialization, and industrial policy more generally (developmentalism) versus privatization, financialization, deregulation, and open trade.

8. To the extent that rival groups may be dependent upon sales in the domestic market, structural adjustment program–mandated trade liberalization also would have a part to play in this process.

9. Global, regional, and bilateral agreements may still rule out the application of certain protective tariffs and industrial policies.

10. I adopt the term "popular classes," rather than "proletariat" or similar, primarily in recognition that, in most of the Southern societies discussed in the following chapters, the proportion of wage laborers is low in comparison to those in the informal sector or in the (perhaps not adequately labeled) semiproletariat (Schneider and Enste 2000). In discussion of several of the cases, I detail the circumstances under which it may be possible for different configurations of these groups to work together to advance common interests. I therefore use "popular class" in a broad manner, similar to Goran Therborn's (2012) preferred terminology of "plebeian."

11. As occurred during the first term of Alan García in Peru and the administration of Raúl Alfonsín in Argentina.

12. Of course, clientelistic governance is not singular, and much recent literature explores its various forms and their potential implications for development, often, though not

exclusively, in the African context (see, for example, Khan 2010; Kelsall 2012; Abdulai and Hickey 2016; Behuria, Buur, and Gray 2017). Something along the lines of a "political settlement" approach may be a productive avenue through which to extend the analysis of my typology cases, although, with the book's already rather involved theoretical framework, such an effort lies beyond my scope here.

5. Neodevelopmentalist Type: Argentina and Brazil

1. In this respect, neodevelopmentalism is similar to the neostructuralist work that began to emerge from the Economic Commission for Latin America and the Caribbean (commonly known by its Spanish acronym, CEPAL) in the 1990s (Sunkel and Zuleta 1990; Sunkel 1993; Leiva 2008). Certainly most neodevelopmentalist work owes a debt to this school. Where they differ crucially is in the neodevelopmentalist core belief in maintenance of a high exchange rate, implying a more interventionist macroeconomic approach than would be countenanced by the neostructuralists, who regard devaluation-derived competitiveness as "spurious."

2. Indeed, one of the major differences between neodevelopmentalism and older Latin American developmentalist efforts is a partial retreat from concern with the structural underpinnings of global trade.

3. In 2002, general government debt as a percentage of gross domestic product stood at 79 percent in Brazil and 138 percent in Argentina (International Monetary Fund n.d.).

4. It is not at all clear that the commodity boom made corruption worse in either case. In Brazil, for example, the *lava jato* (car wash) scandal has implicated a wide range of politicians from all major parties as well as prominent businesspeople and executives at the state-owned oil company Petrobras. But such bribery is not by any means a novel feature of the boom or the Partido dos Trabalhadores eras. Instead, it has been a pervasive element of Brazilian politics since the return of democracy in the 1980s, rooted in the country's electoral system (Anderson 2016).

5. These being former president Carlos Menem, who had been the chief architect of neoliberal reform during the 1990s, and Ricardo Lopez Murphy, a Chicago-trained economist with strong ties to the international financial institutions (and briefly economy minister, in 2001). In a crowded field, Menem scored a narrow first-round victory, with Nestor Kirchner in second place, though Menem then forfeited the election when it became obvious that Kirchner was set for a second-round landslide.

6. There is a high degree of correspondence and exchange between Brazilian scholars and their Argentinian counterparts, with the neo/post-Keynesian Phoenix Group, formed at the University of Buenos Aires in 2001, being a key source of policy advice in the initial stages of the Nestor Kirchner government (Ferrer, Clemente, and Rofman 2004). However, for the sake of clarity, I rely largely upon Brazilian authors for the theoretical exposition of Latin American neodevelopmentalist thought, since this tradition is arguably more fully developed and has certainly attracted more commentary and debate.

7. There are indications that China may begin to rely upon grain and other agricultural imports in the next decade (*Economist* 2015; Hansen and Gale 2014), at which point it is

possible that a comparable China effect on markets for these products may emerge, with similar potential consequences for exporting countries.

8. As will be discussed in more detail with regard to the Argentinian case, the fact that the vast majority of soy production in both countries is exported enhances this effect, because changes in export taxes on soy therefore have very little direct bearing on domestic markets.

9. The International Monetary Fund also signaled concern—the negotiation of a new $30 billion loan package with the outgoing Cardoso government, in 2002, was explicitly designed to lock any successor administration into fiscal austerity and primary surpluses. The agreement also mandated central bank independence as a key means of maintaining policy continuity (Morais and Saad-Filho 2003).

10. Many of these firms would be those later implicated in the *lava jato* (car wash) scandal, leading to many of their executives being convicted on corruption charges.

11. It is worth clarifying here that two rather distinct groupings benefited from the changes during the Menem era: domestic manufacturing sectors and manufacturers integrated into international supply chains (especially the auto industry); and agribusiness, especially with the introduction of "no tillage" systems and other technologies that greatly increased yield and extended cultivation to the dry Northwestern provinces.

12. Beef and wheat exports were also taxed, and at times even banned, across the two Kirchner administrations, with the intent of depressing prices, as a means of containing both inflation and wages. Soy exports have more than compensated for any impact such measures have had on external trade, however.

13. These sorts of taxes were especially attractive because they could be imposed by presidential decree and were one of the few forms of taxation that did not have to be shared with provincial governments under the terms of the 1990s decentralization.

14. Somewhat ironically, the rents from agricultural export taxes were in part responsible for the ability of the government to maintain the weak peso, which benefited the rural bourgeoisie greatly, though this was a measure mainly meant to help industrial sectors.

15. In 2008, under Cristina Fernandez de Kirchner, agriculturalists did manage to organize themselves into a coherent protest movement in the face of a further tax increase—to an initial, but variable, 44 percent. This move increased cohesion among producer groups. Those representing smaller farmers, who had previously been more accepting of tax increases, began to argue that they might be unable to absorb the new rate (unlike larger farms). Concurrently, the new measure pushed large producer associations away from what had proved fruitless dialogue with the government and more toward the smaller producers' preferred strategy of protest (Fairfield 2010; 2011; 2015, chapter 7). The participation of small producers, many of whom were not affiliated with any group, gave the protests a movement-like character that prevented the government from portraying the protests as elite agitation against progressive taxation. After five months of strikes and roadblocks, much urban middle-class opinion had turned against the government, and Fernandez de Kirchner was forced to back down after a senate vote against the taxes was decided in favor of the protesters—by the single vote of her own vice president. The events around this period certainly seem to have weakened the

bases of the governing coalition, though the previous 35 percent export tax remained in place and both soy production and government revenue continued to increase for several years.

16. The Plan Jefes y Jefas de Hogares Desempleados was initially funded by the first round of export taxes, together with the World Bank. As Nestor Kirchner distanced himself from the IFIs, subsequent programs came to be funded entirely by the central state.

17. The scheme was also meant to help the Peronist political machine reassert some of the control of the *villas* (informal settlements), which, during the 1990s, it had increasingly ceded to *piquetero* groups (Svampa 2007). In part, this was achieved by diverting some of the funds to local Peronist *punteros* (neighborhood fixers) as a "toll" for access to the program.

18. However, the degree to which wages increased, or whether real wages ever returned to pre-neoliberalization levels, is difficult to discern, given disputes over official inflation figures from 2007 onward.

19. Nestor Kirchner's decision to delay settling the outstanding debt until late 2005 actually allowed for a buildup of international reserves, which helped domestic business confidence, boosting the recovery (Grugel and Riggirozzi 2007).

20. At least, interest rates were kept low until 2007, when increasing inflation prompted a return to higher rates.

21. The combination of a maintained devaluation of the peso with agro-export taxes may itself be thought of as industrial policy, since, as Salama (2012) points out, this is effectively the same as a system of multiple exchange rates, in terms of its differential impact upon industry and agriculture.

22. As well as providing a direct energy subsidy to business, of course.

23. This was made a formal part of the bank's charter in 2012.

24. Cristina Fernandez de Kirchner's presidency is often seen as somewhat more radical than that of her husband. For example, she renationalized the national pension scheme and expropriated the former national oil company, Yacimientos Petrolíferos Fiscales, from its Spanish owners. In the case of the pension scheme, this was mainly to ease fiscal pressure on the government. In first place, the central government had, after privatization, kept all pension liabilities up to that point and thus was continuing to pay out while receiving no new pension payments. Second, the newly nationalized pension scheme was mandated to buy up government bonds during times of fiscal stress, providing a work-around in the absence of foreign creditors. The nationalization of YPF (or, more accurately, the expropriation of the 51 percent of its shares controlled by the Spanish company Repsol) was partly meant to inspire nationalistic fervor at a point of declining popularity for the government, and it was timed around similarly inspired saber rattling over the long-dormant Malvinas/Falklands dispute. Even so, there was an economic rationale to the move, born of the belief that electricity price controls and subsidies had led to chronic underinvestment in Argentina's energy infrastructure and that government thus was required to assume this responsibility. Furthermore, acquisition of YPF made the government the major negotiating partner in the prospective deal with Chinese state-owned enterprises regarding Argentina's vast shale gas reserves (the third largest in the world).

25. Vulture funds operate by purchasing, at a low price, debt that is in default and then aggressively pursuing any available legal avenues to recover the full face value of the debt.

26. Delivering budget, or at least primary, surpluses was a policy priority in the first years of Nestor Kirchner's presidency, lining up with neodevelopmentalist recommendations, though in the Argentinian case this was for the specific purpose of strengthening the government's hand in negotiations with creditors.

27. Manufactures as a share of Brazilian exports dropped by 10 percent from 2005 to 2010, even when adjusting for commodity price increases over the period (Jenkins 2014).

6. Extractivist-Redistributive Type: Ecuador, Bolivia, and Venezuela

1. The governing party, initially, was the Movimiento Quinta Republica (Fifth Republic Movement), until the consolidation of various parties of the pro-Chavez coalition into the Partido Socialista Unido de Venezuela (United Socialist Party of Venezuela), in 2007.

2. Classical populism, associated most prominently with Juan Perón in Argentina (though also with a host of other figures), was often identified with industrialization in previously commodity export–driven economies, involving the mass mobilization of new urban masses and associated with nationalist-developmentalist projects. The emergence of neoliberal populist leaders such as Alberto Fujimori and Carlos Menem (Weyland 1996), followed by the likes of Hugo Chavez and Rafael Correa, has led to a broadening of the definition of the term to encompass divergent economic models, largely concentrating, instead, on political style.

3. This might be thought of as including specifically neoliberal institutions, such as a membership in the International Court of Investment Dispute Settlement.

4. The exception here is Bolivia, where the Movimiento al Socialismo heads a coalition of allied social movement groups, both rural and urban, which coalesced around Evo Morales, a representative of coca growers' associations. The Morales government is not typically defined as populist, since it is a social movement–driven government that originated in bottom-up mobilization. However, the political style and tactics of Morales have been extremely similar to those of the other two extractivist-redistributive governments, and the MAS has become increasingly alienated from its social movement base over time.

5. As one example, Ellner (2001) mentions that the previous pledge that there would be no sell-off of any part of the state-owned Petróleos de Venezuela, S.A. was honored, though clauses were added permitting "strategic association" and the sale of subsidiaries to foreign interests.

6. The governments of the time were very much on board with Kennedy's Alliance for Progress.

7. A concurrent process was continuing concentration of capital. Only large businesses, favored by clientelistic networks around the two parties, tended to survive the tough

economic conditions. This paradoxically left the position of capital more unified and stronger relative to the state when facing down neoliberalization, which would lead to cuts in their various privileges. This accounts for the moderate and stop-start character of neoliberalism in Venezuela.

8. Poverty rates stood at an astonishing 77.1 percent in 1996—a rate that, sadly, would eventually be exceeded after the postboom collapse, under Nicolas Maduro.

9. However, the lack of a rival, neoliberally oriented capitalist fraction is also related to the relative unity of Venezuelan capital, compared to the sectoral–geographic divide found in Bolivia and (in a somewhat different manner) in Ecuador.

10. Tony Blair and the "third way" were cited as inspirations for Chavez (Raby 2011).

11. Constitutional changes in 1999 had undermined the power of the two traditional parties (and thus of groups that had received corporatist or clientelistic benefits under the old two-party system) by removing state funding for the parties, weakening the legislature in favor of the executive, and stripping the legislature of the power to appoint the judiciary. Compounding this, the business community was denied its usual representation in government, and the practice of forming regular tripartite (government–business–labor) commissions was discontinued. These changes had already fomented the first widespread opposition to Chavez, though PDVSA's wide-ranging societal influence (Parker 2005) meant that its executives were crucial in solidifying these currents into an intractable opposition that was prepared to confront the government head-on.

12. This sort of rhetoric had resonance along classist and racist lines, as it would in many Latin American states.

13. This included a general strike, an April 2002 coup attempt that briefly saw FEDECA-MARAS head Pedro Carmona installed as president, and then a management lockout at PDVSA.

14. An exception was the Plan Bolivar 2000, under which the army was used to repair roads and build schools, in the tradition of progressive militaries in Latin America. This created resentment among many in the top ranks of the armed forces, which were purged after participation in anti-Chavez agitation during the 2001–2003 period.

15. These included Mision Barrio Adentro (primary health), Mision Robinson (literacy), Mision Sucre (university education), Mision Ribas (adult secondary education), and Mision Habitat (housing). These schemes existed autonomously from and in parallel to traditional ministries of health, education, and others ordinarily responsible for social provision. The Mision Vuelvan Caras, meanwhile, was a training program—including political and ideological formation—designed to help the urban poor organize as a workers' cooperative, a key means of organizing the informal sector.

16. At the conclusion of the strikes and lockout actions, seventeen thousand PDVSA employees were dismissed. The speed at which production was restarted following these moves suggests that the workforce had been somewhat bloated previously. A new board of executives was put in place by Chavez, and the company was made very much subordinate to the Ministry of Energy and Mines. PDVSA was essentially incorporated as an arm of the state, directly funding social programs and diplomatic initiatives, which saw cheap oil being sent to other parts of Latin America and the Caribbean (as well as to poor households in the United States and as subsidized fuel for London buses).

Foreign participation was still permitted in the industry, though on much better terms for the state. As a result, ExxonMobil and Shell pulled out, though Chevron renegotiated its contracts and remained a major player. Venezuela increasingly sought investors from outside the global North, particularly from China, with capital from Sinopec and the China National Offshore Oil Company proving crucial to the opening up of the massive heavy crude deposits of the Orinoco Delta (Dreher et al. 2017).

17. This is yet another example of the use of community organizations to administer public funds, in preference to formal bureaucracies. As with many of Chavez's spending initiatives, this form of infrastructure provision actually tends to be very inefficient. Crucially, though, it bypasses spending on megaprojects, considered a major source of patronage and corruption under *puntofijismo.*

18. There also has been a nationalization of basic industry, a long-standing goal of nationalist movements in Venezuela.

19. In 2018, a deal was signed for the German firm ACI Systems to invest $1.3 billion in the lithium sector, with the intention of partnering in extraction and battery manufacture (Clayton 2018).

20. The 1985 standby agreement with the International Monetary Fund stipulated that Yacimientos Petroliferos Fiscales Bolivianos would be barred from investing in capital goods, with the sector opened up to foreign investment in the early 1990s. Bolivia, as the ER state most impacted by neoliberal conditionality, was also the only one of these states that was pressured into privatizing its hydrocarbon industry. In 1996, much of YPFB was auctioned off in several packages. Rather than paying the state for their newly obtained assets, however, winning bidders were merely required to commit the amount they had bid toward new investment in the industry. With royalty rates also significantly lowered, gas subsequently became a focal issue for social movement mobilization.

21. The separate contributory pension scheme was also overhauled. Pension funds were nationalized, the age of eligibility was lowered from sixty-five to fifty-eight (in a country with a life expectancy of sixty-three), and previous terms that had made access to any retirement benefits unrealistic for the majority were made considerably more generous. Efforts also were made to extend the scheme to previously excluded informal workers.

22. There are complaints that such redistribution as has occurred has made inroads into previously protected national parks and indigenous lands and has favored highlanders by granting them land in the lowlands.

23. Though a staunch free marketeer, it was in fact Jamil Mahuad who presided over Ecuador's temporary estrangement from the international financial institutions, after he suspended the payment of Brady bonds in the face of a banking crisis.

24. It was during this period that Ecuador abandoned the national currency, the sucre, and adopted full dollarization of the economy. The dollar has become increasingly popular, and even Correa has argued that to remove it would do more economic harm than good.

25. The lasting influence of the 1999–2000 economic crisis, and its impact on the banking elites in particular, is still easily observed. Common graffiti seen around Quito in 2013 satirized Bank of Guayaquil vice president Guillermo Lasso's election slogan of

"A different Ecuador is possible" by adding "But a different banker isn't." The Ecuadorian Banker's Association regularly publishes documents that stress how different today's domestic banks are from their counterparts during the 1999 crisis, when withdrawals were suspended before dollarization of accounts proceeded, at an unfavorable exchange rate. It is no surprise that Correa was particularly aggressive in his stance toward the banking sector, given its previous power. Financial institutions are now prohibited from ownership of any media outlets (a previously common structure).

26. A key event was the formation of the constituent assembly, which allowed for a rewriting of the constitution. Congress (for which Correa had nominated no candidates in the 2006 election, as part of his outsider strategy) had sought to block the creation of this body, which is where mass mobilization, enabling an overriding of liberal democratic norms, became highly significant.

27. Gutiérrez probably had no intention of following through on his campaign promises and was simply using this rhetoric to secure the votes of the left-inclined indigenous party Pachakutik (which had scored around 15 percent in the previous election). Certainly, many Partido Sociedad Patriotica (Patriotic Society Party) officials had roots in center-right organizations, and several important ministerial posts went to avowedly neoliberal figures. However, this still leaves unanswered the question of whether Gutiérrez's stated original agenda was politically and economically possible under the conditions of the time.

28. Interview 7e. Details about Ecuador interviews may be found in the appendix, table A.4.

29. Interviews 2e, 7e.

30. Correa's doctoral dissertation argued, from a broadly Keynesian stance, that structural reform in 1980s Latin America had failed to drive growth.

31. In seeking to interview representatives from other arms of the government on matters relating to economic policy or development issues, I was often referred to the Secretaria Nacional, known as SENPLADES. Organizational charts of the Ecuadorian governmental structure show the executive standing directly above SENPLADES, which in turn is placed above all other ministries (SENPLADES 2013).

32. Interview 11e.

33. Correa's move to seize the assets of Roberto and William Isaias, for instance, was highly popular. The brothers are the former owners of Filanbanco, who embezzled bailout funds by making loans to businesses they controlled and then presenting these as losses to the government. They fled to Miami in the wake of the financial crisis and were sentenced to eight years in jail in absentia. After many years living in Florida, they were arrested in early 2019 (Robles 2019).

34. This policy was subsequently implemented, following Correa's easy first-round victory in 2013.

35. This was the extension of a law that outlawed financial companies from media ownership, or vice versa. The prohibition of ownership of other financial companies is essentially a Glass–Steagall type of provision, but the cumulative impact of these two laws is to force a separation of the domestic financial sector from the rest of the capitalist sphere.

36. The government was subsequently able to secure limited loans from more sympathetic multilateral lenders, such as the Inter-American Development Bank.

37. Under this form of loan arrangement, a fixed quantity (rather than value) of oil is sold on the open market and the proceeds are deposited into an escrow account, which is then drawn from in order to pay off the loan (Brautigam and Gallagher 2014).

38. Some of these projects are aimed at making Ecuador self-sufficient in energy generation. With insufficient refinery capacity, it currently imports fuel, and the only real wobble in Correa's popularity occurred after a series of rolling blackouts in 2009, caused by droughts that affected the generation of hydroelectricity.

39. Interview 3e.

40. Interview 11e.

41. Interview 4e.

42. Anti-extraction protests also occur frequently in Bolivia, but they are less frequent in Venezuela, where the historical role of oil in national development imaginaries seems to have prompted a wider acceptance of extractivism.

43. Though business leaders were likely to be unhappy with Correa's continuing anti-oligarchy rhetoric, they were probably much more pleased with his dismissal of indigenous interests. Perhaps one-third of Ecuador's population is indigenous, and the various communities have long been effectively organized as a political actor through the Confederación de Nacionalidades Indígenas del Ecuador (Confederation of Indigenous Nationalities of Ecuador) and the Pachakutik political party. Pachakutik's credibility was seriously damaged by the fallout from its disastrous electoral alliance with Lucio Gutiérrez, in 2002, and indigenous groups were hardly involved in the coup of 2005. Correa drew most of his support from the urban working and middle classes, the majority of whom are mestizos. Though lip service was paid to the indigenous community in the 2008 constitution, which granted rights to Pachamama (Mother Nature) and declared Ecuador to be a plurinational state, many indigenous leaders condemned these provisions as "folklorization." It was fortunate for Correa that his electoral majority did not depend upon rural indigenous populations, because there have been running conflicts with these groups over oil extraction in the Amazon and new copper and gold mining projects. A large-scale march in 2009 was repressed, and several indigenous activists were thrown in jail, convicted of terrorism.

44. Interview 4e.

45. Interview 8e, 9e.

7. Extractivist-Oligarchic Type: Angola and Kazakhstan

1. This is not to define a simple binary between clientelist and capitalist political formations, since all societies display features of both, to some degree. In addition, nascent capitalists, in cases of late development, have almost always depended on their ties to the state to forge processes of accumulation (through the distribution of contracts, licenses, land, subsidies, and so forth). Even when large domestic capitalist classes have

emerged (that is, in schematic terms, an elite with a basis of power in capital accumulation rather than in distribution of rents), a variety of different relationships with the state are observed. In the Gulf countries, for example, public and private political and economic realms are difficult to distinguish. The key aspect of the donor-dependent orthodoxy and the extractivist-oligarchic types, which distinguishes them from the others, is the absence of an economic elite with a base of power that lies (at least to some significant degree) outside direct dependence on the distribution of state largesse. These issues are explored in more detail over this chapter and the next.

2. Rentier states were originally associated with oil-rich Middle Eastern states, and hydrocarbon exporters remain the most obvious examples, though any state dependent upon centralized and externally derived revenue flows (including, for instance, aid receipts) may potentially fit the description (Moore 2001).

3. This is by no means an entirely new endeavor. Boone's (1990) work on Senegal, for example, uses the terminology of a rentier class. Hanieh (2011), whose work will be discussed in more detail here, seeks to marry a rentier state model with Marxian state theory in his study of Gulf capitalism.

4. At times, the RS label has been applied more widely, particularly to oil-rich states with relatively significant domestic capitalist classes, such as Venezuela (Karl 1997). Clearly, this is the case with Venezuela during the years of the Puntofijo settlement, under which patronage resources, much of it ultimately stemming from oil revenues, were divided up between the two main parties and an associated domestic capitalist class, which was weak enough, relative to oil earnings, to become increasingly dependent upon state subsidies and procurement arrangements. Overall, however, the scenario of external-rent-derived relative autonomy for the state is most applicable in cases such as the EO type, in which domestic capital depends heavily on the state for its continuing activity. This is the context in which the RS concept is employed in this chapter, unless otherwise stated.

5. Here, I stress the reliance upon commodity prices as the primary external constraint on rentier state managers, though technological and organizational factors are also at play—foreign investment or management is often necessary, given the technical challenges associated with identifying, developing, and maintaining extractive ventures. Even in times of high commodity prices, such requirements can have a significant impact. For example, various "shallow" nationalizations of resource sectors in Africa during the 1970s left previous managers in charge of operations, given a paucity of local staff able to fill their roles (Shaw 1976).

6. Such downstream industries include Saudi Arabia Basic Industries Corporation (petrochemicals), Etisalat (telecommunications) in Abu Dhabi, and DP World (logistics) in Dubai.

7. Persian Gulf states do, of course, employ large numbers of wage laborers in construction, extraction, and services, but the vast majority of workers are migrants from South Asia and elsewhere who did not directly become workers through processes of dispossession and capitalist development in their destination states.

8. Another distinction should be made with the embedded autonomy framework of state-nurtured (but also disciplined) capitalists in East Asia (Evans 1995), given the persistence

in the Gulf (as well as in EO states) of rent-funded waste, luxury consumption, and patrimonial networks, as well as the difficulty of distinguishing between state and bourgeoisie as separate entities.

9. The Kashagan Field, located in the shallows of the Caspian Sea, is the world's largest offshore oil field. Its development has been beset with technical challenges and delays, though, by 2018, it had begun production (Cohen 2018).

10. However, it should be noted that, following the end of the Cold War and the loss of aid from state socialist countries, the Movimento Popular de Libertação de Angola officially abandoned Marxism in favor of some form of capitalism. During the period immediately following the civil war, the rather uncontrolled primitive accumulation that had occurred during the 1990s was reined in and an essentially orthodox macroeconomic framework was adopted as a means of encouraging foreign direct investment (Soares de Oliveira 2015, 132).

11. The fact that Samruk-Kazyna evolved from two holding companies, one of which was initially set up for the purpose of the managed privatization of utilities, brings Kazakhstan's turn away from neoliberalization more sharply into focus, since the fund has retained all of these companies (including utility monopolies) and has added Air Astana and large real estate holdings, among others.

8. Donor-Dependent Orthodoxy Type:
Zambia, Laos, and Mongolia

1. Vietnamese influence in Laos is also considerable, though the Laotian reform process actually began before that of its larger neighbor to the east.

2. Official development assistance includes both aid and concessional finance from the members of the Organization for Economic Co-operation and Development's Development Assistance Committee.

3. For the rest of the chapter, I will refer to donors and international financial institutions as acting with largely shared goals and strategies in their interactions with recipient countries. Of course, this is not always the case, since bilateral donors may, for example, have particular economic or strategic reasons for more flexible or stringent treatment of particular recipients. However, after the adoption of the participatory agenda by the World Bank and then by the International Monetary Fund, in the late 1990s, major donors and IFIs converged toward a common overarching approach to official development assistance, in terms of both policy and process. This was further advanced by the process of aid harmonization on the part of OECD donors, which began with the Rome Declaration, in 2003 (Thede 2013). There has been considerable debate in recent years around the extent to which such commonalities continue to endure (Güven 2018).

4. Clearly, various forms of bureaucratic and political resistance were attempted and, for a variety of reasons, many structural adjustment program conditions were not fully implemented, but at no point during the SAP era could a government needing IFI funds chart a wholly different political course.

5. As Babb (2013) reports, there were divergent views on this point around the turn of the millennium, with the U.S. congressional Meltzer Report arguing that lack of full implementation lay behind the various adjustment failures. Stiglitz (2002), who was far more critical of the IMF than of the World Bank, where he had previously served, claimed that an inevitable lack of perfect information in developing economies had led to market failures. In terms of policy implications, this thesis departed little from what was to become the "establishment" position—that greater attention needed to be given to the institutional frameworks that would underpin (and to a limited extent correct for) the functioning of markets.

6. In recent years, some more flexibility has been introduced into IFI processes, with "economic development documents" (which can take the form of government-written national development plans) replacing the IMF's PRSP template. There is some disagreement as to how substantive such changes have really been in terms of policy conditionality and overall agenda (Kentikelenis, Stubbs, and King 2016; Güven, 2018). For example, aid and loan disbursements are still often benchmarked against Country Policy and Institutional Assessment scores.

7. Always implicit in the depoliticized goal of poverty alleviation (that is, pushing the largest possible number of people over the current $1.25 per day threshold) is a decrease of aspirations toward short- and medium-term solutions to extreme deprivation and a movement away from a view of development as potentially encompassing society-wide transformation.

8. The concept of reform coalitions is associated with Robert Bates (1981), whose work on sub-Saharan Africa claimed that development had been stunted by the dominance of an urban coalition of the state, the public sector, and wage laborers, which had pursued distortionary, self-interested policies to the detriment of broader development. Bates's proposed solution was to attempt to activate a countervailing reform coalition of peasants and agro-exporters, who might support initially painful adjustment measures if they could be persuaded of a longer-term developmental payoff. IFI qualms over extending their interference with national sovereignty into directly building political coalitions seems to have forestalled the application of Bates's ideas in this area, until the emergence of the participation agenda in the late 1990s presented a more palatable means to similar ends.

9. Clearly, in many cases governments and other participants will share the basic policy assumptions of IFIs, to a greater or lesser degree, and thus, again, Poverty Reduction Strategy Papers rarely involve a simple imposition of external ideas upon unwilling governments.

10. Though the power of transnational capital in Bolivia has declined during the Movimiento al Socialismo years, its participation has still very much been required for the continuation of Evo Morales's project, given Bolivia's need to attract new investment in gas fields if current levels of social spending and redistribution are to be maintained.

11. Clearly, aid can rarely be considered capital, strictly speaking, but ODA flows do tend to broadly follow, at one or several removes, the preferences of Northern capital, through conditionality (except where aid may flow or not flow for geopolitical reasons).

12. Interview 2z. Details about Zambia interviews may be found in the appendix, table A.5.

13. Interview 2z.

14. Interview 2z.

15. Ollawa (1979) also includes senior officials of the Zambian Congress of Trade Unions in his list of ruling class subgroups, based on 1975–1977 survey data. This was probably a valid classification during most of the period of United National Independence Party rule, when trade union leaders were co-opted by a government-instituted closed shop that guaranteed them access to significant economic resources. It is also important to point out that industrial action in Zambia, particularly that of mineworkers, has often tended to come in defiance of the union leadership, including incidents in the past decade, meaning the rank and file should be considered separately from the leadership. I do not list leading trade unionists as part of the ruling elite, though, since their position vis-à-vis this elite has sometimes been oppositional.

16. This included a policy of "ethnic balancing," whereby patronage was, in theory, dispensed equally to representatives of the major linguistic groups in Zambia. Though couched in terms of being antithetical to tribalist tendencies, this was spoils politics, which utilized vertical ethnic networks through traditional leaders and local "big men."

17. Larmer gives Miners' Union of Zambia membership figures of around sixty thousand at the peak, in the late 1980s, with a low of 15,600 during the first years of the twenty-first century. Since the arrival of the breakaway National Union of Miners and Allied Workers, in 2004, the picture has been complicated by the movement of workers between the two unions, but membership in 2008 is reported as twenty-seven thousand for the Miners' Union and perhaps ten thousand for the National Union (Larmer 2010).

18. There also were occasions when the stances of IFIs and private domestic capital were categorically opposed to one another on the issues of specific reforms.

19. Manufacturers for instance, were provided with almost no protection against the sudden opening of the Zambian economy to international competition.

20. Among them was President Michael Sata (2011–2014), who, in common with several of his ministers, belonged successively to UNIP, the Movement for Multiparty Democracy, and the Patriotic Front.

21. This is contrary to the ideas developed by Robert Bates (1981), for whom Zambia served as an exemplar of a rural–urban divide (heavily favoring the urban), which constituted a fundamental obstacle to development. This was to provide the inspiration for many of the World Bank policy recommendations across Africa during the 1980s, which attempted to favor agricultural development, echoing the anti-urban sentiments of the colonial administration and UNIP's notional commitment to the countryside.

22. Today, this would include, for instance, workers in the South Africa–dominated formal retail sector. I do not include public sector workers in this grouping, though their interests may at times be in line with other formal sector workers.

23. Or even to employ informal workers, as was revealed in the 2013 dispute between retail workers and the Shoprite chain, when employees agitated for higher wages partly on the basis of not being able to pay their own domestic workers (*Lusaka Times* 2013b).

24. I refer to these two provinces throughout, since these were the relevant administrative units for the majority of the period discussed. In 2011, however, four districts from Northern Province and one from Eastern Province were broken off to form the new province of Muchinga.

25. Though Cheeseman and Larmer (2015) argue for a dual "ethnopopulist" strategy on the part of the PF, stressing ethnicity in the countryside and populism in the towns, they cite evidence from Cheeseman et al. (2013) that voters in the two Bemba-dominated rural provinces were highly receptive to populist appeals and significantly more likely to respond to these than were their rural compatriots elsewhere. Ostensibly, the PF's repeated message, during multiple elections, of "More jobs, less taxes, and more money in your pocket" has very little to offer to subsistence farmers, especially when compared to MMD fertilizer distribution, which is designed to appeal to precisely these groups. Though there was undoubtedly an element of Sata evoking shared ethnicity when he campaigned in Luapula and Northern Provinces, it is worth pointing out that his attempt to run as a "Bemba" candidate, in 2001, attracted just 3 percent of the national vote and very little success even in his "home" regions. In contrast, the United Party for National Development regularly won majorities in Southern Province, based on appeals to Tonga ethnicity (though rarely much beyond that until UPND's postboom transformation into a broader-based party), again suggesting that a different political logic is at work in the urban/Bembaphone areas than in the rest of the country.

26. In recent years, Lusaka has seen an influx of migration from the Copperbelt, though the majority of its residents are originally from other areas and its lingua franca remains Nyanja rather than Bemba. Nevertheless, despite the absence of mines in Lusaka, urban areas exhibit a core of organized formal labor, combined with a wider, marginalized urban community, that has voted with the Copperbelt in recent elections. This perhaps indicates that more extensive urban class formation may hold the possibility for broader popular class coalitions in the future.

27. Interview 9z.

28. Interviews 8z and 5z.

29. The 2008 election was a presidential by-election, mandated by Zambian law following the death of the MMD incumbent, Levy Mwanawasa, and was won by his vice president, Rupiah Banda, who ran again, unsuccessfully, in 2011.

30. This anti-Chinese rhetoric gained traction in the wake of a 2005 tragedy in which fifty workers were killed in a blast at the BGRIMM explosives factory, part of the Chambishi mines, which was owned by China Nonferrous Metal Mining.

31. The number of people operating informally as city center vendors, selling snacks, mobile phone credit, or produce, especially in Lusaka, had increased so much that it was now becoming physically difficult to navigate many urban streets, sparking widespread complaints, particularly from the middle classes. A crackdown on informal vendors and markets, initiated by the MMD government, came at the same time as the growth in competition from Chinese traders, who often were able to source Chinese goods and sell at lower prices than local vendors.

32. Zambia's Gini coefficient rose alarmingly with its twenty-first-century copper boom, from an already high 0.51 in 2004 to 0.65 in 2010, making it one of the most economically unequal countries in the world.

33. Larmer and Fraser (2007, 613) use the concept of populism, as defined by Laclau (2005), to link the Latin American parties with the Zambian PF, specifically in "the identification of particular unmet demands of distinct social groups, and their re-presentation to those groups not only as legitimate but also as aspects of a wider set of linked and unmet demands, sharing few characteristics beyond their frustration. The suggestion is then made that the frustration of these demands results from a disconnection between a newly imagined 'people' (those whose demands are being frustrated) and 'power' (those on whom demands are made)." Arguably, however, this underestimates the relative coherence of the Latin American examples, which, in different ways, connected the marginalization of the (mainly urban) poor to a relationship between a domestic elite and global capitalism, despite their employment of classically populist, personalist style of campaigning. It is also worth noting that Bolivia's Movimiento al Socialismo began as a broad-based social movement rather than a top-down political party dominated by a charismatic leader. While Sata's campaigning was certainly more ad hoc and less "ideological" than the Latin American cases, the PF had specific policy proposals at each election and this was thus not an entirely "empty" populism. I use the term "populism" more generally here, simply to indicate a style of politics that is designed to connect (whether cynically or not) with the concerns of the urban poor.

34. Interviews 2z, 3z, and 6z.

35. One of the significant features of the windfall tax, as proposed, was that it targeted the global price of copper on the London Metal Exchange rather than on any measure internal to the situation in Zambia.

36. After its closure by a previous Swiss–Israeli joint venture, however, the Luanshya mine was taken over by China Nonferrous Metals Africa.

37. Efforts to improve accounting standards to detect tax avoidance, chiefly funded by Norway, may have yielded some improved revenue, as with reforms banning foreign-denominated transactions within the country. Nevertheless, tax avoidance is a problem that states with access to far greater administrative capacity than Zambia's have found difficult to grapple with. Accounting methods such as transfer pricing allow many companies to underreport profits (or to report a loss) and thus to avoid paying the majority of royalties, which are typically calculated against profits (as contrasted with the windfall tax, which would have targeted the international copper price).

38. This same document alleges that the Chinese government had approached the PF in 2006 to offer funding and indeed that Zimbabwean President Robert Mugabe had lent Sata money for campaign finances in 2008.

39. Local cash transfer programs have been trialed, with donor assistance, and are expanding significantly, but were still small scale as of 2013 (interview 3z).

40. Interview 3z.

41. For instance, in a dispute with the South African retailer Shoprite in 2013, workers went on strike after claiming they had not been awarded the minimum mandated increment.

After the company moved to fire three thousand striking workers, the government threatened the removal of the chain's operating license, resulting in the reinstatement of the workers and the negotiation of pay raises of 15 to 34 percent.

42. The 2014 Zambian budget statement (Government of Zambia 2013) estimated that fifty-eight thousand formal sector jobs were created in the first nine months of 2013, though this may not accurately reflect the total.

43. Sata, formerly a senior MMD figure, originally formed the PF after being passed over for the leadership. As noted, Sata's vice president, Guy Scott (briefly interim president after Sata's death), previously was MMD agriculture minister (and an enthusiastic neo-liberal reformer). As with the MMD victory in 1991, many members of parliament and other officials defected to the new ruling party in the months following the 2011 election.

44. The PF did not have a parliamentary majority following the 2011 election. The switching of allegiance on the part of various MMD members of parliament (enticed in some cases by the prospect of deputy minister positions) triggered by-elections, as did the removal of (usually opposition) members on charges of corruption.

45. This occurred, for instance, in the Southern Province tourist hub of Livingstone, previously a United Party for National Development heartland (Mwenya 2013), and in Mkaika, in Eastern Province (*Lusaka Times* 2013a).

46. The fact that Chinese investors stayed—and, indeed, purchased new mining assets—during the financial crisis went some way to reversing their previously negative image among Zambians that was based on low rates of pay and perceived poor conditions.

47. Clearly, MAS's politics also revolved centrally around the issue of ethnicity. Morales's victory was historic because he was the first Bolivian president from the indigenous majority. However, given the particular course of colonialism in Bolivia, race and class overlap to a very large extent.

48. Though Cox and Negi (2010) are dismissive of "neo-Smithian" approaches, a version of this with the emphasis on exchange rather than on production would instead merely note the lack of penetration of the market into the social relations of rural Zambians, which places them mostly outside (albeit linked to) the world-system, even if "Zambia" as an entity can be considered part of this system, given the participation of Zambia's governing class within it.

49. Even in Northern and Luapula Provinces, patterns of political mobilization seem to indicate expectations of indirect benefits—through, for instance, increased remittances—combined with traditional patronage.

50. Though they suggest markedly divergent underlying causalities, these conclusions are not necessarily antithetical to those of influential authors writing on the African state in markedly different theoretical traditions, such as Mamdani (1996) or Chabal and Daloz (1999). Mamdani stresses the colonial-era origins of what he calls the bifurcated state—a division between a rural populace ruled indirectly through traditional authority and the urban setting that was placed under the direct rule of the colonial power—which set the scene for differentiated social logics in the postcolonial period. For Chabal and Daloz, the persistence of widespread patronage politics relates to specifically African cultural features of patrimonialism.

51. Stuart-Fox (2006) identifies a lack of bureaucratic tradition, in comparison with China and Vietnam, as a major driver of the relatively greater salience of clientelism in contemporary Laos.

52. State socialism in Mongolia had begun in 1921 and effectively constituted a declaration of independence from nationalist China, explaining the country's close relations with the Soviet Union until the 1990s. The experience of Chinese and then Soviet domination seems to be reflected in post-1990 Mongolian foreign and economic policy, which has tried to use the West (and Japan) in an effort to avoid dependence on its two much larger neighbors. Fear of Chinese economic penetration actually prompted one of the few examples of non-neoliberal policy in recent years, in which the prospective sale of a coal mining firm to Chinese investors prompted the identification of several strategic deposits where sales would need to be approved by Parliament (the huge copper and gold deposit at Oyu Tolgoi being the most important of these). The scale of Chinese investment in Mongolia remains surprisingly low, given its proximity and the obvious scope for profitable ventures.

53. Mongolia, during the early 1990s, seems to have been viewed by both external and internal market reformers as a sort of ideal test bed for shock therapy. Jeffrey Sachs visited to give his endorsement to the process in 1991, and, on several occasions, plans have been advanced to erect a statue of Milton Friedman in one of Ulaanbaatar's central squares, in place of the previous occupant, Vladimir Lenin.

54. The phenomenon known as *dzuds*, or patterns of extreme weather over several months, which wipe out livestock herds via some combination of extreme cold, deep snow cover, and/or prolonged drought, have become more frequent in recent decades. In part, this increased incidence is likely driven by climate change. However, water shortages have been exacerbated by increased consumption following the postsocialist growth of herding and by water table pollution caused by the mining industry. Several severe *dzuds* have occurred in recent years, killing millions of animals and forcing large numbers of farmers back to the city, resulting in a growth of perhaps 1.2 million in the population of Ulaanbaatar's peri-urban *gert* (traditional tent) dwellers (Mayer 2015).

55. Depending on the amounts distributed by this kind of unconditional cash transfer, such measures could be looked at as a basic income grant.

9. Homegrown Orthodoxy Type: Jamaica, Peru, South Africa, Colombia, and Indonesia

1. Beyond commodity markets, China does have a significant influence in Jamaica, with loans from People's Republic of China policy banks totaling more than $1.3 billion since 2009 (Gallagher and Myers 2018).

2. Bauxite is extracted through strip mining, before being processed into alumina, or aluminum oxide. Variations in the chemical composition of ores found in different deposits mean that alumina plants tend to be adapted to the processing of ores from particular locations, giving the aluminum value chain a somewhat different character than that of other hard commodities. This has recently been particularly pertinent in

Jamaica, with the dominance for a time of UC RUSAL over the domestic bauxite industry and the efforts of the latter to integrate Jamaican bauxite with processing in Russia (interview 5j; details about Jamaica interviews may be found in the appendix, table A.6.)

3. I use copper as the most appropriate comparator for aluminum because these are the two most widely used industrial metals and because, although substitutability between the two is generally low, a high proportion of applications for either (such as in appliances, construction, or military usages) employs the other in some way.

4. Large quantities of electricity are consumed in the process of transforming alumina into aluminum, meaning that refineries often are located close to cheap energy supplies (in Russia or West Asia, for example).

5. This strategy served to place Jamaica into a persistent trade deficit, which was only compensated for by surges in foreign investment, particularly in the bauxite and tourism industries.

6. Both the People's National Party and the Jamaica Labour Party are rooted in the trade union struggles of the 1930s, from which the eventually successful demands for independence first emerged. Both were essentially multiclass populist–nationalist coalitions, though the JLP was more conservative and drew more support from rural areas.

7. An agreement had, in fact, been reached just prior to the 1976 election, but, with a renewed mandate, Manley instead decided to attempt a homegrown solution, the Emergency Production Plan, announced in 1977, which envisaged a much greater role for the state in the economy. This set the tone for fractious relations between the International Monetary Fund and the PNP, and many in the party blamed the IMF for the electoral defeat in 1980, explaining why later PNP governments attempted to avoid IMF agreements where possible.

8. Initially under Manley, until his failing health forced him to step down in favor of P. J. Patterson, in 1992.

9. An option which was itself possible because of the IMF-mandated liberalization of the financial sector from 1991, which led to a mushrooming of domestic credit.

10. This was seen, for example, under neoliberal populist governments in Peru and Argentina. These governments, as in Jamaica, tended to dole out relief on a clientelistic basis to supporters of the ruling party.

11. Interview 3j.

12. In the rather particular circumstances of postapartheid South Africa, the existence of such constraints is far more arguable, though the heterodox Growth, Employment, and Redistribution plan, which was developed prior to the democratic changeover, was eventually rejected in the face of business opposition (Freund 2013).

13. Patterson is sometimes referred to as Jamaica's first elected black prime minister (though following Hugh Shearer, in 1967, who was appointed to the role following the death of Donald Sangster). This can be a contentious issue in Jamaica, depending on how ideas around race and ethnicity are understood. Nevertheless, it seems fair to say that Patterson was the first to place such stress upon an ethnic and cultural appeal to the disadvantaged black majority population (Robotham 2000).

14. The JLP, by this stage, with attitudes tempered by a traditional paternalism and a concern for agricultural unemployment in their rural base, were less enthusiastic liberalizers than the PNP.

15. Interview 5j.

16. Though the cases of Jamaica and Brazil clearly are extremely different in almost all respects, it is worth noting that, in Brazil, another state where domestic debt has been relatively important, the financial sector has played an important role in the continuation of elements of neoliberal policy, despite a neodevelopmentalist turn (Morais and Saad-Filho 2011).

17. Much of the information here is taken from anonymous interviews with a private consultant in the bauxite industry, who was formerly a senior manager at a parastatal (interview 4j).

18. Noranda was 49 percent owned by the U.S. firm Noranda Holdings until Noranda's bankruptcy in 2016 and the acquisition of its stake by New Day Aluminum (also based in the United States). The Jamaican government sold its minority share in Windalco (which comprises two mines, two alumina refineries, and a port facility) to UC RUSAL in 2014 (Drakapoulos 2018).

19. Interview 4j.

20. Government divestment in the bauxite industry has been a condition of IMF agreements (which will be discussed in the next section), though the Jamaican government held on to its 45 percent stake in Jamalco while divesting from Winalco. U.S.-based, Alcoa World Alumina and Chemicals owned the other 55 percent of Jamalco, until selling to Hong Kong–based commodities trader Noble Group Holdings in 2014. At one point, it appeared that UC RUSAL was poised to take over the entire Jamaican bauxite/alumina industry, though attempts to acquire Jamalco came to nothing. Alpart's refinery has since been reopened by new owners Jinquan Iron and Steel, which apparently plans a $3 billion special economic zone around the refinery for the manufacture of aluminum products (Drakapoulos 2019).

21. Interview 2j.

22. Interview 7z.

23. Interview 3j, 7j.

24. This target was achieved at the expense of non-execution of 5 percent of the already skeletal budget, allowing Jamaica to run a 0.1 percent surplus, the first positive fiscal balance in two decades (Government of Jamaica 2014, 36).

25. Peru also exports gold, which is not included as one of the commodities considered toward resource dependence for the purposes of the typology, given the metal's distinctive demand determinants.

26. Unusually, though not uniquely, among the cases examined in this research, the presence of an important domestic mining bourgeoisie, which acts as junior partner to external extractive capital, seems to be of significance in accounting for a strengthening of domestic, though externally oriented capital during the course of the commodity boom. This contrasts sharply with the situation in Argentina, where the aftermath of the 2001–2002 crisis strengthened the voice of an internally oriented capitalist fraction.

27. Unlike Hugo Chavez's coup attempt, which appears to have had some realistic hope of success, Ollanta Humala's uprising involved fewer than one hundred soldiers in the southern city of Tacna. Humala was pardoned by Congress, following Alberto Fujimori's fall a few months later, and seems to have gained a degree of public sympathy.

28. Alan García's victory represented a remarkable political comeback following his first presidency (1985–1990), during which, elected on an anti-neoliberal platform, his attempts at economic heterodoxy had resulted in hyperinflation and a 20 percent fall in gross domestic product. Though he was at the head of the Alianza Popular Revolucionaria Americana, Latin America's oldest populist party, by the time of his second presidency García had fundamentally reoriented his program toward neoliberal orthodoxy.

29. The 1994 Popular Participation Law.

30. Madrid (2011) notes the tendency of these regions to all vote for the same candidate in elections going back to 1990, explaining this mainly in terms of "ethnic proximity"— that is, indigenous voters choosing Fujimori, Alejandro Toledo, and then Humala based upon their nonwhite ethnicity.

31. The failure of land reform also set the scene for the emergence of the Maoist *Sendero Luminoso* (Shining Path) guerrilla movement.

32. Ecuador's experience lies somewhere between that of Peru and Bolivia. Land reform under the military government of Rodriguez Lara (1972–1976) deprived the hacienda-owning highland classes of much of their holdings and eventually saw power shift toward coastal capitalists, but it left the Quito bourgeoisie in a position to diversify into commerce and finance, leading to substantially overlapping interests with their Guayaquil counterparts. Thus, while rivalry between littoral and Andes continued throughout the neoliberal era, complex coalitions of elements of the two factions often formed to temporarily gain political power, crosscut with alternating "classical" populist and antipopulist dynamics.

33. See, for example, Maxwell Cameron's (1997) *The Eighteenth Brumaire of Alberto Fujimori*.

34. There also was an element of nationalism in this. For many protesters, a major objection to proposed arrangements for natural gas sales was a plan to export the gas via a pipeline that would end in a port and liquid natural gas facility in an area of the Chilean coast, which Bolivia had ceded to Chile following the War of the Pacific in 1904.

35. There certainly has been a far greater incidence of indigenous antigovernment protest in the lowlands in recent years. The 2011 clashes over the proposed Trans-Amazonian Highway saw highland and lowland groups on opposite sides of the dispute, with one grievance of the lowland groups being a fear of increasing migration from the Andes.

36. Clearly, in Bolivia, the Movimiento al Socialismo gained success through an alliance of all these sectors, plus rural elements, contrary to any assumptions that conflicting class interests would make such a coalition unworkable, as in the earlier Peruvian case. Appeals to indigenous ethnicity in Bolivia, combined with the catalytic effect of the gas export issue, may well have been important in transcending various segmented interests, though there is evidence that ethnic identification as nonwhite can be an important analogous factor in Peruvian politics as well (Madrid 2011). Perhaps more important, though, is that the MAS emerged over time, from a relatively weak and fragmented popular sector, without a formal worker base. It began with local issues but gradually

moved toward a national alliance, the formation of which required experimentation with relatively novel organizational forms. In Peru, the Izquierda Unida looked much more like a traditional leftist party, which was unable to adapt once its worker base began to be undermined. Without the legacy of both the Shining Path and the Fujimori years to contend with, it is certainly possible that Peru might have acquired a political force equivalent to the MAS (or, for that matter, an urban middle class–radical alliance, as in Ecuador).

37. The association between leftism and the specter of the Shining Path is evident in the common use of the term "watermelon" to dismiss anti-mining protesters in rural areas, with the implication that the sheen of an environmental cause is being used to hide a (necessarily) sinister socialist agenda (Arellano-Yanguas 2011).

38. It is worth pointing out that Fujimori's original platform was strongly against the shock therapy approach advocated by his main challenger, Mario Vargas Llosa. Once in office, however, Fujimori quickly implemented a thoroughgoing shock, making his government one of the most prominent examples of the apparently contradictory phenomenon of neoliberal populism.

39. A precipitous decline in support for incumbent presidents is an enduring feature of Peruvian politics and arguably reflects the contradictions of neoliberal populism: antisystem candidates, once in office, act to perpetuate the very system whose unpopularity had precipitated their support in the first place. In Toledo's case, in addition to growing waves of protest, media attention tended to highlight increasing perceptions of corruption, not unconnected to his apparently lavish lifestyle and taste for luxury consumer goods (McClintock 2006).

40. While most of the fruits of the commodity boom undoubtedly flowed upward and outward, some of the urban poor of the coast were beginning to see a degree of greater prosperity, as shown by a huge gap in poverty rates—20 percent in Lima and 61 percent in rural areas (Eaton 2015).

41. Several accusations of human rights abuses committed by Humala during his military service began to emerge during the campaign, some of which (though perhaps not all) were almost certainly inaccurate. Increasingly, during the second round, Humala was portrayed by the media in Lima as a stooge of Chavez, a perception which García sought to highlight at every opportunity.

42. Levitsky (2011) notes that while the Lima elite voted overwhelmingly for Keiko Fujimori, Humala was able to split the city's middle classes. This, together with a greater majority in the areas that had supported him in 2006, was enough for a second-round victory. The votes of wealthy areas and backing from the influential *El Comerico* daily (itself part of a large *grupo*) goes some way to indicating a favoring of Fujimori by Peruvian business. Nevertheless, Humala's alliance with Toledo and his team does reveal that at least some of the externally oriented technocratic stratum, which had shaped economic policy for most of the Alberto Fujimori, Toledo, and García governments, preferred Humala. The elder Fujimori had, of course, been the first to imprint Peruvian government with its persistent neoliberal technocratic bent. Nevertheless, the latter years of his reign had seen rising concerns over both a briefly resurgent "populist" wing of advisers (favoring domestic industry) and the incompatibility of his centralized,

authoritarian rule with the second-generation neoliberal institutional reform advanced by technocrats at home and abroad (Durand 2002). Toledo's presidency (as well as García's) saw the restoration of technocrats in key positions and the (at least partial) self-fulfilling of these reform demands. Speculatively, then, Toledo's campaign team, together with other technocrats, may have feared a rollback of these policies under a new Fujimori government. Since Toledo had been Alberto Fujimori's opponent in the fraudulent 2000 presidential election, however, Toledo also would have had his own reasons to side with Humala.

43. Humala's father had been a member of the Communist Party and, in 2006, had spoken in support of pardoning imprisoned Shining Path leader Abimael Guzman.

44. Toledo appointed U.S.-educated former members of the Fernando Belaunde-Terry cabinet to senior posts, while García signaled his desire for neoliberal continuity by selecting Luis Carranza as his first finance minister, in 2006. Carranza, at the time, was working as an economist for Banco Bilbao Vizcaya Argentaria, having previously resigned as deputy finance minister in Toledo's government over a reluctance to increase public spending (Weitzman 2006).

45. Reshuffles also tended to bring a change of political style. For example, the move from business leader Salomon Lerner to Humala's former army instructor, Oscar Valdes, as prime minister, in late 2011, signaled a more hard-line approach to law-and-order matters (Kozak and Moffett 2011). At times, there was undoubtedly some change in terms of policy emphasis, also, though this was largely limited to tinkering at the margins.

46. Castilla's resignation is usually blamed on pressure from the right in Congress, after a slowdown in economic growth, coinciding with a dip in global mineral prices. It is interesting to note that Castilla had earlier stayed in his post when Humala's fourth prime minister, Cesar Villanueva, was forced to resign, after Castilla opposed Villanueva's plans for a hike in the minimum wage (Dube 2014b).

47. "English" here, in the South African context, denotes white native English speakers, as juxtaposed with Afrikaans speakers.

48. The centrality of the energy sector in South Africa is especially notable. This includes the conversion of domestically mined coal into liquid fuel, the majority of which is used in electricity generation.

49. The World Bank showed remarkable flexibility in suggesting an initial postapartheid budget deficit of up to 10 percent. The IMF, however—with whom a joint National Party/African National Congress transition team negotiated an $850 million loan, in 1993—produced a more typical analysis, which stressed external liberalization and fiscal conservatism (Pons-Vignon and Segatti 2013).

50. Unlike the Shining Path in Peru, the Fuerzas Armadas Revolucionarias de Colombia, the major Colombian guerrilla group, at times showed an inclination toward electoral participation, as in the mid-1980s, when its leaders set up the Union Patriotica (Patriotic Union) party, which was then largely destroyed during the subsequent decade by a wave of assassinations by security and paramilitary forces (Aviles 2008). As part of the 2017 peace accords, the FARC rebranded as Fuerza Alternativa Revolucionaria del Común (Common Alternative Revolutionary Force) and contested the 2018 elections, without much success. However, trade unions and other movements have proved

remarkably resilient in their ability to organize protests against neoliberalization. A $2.7 billion IMF loan, which stipulated wage freezes and public sector lay-offs, for example, brought a twenty-four-hour general strike at the height of anti–trade union violence. The potential for widespread protest has often been met with police crackdowns, as in 2013, when two hundred thousand joined rural protests against the impact of free trade deals with the European Union and the United States (BBC 2013). With political polarization following the peace accords, leftist Gustavo Petro was able to make the make the second round of the 2018 presidential election.

51. The frequency of trade unionist murders appears to have slowed somewhat in recent years, but figures are still high, with twenty-seven killed in 2013 and twenty in 2014 (Amnesty International 2015).

52. In Peru and Bolivia, widespread traditional usage of coca, the plant from which cocaine is extracted, makes it important to distinguish between cultivation of the source plant and the manufacture of its far more powerful and lucrative alkaloid. Some indigenous groups in Colombia have historically used coca for chewing and tea and are permitted to grow small amounts for these purposes. Nevertheless, the lack of a widespread tradition of coca use in Colombia makes it far less controversial to identify the vast majority of Colombia's coca industry with cultivation for processing into cocaine.

53. Álvaro Uribe, however, bridges the divide between nationalist and transnationalized elites in Colombia, as the son of a cattle rancher (killed by the FARC) and a lawyer educated at Harvard and Oxford.

54. Richani (2010) cites Santiago Montenegro, ex-president of the National Association of Finance Institutions, in 2002, as making the case for increased military spending by arguing that the costs would be recouped through investment attracted by the better investment conditions that would result from improved security.

55. Some privatization and liberalization of elements of this system did occur during the 1990s (Robison 1993), though, for the most part, this left the patronage relationships that underpinned it largely unaffected.

56. However, the export ban would not be implemented until 2014. Rules on divestment were hardened significantly in 2012, to a mandatory 51 percent over ten years.

10. China and Global Transformation

1. The figure for oil is lower than might be expected, owing to China's continued reliance on coal as a fuel source. Concern over climate change and, particularly, urban pollution has brought efforts to shift the Chinese energy mix away from coal, though so far these attempts have met with only limited success (Hao and Baxter 2019).

2. As discussed in chapter 8, the later replacement of structural adjustment programs with Poverty Reduction Strategy Papers altered the process of conditionality, but it offered no fundamental changes to the policy orientation required in exchange for international financial institution loans and Development Assistance Committee aid.

3. It is worth repeating that here I am not solely referring to states that conduct significant direct trade with China or that house Chinese-owned extractive industry. More

important is that China's impact on global demand for energy, metals, and soybeans has upped world prices as a whole, meaning that similar effects are observed for exporters of these goods, no matter their trading partners.

4. As discussed in chapter 7, in the wake of the 2008 crisis, Angola did turn to the International Monetary Fund for help and, as a result, made some concessions on policy. However, the fund was far more flexible on terms than creditors had been in the early 2000s, signaling a turnaround whereby, in many respects, a deal with Angola, now a major oil producer, was more important for the IMF than for the recipient country. The 2009 agreement did little to substantively change Angola's political-economic model.

5. Part of this equation is the increasing interconnectedness of commodity markets, given possible substitution across categories (such as converting sugarcane into ethanol to be used in place of fossil fuels) and the increasing energy inputs required to explore for, extract, and transport increasingly remote reserves.

6. Many such systems, of course, were heavily criticized for setting prices for peasant production artificially low, which often led producers to abandon cash crops in favor of other activities (Ellis 1983).

Bibliography

Abdulai, A. G., and S. Hickey. 2016. "The Politics of Development Under Competitive Clientelism: Insights from Ghana's Education Sector." *African Affairs* 115 (458): 44–72.

Achcar, G. 2013. *People Want: A Radical Exploration of the Arab Uprising.* Berkeley: University of California Press.

Achtenberg, E. 2011. "Peru's Mining Conflicts: Ollanta Humala's Ticking Time Bomb." NACLA, July 29, 2011. https://nacla.org/blog/2011/7/29/peru%25E2%2580%2599s -mining-conflicts-ollanta-humala%25E2%2580%2599s-ticking-time-bomb.

Achtenberg, E. 2018. "Tensions Roil Bolivia as Electoral Court Says Morales Can Run Again." NACLA, December 27, 2018. https://nacla.org/blog/2018/12/29/tensions-roil -bolivia-electoral-court-says-morales-can-run-again.

Africa Confidential. 2016. "Lungu Schemes to Survive." *Africa Confidential* 57 (5). March 4.

Africa Confidential. 2018. "Bonds, Bills, and Ever Bigger Debts." *Africa Confidential* 59 (18). September 1.

Africa Confidential. 2019. "Debt and Discontent." *Africa Confidential* 60(2). January 25.

Agarwala, P. N. 1983. *The New International Economic Order: An Overview.* New York: Pergamon.

Aiello, K. 2010. "Bagua, Peru: A Year After." NACLA, June 25, 2010. https://nacla.org /news/bagua-peru-year-after.

Albro, R. 2005. "The Indigenous in the Plural in Bolivian Oppositional Politics." *Bulletin of Latin American Research* 24 (4): 433–53.

Al-Chalabi, F. J. 1988. "OPEC and the Present Structural Limitations on Its Oil Price Control." *OPEC Review* 12 (2): 115–21.

Alden, C., and D. Large. 2015. "On Becoming a Norms Maker: Chinese Foreign Policy, Norms Evolution, and the Challenges of Security in Africa." *China Quarterly* 221: 123–42.

Allinson, J. 2015. "Class Forces, Transition, and the Arab Uprisings: A Comparison of Tunisia, Egypt, and Syria." *Democratization* 22 (2): 294–314.

Alper, A. 2017. "Bolivia Seeks Investors to Power Up Lagging Lithium Output." Reuters, December 27, 2017. https://www.reuters.com/article/us-bolivia-lithium-analysis/bolivia-seeks-investors-to-power-up-lagging-lithium-output-idUSKBN1EL1JB.

Álvarez, R., and S. Claro. 2009. "David Versus Goliath: The Impact of Chinese Competition on Developing Countries." *World Development* 37 (3): 560–71.

Al Jazeera. 2019. "Hundreds Arrested in Kazakhstan Over Election Protests." June 13, 2019. https://www.aljazeera.com/news/2019/06/hundreds-arrested-kazakhstan-election-protests-190613201849137.html.

Amann, E., and W. Baer. 2000. "The Illusion of Stability: The Brazilian Economy Under Cardoso." *World Development* 28 (10): 1805–19.

Amnesty International. 2015. *Amnesty International Report 2014/15—Colombia.* https://www.refworld.org/docid/54f07e066.html.

Amsden, A. H. 1994. "Why Isn't the Whole World Experimenting with the East Asian Model to Develop? Review of the East Asian Miracle." *World Development* 22 (4): 627–33.

Amsden, A. H. 2001. *The Rise of the Rest: Challenges to the West from Late-Industrializing Economies.* Oxford: Oxford University Press.

Anderlini, J. 2014. "'Ghost Cities' Bear Witness to 'Wasted' $6.8tn." *Financial Times,* November 28, 2014.

Anderson, P. 2011. "Lula's Brazil." *London Review of Books* 33 (7) 3–12.

Anderson, P. 2016. "Crisis in Brazil." *London Review of Books* 38 (8): 15–22.

Anderson, P. 2019. "Bolsonaro's Brazil." *London Review of Books* 41 (3): 11–22.

Arce, M. 2006. "The Societal Consequences of Market Reform in Peru." *Latin American Politics and Society* 48 (1): 27–54.

Arce, M. 2008. "The Repoliticization of Collective Action After Neoliberalism in Peru." *Latin American Politics and Society* 50 (3): 37–62.

Arellano-Yanguas, J. 2011. "Aggravating the Resource Curse: Decentralisation, Mining and Conflict in Peru." *Journal of Development Studies* 47 (4): 617–38.

Arestis, P., and T. Pelagidis. 2010. "Absurd Austerity Policies in Europe." *Challenge* 53 (6): 54–61.

Arrighi, G. 1994. *The Long Twentieth Century: Money, Power, and the Origins of Our Times.* London: Verso.

Arrighi, G. 2002. "The African Crisis." *New Left Review* 15 (May/June): 5–36.

Arrighi, G. 2003. "The Social and Political Economy of Global Turbulence." *New Left Review* 20 (2): 5–71.

Arrighi, G. 2007. *Adam Smith in Beijing: Lineages of the Twenty-First Century.* London: Verso.

Arrighi, G. 2010. *The Long Twentieth Century: Money, Power and the Origins of Our Times.* 2nd ed. London: Verso.

Arrighi, G., and J. Drangel. 1986. "The Stratification of the World-Economy: An Exploration of the Semiperipheral Zone." *Review (Fernand Braudel Center)* 10 (1): 9–74.

Arrighi, G., and B. J. Silver. 1999. *Chaos and Governance in the Modern World System.* Minneapolis: University of Minnesota Press.

Arrighi, G., B. J. Silver, and B. D. Brewer. 2003. "Industrial Convergence, Globalization, and the Persistence of the North–South Divide." *Studies in Comparative International Development* 38 (1): 3–31.

Ashman, S., and B. Fine. 2013. "Neo-liberalism, Varieties of Capitalism, and the Shifting Contours of South Africa's Financial System." *Transformation: Critical Perspectives on Southern Africa* 81 (1): 144–78.

Ashman, S., B. Fine, and S. Newman. 2010. "The Developmental State and Post-liberation South Africa." In *Testing Democracy: Which Way Is South Africa Going?*, ed. N. Misra-Dexter and J. February, 23–45. Cape Town: Institute for Democratic Alternatives in South Africa.

Ashman, S., B. Fine, and S. Newman. 2011. "Amnesty International? The Nature, Scale and Impact of Capital Flight from South Africa." *Journal of Southern African Studies* 37 (1): 7–25.

Aspinall, E. 2013. "A Nation in Fragments: Patronage and Neoliberalism in Contemporary Indonesia." *Critical Asian Studies* 45 (1): 27–54.

Auty, R. M. 1993. *Sustaining Development in Mineral Economies: The Resource Curse Thesis.* London: Routledge.

Auty, R. 2002. *Sustaining Development in Mineral Economies: The Resource Curse Thesis.* London: Routledge.

Aviles, W. 2006. *Global Capitalism, Democracy, and Civil–Military Relations in Colombia.* Albany: State University of New York Press.

Aviles, W. 2008. "US Intervention in Colombia: The Role of Transnational Relations." *Bulletin of Latin American Research* 27 (3): 410–29.

Azmeh, S., and K. Nadvi. 2013. "Greater Chinese Global Production Networks in the Middle East: The Rise of the Jordanian Garment Industry." *Development and Change* 44 (6): 1317–40.

Azpiazu, D., E. M. Basualdo, and H. J. Nochteff. 1998. "Menem's Great Swindle: Convertibility, Inequality and the Neoliberal Shock." *NACLA Report on the Americas* 31 (6): 16.

Babb, S. 2009. *Behind the Development Banks: Washington Politics, World Poverty, and the Wealth of Nations.* Chicago: University of Chicago Press.

Babb, S. 2013. "The Washington Consensus as Transnational Policy Paradigm: Its Origins, Trajectory and Likely Successor." *Review of International Political Economy* 20 (2): 268–97.

Babones, S. 2011. "The Middling Kingdom." *Foreign Affairs* 90 (5): 66–78.

Bacha, E., and A. Fishlow. 2011. "The Recent Commodity Price Boom and Latin American Growth: More Than New Bottles for an Old Wine?" In *The Oxford Handbook of Latin American Economics*, ed. J. A. Ocampo and J. Ros. Oxford: Oxford University Press.

Baer, W. 1972. "Import Substitution and Industrialization in Latin America: Experiences and Interpretations." *Latin American Research Review* 7 (1): 95–122.

Baer, W., and P. Beckerman. 1989. "The Decline and Fall of Brazil's Cruzado." *Latin American Research Review* 24 (1): 35–64.

Baffes, J., A. Kabundi, P. Nagle, and F. Ohnsorge. 2018. "Special Focus 1: The Role of Major Emerging Markets in Global Commodity Demand." *Global Economic Prospects*, June 2018. Washington, DC: World Bank. http://pubdocs.worldbank.org/en/184021

526414119243/Global-Economic-Prospects-June-2018-Topical-Issue-global-commo
dity-demand.pdf.

Baker, J. 2016. "The Middle Class President." *New Mandala*, August 5, 2016. http://www
.newmandala.org/comfortable-uncomfortable-accommodations.

Balbi S., C. R. 2008. "Violencia, democracia y Gobernabilidad de los países andinos de la
subregión (Bolivia, Ecuador, Perú)." *Temas Sociales* 28: 273–95.

Ban, C. 2013. "Brazil's Liberal Neo-developmentalism: New Paradigm or Edited Orthodoxy?" *Review of International Political Economy* 20 (2): 298–331.

Ban, C., and M. Blyth. 2013. "The BRICs and the Washington Consensus: An Introduction." *Review of International Political Economy* 20 (2): 241–55.

Bates, R. H. 1981. *Markets and States in Tropical Africa: The Political Basis of Agricultural Policies*. Berkeley: University of California Press.

BBC. 2003. "Ecuador Set for Fresh IMF Funds." February 7, 2003. http://news.bbc.co.uk
/1/hi/business/2738791.stm.

BBC. 2013. "Colombia Agricultural Strike Sparks Fear of Shortages." August 24, 2013.
http://www.bbc.co.uk/news/world-latin-america-23829482.

BBC. 2014. "The MINT Countries: Next Economic Giants?" January 6, 2014. https://
www.bbc.co.uk/news/magazine-25548060.

Beardsworth, N. 2018. "Zambian Economy on Slippery Slope." *Mail & Guardian*, October 12, 2018. https://mg.co.za/article/2018-10-12-00-zambian-economy-on-slippery
-slope.

Bebbington, D. H., and A. Bebbington. 2010. "Anatomy of a Regional Conflict: Tarija and
Resource Grievances in Morales's Bolivia." *Latin American Perspectives* 37 (4): 140–60.

Beblawi, H., and G. Luciani, eds. 1987. *The Rentier State*. London: Croom Helm.

Becker, D. G. 1982. "'Bonanza Development' and the 'New Bourgeoisie': Peru Under
Military Rule." *Comparative Political Studies* 15 (3): 243–88.

Becker, M. 2013. "The Stormy Relations Between Rafael Correa and Social Movements
in Ecuador." *Latin American Perspectives* 40 (3): 43–62.

Becker, M., and T. N. Riofrancos. 2018. "A Souring Friendship, a Left Divided." *NACLA
Report on the Americas* 50 (2): 124–27.

Behuria, P., L. Buur, and H. Gray. 2017. "Studying Political Settlements in Africa." *African
Affairs* 116 (464): 508–25.

Bergesen, A. 2015. "World-System Theory After Andre Gunder Frank." *Journal of World-
Systems Research* 21 (1): 147–61.

Bernal, R. L. 1984. "The IMF and Class Struggle in Jamaica, 1977–1980." *Latin American
Perspectives* 11 (3): 53–82.

Bernstein, H. 1971. "Modernization Theory and the Sociological Study of Development."
Journal of Development Studies 7 (2): 141–60.

Bird, K., and H. Hill. 2010. "Tiny, Poor, Land-Locked, Indebted, But Growing: Lessons
for Late Reforming Transition Economies from Laos." *Oxford Development Studies* 38
(2): 117–43.

Bissessar, A. M. 2014. "Whose Governance? IMF Austerities in a Small Island State: The
Case of Jamaica." *Journal of Reviews on Global Economics* 3: 190–99.

Block, F. 1977. "The Ruling Class Does Not Rule: Notes on the Marxist Theory of the State." *Socialist Revolution* 33 (7): 6–28.

Block, F. 2001. "Using Social Theory to Leap Over Historical Contingencies: A Comment on Robinson." *Theory and Society* 30 (2): 215–21.

Blyth, M. 2013. *Austerity: The History of a Dangerous Idea*. Oxford: Oxford University Press.

Boas, T. C., and J. Gans-Morse. 2009. "Neoliberalism: From New Liberal Philosophy to Anti-liberal Slogan." *Studies in Comparative International Development* 44 (2): 137–61.

Boito, A., and T. Berringer. 2014. "Social Classes, Neodevelopmentalism, and Brazilian Foreign Policy Under Presidents Lula and Dilma." *Latin American Perspectives* 41 (5): 94–109.

Boito, A., and A. Saad-Filho. 2016. "State, State Institutions, and Political Power in Brazil." *Latin American Perspectives* 43 (2): 190–206.

Bond, P. 2000. *Elite Transition: From Apartheid to Neoliberalism in South Africa*. Pietermaritzburg: Pluto Press.

Bonini, A. 2012. "Complementary and Competitive Regimes of Accumulation: Natural Resources and Development in the World-System." *Journal of World Systems Research* 18 (1): 50–68.

Boone, C. 1990. "The Making of a Rentier Class: Wealth Accumulation and Political Control in Senegal." *Journal of Development Studies* 26 (3): 425–49.

Boschi, R., and F. Gaitán. 2009. "Politics and Development: Lessons from Latin America." *Brazilian Political Science Review*, 4 (selected edition).

Botiveau, R. 2013. "Longevity of the Tripartite Alliance: The Post-Mangaung Sequence." *Review of African Political Economy* 40 (138): 620–27.

Braudel, F. 1982. *Civilization and Capitalism, 15th–18th Century: The Perspective of the World*. Berkeley: University of California Press.

Brautigam, D. 2009. *The Dragon's Gift: The Real Story of China in Africa*. Oxford: Oxford University Press.

Brautigam, D. 2011. "Aid 'with Chinese Characteristics': Chinese Foreign Aid and Development Finance Meet the OECD–DAC Aid Regime." *Journal of International Development* 23 (5): 752–64.

Brautigam, D. 2013. "Rubbery Numbers for Chinese Aid to Africa." China in Africa the Real Story, April 30, 2013. http://www.chinaafricarealstory.com/2013/04/rubbery-numbers-on-chinese-aid.html.

Brautigam, D., and K. P. Gallagher. 2014. "Bartering Globalization: China's Commodity-Backed Finance in Africa and Latin America." *Global Policy* 5 (3): 346–52.

Brautigam, D., and S. Knack. 2004. "Foreign Aid, Institutions, and Governance in Sub-Saharan Africa." *Economic Development and Cultural Change* 52 (2): 255–85.

Brautigam, D., and H. Zhang. 2013. "Green Dreams: Myth and Reality in China's Agricultural Investment in Africa." *Third World Quarterly* 34 (9): 1676–96.

Bremmer, I. 2017. "The Mixed Fortunes of the BRICS Countries in 5 Facts." *Time*, September 1, 2017. http://time.com/4923837/brics-summit-xiamen-mixed-fortunes.

Bremmer, I., and R. Johnston. 2009. "The Rise and Fall of Resource Nationalism." *Survival* 51 (2): 149–58.

Brenner, R. 1977. "The Origins of Capitalist Development: A Critique of Neo-Smithian Marxism." *New Left Review* (104): 25–92.

Brenner, R. 2003. *The Boom and the Bubble: The US in the World Economy.* London: Verso.

Brenner, N., J. Peck, and N. Theodore. 2010. "Variegated Neoliberalization: Geographies, Modalities, Pathways." *Global Networks* 10 (2): 182–222.

Breslin, S. 2011a. "China and the Crisis: Global Power, Domestic Caution and Local Initiative." *Contemporary Politics* 17 (2): 185–200.

Breslin, S. 2011b. "The 'China Model' and the Global Crisis: From Friedrich List to a Chinese Mode of Governance?" *International Affairs* 87 (6): 1323–43.

Breslin, S. 2013. "Xi-ing Is Believing: Political and Economic Reforms Under China's New Leadership." ISPI analysis no. 210, November 2013. Istituto per gli Studi di Politica Internazionale. http://www.ispionline.it/sites/default/files/pubblicazioni/analysis_210 _2013.pdf.

Breslin, S. 2014. "Financial Transitions in the PRC: Banking on the State?" *Third World Quarterly* 35 (6): 996–1013.

Bresser-Pereira, L. C. 2012. "Structuralist Macroeconomics and the New Developmentalism." *Brazilian Journal of Political Economy* 32 (3): 347–66.

Bresser-Pereira, L. C. 2015. "State-Society Cycles and Political Pacts in a National-Dependent Society: Brazil." *Latin American Research Review* 50 (2): 3–22.

Bril-Mascarenhas, T., and A. E. Post. 2015. "Policy Traps: Consumer Subsidies in Post-crisis Argentina." *Studies in Comparative International Development* 50 (1): 98–120.

Brown, A. 2018. "Supporting Kazakhstan's Commitment to Fiscal Consolidation and Long-Term Economic Transformation." World Bank, January 12, 2018. https://www .worldbank.org/en/news/opinion/2018/01/12/supporting-kazakhstans-commitment -to-fiscal-consolidation-and-long-term-economic-transformation.

Bunker, S. G. 1988. *Underdeveloping the Amazon: Extraction, Unequal Exchange, and the Failure of the Modern State.* Chicago: University of Chicago Press.

Bunker, S. G., and P. S. Ciccantell. 2005. *Globalization and the Race for Resources.* Baltimore: Johns Hopkins University Press.

Bunker, S. G., and P. S. Ciccantell. 2007. *East Asia and the Global Economy: Japan's Ascent, with Implications For China's Future.* Baltimore: Johns Hopkins University Press.

Burawoy, M. 1972. *The Colour of Class on the Copper Mines: From African Advancement to Zambianization.* Manchester: Manchester University Press for the Institute for African Studies, University of Zambia.

Burron, N. 2011. "Curbing 'Anti-Systemic' Tendencies in Peru: Democracy Promotion and the US Contribution to Producing Neoliberal Hegemony." *Third World Quarterly* 32 (9): 1655–72.

Busch, M. 2015. "Tinkerer in Chief: One Year of Economic Leadership Under Joko Widodo." *The Interpreter*, November 5, 2015. https://www.lowyinstitute.org/the -interpreter/tinkerer-chief-one-year-economic-leadership-under-joko-widodo.

Buxton, J. 2008. "Venezuela's Bolivarian Revolution." *Global Dialogue* 10: 11–22.

Buxton, J. 2016. "Venezuela After Chavez." *New Left Review* 99. https://newleftreview.org/issues/II99/articles/julia-buxton-venezuela-after-chavez.

Cai, P. 2017. "Understanding China's Belt and Road Initiative." Sydney: Lowy Institute for International Policy. http://hdl.handle.net/11540/6810.

Cameron, M. 1997. "Political and Economic Origins of Regime Change in Peru: The Eighteenth Brumaire of Alberto Fujimori." In *The Peruvian Labyrinth: Polity, Society, Economy*, ed. M. Cameron and P. Mauceri, 37–69. University Park: Penn State University Press.

Cameron, M. A. 2008. "Peru's Left and APRA's Victory." Paper presented at the conference Latin America's "Left Turn": Causes and Implications, Harvard University, Boston, April 4–5, 2008.

Cameron, P. D., and M. C. Stanley. 2017. *Oil, Gas, and Mining: A Sourcebook for the Extractive Industries*. Washington, DC: World Bank Group.

Cammack, P. 2004. "What the World Bank Means by Poverty Reduction, and Why It Matters." *New Political Economy* 9 (2): 189–211.

Campello, D. 2007. "Do Markets Vote? A Systematic Analysis of Portfolio Investors' Response to National Elections." Unpublished, Department of Political Science, University of California, Los Angeles.

Campello, D. 2015. *The Politics of Market Discipline in Latin America: Globalization and Democracy*. New York: Cambridge University Press.

Canuto, O. 2014. "The Commodity Super Cycle: Is This Time Different?" *World Bank—Economic Premise* 150: 1–3.

Cardoso, F. H., and E. Faletto. 1979. *Dependency and Development in Latin America*. Trans. M. Mattingly Urquidi. Berkeley: University of California Press.

Carmody, D. P. 2013. *The Rise of the BRICS in Africa: The Geopolitics of South-South Relations*. London: Zed.

Carrillo, I. R. 2014. "The New Developmentalism and the Challenges to Long-Term Stability in Brazil." *Latin American Perspectives* 41 (5): 59–74.

Casteñeda, J. G. 2006. "Latin America's Left Turn." *Foreign Affairs* 85 (3): 28–43.

CEMOTEV. n.d. "'Primary Commodities' Access." Centre d'études sur la mondialisation, les conflits, les territoires et les vulnérabilités. Accessed July 8, 2019. http://www.cemotev.uvsq.fr/cemotev/langue-en/primary-commodities-access/primary-commodities-access-405955.kjsp?RH=1274103082759.

Chabal, P., and J.-P. Daloz. 1999. *Africa Works: Disorder as Political Instrument*. London: James Currey.

Chang, H. J. 2002. *Kicking Away the Ladder: Development Strategy in Historical Perspective*. London: Anthem.

Chatham House. n.d. Resourcetrade.earth database. Accessed April 29, 2019. http://resourcetrade.earth/data.

Chavez O'Brien, E. 1992. "El mercado de trabajo y las nuevas tendencias en la estructura del empleo en el Perú." *Socialismo y participación* 60 (20).

Cheeseman, N., R. Ford, and N. Simutanyi. 2013. "Is There a 'Populist' Threat in Zambia?" In *Zambia: Building Prosperity from Resource Wealth*, ed. C. S. Adam, P. Collier, and M. Gondwe, 493–512. Oxford: Oxford University Press.

Cheeseman, N., and M. Hinfelaar. 2010. "Parties, Platforms, and Political Mobilization: The Zambian Presidential Election of 2008." *African Affairs* 109 (434): 51–76.

Cheeseman, N., and M. Larmer. 2015. "Ethnopopulism in Africa: Opposition Mobilization in Diverse and Unequal Societies." *Democratization* 22 (1): 22–50.

Chen, M. S., and J. S. Kang. 2018. "Credit Booms: Is China Different?" IMF Working Paper 18/2. Washington, DC: International Monetary Fund.

Cheremukhin, A., M. Golosov, S. Guriev, and A. Tsyvinski. 2015. *The Economy of People's Republic of China from 1953*. NBER Working Paper No. 21397. Cambridge, MA: National Bureau of Economic Research.

Chibber, V. 2002. "Bureaucratic Rationality and the Developmental State." *American Journal of Sociology* 107 (4): 951–89.

Chibber, V. 2003. *Locked in Place: State-Building and Late Industrialization in India*. Princeton, NJ: Princeton University Press.

Chibber, V. 2005. "Reviving the Developmental State? The Myth of the 'National Bourgeoisie.'" *Socialist Register* 41: 144–65.

Chin, G. T., and K. P. Gallagher. 2019. "Coordinated Credit Spaces: The Globalization of Chinese Development Finance." *Development and Change* 50 (1): 245–74.

Choi, N. 2014. "Local Political Elites in Indonesia: 'Risers' and 'Holdovers.'" *Sojourn: Journal of Social Issues in Southeast Asia* 29 (2): 364–407.

Chua, C. 2008. *Chinese Big Business in Indonesia: The State of Capital*. London: Routledge.

Chwieroth, J. 2007. "Neoliberal Economists and Capital Account Liberalization in Emerging Markets." *International Organization* 61 (2): 443–63.

Clark, P. 2010. "Sowing the Oil? The Chavez Government's Policy Framework for an Alternative Food System in Venezuela." *Humboldt Journal of Social Relations* 33 (1/2): 135–65.

Clayton, F. 2018. "As Others Snub Bolivia's Lithium, Will Morales' Gamble on Germany Pay Off?" *Americas Quarterly*, May 22, 2018. https://www.americasquarterly.org/content /others-snub-bolivias-lithium-will-morales-gamble-germany-pay.

Clemente, J. 2015. "China's Car, Gasoline, and Oil Markets to 2020." *Forbes*, March 18, 2015. http://www.forbes.com/sites/judeclemente/2015/03/18/chinas-car-gasoline-and -oil-markets-to-2020.

CNBC Africa. 2018. "This Is What Angola Is Telling Investors to Get Them to Invest in Its Eurobonds." May 11, 2018. https://www.cnbcafrica.com/news/southern-africa/2018 /05/11/angola-telling-investors-get-invest-eurobonds.

Coates, B., and N. Luu. 2012. "China's Emergence in Global Commodity Markets." *Economic Round-up* 1: 1–30.

Cohen, A. 2018. "Exxon and Chevron Hope to Cash in After New Caspian Summit." *Forbes*, August 9, 2018. https://www.forbes.com/sites/arielcohen/2018/08/09/exxon-and -chevron-hope-to-cash-in-after-new-caspian-summit/#6854f0793119.

Conaghan, C. M. 1988. *Restructuring Domination: Industrialists and the State in Ecuador*. Pittsburgh, PA: University of Pittsburgh Press.

Conaghan, C. M. 1996. "A Deficit of Democratic Authenticity: Political Linkage and the Public in Andean Polities." *Studies in Comparative International Development* 31 (3): 32–55.

Conaghan, C. M., and R. Espinal. 1990. "Unlikely Transitions to Uncertain Regimes? Democracy Without Compromise in the Dominican Republic and Ecuador." *Journal of Latin American Studies* 22 (3): 553–74.

Conaghan, C. M., J. M. Malloy, and L. A. Abugattas. 1990. "Business and the 'Boys': The Politics of Neoliberalism in the Central Andes." *Latin American Research Review* 25 (2): 3–30.

Conceição, P., and H. Marone. 2008. *Characterizing the 21st Century First Commodity Boom: Drivers and Impact*. Office of Development Studies Working Paper. New York: United Nations Development Programme.

Cook, M. L., and J. C. Bazler. 2013. "Bringing Unions Back In: Labour and Left Governments in Latin America." Working paper. Cornell University ILR School. http://digitalcommons.ilr.cornell.edu/workingpapers/166.

Cooley, A. 2003. "Western Conditions and Domestic Choices: The Influence of External Actors on the Post-communist Transition." In *Nations in Transit 2003: Democratization in East Central Europe and Eurasia*, ed. A. Karatnycky, A. Motyl, and A. Schnetzer. Washington, DC: Freedom House.

Cooper, F. 2002. *Africa Since 1940: The Past of the Present*. Cambridge: Cambridge University Press.

Corkin, L. 2011. "Uneasy Allies: China's Evolving Relations with Angola." *Journal of Contemporary African Studies* 29 (2): 169–80.

Corkin, L. 2012. "Chinese Construction Companies in Angola: A Local Linkages Perspective." *Resources Policy* 37 (4): 475–83.

Cornia, A., R. Jolly, and F. Stewart. 1987. *Adjustment with a Human Face*. Vol. 1, *Protecting the Vulnerable and Promoting Growth*. Oxford: Clarendon.

Cornwall, A., and K. Brock. 2005. "What Do Buzzwords Do for Development Policy? A Critical Look at 'Participation,' 'Empowerment,' and 'Poverty Reduction.'" *Third World Quarterly* 26 (7): 1043–60.

Coronil, F. 1997. *The Magical State: Nature, Money, and Modernity in Venezuela*. Chicago: University of Chicago Press.

Cotula, L. 2012. "The International Political Economy of the Global Land Rush: A Critical Appraisal of Trends, Scale, Geography, and Drivers." *Journal of Peasant Studies* 39 (3–4): 649–80.

Cox, K. R., and R. Negi. 2010. "The State and the Question of Development in Sub-Saharan Africa." *Review of African Political Economy* 37 (123): 71–85.

Cox, R. W. 1979. "Ideologies and the New International Economic Order: Reflections on Some Recent Literature." *International Organization* 33 (2): 257–302.

Craig, D., and D. Porter. 2003. "Poverty Reduction Strategy Papers: A New Convergence." *World Development* 31 (1): 53–69.

Crowson, P. 2018. "Intensity of Use Reexamined." *Mineral Economics* 31 (1–2): 61–70.

Cummings, S. N., and O. Nørgaard. 2004. "Conceptualising State Capacity: Comparing Kazakhstan and Kyrgyzstan." *Political Studies* 52 (4): 685–708.

Cunha Filho, C. M., R. S. Gonçalves, and A. D. Déa. 2010. "The National Development Plan as a Political Economic Strategy in Evo Morales's Bolivia: Accomplishments and Limitations." *Latin American Perspectives* 37 (4): 177–96.

Curado, M. 2015. "China Rising: Threats and Opportunities for Brazil." *Latin American Perspectives* 42 (6): 88–104.

Dauvergne, P., and D. BL Farias. 2012. "The Rise of Brazil as a Global Development Power." *Third World Quarterly* 33 (5): 903–17.

Davies, O. 1986. "An Analysis of the Management of the Jamaican Economy: 1972–1985." *Social and Economic Studies* 35 (1): 73–109.

de Echave C., José. 2013. "La minería y la protección ambiental en el discurso presidencial." *Observatorio de conflictos mineros de América Latina.* July 31, 2013. https://www.ocmal .org/la-mineria-y-la-proteccion-ambiental-en-el-discurso-presidencial.

de la Torre, C. 1997. "Populism and Democracy: Political Discourses and Cultures in Contemporary Ecuador." *Latin American Perspectives* 24 (3): 12–24.

de la Torre, C. 2010. *Populist Seduction in Latin America.* 2nd ed. Athens: Ohio University Press.

de la Torre, C. 2013. "El tecnopopulismo de Rafael Correa: Es compatible el carisma con la tecnocracia?" *Latin American Research Review* 48 (1): 24–43.

de Oliveira, R. S. 2011. "Illiberal Peacebuilding in Angola." *Journal of Modern African Studies* 49 (2): 287–314.

de Waal, A. 2013. "The Theory and Practice of Meles Zenawi." *African Affairs* 112 (446): 148–55.

Dieter, H. 2006. "The Decline of the IMF: Is It Reversible? Should It Be Reversed?" *Global Governance: A Review of Multilateralism and International Organizations* 12 (4): 343–49.

Dinerstein, A. C. 2003. "Power or Counter Power? The Dilemma of the Piquetero Movement in Argentina Post-crisis." *Capital & Class* 27 (3): 1–8.

Dinerstein, A., M. Deledicque, and D. Contartese. 2008. "Notas de investigación sobre la innovación organizacional en entidades de trabajadores desocupados en la Argentina." *Realidad Económica* 234: 50–79.

Dobbs, R., J. Oppenheim, F. Thompson, S. Mareels, S. Nyquist, and S. Sanghvi. 2013. "Resource Revolution: Tracking Global Commodity Markets." McKinsey & Company, September 2013. http://www.mckinsey.com/insights/energy_resources_materials /resource_revolution_tracking_global_commodity_markets.

Doctor, M. 2015. "Assessing the Changing Roles of the Brazilian Development Bank." *Bulletin of Latin American Research* 34 (2): 197–213.

Dollar, D. 2018. "Is China's Development Finance a Challenge to the International Order?" *Asian Economic Policy Review* 13 (2): 283–98.

Domjan, P., and M. Stone. 2010. "A Comparative Study of Resource Nationalism in Russia and Kazakhstan, 2004–2008." *Europe-Asia Studies* 62 (1): 35–62.

Drahokoupil, J., ed. 2017. *Chinese Investment in Europe: Corporate Strategies and Labour Relations.* Brussels: European Trade Union Institute.

Drakapoulos, Y. 2018. "The Evolution of Bauxite Mining in Jamaica: Modern Challenges for a Mature Industry." In *Travaux 47.* Proceedings of the 36th International ICSOBA Conference, Belem, Brazil, October 29–November 1, 2018. https://icsoba.org/sites /default/files/Papers2018/BAUXITE/BX05%20-%20The%20Evolution%20of%20Bau xite%20Mining%20in%20Jamaica%20-%20Modern%20Challenges%20for%20a%20 Mature%20Industry.pdf.

Dreher, A., A. Fuchs, B. C. Parks, A. M. Strange, and M. J. Tierney. 2017. "Aid, China, and Growth: Evidence from a New Global Development Finance Dataset." AidData Working Paper no. 46. Williamsburg, VA: AidData. https://china.aiddata.org/projects /38053?iframe=y.

Dube, R. 2014a. "Bolivia to Appeal Ruling Favoring India's Jindal in El Mutún Dispute." *Wall Street Journal*, August 26, 2014. http://www.wsj.com/articles/bolivia-to-appeal -ruling-favoring-indias-jindal-in-el-mutun-dispute-1409074729.

Dube, R. 2014b. "Peruvian Prime Minister César Villanueva Resigns." *Wall Street Journal*, February 24, 2014. http://www.wsj.com/articles/SB100014240527023046104045794031 43968816858.

Duménil, G., and D. Lévy. 2001. "Costs and Benefits of Neoliberalism: A Class Analysis." *Review of International Political Economy* 8 (4): 578–607.

Duménil, G., and D. Lévy. 2004. *Capital Resurgent: Roots of the Neoliberal Revolution*. Cambridge, MA.: Harvard University Press.

Durand, F. 2002. "Business and the Crisis of Peruvian Democracy." *Business and Politics* 4 (3): 319–41.

Dymond, A. 2007. *Undermining Development? Copper Mining in Zambia*. Scottish Catholic International Aid Fund, Christian Aid, and Action for Southern Africa.

Eaton, K. 2011. "Conservative Autonomy Movements: Territorial Dimensions of Ideological Conflict in Bolivia and Ecuador." *Comparative Politics* 43 (3): 291–310.

Eaton, K. 2015. "Disciplining Regions: Subnational Contention in Neoliberal Peru." *Territory, Politics, Governance* 3 (2): 124–46.

Ebenau, M., and V. Liberatore. 2013. "Neodevelopmentalist State Capitalism in Brazil and Argentina: Chances, Limits, and Contradictions." *Der Moderne staat—Zeitschrift Für Public Policy, Recht Und Management* 6 (1): 105–25.

Economic Commission for Latin America and the Caribbean. n.d. CEPALSTAT. Accessed June 21 2019. https://estadisticas.cepal.org/cepalstat/WEB_CEPALSTAT/estadisticas Indicadores.asp?idioma=i.

Economist. 2013. "Peak Oil." March 5, 2013. http://www.economist.com/blogs/graphicdetail /2013/03/focus-0.

Economist. 2014. "Building the Dream." April 19, 2014. https://www.economist.com/special -report/2014/04/19/building-the-dream.

Economist. 2015. "Cornering the Markets." July 4, 2015. http://www.economist.com/news /finance-and-economics/21656721-how-china-continues-reshape-world-commodities -cornering-markets.

Economist. 2018. "Why Commodity Prices Are Surging." The Economist Explains, January 11, 2018. https://www.economist.com/the-economist-explains/2018/01/11 /why-commodity-prices-are-surging.

Economist Intelligence Unit. 2013. "Peru: Part Privatisation of State Energy Firm Approved." December 17, 2013. http://www.eiu.com/industry/article/221345806/peru-part -privatization-of-state-energy-firm-approved/2013-12-17.

Edwards, L., and R. Jenkins. 2015. "The Impact of Chinese Import Penetration on the South African Manufacturing Sector." *Journal of Development Studies* 51 (4): 447–63.

El Comercio. 2009. "Correa dice que es peor negociar con China que con el FMI." December 5, 2009. http://www.elcomercio.com/actualidad/correa-dice-peor-negociar-china .html.

El Comercio. 2014. "Los incentivos no son suficientes para la minería." December 2, 2014. http://www.elcomercio.com/actualidad/incentivos-impuestos-insuficientes-mineria -inversion.html.

Ellis, F. 1983. "Agricultural Marketing and Peasant–State Transfers in Tanzania." *Journal of Peasant Studies* 10 (4): 214–42.

Ellner, S. 2001. "The Radical Potential of Chavismo in Venezuela: The First Year and a Half in Power." *Latin American Perspectives* 28 (5): 5–32.

Ellner, S. 2004. "Introduction: The Search for Explanations." In *Venezuelan Politics in the Chávez Era: Class, Polarization, and Conflict,* ed. S. Ellner and D. Hellinger, 7–26. Boulder, CO: Lynne Rienner.

Ellner, S. 2012. "The Distinguishing Features of Latin America's New Left in Power: The Chávez, Morales, and Correa Governments." *Latin American Perspectives* 39 (1): 96–114.

Ellner, S. 2013. "Social and Political Diversity and the Democratic Road to Change in Venezuela." *Latin American Perspectives* 40 (3): 63–82.

El Telégrafo. 2014. "Ecuador aplicará nuevas reformas al sector minero." June 7, 2014. http:// www.telegrafo.com.ec/economia/item/ecuador-aplicara-nuevas-reformas-al-sector -minero-2.html.

Enerdata. 2018. EnerOutlook 2018. Accessed April 29, 2019. https://eneroutlook.ener data.net.

Eom, J., D. Brautigam, and L. Benabdallah. 2018. "The Path Ahead: The 7th Forum on China–Africa Cooperation." Briefing Paper 1/2018. Washington, DC: China Africa Research Initiative.

Erten, B., and J. A. Ocampo. 2013. "Super-Cycles of Commodity Prices Since the Mid-nineteenth Century." *World Development* 44: 14–30.

Escribano, G. 2013. "Ecuador's Energy Policy Mix: Development Versus Conservation and Nationalism with Chinese Loans." *Energy Policy* 57: 152–59.

Evans, P. 1979. *Dependent Development: The Alliance of Multinational, State, and Local Capital in Brazil.* Princeton, NJ: Princeton University Press.

Evans, P. 1989. "Predatory, Developmental, and Other Apparatuses: A Comparative Political Economy Perspective on the Third World State." *Sociological Forum* 4 (4): 561–87.

Evans, P. 1995. *Embedded Autonomy: States and Industrial Transformation.* Princeton, NJ: Princeton University Press.

Fairfield, T. 2010. "Business Power and Tax Reform: Taxing Income and Profits in Chile and Argentina." *Latin American Politics and Society* 52 (2): 37–71.

Fairfield, T. 2011. "Business Power and Protest: Argentina's Agricultural Producers Protest in Comparative Context." *Studies in Comparative International Development* 46 (4): 424–53.

Fairfield, T. 2015. *Private Wealth and Public Revenue in Latin America: Business Power and Tax Politics.* New York: Cambridge University Press.

Farchy, J. 2011. "China's Aluminium Imports Predicted to Soar by 2020." *Financial Times,* November 15, 2011.

Farooki, M. 2012. "China's Metals Demand and Commodity Prices: A Case of Disruptive Development?" *European Journal of Development Research* 24 (1): 56–70.

Farooki, M., and R. Kaplinsky. 2013. *The Impact of China on Global Commodity Prices: The Global Reshaping of the Resource Sector.* London: Routledge.

Féliz, M. 2011. "Neoliberalismos, neodesarrollismos y proyectos contrahegemonicos en sudamerica." *Astrolabio* 7. http://revistas.unc.edu.ar/index.php/astrolabio/article/view /490.

Feliz, M. 2012. "Neo-Developmentalism: Beyond Neoliberalism? Capitalist Crisis and Argentina's Development Since the 1990s." *Historical Materialism* 20 (2): 105–23.

Féliz, M. 2015. "Limits and Barriers of Neodevelopmentalism: Lessons from the Argentinean Experience, 2003–2011." *Review of Radical Political Economics* 47 (1): 70–89.

Fernando Jilberto, A. E. and B. Hogenboom. 2012. *Latin America Facing China: South–South Relations Beyond the Washington Consensus.* Oxford: Berghahn.

Ferrari-Filho, F., and L. F. De Paula. 2003. "The Legacy of the Real Plan and an Alternative Agenda for the Brazilian Economy." *Investigación económica* 62 (244): 57–92.

Ferrer, A., A. Clemente, and A. B. Rofman. 2004. *Sociedad y deuda externa. Dimensiones sociales, políticas, económicas y jurídicas.* Buenos Aires: University of Buenos Aires. http:// biblioteca.unm.edu.ar/cgi-bin/koha/opac-detail.pl?biblionumber=7984.

Figueroa, A. 2012. "Competencia y circulación de las elites económicas." *Economía* 27 (53–54): 255–91.

Financial Times. 2013. "A Timely Chance to Revive World Trade: Brazil's Roberto Azevedo Must Show He Is His Own Man." May 9, 2013.

Findlay, R. 1980. "On W. Arthur Lewis' Contributions to Economics." *Scandinavian Journal of Economics* 82 (1): 62–79.

Fine, B. 2010. "Engaging the MEC: Or a Few of My Views on a Few Things." *Transformation: Critical Perspectives on Southern Africa* 71 (1): 26–49.

Fine, B. 2012. "Assessing South Africa's New Growth Path: Framework for Change?" *Review of African Political Economy* 39 (134): 551–68.

Fine, B., and Z. Rustomjee. 1996. *The Political Economy of South Africa: From Minerals-Energy Complex to Industrialization.* London: C. Hurst.

Fischer, A. M. 2015. "The End of Peripheries? On the Enduring Relevance of Structuralism for Understanding Contemporary Global Development." *Development and Change* 46 (4): 700–732.

Fitch, J. S. 2005. "Post-transition Coups: Ecuador 2000." *Journal of Political and Military Sociology* 33 (1): 39.

Fogel, B., and Jacobs, S. 2018. "From Zuma to Ramaphosa." *Africa Is a Country,* August 22, 2018. https://africasacountry.com/2018/02/from-zuma-to-ramaphosa.

Fornes, G., and A. Mendez. 2018. *The China–Latin America Axis: Emerging Markets and Their Role in an Increasingly Globalised World.* London: Palgrave Macmillan.

Fourcade-Gourinchas, M., and S. L. Babb. 2002. "The Rebirth of the Liberal Creed: Paths to Neoliberalism in Four Countries." *American Journal of Sociology* 108 (3): 533–79.

Frank, A. G. 1966. *The Development of Underdevelopment .* Boston: New England Free Press.

Frank, A. G. 1998. *ReOrient: Global Economy in the Asian Age*. Berkeley: University of California Press.

Franke, A., A. Gawrich, and G. Alakbarov. 2009. "Kazakhstan and Azerbaijan as Post-Soviet Rentier States: Resource Incomes and Autocracy as a Double 'Curse' in Post-Soviet Regimes." *Europe-Asia Studies* 61 (1): 109–40.

Fraser, A. 2005. "Poverty Reduction Strategy Papers: Now Who Calls the Shots?" *Review of African Political Economy* 32 (104–105): 317–40.

Fraser, A. 2007. "Zambia: Back to the Future?" GEG Working Paper 2007/30. Global Economic Governance Programme, Managing Aid Dependency Project, June 2007. http://www.globaleconomicgovernance.org/docs/Fraser Zambia_2007-30.

Fraser, A. 2010. "Zambia, Mining, and Neoliberalism." In *Zambia, Mining, and Neoliberalism: Boom and Bust on the Globalized Copperbelt*, ed. M. Larmer and A. Fraser. London: Palgrave Macmillan.

Fraser Institute. n.d. Economic Freedom. Accessed April 29, 2019. https://www.fraserinstitute.org/economic-freedom/dataset.

French, H. W. 2015. *China's Second Continent: How a Million Migrants Are Building a New Empire in Africa*. New York: Vintage.

Freund, B. 1978. "Oil Boom and Crisis in Contemporary Nigeria." *Review of African Political Economy* 5 (13): 91–100.

Freund, B. 2007. "South Africa: The End of Apartheid and the Emergence of the 'BEE Elite.'" *Review of African Political Economy* 34 (114): 661–78.

Freund, W. 1981. "Class Conflict, Political Economy, and the Struggle for Socialism in Tanzania." *African Affairs* 80 (321): 483–99.

Freund, W. 2013. "Swimming Against the Tide: The Macro-Economic Research Group in the South African Transition, 1991–94." *Review of African Political Economy* 40 (138): 519–36.

Frieden, J. 1981. "Third World Indebted Industrialization: International Finance and State Capitalism in Mexico, Brazil, Algeria, and South Korea." *International Organization* 35 (3): 407–31.

Fuentes, F. 2012. "The Morales Government: Neoliberalism in Disguise?" *International Socialism* 134. http://isj.org.uk/the-morales-government-neoliberalism-in-disguise.

Fuentes, F. 2015. "How Rejecting Neoliberalism Rescued Bolivia's Economy." *Green Left Weekly*, August 9, 2015. https://www.greenleft.org.au/node/59730.

Gacs, D. 2014. "How Peru Could Survive the End of the Commodities Boom." *Business Insider*, January 7, 2014. https://www.businessinsider.com/peru-after-the-end-of-commodities-boom-2014-1.

Gak, A. L. 2011. "Luces y sombras de la salida de la crisis en la República Argentina." *Iztapalapa: Revista de ciencias sociales y humanidades* 70: 69–91.

Gallagher, K., ed. 2005. *Putting Development First: The Importance of Policy Space in the WTO and IFIs*. London: Zed.

Gallagher, K. 2016. *The China Triangle: Latin America's China Boom and the Fate of the Washington Consensus*. Oxford: Oxford University Press.

Gallagher, K., and M. Myers. 2018. China–Latin America Finance Database. Washington, DC: Inter-American Dialogue. https://www.thedialogue.org/map_list.

Gallagher, K. P., A. Irwin, and K. Koleski. 2012. "The New Banks in Town: Chinese Finance in Latin America." Washington, DC: Inter-American Dialogue.

Gallagher, K., and R. Porzecanski. 2010. *The Dragon in the Room: China and the Future of Latin American Industrialization.* Stanford, CA: Stanford University Press.

Garcia, A., and P. Bond, eds. 2017. *BRICS: An Anticapitalist Critique.* Chicago: Haymarket.

Garrett, R. D., E. F. Lambin, and R. L. Naylor. 2013. "Land Institutions and Supply Chain Configurations as Determinants of Soybean Planted Area and Yields in Brazil." *Land Use Policy* 31: 385–96.

George, S., and F. Sabelli. 1994. *Faith and Credit: The World Bank's Secular Empire.* London: Penguin.

Gereffi, G. 1989. "Rethinking Development Theory: Insights from East Asia and Latin America." *Sociological Forum* 4 (4): 505–33.

Gereffi, G. 2014. "Global Value Chains in a Post-Washington Consensus World." *Review of International Political Economy* 21 (1): 9–37.

Geronimi, V., E. Anani, and A. Taranco. 2017. "Notes on Updating Price Indices and Terms of Trade for Primary Commodities." Working paper cahier du CEMOTEV no. 2017–03, December 8, 2017.

Gilbert, C. L. 2006. "International Commodity Agreements." In *Handbook on International Trade Policy*, ed. W. Kerr and J. Gaisford, 470–81. Cheltenham, UK: Edward Elgar.

Gill, L. 2015. "State Formation and Class Politics in Colombia." In *State Theory and Andean Politics: New Approaches to the Study of Rule*, ed. C. Krupa and D. Nugent, 78–98. Philadelphia: University of Pennsylvania Press.

Gill, S. 1995. "Globalisation, Market Civilisation, and Disciplinary Neoliberalism." *Millennium* 24 (3): 399–423.

Gillespie, P. 2018. "IMF Board Approves Argentina's $50 Billion Stand-by Accord." Bloomberg, June 20, 2018. https://www.bloomberg.com/news/articles/2018-06-20/imf-board -approves-argentina-s-50-billion-stand-by-arrangement.

Gillespie, P., and I. Olivera Doll. 2018. "Argentina Gets $57 Billion as IMF Doubles Down on Record Bailout." Bloomberg, September 26, 2018. https://www.bloomberg.com /news/articles/2018-09-26/argentina-gets-57-billion-as-imf-doubles-down-on-record -bailout.

Glassman, J. 2010. *Bounding the Mekong: The Asian Development Bank, China, and Thailand.* Honolulu: University of Hawai'i Press.

Gleaner. 2010. "More to the Ruling than Back-Pay." Editorial, August 5, 2010. http://jamaica -gleaner.com/gleaner/20100805/cleisure/cleisure1.html.

Gleaner. 2014. "RUSAL Acquires Remaining Government Stake in WINDALCO." December 12, 2014. http://jamaica-gleaner.com/article/news/20141212/rusal-acquires -remaining-government-stake-windalco.

Global Financial Integrity. 2012. *Illicit Financial Flows from Africa: Hidden Resource for Development.* Washington, DC: Global Financial Integrity. http://www.gfintegrity.org /storage/gfip/documents/reports/gfi_africareport_web.pdf.

Goertz, G. 2006. *Social Science Concepts: A User's Guide.* Princeton, NJ: Princeton University Press.

Goldfrank, W. L. 2000. "Paradigm Regained? The Rules of Wallerstein's World-System Method." *Journal of World-Systems Research* 6 (2): 150–95.

Goldman, M. 2006. *Imperial Nature: The World Bank and Struggles for Social Justice in the Age of Globalization.* New Haven, CT: Yale University Press.

Gonzalez-Vicente, R. 2012. "Mapping Chinese Mining Investment in Latin America: Politics or Market?" *China Quarterly* 209: 35–58.

Government of Jamaica. 2014. *Fiscal Policy Paper FY 2014/15.* April 17, 2014. Kingston: Government of Jamaica. http://www.mof.gov.jm/budgets/fiscal-policy-papers/file/7-fiscal -policy-paper-2014-15.html

Government of Zambia. 2013. "2014 Budget address by Hon. Alexander B. Chikwanda MP, Minister of Finance." Delivered to the National Assembly on Friday 11th October, 2013. http://www.sapayroll.co.za/Portals/12/Documents/TaxInfo/2014%20Final%20 Budget%20Speech%20-%20Zambia.pdf.

Grabel, I. 2018. *When Things Don't Fall Apart: Global Financial Governance and Developmental Finance in an Age of Productive Incoherence.* Cambridge, MA: MIT Press.

GRAIN. 2013. "The United Republic of Soybeans: Take Two." *Against the Grain,* June 2013. https://www.grain.org/article/entries/4749-the-united-republic-of-soybeans-take-two.

Griffith-Jones, S. 2014. *A BRICS Development Bank: A Dream Coming True?* United Nations Conference on Trade and Development Discussion Papers. No. 215 (March 2014). New York: United Nations Conference on Trade and Development.

Griffith-Jones, S., and J. A. Ocampo. 2009. *The Financial Crisis and Its Impact on Developing Countries.* Poverty Reduction Discussion Paper PG/2009/001. New York: United Nations Development Programme.

Grigoryan, A. 2016. "The Ruling Bargain: Sovereign Wealth Funds in Elite-Dominated Societies." *Economics of Governance* 17 (2): 165–84.

Grosfoguel, R. 2000. "Developmentalism, Modernity, and Dependency Theory in Latin America." *Nepantla: Views from South* 1 (2): 347–74.

Grugel, J., and M. P. Riggirozzi. 2007. "The Return of the State in Argentina." *International Affairs* 83 (1): 87–107.

Gulick, J. 2011. "The Long Twentieth Century and Barriers to China's Hegemonic Accession." *Journal of World-Systems Research* 17 (1): 4–38.

Güven, A. B. 2018. "Whither the Post-Washington Consensus? International Financial Institutions and Development Policy Before and After the Crisis." *Review of International Political Economy* 25 (3): 392–417.

Gwynne, R. N., and C. Kay. 2000. "Views from the Periphery: Futures of Neoliberalism in Latin America." *Third World Quarterly* 21 (1): 141–56.

Hadiz, V. R., and R. Robison. 2013. "The Political Economy of Oligarchy and the Reorganization of Power in Indonesia." *Indonesia* (96): 35–57.

Hadiz, V. R., and R. Robison. 2017. "Competing Populisms in Post-authoritarian Indonesia." *International Political Science Review* 38 (4): 488–502.

Haggard, S., and R. Kaufman. 1989. "The Politics of Stabilization and Structural Adjustment." In *Developing Country Debt and Economic Performance,* ed. J. Sachs, vol. 1, *The International Financial System,* 209–54. Chicago: University of Chicago Press.

Haglund, D. 2011. *Blessing or Curse? The Rise of Mineral Dependence Among Low- and Middle-Income Countries*. Oxford: Oxford Policy Management.

Hakim, P. 2003. "Latin America's Lost Illusions: Dispirited Politics." *Journal of Democracy* 14 (2): 108–22.

Hall, P. A., and D. Soskice, eds. 2001. *Varieties of Capitalism: The Institutional Foundations of Comparative Advantage*. Oxford: Oxford University Press.

Handley, P. A. 2008. *Business and the State in Africa: Economic Policy-Making in the Neo-liberal Era*. Cambridge: Cambridge University Press.

Hanieh, A. 2011. *Capitalism and Class in the Gulf Arab States*. New York: Palgrave Macmillan.

Hansen, J. and F. Gale. 2014. "China in the Next Decade: Rising Meat Demand and Growing Imports of Feed." *Amber Waves*, April 7, 2014. USDA Economic Research Service. http://www.ers.usda.gov/amber-waves/2014/april/china-in-the-next-decade-rising -meat-demand-and-growing-imports-of-feed.

Hao, F., and T. Baxter. 2019. "China's Coal Consumption on the Rise." *Chinadialogue*, January 3, 2019. https://www.chinadialogue.net/article/show/single/en/11107-China-s-coal -consumption-on-the-rise.

Harrison, G. 2004. *The World Bank and Africa: The Construction of Governance States*. London: Routledge.

Harrison, G. 2005. "Economic Faith, Social Project, and a Misreading of African Society: The Travails of Neoliberalism in Africa." *Third World Quarterly* 26 (8): 1303–20.

Hart, G. 2003. *Disabling Globalization: Places of Power in Post-apartheid South Africa*. Berkeley: University of California Press.

Harvey, D. 2005. *A Brief History of Neoliberalism*. Oxford: Oxford University Press.

Hawkins, K. 2003. "Populism in Venezuela: The Rise of Chavismo." *Third World Quarterly* 24 (6): 1137–60.

Hay, C. 2004. "The Normalizing Role of Rationalist Assumptions in the Institutional Embedding of Neoliberalism." *Economy and Society* 33 (4): 500–527.

Haydu, J. 1998. "Making Use of the Past: Time Periods as Cases to Compare and as Sequences of Problem Solving." *American Journal of Sociology* 104 (2): 339–71.

Heidenreich, G. 2007. "Trade Unions and the Informal Economy in Zambia: Building Strength or Losing Ground?" Bayreuth African Studies Working Papers No. 5. Bayreuth: Bayreuth University.

Helbling, T. 2008. "The Current Commodity Price Boom in Perspective." In *World Economic Outlook 2008: Housing and the Business Cycle*, 198–99. April 2008. Washington, DC: International Monetary Fund.

Hellinger, D. 2004a. "Chile, CIPEC and the Neoliberal Regime in the Production and Trade in Copper." Presented at the 25th International Congress of the Latin American Studies Association, Las Vegas, October 6–8, 2004.

Hellinger, D. 2004b. "Political Overview: The Breakdown of Puntofijismo and the Rise of Chavismo." *Venezuelan Politics in the Chávez Era: Class, Polarization, and Conflict*, ed. S. Ellner and D. Hellinger. Boulder, CO: Lynne Rienner.

Henderson, J. 2008. "China and Global Development: Towards a Global-Asian Era?" *Contemporary Politics* 14 (4): 375–92.

Henderson, J. 2011. *East Asian Transformation: On the Political Economy of Dynamism, Governance, and Crisis.* London: Taylor & Francis.

Henderson, J., R. P. Appelbaum, and S. Y. Ho. 2013. "Globalization with Chinese Characteristics: Externalization, Dynamics, and Transformations." *Development and Change* 44 (6): 1221–53.

Heritage Foundation. n.d. Index of Economic Freedom. Accessed April 29, 2019. https://www.heritage.org/index/explore?view=by-region-country-year&u=63689989170599 3387.

Hertog, S. 2010. "Defying the Resource Curse: Explaining Successful State-Owned Enterprises in Rentier States." *World Politics* 62 (2): 261–301.

Hetland, G. 2017. "Why Is Venezuela Spiraling Out of Control?" NACLA, April 28, 2017. https://nacla.org/news/2018/05/18/why-venezuela-spiraling-out-control.

Hetland, G. 2019. "Venezuela and the Left." *Jacobin*, February 5, 2019. https://www.jacobinmag.com/2019/02/venezuela-noninterventionism-self-determination-solidarity.

Heydarian, R. J. 2015. "China's Economy: Back to Reality." *Aljazeera*, August 16, 2015. http://www.aljazeera.com/indepth/opinion/2015/08/china-economy-reality-150815165145072.html.

Hill, M. 2011. "Oyu Tolgoi to Account for 33% of Mongolia's GDP in 2020." *Mining Weekly*, September 8, 2011. http://www.miningweekly.com/article/oyu-tolgoi-to-account-for-33-of-mongolias-gdp-in-2020-2011-09-08.

Hirsch, A. 2005. *Season of Hope: Economic Reform Under Mandela and Mbeki.* Scottsville and Ottawa: University of KwaZulu-Natal Press and International Development Research Centre.

Hirschman, A. O. 1968. "The Political Economy of Import-Substituting Industrialization in Latin America." *Quarterly Journal of Economics* 82 (1): 1–32.

Hobsbawm, E. 1989. *The Age of Empire: 1875–1914.* New York: Vintage.

Hochstetler, K., and A. P. Montero. 2013. "The Renewed Developmental State: The National Development Bank and the Brazil Model." *Journal of Development Studies* 49 (11): 1484–99.

Hopkins, T. K., and I. Wallerstein. 1977. "Patterns of Development of the Modern World-System." *Review (Fernand Braudel Center)* 1 (2): 111–45.

Hornbeck, J. F. 2013. "Argentina's Post-crisis Economic Reform: Challenges for US Policy." Washington, DC: Congressional Research Service. http://digital.library.unt.edu/ark:/67531/metadc463111/m1/1/high_res_d/R43022_2013Mar26.pdf.

Horner, R., and K. Nadvi. 2018. "Global Value Chains and the Rise of the Global South: Unpacking Twenty-First-Century Polycentric Trade." *Global Networks* 18 (2): 207–37.

Huber, E., and J. D. Stephens. 1992. "Changing Development Models in Small Economies: The Case of Jamaica from the 1950s to the 1990s." *Studies in Comparative International Development* 27 (3): 57–92.

Hume, N., and J. Wilson. 2014. "Rio Seeks to Blend Mining with Marketing." *Financial Times*, December 2, 2014.

Humphreys, D. 2018. "In Search of a New China: Mineral Demand in South and Southeast Asia." *Mineral Economics* 31 (1–2): 103–12.

Hung, H.-F. 2008. "Rise of China and the Global Overaccumulation Crisis." *Review of International Political Economy* 15 (2): 149–79.

Hung, H.-F., ed. 2009. *China and the Transformation of Global Capitalism.* Baltimore: Johns Hopkins University Press.

Hung, H.-F. 2013. "China: Saviour or Challenger of the Dollar Hegemony?" *Development and Change* 44 (6): 1341–61.

Hung, H.-F. 2016. *The China Boom: Why China Will Not Rule the World.* New York: Columbia University Press.

Hunter, W., and T. J. Power. 2005. "Lula's Brazil at Midterm." *Journal of Democracy* 16 (3): 127–39.

Hunter, W., and T. J. Power. 2007. "Rewarding Lula: Executive Power, Social Policy, and the Brazilian Elections of 2006." *Latin American Politics and Society* 49 (1): 1–30.

Hurley, J., S. Morris, and G. Portelance. 2018. "Examining the Debt Implications of the Belt and Road Initiative from a Policy Perspective." CGD Policy Paper 121, March 2018. Washington, DC: Center for Global Development.

Ikenberry, J. G. 2008. "The Rise of China and the Future of the West: Can the Liberal System Survive?" *Foreign Affairs* 87 (1): 23–37.

International Energy Agency. 2015. *World Energy Outlook 2015.* Paris: International Energy Agency.

International Energy Agency. 2017. *World Energy Outlook 2017.* Paris: International Energy Agency.

International Energy Agency. 2018. *Global Energy Statistical Yearbook 2018.* Paris: International Energy Agency.

International Monetary Fund. n.d. World Economic Outlook Database, April 2018 edition. Washington, DC: International Monetary Fund. Accessed April 29, 2019. https://www.imf.org/external/pubs/ft/weo/2018/01/weodata/index.aspx.

International Monetary Fund. 2006. "World Economic Outlook, September 2006: Financial Systems and Economic Cycles." Washington, DC: International Monetary Fund. https://www.imf.org/en/Publications/WEO/Issues/2016/12/31/World-Economic-Outlook-September-2006-Financial-Systems-and-Economic-Cycles-19774.

International Monetary Fund. 2012. *Zambia: 2012 Article IV Consultation.* IMF Country Report No. 12/200, July 2012. Washington, DC: International Monetary Fund. https://www.imf.org/external/pubs/ft/scr/2012/cr12200.pdf.

International Monetary Fund. 2014a. *Republic of Kazakhstan: 2014 Article IV Consultation— Staff Report; Press Release.* IMF Country Report No. 14/242, August 2014. Washington, DC: International Monetary Fund.

International Monetary Fund. 2014b. *World Economic Outlook: Recovery Strengthens, Remains Uneven.* April 2014. Washington, DC: International Monetary Fund.

International Monetary Fund. 2015. *World Economic Outlook: Adjusting to Lower Commodity Prices.* October 2015. Washington, DC: International Monetary Fund.

International Monetary Fund. 2017. *Angola: 2016 Article IV Consultation—Press Release; Staff Report; and Statement by the Executive Director for Angola.* IMF Country Report No. 17/39, February 2017. Washington, DC: International Monetary Fund. https://www.imf.org

/en/Publications/CR/Issues/2017/02/06/Angola-2016-Article-IV-Consultation-Press-Release-Staff-Report-and-Statement-by-the-44628.

International Monetary Fund. 2018. *Angola: 2018 Article IV Consultation—Press Release; Staff Report; and Statement by the Executive Director for Angola.* IMF Country Report No. 18/156, June 2018. Washington, DC: International Monetary Fund. https://www.imf.org/en/Publications/CR/Issues/2018/06/11/Angola-2018-Article-IV-Consultation-Press-Release-Staff-Report-and-Statement-by-the-45957.

Isaacs, R. 2008. "The Parliamentary Election in Kazakhstan, August 2007." *Electoral Studies* 27 (2): 381–85.

Isaacs, R. 2010. "Informal Politics and the Uncertain Context of Transition: Revisiting Early Stage Non-democratic Development in Kazakhstan." *Democratization* 17 (1): 1–25.

Isaacs, R. 2013. "Nur Otan, Informal Networks, and the Countering of Elite Instability in Kazakhstan: Bringing the 'Formal' Back In." *Europe-Asia Studies* 65 (6): 1055–79.

Isakova, A., A. Plekhanov, and J. Zettelmeyer. 2012. *Managing Mongolia's Resource Boom.* London: European Bank for Reconstruction and Development. http://www.researchgate.net/profile/Alexander_Plekhanov/publication/241755949_Managing_Mongolias_resource_boom/links/0f317531c526a7c79e000000.pdf.

Ismail, Z. 2017. "How Zambia's Once Insuperable MMD Returned to Power by Disappearing." *African Arguments*, February 14, 2017. https://africanarguments.org/2017/02/14/how-zambias-once-insuperable-mmd-returned-to-power-by-disappearing.

Jackson, S. L. 2015. "Imagining the Mineral Nation: Contested Nation-Building in Mongolia." *Nationalities Papers* 43 (3): 437–56.

Jackson, S. L., and Dear, D. 2016. "Resource Extraction and National Anxieties: China's Economic Presence in Mongolia. *Eurasian Geography and Economics* 57 (3): 343–73.

Jacques, M. 2009. *When China Rules the World: The End of the Western World and the Birth of a New Global Order.* London: Allen Lane.

Jamal, U. 2019. "Pakistan's Governance Changes Won't Be Enough to Offer It Economic Salvation." *Diplomat*, February 22, 2019. https://thediplomat.com/2019/02/pakistans-governance-changes-wont-be-enough-to-offer-it-economic-salvation.

Jenkins, R. 1991. "The Political Economy of Industrialization: A Comparison of Latin American and East Asian Newly Industrializing Countries." *Development and Change* 22 (2): 197–231.

Jenkins, R. 2012. "Latin America and China: A New Dependency?" *Third World Quarterly* 33 (7): 1337–58.

Jenkins, R. 2014. "Chinese Competition and Brazilian Exports of Manufactures." *Oxford Development Studies* 42 (3): 395–418.

Jenkins, R. 2018. *How China Is Reshaping the Global Economy: Development Impacts in Africa and Latin America.* Oxford: Oxford University Press.

Jensen, N., and L. Wantchekon. 2004. "Resource Wealth and Political Regimes in Africa." *Comparative Political Studies* 37 (7): 816–41.

Jepson, N., and J. Henderson. 2016. "Critical Transformations: Rethinking Zambian Development." SPERI Paper No. 33. Sheffield: Sheffield Political Economy Research Institute.

Johnson, K. 2018. "Why Is China Buying Up Europe's Ports?" *Foreign Policy*, February 2, 2018. https://foreignpolicy.com/2018/02/02/why-is-china-buying-up-europes-ports.

Johnston, J. 2013. "The Multilateral Debt Trap in Jamaica." Issue brief, June 2013. Washington, DC: Center for Economic Policy Research. http://www.cepr.net/documents/publications/jamaica-debt-2013-06.pdf.

Johnston, J. 2015. "Partners in Austerity: Jamaica, the United States, and the International Monetary Fund." April 2015. Washington, DC: Center for Economic Policy Research. http://www.cepr.net/publications/reports/partners-in-austerity-jamaica-the-united-states-and-the-international-monetary-fund.

Johnston, J., and S. Lefebvre. 2014. "Bolivia's Economy Under Evo in 10 Graphs." The Americas Blog, October 8, 2014. Washington, DC: Center for Economic Policy Research. http://www.cepr.net/blogs/the-americas-blog/bolivias-economy-under-evo-in-10-graphs.

Johnston, J., and J. A. Montecino. 2011. "Jamaica: Macroeconomic Policy, Debt, and the IMF." Washington, DC: Center for Economic and Policy Research. https://www.monroecoll.edu/uploadedFiles/_Site_Assets/PDF/cepr-jamaica-study.pdf.

Jones, M. 2018. "Why Turkey and Argentina Are the Main Emerging Market Weak Links." Reuters, May 18, 2018. https://www.reuters.com/article/us-emerging-markets-reserves-analysis/why-turkey-and-argentina-are-the-main-emerging-market-weak-links-idUSKCN1IJ1TX.

Junisbai, B. 2010. "A Tale of Two Kazakhstans: Sources of Political Cleavage and Conflict in the Post-Soviet Period." *Europe-Asia Studies* 62 (2): 235–69.

Junisbai, B. 2012. "Improbable But Potentially Pivotal Oppositions: Privatization, Capitalists, and Political Contestation in the Post-Soviet Autocracies." *Perspectives on Politics* 10 (4): 891–916.

Kanai, J. M., and S. Schindler. 2018. "Peri-Urban Promises of Connectivity: Linking Project-Led Polycentrism to the Infrastructure Scramble." *Environment and Planning A: Economy and Space* 51 (2): 302–22.

Kaplan, S. B. 2014. "The China Boom in Latin America: An End to Austerity?" SSRN Scholarly Paper No. ID 2552280. Rochester, NY: Social Science Research Network.

Kaplan, S. B. 2016. "Banking Unconditionally: The Political Economy of Chinese Finance in Latin America." *Review of International Political Economy* 23 (4): 643–76.

Kaplinsky, R. 2013. "What Contribution Can China Make to Inclusive Growth in Sub-Saharan Africa?" *Development and Change* 44 (6): 1295–1316.

Kaplinsky, R., and D. Messner. 2008. "Introduction: The Impact of Asian Drivers on the Developing World." *World Development* 36 (2), 197–209.

Kaplinsky, R., and M. Morris. 2009. "Chinese FDI in Sub-Saharan Africa: Engaging with Large Dragons." *European Journal of Development Research* 21 (4): 551–69.

Karl, T. L. 1997. *The Paradox of Plenty: Oil Booms and Petro-States*. Berkeley: University of California Press.

Kaup, B. Z. 2008. "Negotiating Through Nature: The Resistant Materiality and Materiality of Resistance in Bolivia's Natural Gas Sector." *Geoforum* 39 (5): 1734–42.

Kaup, B. Z. 2010. "A Neoliberal Nationalization? The Constraints on Natural-Gas-Led Development in Bolivia." *Latin American Perspectives* 37 (3): 123–38.

Kaup, B. Z. 2013a. "In Spaces of Marginalization: Dispossession, Incorporation, and Resistance in Bolivia." *Journal of World Systems Research* 19 (1): 108–29.

Kaup, B. Z. 2013b. *Market Justice: Political Economic Struggle in Bolivia.* Cambridge: Cambridge University Press.

Kaup, B. Z. 2013c. "Transnational Class Formation and Spatialities of Power: The Case of Elite Competition in Bolivia." *Global Networks* 13 (1): 101–19.

Kay, C. 2007. "Land, Conflict, and Violence in Latin America." *Peace Review: A Journal of Social Justice* 19 (1): 5–14.

Kayizzi-Mugerwa, S. 1990. "Growth From Own Resources: Zambia's Fourth National Development Plan in Perspective." *Development Policy Review* 8 (1): 59–76.

Kelsall, T. 2012. "Neo-patrimonialism, Rent-Seeking, and Development: Going with the Grain?" *New Political Economy* 17 (5): 677–82.

Kemme, D. 2012. "Sovereign Wealth Fund Issues and The National Fund(s) of Kazakhstan." SSRN Scholarly Paper No. ID 2188391. Rochester, NY: Social Science Research Network.

Kennemore, A., and G. Weeks. 2011. "Twenty-First Century Socialism? The Elusive Search for a Post-neoliberal Development Model in Bolivia and Ecuador." *Bulletin of Latin American Research* 30 (3): 267–81.

Kentikelenis, A. E., T. H. Stubbs, and L. P. King. 2016. "IMF Conditionality and Development Policy Space, 1985–2014." *Review of International Political Economy* 23 (4): 543–82.

Khan, M. 2010. *Political Settlements and the Governance of Growth-enhancing Institutions.* London: SOAS University of London.

Khan, M. S., and S. Sharma. 2003. "IMF Conditionality and Country Ownership of Adjustment Programs." *World Bank Research Observer* 18 (2): 227–48.

King, D., and L. Richards. 2008. *Jamaica's Debt: Exploring Causes and Strategies.* Kingston: Caribbean Policy Research Institute.

Kirchherr, J., K. J. Charles, and M. J. Walton. 2016. "Multi-causal Pathways of Public Opposition to Dam Projects in Asia: A Fuzzy Set Qualitative Comparative Analysis (fsQCA)." *Global Environmental Change* 41: 33–45.

Klare, M. 2012. *The Race for What's Left: The Global Scramble for the World's Last Resources.* New York: Picador.

Koch, N. 2013. "Kazakhstan's Changing Geopolitics: The Resource Economy and Popular Attitudes About China's Growing Regional Influence." *Eurasian Geography and Economics* 54 (1): 110–33.

Kohl, B. 2010. "Bolivia Under Morales: A Work in Progress." *Latin American Perspectives* 37 (3): 107–122.

Kohli, A. 2004. *State-Directed Development: Political Power and Industrialization in the Global Periphery.* Cambridge: Cambridge University Press.

Kong, B., and K. Gallagher. 2017. "Globalizing Chinese Energy Finance: The Role of Policy Banks." *Journal of Contemporary China* 26 (108): 834–51.

Korves, R. 2013. "Brazil's Agricultural Subsidies." Global Farmers Network, May 2, 2013. https://globalfarmernetwork.org/2013/05/brazils-agricultural-subsidies.

Kozak, R. 2015. "Peru's President Humala Names Pedro Cateriano as Prime Minister." *Wall Street Journal*, April 3, 2015. http://www.wsj.com/articles/perus-president-humala-names-pedro-cateriano-as-prime-minister-1428029177.

Kozak, R., and M. Moffett. 2011. "Ex-brass to Head Peruvian Cabinet." *Wall Street Journal*, December 12, 2011. http://www.wsj.com/articles/SB10001424052970203430404577092663973502538.

Kragelund, P. 2014. "'Donors Go Home': Non-traditional State Actors and the Creation of Development Space in Zambia." *Third World Quarterly* 35 (1): 145–62.

Kragelund, P. 2015. "Towards Convergence and Cooperation in the Global Development Finance Regime: Closing Africa's Policy Space?" *Cambridge Review of International Affairs* 28 (2): 246–62.

Krippner, G. R. 2005. "The Financialization of the American Economy." *Socio-Economic Review* 3 (2): 173–208.

Kröger, M. 2012. "Neo-mercantilist Capitalism and Post-2008 Cleavages in Economic Decision-Making Power in Brazil." *Third World Quarterly* 33 (5): 887–901.

Krugman, P. 1998. "It's Baaack: Japan's Slump and the Return of the Liquidity Trap." Brookings Papers on Economic Activity 2. Washington, DC: Brookings Institution.

Krusekopf, C. 2015. "State Ownership and the Development of Natural Resources in Mongolia." http://sites.socialsciences.manoa.hawaii.edu/css/demr2015/_papers/krusekopf-charles.pdf.

Kuncoro, M., T. Widodo, and R. H. McLeod. 2009. "Survey of Recent Developments." *Bulletin of Indonesian Economic Studies* 45 (2): 151–76.

Kuo, M. 2018. "The US–China Trade War: Winners and Losers." *Diplomat*, July 11, 2018. https://thediplomat.com/2018/07/the-us-china-trade-war-winners-and-losers.

Laclau, E. 1977. "Towards a Theory of Populism." In *Politics and Ideology in Marxist Theory*, ed. E. Laclau. London: New Left.

Laclau, E. 2005. *On Populist Reason*. London: Verso.

Lander, E. 2005. "Venezuelan Social Conflict in a Global Context." *Latin American Perspectives* 32 (2): 20–38.

Lander, E. 2007. "El estado y las tensiones de la participación popular en Venezuela." *OSAL* 8 (22): 65–86.

Lander, E., and P. Navarrete. 2007. "The Economic Policy of the Latin American Left in Government: Venezuela." Amsterdam: Transnational Institute, November 23, 2007. https://www.tni.org/es/briefing/la-pol%C3%ADtica-econ%C3%B3mica-de-la-izquierda-latinoamericana-en-el-gobierno-venezuela?content_language=en.

Large, D. 2013. "China, Africa, and Beyond." *Journal of Modern African Studies* 51 (4): 707–14.

Larmer, B. 2017. "Is China the World's New Colonial Power?" *New York Times*, May 2, 2017. https://www.nytimes.com/2017/05/02/magazine/is-china-the-worlds-new-colonial-power.html.

Larmer, M. 2005a. "Reaction and Resistance to Neo-liberalism in Zambia." *Review of African Political Economy* 32 (103): 29–45.

Larmer, M. 2005b. "Unrealistic Expectations?: Zambia's Mineworkers from Independence to the One-Party State, 1964–1972." *Journal of Historical Sociology* 18 (4): 318–52.

Larmer, M. 2010. "Historical Perspectives on Zambia's Mining Booms and Busts." In *Zambia, Mining, and Neoliberalism: Boom and Bust on the Globalized Copperbelt*, ed. A. Fraser and M. Larmer, 31–58. New York: Palgrave Macmillan.

Larmer, M., and A. Fraser. 2007. "Of Cabbages and King Cobra: Populist Politics and Zambia's 2006 Election." *African Affairs* 106 (425): 611–37.

Latin American Herald Tribune. 2013. "Morales Inaugurates Bolivia's 1st Natural Gas Liquids Separation Plant." http://www.laht.com/article.asp?ArticleId=775148&CategoryId=14919.

le Billon, P. 2001. "Angola's Political Economy of War: The Role of Oil and Diamonds, 1975–2000." *African Affairs* 100 (398): 55–80.

Lee, C. K. 2009. "Raw Encounters: Chinese Managers, African Workers, and the Politics of Casualization in Africa's Chinese Enclaves." *China Quarterly* 199: 647–66.

Lee, C. K. 2010. "Raw Encounters: Chinese Managers, African Workers, and the Politics of Casualization in Africa's Chinese Enclaves." In *Zambia, Mining, and Neoliberalism: Boom and Bust on the Globalized Copperbelt*, ed. A. Fraser and M. Larmer, 127–54. New York: Palgrave Macmillan.

Lee, C. K. 2014. "The Spectre of Global China." *New Left Review* 89: 29–65.

Lee, C. K. 2017. *The Specter of Global China: Politics, Labor, and Foreign Investment in Africa*. Chicago: University of Chicago Press.

Leibbrandt, M., I. Woolard, A. Finn, and J. Argent. 2010. "Trends in South African Income Distribution and Poverty Since the Fall of Apartheid." OECD Social, Employment and Migration Working Papers. Paris: Organisation for Economic Co-operation and Development.

Leiva, F. I. 2008. *Latin American Neostructuralism: The Contradictions of Post-neoliberal Development*. Minneapolis: University of Minnesota Press.

Leuz, C., and F. Oberholzer-Gee. 2006. "Political Relationships, Global Financing, and Corporate Transparency: Evidence from Indonesia." *Journal of Financial Economics* 81 (2): 411–39.

Levitsky, S. 2011. "A Surprising Left Turn." *Journal of Democracy* 22 (4): 84–94.

Levitsky, S., and J. Loxton. 2013. "Populism and Competitive Authoritarianism in the Andes." *Democratization* 20 (1): 107–36.

Li, M. (2016). *China and the 21st Century Crisis*. London: Pluto Press.

Libman, A. 2010. "Governments and Companies in the Post-Soviet World: Power, Intentions, and Institutional Consistency." *Eurasian Review* 3: 41–66.

Lieberman, E. S. 2005. "Nested Analysis as a Mixed-Method Strategy for Comparative Research." *American Political Science Review* 99 (3): 435–52.

Lin, J. Y. 2011. "New Structural Economics: A Framework for Rethinking Development." *World Bank Research Observer* 26 (2): 193–221.

Lin, J. Y. 2012. "From Flying Geese to Leading Dragons: New Opportunities and Strategies for Structural Transformation in Developing Countries." *Global Policy* 3 (4): 397–409.

Lin, J., D. Fridley, H. Lu, L. Price, and N. Zhou. 2018. "Has Coal Use Peaked in China? Near-Term Trends in China's Coal Consumption." *Energy Policy* 123: 208–14.

Liu, W., and M. Dunford. 2016. "Inclusive Globalization: Unpacking China's Belt and Road Initiative." *Area Development and Policy* 1 (3): 323–40.

Loewenstein, A. 2015. "Afghanistan Should Leave Its Copper in the Ground to Avoid Further Strife." *Guardian*, June 15, 2015. http://www.theguardian.com/commentisfree /2015/jun/15/afghanistan-should-leave-its-copper-in-the-ground-to-avoid-further -strife.

Lora, E. 2012. "Structural Reforms in Latin America: What Has Been Reformed and How to Measure It (Updated Version)." IDB Working Paper IDB-WP-346. Washington, DC: Inter-American Development Bank.

Loureiro, P. M., and A. Saad-Filho. 2019. "The Limits of Pragmatism: The Rise and Fall of the Brazilian Workers' Party (2002–2016)." *Latin American Perspectives* 46 (1): 66–84.

Love, J. L. 2010. "Latin America, UNCTAD, and the Postwar Trading System." In *Economic Development in Latin America: Essay in Honor of Werner Baer*, ed. H. S. Esfahani, G. Facchini, and G. Hewings, 22–33. London: Palgrave Macmillan.

Lundstøl, O., and Isaksen, J. 2018. "Zambia's Mining Windfall Tax." WIDER Working Paper No. 2018/51. Helsinki: United Nations University–World Institute for Development Economic Research.

Lungu, J. 2008a. "Copper Mining Agreements in Zambia: Renegotiation or Law Reform?" *Review of African Political Economy* 35 (117): 403–15.

Lungu, J. 2008b. "Socio-Economic Change and Natural Resource Exploitation: A Case Study of the Zambian Copper Mining Industry." *Development Southern Africa* 25 (5): 543–60.

Lupu, N. 2012. "The 2011 General Elections in Peru." *Electoral Studies* 31 (3): 621–24.

Lusaka Times. 2012. "Zambia: Collum Coal Miner Dies as Chinese Supervisor Allegedly Forced Workers into Unsafe Tunnel." January 18, 2012. https://www.lusakatimes.com /2012/01/18/collum-coal-miner-dies-chinese-supervisor-allegedly-forced-workers -unsafe-tunnel.

Lusaka Times. 2013a. "Sata Promises Development to People of Mkaika Constituency If They Vote PF." March 9, 2013. https://www.lusakatimes.com/2013/09/03/sata-promises -development-to-people-of-mkaika-constituency-if-they-vote-pf.

Lusaka Times. 2013b. "Shoprite Workers Go On Countrywide Strike." October 14, 2013. https://www.lusakatimes.com/2013/10/14/shoprite-workers-go-on-countrywide -strike.

MacEwan, A. 2002. "Economic Debacle in Argentina." *Dollars & Sense* 240: 22–25.

Madrid, R. L. 2011. "Ethnic Proximity and Ethnic Voting in Peru." *Journal of Latin American Studies* 43 (2): 267–97.

Madrid, R. L. 2012. *The Rise of Ethnic Politics in Latin America*. New York: Cambridge University Press.

Mahdavy, H. 1970. "The Patterns and Problems of Economic Development in Rentier States: The Case of Iran." In *Studies in the Economic History of the Middle East*. ed. M. A. Cook, 428–67. Oxford: Oxford University Press.

Makki, F. 2004. "The Empire of Capital and the Remaking of Center–Periphery Relations." *Third World Quarterly* 25 (1): 149–68.

Mamdani, M. 1996. *Citizen and Subject: Contemporary Africa and the Legacy of Late Colonialism*. Princeton, NJ: Princeton University Press.

Mander, B. 2014. "Fernández Wanes as Argentines Struggle." *Financial Times*, August 18, 2014.

Marais, H. 2011. *South Africa Pushed to the Limit: The Political Economy of Change*. London: Zed.

Mawdsley, E. 2008. "Fu Manchu Versus Dr. Livingstone in the Dark Continent? Representing China, Africa, and the West in British Broadsheet Newspapers." *Political Geography* 27 (5): 509–29.

Mayer, B. 2015. "Managing 'Climate Migration' in Mongolia: The Importance of Development Policies." In *Climate Change in the Asia-Pacific Region*, ed. W. L. Filho, 191–204. New York: Springer.

Mayer, J. 2009. "Policy Space: What, for What, and Where?" *Development Policy Review* 27 (4): 373–95.

McClintock, C. 2006. "An Unlikely Comeback in Peru." *Journal of Democracy* 17 (4): 95–109.

McEwan, C., and E. Mawdsley. 2012. "Trilateral Development Cooperation: Power and Politics in Emerging Aid Relationships." *Development and Change* 43 (6): 1185–1209.

McFarlane, I., and E. A. O'Connor. 2014. "World Soybean Trade: Growth and Sustainability." *Modern Economy* 5 (5): 580–88.

McKeown, A. 2011. "The Structural Production of State Terrorism: Capitalism, Imperialism, and International Class Dynamics." *Critical Studies on Terrorism* 4 (1): 75–93.

McMichael, P. 1990. "Incorporating Comparison Within a World-Historical Perspective: An Alternative Comparative Method." *American Sociological Review* 55 (3): 385–97.

McMichael, P. 1996. "Globalization: Myths and Realities." *Rural Sociology* 61 (1): 25–55.

McMichael, P. 2000. "World-Systems Analysis, Globalization, and Incorporated Comparison." *Journal of World-Systems Research* 6 (3): 668–90.

McMichael, P. 2001. "Revisiting the Question of the Transnational State: A Comment on William Robinson's 'Social Theory and Globalization.'" *Theory and Society* 30 (2): 201–10.

Mfula, C. 2013. "Zambia Revokes Visa for Vedanta Unit's CEO as Job Cuts Row Deepens." Reuters, November 11, 2013. http://uk.reuters.com/article/2013/11/11/uk-zambia-konkola-idUKBRE9AA08220131111.

Mfula, C. 2017. "Zambian Opposition Leader Walks Free in Treason Case." Reuters, August 16, 2017. https://uk.reuters.com/article/uk-zambia-politics/zambian-opposition-leader-walks-free-in-treason-case-idUKKCN1AW0KT.

Mining Journal. 2019. "Mongolian Push for Oyu Tolgoi Deal Changes." April 8, 2019. https://www.mining-journal.com/politics/news/1360458/mongolian-push-for-oyu-tolgoi-deal-changes.

Mohan, G., and B. Lampert. 2013. "Negotiating China: Reinserting African Agency into China–Africa Relations." *African Affairs* 112 (446): 92–110.

Mollo, M. de L. R., and A. Saad-Filho. 2006. "Neoliberal Economic Policies in Brazil (1994–2005): Cardoso, Lula, and the Need for a Democratic Alternative." *New Political Economy* 11 (1): 99–123.

Moore, M. 2001. "Political Underdevelopment: What Causes 'Bad Governance.'" *Public Management Review* 3 (3): 385–418.

Moore, M. 2004. "Revenues, State Formation, and the Quality of Governance in Developing Countries." *International Political Science Review* 25 (3): 297–319.

Moore Stephens. 2014. *Zambia Extractive Industries Transparency Initiative: Reconciliation Report for the Year 2011.* February 2014. https://eiti.org/sites/default/files/migrated_files/Zambia -2011-EITI-Report.pdf.

Morais, L., and A. Saad-Filho. 2003. "Snatching Defeat From the Jaws of Victory? Lula, the 'Losers' Alliance,' and the Prospects for Change in Brazil." *Capital & Class* 27 (3): 17–23.

Morais, L., and A. Saad-Filho. 2011. "Brazil Beyond Lula: Forging Ahead or Pausing for Breath?" *Latin American Perspectives* 38 (2): 31–44.

Morais, L., and A. Saad-Filho. 2012. "Neo-developmentalism and the Challenges of Economic Policy-Making Under Dilma Rousseff." *Critical Sociology* 38 (6): 789–98.

Morley, S. A., R. Machado, and S. Pettinato. 1999. *Indexes of Structural Reform in Latin America.* Vol. 12. Santiago: United Nations, Economic Commission for Latin America and the Caribbean.

Morris, M., and J. Fessehaie. 2014. "The Industrialisation Challenge for Africa: Towards a Commodities-Based Industrialisation Path." *Journal of African Trade* 1 (1): 25–36.

Morris, M., R. Kaplinsky, and D. Kaplan. 2012. "'One Thing Leads to Another': Commodities, Linkages, and Industrial Development." *Resources Policy* 37 (4): 408–16.

Mosley, P., J. Harrigan, and J. F. J. Toye. 1991. *Aid and Power: The World Bank and Policy-Based Lending: Analysis and Policy Proposals.* Vol. 1. London: Routledge.

Moyo, D. 2012. *Winner Take All: China's Race for Resources and What It Means for the World.* London: Allen Lane.

Muchapondwa, E., D. Nielson, B. Parks, A. M. Strange, and M. J. Tierney. 2016. "'Ground-Truthing' Chinese Development Finance in Africa: Field Evidence from South Africa and Uganda." *Journal of Development Studies* 52 (6): 780–96.

Muggah, R., and E. Passarelli Hamann. 2012. "Brazil's Generous Diplomacy: Friendly Dragon or Paper Tiger?" *International Development Policy/Revue Internationale de Politique de Développement* 3.

Munck, R. 2001. "Argentina, or the Political Economy of Collapse." *International Journal of Political Economy* 31 (3): 67–88.

Munck, R. 2003. "Neoliberalism, Necessitarianism, and Alternatives in Latin America: There Is No Alternative (TINA)?" *Third World Quarterly* 24 (3): 495–511.

Mundy, S., and K. Hille. 2019. "Maldives Seeks to Renegotiate with China Over Belt and Road Debt." *Financial Times*, January 31, 2019. https://www.ft.com/content/fcab0410 -2461-11e9-8ce6-5db4543da632.

Mussa, M. 2002. *Argentina and the Fund: From Triumph to Tragedy.* Washington, DC: Peterson Institute.

Mwenya, G. 2013. "Sata Threatens to Withhold Development From Southern Province." *Zambia Reports*, February 24, 2013. https://zambiareports.com/2013/02/24/sata-threatens -to-withhold-development-from-Southern-province.

National Intelligence Council. 2012. *Global Trends 2030: Alternative Worlds.* NIC 2012–001. December 2012. Washington, DC: National Intelligence Council. https://www.dni.gov /files/documents/GlobalTrends_2030.pdf.

National Intelligence Council. 2017. *Global Trends: Paradox of Progress*. NIC 2017–001, January 2017. Washington, DC: National Intelligence Council. https://www.dni.gov/files/documents/nic/GT-Full-Report.pdf.

Naughton, B. 2009. "Understanding the Chinese Stimulus Package." *China Leadership Monitor* 28.

Naughton, B. 2010. "China's Distinctive System: Can It Be a Model for Others?" *Journal of Contemporary China* 19 (65): 437–60.

Neems, Mitchell. 2015. "Rio Tinto, Mongolia Sign Oyu Tolgoi Deal." *Australian*, May 19, 2015. http://www.theaustralian.com.au/business/mining-energy/rio-tinto-mongolia-sign-oyu-tolgoi-deal/story-e6frg9df-1227359732791.

Nem Singh, J. T. 2012. "Who Owns the Minerals? Repoliticizing Neoliberal Governance in Brazil and Chile." *Journal of Developing Societies* 28 (2): 229–56.

Nölke, A., and S. Claar. 2013. "Varieties of Capitalism in Emerging Economies." *Transformation: Critical Perspectives on Southern Africa* 81 (1): 33–54.

Nye, J. S., Jr. 2015. *Is the American Century Over?*. Cambridge: Polity.

Observatory of Economic Complexity. n.d. Accessed April 29, 2019. https://atlas.media.mit.edu.

Ocampo, J. A. 2014. "Trade and Finance in Development Thinking." In *International Development: Ideas, Experience, and Prospects*, ed. B. Currie-Alder, R. Kanbur, D. M. Malone, and R. Medhora, 277–94. Oxford: Oxford University Press.

O'Donnell, G. 1978. "State and Alliances in Argentina, 1956–1976." *Journal of Development Studies* 15 (1): 3–33.

O'Hearn, D. 2001. *The Atlantic Economy: Britain, the US, and Ireland*. Manchester: Manchester University Press.

O'Hearn, D. 2005. "Cycles of Accumulation, Crisis, Materials, and Space: Can Different Theories of Change Be Reconciled?" In *Research in Development and Rural Sociology*. Vol. 10, *Nature, Raw Materials, and Political Economy*, ed. P. S. Ciccantell, D. A. Smith, and G. Seidman, 113–40. Bingley: Emerald Group.

Okeowo, A. 2013. "China, Zambia, and a Clash in a Coal Mine." *New Yorker*, October 9, 2013. http://www.newyorker.com/business/currency/china-zambia-and-a-clash-in-a-coal-mine.

Ollawa, P. E. 1979. *Participatory Democracy in Zambia*. Ilfracombe: Stockwell.

Organisation for Economic Cooperation and Development. 2011. "Brazil: Agricultural Policy Monitoring and Evaluation." Paris: Organisation for Economic Cooperation and Development. http://www.oecd.org/brazil/brazil-agriculturalpolicymonitoringandevaluation.htm.

Ostrowski, W. 2009. "The Legacy of the 'Coloured Revolutions': The Case of Kazakhstan." *Journal of Communist Studies and Transition Politics* 25 (2–3): 347–68.

Ostry, J. D., P. Loungani, and D. Furceri. 2016. "Neoliberalism: Oversold?" *Finance & Development* 53 (2): 38–41.

Ovadia, J. S. 2013. "The Reinvention of Elite Accumulation in the Angolan Oil Sector: Emergent Capitalism in a Rentier Economy." *Cadernos de estudos africanos* 25: 33–63.

Ovadia, J. S. 2016. *The Petro-Developmental State in Africa: Making Oil Work in Angola, Nigeria and the Gulf of Guinea*. London: Hurst.

Ovadia, J. S. 2018. "State-Led Industrial Development, Structural Transformation and Elite-Led Plunder: Angola (2002–2013) as a Developmental State." *Development Policy Review* 36 (5): 587–606.

Overbeek, H. W. 1993. *Restructuring Hegemony in the Global Political Economy: The Rise of Transnational Neo-liberalism in the 1980s.* London: Routledge.

Paige, J. M. 1978. *Agrarian Revolution.* New York: Simon and Schuster.

Parker, D. 2001. "El chavismo: populismo radical y potencial revolucionario." *Revista Venezolana de economía y ciencias sociales* 7 (1): 13–44.

Parker, D. 2003. "Representa Chávez una alternativa al neoliberalismo?" *Revista Venezolana de Economía y ciencias sociales* 9 (3): 83–110.

Parker, D. 2005. "Chávez and the Search for an Alternative to Neoliberalism." *Latin American Perspectives* 32 (2): 39–50.

Peet, R. 2002. "Ideology, Discourse, and the Geography of Hegemony: From Socialist to Neoliberal Development in Postapartheid South Africa." *Antipode* 34 (1): 54–84.

Peine, E. K. 2013. "Trading on Pork and Beans: Agribusiness and the Construction of the Brazil–China–Soy–Pork Commodity Complex." In *The Ethics and Economics of Agrifood Competition,* ed. H. S. James Jr., 193–210. Dordrecht: Springer.

Peru Support Group. 2013. "Repsol, Energy Sovereignty, and Economic Policy Space in Peru." June 3, 2013. http://www.perusupportgroup.org.uk/article-637.html.

Peru Support Group. 2014. "State Capture or the 'Reprivada.'" September 28, 2014. http://www.perusupportgroup.org.uk/article-758.html.

Petkoff, T. 2005. *Dos izquierdas.* Caracas: Editorial Alfa.

Peyrouse, S. 2012. "The Kazakh Neopatrimonial Regime: Balancing Uncertainties Among the 'Family,' Oligarchs, and Technocrats." *Demokratizatsiya* 20 (4): 345.

Phillips, R., J. Henderson, L. Andor, and D. Hulme. 2006. "Usurping Social Policy: Neoliberalism and Economic Governance in Hungary." *Journal of Social Policy* 35 (4): 585–606.

Pieterse, J. N. 1988. "A Critique of World System Theory." *International Sociology* 3 (3): 251–66.

Pieterse, J. N. 2011. "Global Rebalancing: Crisis and the East–South Turn." *Development and Change* 42 (1): 22–48.

Pieterse, J. N. 2015. "China's Contingencies and Globalisation." *Third World Quarterly* 36 (11): 1985–2001.

Pomfret, R. 2012. "Resource Management and Transition in Central Asia, Azerbaijan, and Mongolia." *Journal of Asian Economics* 23 (2): 146–56.

Pomfret, R., and K. Anderson. 2001. "Economic Development Strategies in Central Asia Since 1991." *Asian Studies Review* 25 (2): 185–200.

Pons-Vignon, N., and A. Segatti. 2013. "'The Art of Neoliberalism': Accumulation, Institutional Change, and Social Order Since the End of Apartheid." *Review of African Political Economy* 40 (138): 507–18.

Ponte, S., S. Roberts, and L. van Sittert. 2007. "'Black Economic Empowerment,' Business, and the State in South Africa." *Development and Change* 38 (5): 933–55.

Posner, D. N. 2005. *Institutions and Ethnic Politics in Africa.* Cambridge: Cambridge University Press.

Postero, N. 2010. "The Struggle to Create a Radical Democracy in Bolivia." *Latin American Research Review* 45 (4): 59–78. http://doi.org/10.1353/lar.2010.0035.

Poulantzas, N. 1975. *Classes in Contemporary Capitalism.* New edition. Trans. D. Fernbach. London: Verso.

Power, M. 2012. "Angola 2025: The Future of the 'World's Richest Poor Country' as Seen Through a Chinese Rear-View Mirror." *Antipode* 44 (3): 993–1014.

Prasad, E. S. 2017. *Gaining Currency: The Rise of the Renminbi.* Oxford: Oxford University Press.

Prebisch, R. 1949. *The Economic Development of Latin America and Its Principal Problems.* New York: Economic Commission for Latin America.

PriceWaterhouseCoopers. 2013. *Mining Industry: Doing Business in Peru.* Lima: PriceWater-houseCoopers. http://www.pwc.de/de/internationale-maerkte/assets/doing-business -in-mining-peru.pdf.

Pritchett, L., and L. H. Summers. 2014. "Asiaphoria Meets Regression to the Mean." NBER Working Paper No. 20573. Cambridge, MA: National Bureau of Economic Research.

Pushak, N., and V. Foster. 2011. *Angola's Infrastructure: A Continental Perspective.* Policy Research Working Paper, September 2011. Washington, DC: World Bank. https://doi .org/10.1596/1813-9450-5813.

Raby, D. 2011. "Venezuelan Foreign Policy Under Chávez, 1999–2010: The Pragmatic Success of Revolutionary Ideology?" In *Latin American Foreign Policies: Between Ideology and Pragmatism,* ed. G. Gardini and P. Lambert, 159–178. New York: Palgrave Macmillan.

Rachman, G. 2016. *Easternisation: War and Peace in the Asian Century.* London: Random House.

Ragin, C. C. 1989. *The Comparative Method: Moving Beyond Qualitative and Quantitative Strategies.* Berkeley: University of California Press.

Ragin, C. C. 2008. *Redesigning Social Inquiry: Fuzzy Sets and Beyond.* Chicago: University of Chicago Press.

Rakner, L. 2012. "Foreign Aid and Democratic Consolidation in Zambia." WIDER Working Paper No. 2012/16. Helsinki: United Nations University–World Institute for Development Economic Research.

Rathbone, J. P., and K.-Y. Pan. 2018. "Trump Bans Purchase of Venezuelan Debt in New Sanctions." *Financial Times,* May 21, 2018. https://www.ft.com/content/3202dad2-5d27 -11e8-9334-2218e7146b04.

Ray, R., and S. Kozameh. 2012. *Ecuador's Economy Since 2007.* Washington, DC: Center for Economic and Policy Research. http://cepr.net/documents/publications/ecuador-2012– 05.pdf.

Readhead, A., and D. Mihalyi. 2018. "A Withhold Up in Mongolia? Thoughts on the Renewed Tax Debate Around Oyu Tolgoi." International Centre for Tax and Development. https://www.ictd.ac/blog/a-withhold-up-in-mongolia-thoughts-on-the-renewed -tax-debate-around-oyu-tolgoi.

Reilly, J. 2012. "A Norm-Taker or a Norm-Maker? Chinese Aid in Southeast Asia." *Journal of Contemporary China* 21 (73): 71–91.

Resnick, D. 2012. "Opposition Parties and the Urban Poor in African Democracies." *Comparative Political Studies* 45 (11): 1351–78.

Resnick, D., and J. Thurlow. 2014. "The Political Economy of Zambia's Recovery: Structural Change Without Transformation?" SSRN Scholarly Paper No. ID 2405715. Rochester, NY: Social Science Research Network.

Reuters. 2011. "Peru Approves New Mining Royalty Scheme." September 14, 2011. http://www.reuters.com/article/2011/09/14/peru-mining-royalties-idUSS1E78C2AF2011 0914.

Reuters. 2015. "Rio Shuns Mongolia Plan to Swap Oyu Tolgoi Equity for Royalties." February 12, 2015. http://www.reuters.com/article/2015/02/12/rio-tinto-mongolia-idUS L5N0VL5FG20150212.

Reuters. 2019. "Factbox: China Rolls Out Fiscal, Monetary Stimulus to Spur Economy." January 25, 2019. https://www.reuters.com/article/us-china-economy-policy-factbox /factbox-china-rolls-out-fiscal-monetary-stimulus-to-spur-economy-idUSKCN1 PJ1LK.

Richani, N. 2010. "Colombia: Predatory State and Rentier Political Economy." *Labor, Capital and Society/Travail, Capital et Société* 43 (2): 119–41.

Richardson, N. P. 2009. "Export-Oriented Populism: Commodities and Coalitions in Argentina." *Studies in Comparative International Development* 44 (3): 228–55.

Richardson, N. 2012. *The Politics of Abundance: Export Agriculture and Redistributive Conflict in South America.* PhD diss., University of California, Berkeley.

Riggirozzi, P. 2009. "After Neoliberalism in Argentina: Reasserting Nationalism in an Open Economy." In *Governance After Neoliberalism in Latin America,* ed. J. Grugel and P. Riggirozzi, 89–112. New York: Palgrave Macmillan.

Rihoux, B., P. Álamos-Concha, D. Bol, A. Marx, and I. Rezsöhazy. 2013. "From Niche to Mainstream Method? A Comprehensive Mapping of QCA Applications in Journal Articles from 1984 to 2011." *Political Research Quarterly* 66 (1): 175–84.

Rihoux, B., and B. Lobe. 2009. "The Case for Qualitative Comparative Analysis (QCA): Adding Leverage for Thick Cross-Case Comparison." In *The Sage Handbook of Case-Based Methods,* ed. D. Byrne and C. Ragin, 222–42. London: Sage.

Roberts, C. A., L. E. Armijo, and S. N. Katada. 2018. *The BRICS and Collective Financial Statecraft.* Oxford: Oxford University Press.

Roberts, K. M. 1995. "Neoliberalism and the Transformation of Populism in Latin America: The Peruvian Case." *World Politics* 48 (1): 82–116.

Roberts, K. M. 1996. "Economic Crisis and the Demise of the Legal Left in Peru." *Comparative Politics* 29 (1): 69–92.

Roberts, K. M. 2007. "Latin America's Populist Revival." *SAIS Review of International Affairs* 27 (1): 3–15.

Robinson, N. 2007. "The Political Is Personal: Corruption, Clientelism, Patronage, Informal Practices, and the Dynamics of Post-communism." *Europe-Asia Studies* 59 (7): 1217–24.

Robinson, W. I. 2001. "Social Theory and Globalization: The Rise of a Transnational State." *Theory and Society* 30 (2): 157–200.

Robinson, W. I. 2002. "Remapping Development in Light of Globalization: From a Territorial to a Social Cartography." *Third World Quarterly* 23 (6): 1047–71.

Robinson, W. I. 2004. *A Theory of Global Capitalism: Production, Class, and State in a Transnational World.* Baltimore: Johns Hopkins University Press.

Robinson, W. I. 2008. *Latin America and Global Capitalism: A Critical Globalization Perspective.* Baltimore: Johns Hopkins University Press.

Robinson, W. I., and J. Harris. 2000. "Towards a Global Ruling Class? Globalization and the Transnational Capitalist Class." *Science & Society* 64 (1): 11–54.

Robison, R. 1986. *Indonesia: The Rise of Capital.* Singapore: Equinox.

Robison, R. 1988. "Authoritarian States, Capital-Owning Classes, and the Politics of Newly Industrializing Countries: The Case of Indonesia." *World Politics* 41 (1): 52–74.

Robison, R. 1993. "Indonesia: Tensions in State and Regime. In *Southeast Asia in the 1990s: Authoritarianism, Democracy, and Capitalism,* ed. K. Hewison, R. Robison, and G. Rodan, 39–74. Saint Leonards: Allen & Unwin.

Robison, R., and V. Hadiz. 2004. *Reorganising Power in Indonesia: The Politics of Oligarchy in an Age of Markets.* London: Routledge.

Robles, F. 2019. "Millionaire Brothers Wanted by Ecuador Are Arrested in Miami by ICE." *New York Times,* February 15, 2019. https://www.nytimes.com/2019/02/15/world/americas/isaias-brothers-arrested-ecuador.html.

Robotham, D. 2000. "Blackening the Jamaican Nation: The Travails of a Black Bourgeoisie in a Globalized World." *Identities* 7 (1): 1–37.

Rodney, W. 1972. *How Europe Underdeveloped Africa.* London: Bogle-L'Ouverture and Tanzania Publishing House.

Rodrigues, V., and A. Schipani. 2014. "Ecuador and Bond Markets: Defaulter Is Back with a $2bn Vengeance." *Financial Times,* June 17, 2014.

Rodrik, D. 2016. "Premature Deindustrialization." *Journal of Economic Growth* 21 (1): 1–33.

Romero, S. 2012. "YPF Nationalization Draws Praise in Argentina." *New York Times,* April 27, 2012. https://www.nytimes.com/2012/04/27/world/americas/ypf-nationalization-draws-praise-in-argentina.html.

Ross, M. L. 2001. "Does Oil Hinder Democracy?" *World Politics* 53 (3): 325–61.

Rossabi, M. 2005. *Modern Mongolia: From Khans to Commissars to Capitalists.* Berkeley: University of California Press.

Rosser, A. 2002. *The Politics of Economic Liberalisation in Indonesia: State Market and Power.* Richmond: Curzon.

Rosser, A. 2007. "Escaping the Resource Curse: The Case of Indonesia." *Journal of Contemporary Asia* 37 (1): 38–58.

Roubini, N. 2014. "Are the BRICS in Midlife Crisis?" World Economic Forum, January 24, 2014. https://www.weforum.org/agenda/2014/01/brics-midlife-crisis.

Ruckert, A. 2007. "Development Beyond Neoliberalism? Governance, Poverty Reduction, and Political Economy." *Canadian Journal of Political Science / Revue Canadienne de Science Politique* 40 (4): 1050–52.

Rueschemeyer, D., E. H. Stephens, and J. D. Stephens. 1992. *Capitalist Development and Democracy.* Chicago: University of Chicago Press.

Ruggie, J. G. 1982. "International Regimes, Transactions, and Change: Embedded Liberalism in the Postwar Economic Order." *International Organization* 36 (2): 379–415.

Saad-Filho, A. 2005. "The Rise and Decline of Latin American Structuralism and Dependency Theory." In *Origins of Development Economics: How Schools of Economic Thought Addressed Development,* ed. E. S. Reinert. London: Zed.

Sachs, J. D., and A. Warner. 1995. "Economic Reform and the Process of Global Integration." *Brookings Papers on Economic Activity* 1 (25): 1–118.

Salama, P. 2012. "Economic Growth and Inflation in Argentina Under Kirchner's Government." Centro Editorial FCE-CID, Documento Escuela de Economía 28. Bogota: Centro de Investigaciones de Desarollo.

Scarritt, J. R. 1983. "The Analysis of Social Class, Political Participation, and Public Policy in Zambia." *Africa Today* 30 (3): 5–22.

Schiipani, A., and V. Rodrigues. 2014. "Peru Seeks to Revive Economic Miracle as Supercycle Slows." *Financial Times*, September 25, 2014.

Schneider, B. R. 2004. *Business Politics and the State in Twentieth-Century Latin America*. New York: Cambridge University Press.

Schneider, B. R., and D. Soskice. 2009. "Inequality in Developed Countries and Latin America: Coordinated, Liberal, and Hierarchical Systems." *Economy and Society* 38 (1): 17–52.

Schneider, C. Q., and I. Rohlfing. 2013. "Combining QCA and Process Tracing in Set-Theoretic Multi-method Research." *Sociological Methods & Research* 42 (4): 559–97.

Schneider, F., and D. H. Enste. 2000. "Shadow Economies: Size, Causes, and Consequences." *Journal of Economic Literature* 38 (1): 77–114.

School of Advanced International Studies–China Africa Research Initiative. 2018. "Chinese Loans to Africa Database." http://www.sais-cari.org/data-chinese-loans-and-aid -to-africa.

Schrank, A. 2004. *Reconsidering the "Resource Curse": Sociological Analysis Versus Ecological Determinism*. Albuquerque: University of New Mexico.

Scissors, D. 2018. China Global Investment Tracker. Washington, DC: American Enterprise Institute. http://www.aei.org/china-global-investment-tracker.

Segatti, A., and N. Pons-Vignon. 2013. "Stuck in Stabilization? South Africa's Post-apartheid Macro-economic Policy Between Ideological Conversion and Technocratic Capture." *Review of African Political Economy* 40 (138): 537–55.

Seidman, G. 2010. "Brazil's 'Pro-Poor' Strategies: What South Africa Could Learn." *Transformation: Critical Perspectives on Southern Africa* 72 (1): 86–103.

Senghaas, D. 1985. *The European Experience: A Historical Critique of Development Theory*. Dover, NH: Berg.

SENPLADES. 2013. *Plan Nacional Buen Vivir, 2013–2017*. Quito: Secretaría Nacional de Planificación y Desarrollo. http://documentos.senplades.gob.ec/Plan%20Nacional%20 Buen%20Vivir%202013-2017.pdf.

Serrano, F., and R. Summa. 2011. "Macroeconomic Policy, Growth, and Income Distribution in the Brazilian Economy in the 2000s." Washington, DC: Center for Economic and Policy Research. http://www.insightweb.it/web/files/macroeconomic_policy _growth_and_income_distribution_in_the_brazilian_economy.pdf.

Sewell, W. H. 2012. "Economic Crises and the Shape of Modern History." *Public Culture* 24 (2 (67)): 303–27.

Shafer, M. 1983. "Capturing the Mineral Multinationals: Advantage or Disadvantage?" *International Organization* 37 (1): 93–119.

Shaw, T. M. 1976. "Zambia: Dependence and Underdevelopment." *Canadian Journal of African Studies/La Revue Canadienne Des études Africaines* 10 (1): 3–22.

Shaxson, N. 2007. "Oil, Corruption, and the Resource Curse." *International Affairs* 83 (6): 1123–40.

Shearer, C., M. Brown, and T. Buckley. 2019. *China at a Crossroads: Continued Support for Coal Power Erodes Country's Clean Energy Leadership.* Cleveland, OH: Institute for Energy Economics and Financial Analysis. http://ieefa.org/wp-content/uploads/2019/01/China -at-a-Crossroads_January-2019.pdf.

Sidaway, J. D. 2007. "Spaces of Postdevelopment." *Progress in Human Geography* 31 (3): 345–61.

Sidel, J. T. 2015. "Men on Horseback and Their Droppings: Yudhoyono's Presidency and Legacies in Comparative Regional Perspective." In *The Yudhoyono Presidency: Indonesia's Decade of Stability and Stagnation*, ed. E. Aspinall, M. Mietzner, and D. Tomsa, 55–72. Singapore: Institute of Southeast Asian Studies.

Silva, E. 2013. "Social Movements, Policy, and Conflict in Post-neoliberal Latin America: Bolivia in the Time of Evo Morales." *Research in Political Sociology* 21: 51–76.

Singer, H. 1950. "The Distribution of Gains Between Investing and Borrowing Countries." *American Economic Review* 40 (2): 473–85.

Singer, H. 1984. "Ideas and Policy: The Sources of UNCTAD." *IDS Bulletin* 15 (3): 14–17.

Singer, A. 2017. "The Failure of the Developmentalist Experiment in Three Acts." *Critical Policy Studies* 11 (3): 358–64.

Sklair, L. 2001. *The Transnational Capitalist Class.* London: Wiley.

Skocpol, T. 1977. "Wallerstein's World Capitalist System: A Theoretical and Historical Critique." *American Journal of Sociology* 82 (5): 1075–90.

Skocpol, T. 1982. "Rentier State and Shi'a Islam in the Iranian Revolution." *Theory and Society* 11 (3): 265–83.

Slobodian, Q. 2018. *Globalists: The End of Empire and the Birth of Neoliberalism.* Cambridge, MA: Harvard University Press.

Soares de Oliveira, R. 2007. "Business Success, Angola-Style: Postcolonial Politics and the Rise and Rise of Sonangol." *Journal of Modern African Studies* 45 (4): 595–619.

Soares de Oliveira, R. 2015. *Magnificent and Beggar Land: Angola Since the Civil War.* London: Hurst.

Soeriaatmadja, W. 2019. "Indonesia Calls for 'Belt and Road' Projects to be Private-Sector Driven." *Caixin*, April 26, 2019. https://www.caixinglobal.com/2019-04-26/indonesia -calls-for-belt-and-road-projects-to-be-private-sector-driven-101408892.html.

Sogge, D. 2011. "Angola: Reinventing Pasts and Futures." *Review of African Political Economy* 38 (127): 85–92.

Solidarity Center. 2006. "The Struggle for Worker Rights in Colombia." May 2006. Washington, DC: American Center for International Labor Solidarity. http://www.solidarity center.org/wp-content/uploads/2015/02/ColombiaFinal-1.pdf.

South China Morning Post. 2016. "Xi Jinping's 'New Normal' with Chinese Characteristics." Reuters, May 30, 2016. http://www.scmp.com/business/economy/article/1511855 /xi-jinpings-new-normal-chinese-characteristics.

Spechler, M. C. 2008. "The Economies of Central Asia: A Survey." *Comparative Economic Studies* 50 (1): 30–52.

Spence, M. 2011. *The Next Convergence: The Future of Economic Growth in a Multispeed World.* New York: Farrar, Straus and Giroux.

Stang, G. 2014. *China's Energy Demands: Are They Reshaping the World?* Paris: European Union Institute for Security Studies.

Stark, M., and J. Ahrens. 2012. "Economic Reform and Institutional Change in Central Asia: Towards a New Model of the Developmental State?" PFH Forschungspapiere/Research Papers. Göttingen: Private Hochschule Göttingen.

Stephens, E. H. 1987. "Minerals Strategies and Development: International Political Economy, State, Class, and the Role of the Bauxite/Aluminum and Copper Industries in Jamaica and Peru." *Studies in Comparative International Development* 22 (3): 60–102.

Stiglitz, J. 2002. *Globalization and Its Discontents.* New York: Norton.

Stiglitz, J. 2006. "Is Populism Really So Bad for Latin America?" *New Perspectives Quarterly* 23 (2): 61–62.

Stokes, D. 2006. "'Iron Fists in Iron Gloves': The Political Economy of US Terrorocracy Promotion in Colombia." *British Journal of Politics & International Relations* 8 (3): 368–87.

Stokes, S. C. 2001. *Mandates and Democracy: Neoliberalism by Surprise in Latin America.* Cambridge: Cambridge University Press.

Stone, C. 1985. "Jamaica in Crisis: From Socialist to Capitalist Management." *International Journal* 40 (2): 282–311.

Strange, S. 1987. "The Persistent Myth of Lost Hegemony." *International Organization* 41 (4): 551–74.

Stuart-Fox, M. 2005. "Politics and Reform in the Lao People's Democratic Republic." Working Paper No. 126. Perth: Asia Research Center, Murdoch University.

Stuart-Fox, M. 2006. "The Political Culture of Corruption in the Lao PDR." *Asian Studies Review* 30 (1): 59–75.

Stuenkel, O. 2016. *Post-Western World: How Emerging Powers are Remaking Global Order.* Malden, MA: Polity.

Subacchi, P. 2017. *The People's Money: How China Is Building a Global Currency.* New York: Columbia University Press.

Suni P. 2007. "World Commodity Prices, 2006–2008." Report presented to the AIECE Spring Meeting in Helsinki, Finland, May 2007. Association of European Conjuncture Institutes, Working Group on Commodity Prices.

Sunkel, O. 1993. *Development From Within: Toward a Neostructuralist Approach for Latin America.* Boulder, CO: Lynne Rienner.

Sunkel, O., and G. Zuleta. 1990. "Neo-structuralism Versus Neo-liberalism in the 1990s." *CEPAL Review* 42 (December): 35–51.

Svampa, M. 2007. "Las fronteras del gobierno de Kirchner: Entre la consolidación de lo viejo y las aspiraciones de lo nuevo." *Cuadernos Del CENDES* 65: 39–61.

Szeftel, M. 2000. "'Eat with Us': Managing Corruption and Patronage Under Zambia's Three Republics, 1964–99." *Journal of Contemporary African Studies* 18 (2): 207–24.

Tangri, R., and R. Southall. 2008. "The Politics of Black Economic Empowerment in South Africa." *Journal of Southern African Studies* 34 (3): 699–716.

Tan-Mullins, M., G. Mohan, and M. Power. 2010. "Redefining 'Aid' in the China–Africa Context." *Development and Change* 41 (5): 857–81.

Teichman, J. 2004. "The World Bank and Policy Reform in Mexico and Argentina." *Latin American Politics and Society* 46 (1): 39–74.

Telesur. 2015. "Venezuela's Maduro Hails China–CELAC Forum as 'Historic.'" January 8, 2015. https://www.telesurenglish.net/news/Venezuelas-Maduro-Hails-China-CELAC-Forum-as-Historic-20150108-0004.html.

ten Brink, T. 2014. "Paradoxes of Prosperity in China's New Capitalism." *Journal of Current Chinese Affairs* 42 (4): 17–44.

Thede, N. 2013. "Policy Coherence for Development and Securitization: Competing Paradigms or Stabilising North–South Hierarchies?" *Third World Quarterly* 34 (5): 784–99.

Therborn, G. 2012. "Class in the 21st Century." *New Left Review* 78: 5–29.

Thomas, M., and M. Trevino. 2013. *Resource Dependence and Fiscal Effort in Sub-Saharan Africa.* IMF Working Paper 13-188. August 2013. Washington, DC: International Monetary Fund.

Thomas, A., I. Viciani, J. Tench, R. Sharpe, M. Hall, M. Martin, and R. Watts. 2011. *Real Aid: Ending Aid Dependency.* ActionAid, September 2011. http://www.actionaid.org.uk/sites/default/files/doc_lib/real_aid_3.pdf.

Thoumi, F. E. 2002. "Illegal Drugs in Colombia: From Illegal Economic Boom to Social Crisis." *Annals of the American Academy of Political and Social Science* 582 (1): 102–16.

Tisdall, S. 2016. "Has the BRICS Bubble Burst?" *Guardian*, March 27, 2016. https://www.theguardian.com/business/2016/mar/27/brics-bubble-burst-brazil-russia-india-china-south-africa.

Tordo, S., M. Warner, O. Manzano, and Y. Anouti. 2013. *Local Content Policies in the Oil and Gas Sector.* Washington, DC: World Bank Group. https://doi.org/10.1596/978-0-8213-9931-6.

Toro, F. 2019. "With U.S. Military Action, Venezuela Could Become the Libya of the Caribbean." *Washington Post*, February 25, 2019. https://www.washingtonpost.com/opinions/2019/02/25/with-us-military-action-venezuela-could-become-libya-caribbean/?utm_term=.3c715c4525de.

Toye, J. 2014. "Assessing the G77: 50 Years After UNCTAD and 40 Years After the NIEO." *Third World Quarterly* 35 (10): 1759–74.

United Nations Comtrade. n.d. UN Comtrade Database. Accessed April 29, 2019. http://comtrade.un.org.

United Nations Conference on Trade and Development. n.d. UNCTADStat data center. Accessed April 29, 2019. http://unctadstat.unctad.org/wds/ReportFolders/reportFolders.aspx?sCS_ChosenLang=en.

United Nations Conference on Trade and Development. 2006. *Trade and Development Report 2006: Global Partnership and National Policies for Development.* Geneva: United Nations Conference on Trade and Development.

United Nations Conference on Trade and Development. 2014. *Trade and Development Report, 2014.* New York: United Nations Conference on Trade and Development. http://unctad.org/en/pages/PublicationWebflyer.aspx?publicationid=981.

U.S. Embassy Lusaka. 2008. "Michael Sata: Who Is King Cobra and Will He Be Crowned?" Telegram (cable), October 6, 2008. Public Library of U.S. Diplomacy. Canonical ID 08LUSAKA986_a. https://wikileaks.org/cable/2008/10/08LUSAKA986.html.

U.S. Energy Information Administration. n.d. "Open Data." Accessed April 29, 2019. https://www.eia.gov/opendata.

U.S. Energy Information Administration. 2014. "China Is Now the World's Largest Net Importer of Petroleum and Other Liquid Fuels." *Today in Energy*, March 24, 2014. http://www.eia.gov/todayinenergy/detail.cfm?id=15531.

Valdes, J. G. 1995. *Pinochet's Economists: The Chicago School of Economics in Chile*. Cambridge: Cambridge University Press.

Valle, V. M., and H. C. Holmes. 2013. "Bolivia's Energy and Mineral Resources Trade and Investments with China: Potential Socioeconomic and Environmental Effects of Lithium Extraction." *Latin American Policy* 4 (1): 93–122.

Vaughan, A. 2014. "Ecuador Signs Permits for Oil Drilling in Amazon's Yasuni National Park." *Guardian*, May 23, 2014. http://www.theguardian.com/environment/2014/may/23/ecuador-amazon-yasuni-national-park-oil-drill.

Velasco, A. 2016. "Explaining Venezuela's Crisis." NACLA, October 28, 2016. https://nacla.org/news/2017/04/28/explaining-venezuelan-crisis.

Veltmeyer, H. 2012. "The Natural Resource Dynamics of Postneoliberalism in Latin America: New Developmentalism or Extractivist Imperialism?" *Studies in Political Economy* 90 (1): 57–85.

Vera, L. 2001. "El balance es neoliberal!" *Venezuela Analítica*, June 23, 2001.

Vivanco, P. 2018. "Ecuador's Great Betrayal: An Interview with Guillaume Long." *Jacobin*, August 28, 2018. https://www.jacobinmag.com/2018/08/ecuador-correa-moreno-alianza-pais.

Vivoda, V. 2009. "Resource Nationalism, Bargaining, and International Oil Companies: Challenges and Change in the New Millennium." *New Political Economy* 14 (4): 517–34.

Vreeland, J. R. 2003. *The IMF and Economic Development*. Cambridge: Cambridge University Press.

Wacziarg, R., and K. H. Welch. 2008. "Trade Liberalization and Growth: New Evidence." *World Bank Economic Review* 22 (2): 187–231.

Wade, R. 1990. *Governing the Market: Economic Theory and the Role of Government in East Asian Industrialization*. Princeton, NJ: Princeton University Press.

Wade, R. 2003. "What Strategies Are Viable for Developing Countries Today? The World Trade Organization and the Shrinking of 'Development Space.'" *Review of International Political Economy* 10 (4): 621–44.

Wade, R. 2004. "On the Causes of Increasing World Poverty and Inequality, or Why the Matthew Effect Prevails." *New Political Economy* 9 (2): 163–88.

Wade, R. 2006. "Choking the South." *New Left Review* 38: 115–27.

Wade, R. 2010. "Is the Globalization Consensus Dead?" *Antipode* 41: 142–65.

Wade, R. 2012. "Return of Industrial Policy?" *International Review of Applied Economics* 26 (2): 223–39.

Wallerstein, I. 1974. "The Rise and Future Demise of the World Capitalist System: Concepts for Comparative Analysis." *Comparative Studies in Society and History* 16 (4): 387–415.

Wallerstein, I. 2003. *The Decline of American Power: The US in a Chaotic World*. New York: New Press.

Wallerstein, I. M. 2005. "After Developmentalism and Globalization, What?" *Social Forces* 83 (3): 1263–78.

Warburton, E. 2016. "Jokowi and the New Developmentalism." *Bulletin of Indonesian Economic Studies* 52 (3): 297–320.

Warburton, E. 2017. "Resource Nationalism in Indonesia: Ownership Structures and Sectoral Variation in Mining and Palm Oil. *Journal of East Asian Studies* 17 (3): 285–312.

Warner, M. 2017. "On Globalization 'with Chinese Characteristics'?" *Asia Pacific Business Review* 23 (3): 309–16.

Webber, J. R. 2010. "Bolivia in the Era of Evo Morales." *Latin American Research Review* 45 (3): 248–60.

Weimer, M., and A. Vines. 2012. "China's Angolan Oil Deals, 2003–11." In *China and Angola: A Marriage of Convenience?*, ed. M. Power and A. Alves, 85–104. Cape Town: Fahamu/Pambazuka.

Weisbrot, M. 2014a. "How to Fix Venezuela's Troubled Exchange Rate." *Fortune*, July 22, 2014.

Weisbrot, M. 2014b. "U.S. Foreign Policy in Latin America Leaves an Open Door for China. *Guardian*, January 31, 2014. http://www.theguardian.com/commentisfree/2014/jan/31/latin-america-china-us-foreign-policy-reserve.

Weisbrot, M., J. Johnston, and S. Lefebvre. 2013. *Ecuador's New Deal*. Washington, DC: Center for Economic and Policy Research.

Weisbrot, M., J. Johnston, and S. Lefebvre. 2014. *The Brazilian Economy in Transition: Macroeconomic Policy, Labor and Inequality*. Washington, DC: Center for Economic and Policy Research.

Weisbrot, M., J. Johnston, J. Villarruel Carrillo, and V. Mello. 2017. *Brazil's Enormous Interest Rate Tax: Can Brazilians Afford It?* Washington, DC: Center for Economic and Policy Research. http://cepr.net/images/stories/reports/brazil-interest-rates-2017–04.pdf.

Weisbrot, M., R. Ray, J. A. Montecino, and S. Kozameh. 2011. *The Argentine Success Story and Its Implications*. Washington, DC: Center for Economic Policy and Research. http://cepr.net/publications/reports/the-argentine-success-story-and-its-implications.

Weisbrot, M., and L. Sandoval. 2008. *The Distribution of Bolivia's Most Important Natural Resources and the Autonomy Conflicts*. Washington, DC: Center for Economic and Policy Research.

Weisbrot, M., L. Sandoval, and B. Cadena. 2006. *Ecuador's Presidential Election: Background on Economic Issues*. Washington, DC: Center for Economic and Policy Research.

Weiss, L. 2010. "The State in the Economy: Neoliberal or Neoactivist?" In *Oxford Handbook of Comparative Institutional Analysis*, ed. G. Morgan, J. Campbell, C. Crouch, O. K. Pedersen, and R. Whitley, 183–210. Oxford: Oxford University Press.

Weyland, K. 1996. "Neopopulism and Neoliberalism in Latin America: Unexpected Affinities." *Studies in Comparative International Development* 31 (3): 3–31.

Weyland, K. 2003. "Neopopulism and Neoliberalism in Latin America: How Much Affinity?" *Third World Quarterly* 24 (6): 1095–1115.

Weyland, K. 2009. "The Rise of Latin America's Two Lefts: Insights from Rentier State Theory." *Comparative Politics* 41 (2): 145–64.

White, B., S. M. Borras Jr., R. Hall, I. Scoones, and W. Wolford, eds. 2012. *The New Enclosures: Critical perspectives on Corporate Land Deals.* London: Routledge.

Whitfield, L., and A. Fraser. 2010. "Negotiating Aid: The Structural Conditions Shaping the Negotiating Strategies of African Governments." *International Negotiation* 15 (3): 341–66.

Wiig, A., and I. Kolstad. 2012. "Assigned Corporate Social Responsibility in a Rentier State: The Case of Angola." In *High-Value Natural Resources and Post-conflict Peacebuilding,* ed. P. Lujala and S. A. Rustad, 147–153. New York: Earthscan.

Williams, P., and I. Taylor. 2000. "Neoliberalism and the Political Economy of the 'New' South Africa." *New Political Economy* 5 (1): 21–40.

Winters, J. A. 1996. *Power in Motion: Capital Mobility and the Indonesian State.* Ithaca, NY: Cornell University Press.

Wise, C., and V. Chonn Ching. 2018. "Conceptualizing China–Latin America Relations in the Twenty-First Century: The Boom, the Bust, and the Aftermath." *Pacific Review* 31 (5): 553–72.

Wolf, E. 1982. *Europe and the People Without History.* Berkeley: University of California Press.

Wolff, J. 2016. "Business Power and the Politics of Postneoliberalism: Relations Between Governments and Economic Elites in Bolivia and Ecuador." *Latin American Politics and Society* 58 (2): 124–47.

Wood, E. M. 2002. *The Origin of Capitalism: A Longer View.* London: Verso.

Woods, N. 2008. "Whose Aid? Whose Influence? China, Emerging Donors and the Silent Revolution in Development Assistance." *International Affairs* 84 (6): 1205–21.

Woolard, I., and M. Leibbrandt. 2013. "The Evolution and Impact of Unconditional Cash Transfers in South Africa." In *Development Challenges in a Post-crisis World,* ed. C. P. Sepulveda, A. Harrison. and J. Y. Lin, 363–84. Annual World Bank Conference on Development Economics Global (2011). Washington, DC: International Bank for Reconstruction and Development/World Bank.

World Bank. n.d. "Commodity Price Data—Pink Sheet Data." Washington, DC: World Bank. Accessed April 29, 2019. http://www.worldbank.org/en/research/commodity -markets#1

World Bank. n.d. "World Development Indicators." Washington, DC: World Bank. Accessed April 29, 2019. https://data.worldbank.org/products/wdi.

World Bank. 1993. *Kazakhstan: The Transition to a Market Economy.* Washington, DC: World Bank. http://documents.worldbank.org/curated/en/1993/08/698920/kazakstan-transi tion-market-economy.

World Bank. 2009. *Indonesia Development Policy Review: Enhancing Government Effectiveness in a Democratic and Decentralized Indonesia.* November 2009. Washington, DC: World Bank Group. http://documents.worldbank.org/curated/en/185451468258286286/pdf/5 34510WPoindon10Box345611B01PUBLIC1.pdf.

World Bank. 2014. *Commodity Markets Outlook.* October 2014. Washington, DC: World Bank Group.

World Bank. 2015. "Indonesia: Rising Inequality Risks Long-Term Growth Slowdown." Press release. December 8, 2015. Washington, DC: World Bank. http://www.worldbank

.org/en/news/press-release/2015/12/08/rising-inequality-risks-long-term-growth
-slowdown.

World Bank. 2018. "Commodity Prices to Rise More Than Expected in 2018." Press release, April 24, 2018. Washington, DC: World Bank. https://www.worldbank.org/en/news /press-release/2018/04/24/commodity-prices-to-rise-more-than-expected-in-2018 -world-bank.

World Bank Group. n.d. Worldwide Governance Indicators. Washington, DC: World Bank. Accessed April 29, 2019. www.govindicators.org.

World Bank Group. 2018a. *Commodity Markets Outlook—Oil Exporters: Policies and Challenges.* Washington, DC: World Bank. http://pubdocs.worldbank.org/en/2710415243 26092667/CMO-April-2018-Full-Report.pdf.

World Bank Group. 2018b. *Commodity Markets Outlook—The Changing of the Guard: Shifts in Commodity Demand.* Washington, DC: World Bank. http://pubdocs.worldbank.org /en/236551540394193458/CMO-October-2018-Full-Report.pdf

Wright, G., and J. Czelusta. 2004. "Why Economies Slow: The Myth of the Resource Curse." *Challenge* 47 (2): 6–38.

Wylde, C. 2011. "State, Society and Markets in Argentina: The Political Economy of Neodesarrollismo Under Néstor Kirchner, 2003–2007." *Bulletin of Latin American Research* 30 (4): 436–52.

Wylde, C. 2016. "Post-neoliberal Developmental Regimes in Latin America: Argentina Under Cristina Fernandez De Kirchner." *New Political Economy* 21 (3): 322–41.

Yang, C. 2014. "Market Rebalancing of Global Production Networks in the Post-Washington Consensus Globalizing Era: Transformation of Export-Oriented Development in China." *Review of International Political Economy* 21 (1): 130–56.

Yao, A. 2018. "China Isn't About to Have a Japan-Style Lost Decade." *South China Morning Post,* July 20, 2018. https://www.scmp.com/business/article/2108821/china-isnt-about -have-japan-style-lost-decade.

Yates, D. A. 1996. "The Rentier State in Africa: Oil Rent Dependency and Neocolonialism in the Republic of Gabon." Trenton, NJ: Africa World Press.

Young, K. 2013. "Purging the Forces of Darkness: The United States, Monetary Stabilization, and the Containment of the Bolivian Revolution." *Diplomatic History* 37 (3): 509–37.

Yu, Z. 2011. *Identifying the Linkages Between Major Mining Commodity Prices and China's Economic Growth:Implications for Latin America.* IMF Working Paper 11/86. Washington, DC: International Monetary Fund.

Zack-Williams, T., and G. Mohan. 2005. "Africa from SAPs to PRSP: Plus ca change plus C'est la Meme Chose." *Review of African Political Economy* 32 (106): 501–3.

Zakaria, F. 2008. "The Future of American Power: How America Can Survive the Rise of the Rest." *Foreign Affairs* 87 (3): 18–43.

Zamosc, L. 2007. "The Indian Movement and Political Democracy in Ecuador." *Latin American Politics and Society* 49 (3): 1–34.

Zand, B. 2013. "Mining the Gobi: The Battle for Mongolia's Resources." *Spiegel Online,* August 7, 2013. http://www.spiegel.de/international/world/mining-the-gobi-desert-rio -tinto-and-mongolia-fight-over-profits-a-915021.html.

Zhan, S., and L. Huang. 2013. "Rural Roots of Current Migrant Labor Shortage in China: Development and Labor Empowerment in a Situation of Incomplete Proletarianization." *Studies in Comparative International Development* 48 (1): 81–111.

Zhao, S. 2010. "The China Model: Can It Replace the Western Model of Modernization?" *Journal of Contemporary China* 19 (65): 419–36.

Zhou, C., and D. Banik. 2014. "Access to Justice and Social Unrest in China's Countryside: Disputes on Land Acquisition and Compensation." *Hague Journal on the Rule of Law* 6 (2): 254–75.

Index

Chinese (ethnic group): in Indonesia, 228, 229; in Zambia, 178, 181
Ciccantell, P. S., 25–26
class analysis, 64
climate change, 250, 251, 295n54, 301n1
coal, Chinese consumption of, 20, 251, 301n1
cocaine, 225, 301n52
coffee, 37
Cold War, 33
Colombia, 193; cocaine in, 301n52; FARC in, 300–301n50; as homegrown orthodoxy state, 224–27
colonization, 29
commodities: Chinese consumption of, 238–39; current prices for, 236; future demand for, by China, 253; increase in Chinese demand for, 8; shifts in demand for, 251; structuralist theory on, 30–31
commodity booms, 14, 49, 238–39, 274n1; neodevelopmentalism and, 74
commodity markets, China's effects on, 16–22
Confederación de Nacionalidades Indígenas del Ecuador (Confederation of Indigenous Nationalities of Ecuador), 107
Confederación Nacional de Instituciones Empresariales Privadas (National Confederation of Private Enterprise Institutions, CONFIEP), 208, 217, 218
Congress of South African Trade Unions, 223–24
copper, 17, 296n3; China's imports of, 18, 19; in Indonesia, 230; in Mongolia, 186–87; in Zambia, 166–71, 174, 180–81, 184, 204
Correa, Rafael, 105, 107, 219; Ecuador under, 125–32, 241, 247; following

Chavez, 109; indigenous community and, 287n3; populism of, 107–8; succeeded by Moreno, 134
corruption: in Brazil, 89, 90, 280n4; in rentier states, 141; in Zambia, 173, 180
Cox, K. R., 183, 294n48
Cuba, 148

Daloz, J.-P., 294n50
Declaration for a New International Economic Order (NIEO), 36–37
de Echave, José, 217
de la Rua, Fernando, 92–93
de la Torre, C., 128–29
democratic socialism, in Jamaica, 199
Deng Xiaoping, 1
de Soto, Hernando, 116
development. See economic development
developmentalism, 33, 274n3; in extractivist-oligarchic type, 137; in Jamaica, 199
diamonds, 275n3
dollar: Chinese underwriting of, 254; as Ecuadorian currency, 285n24
donor-dependent orthodoxy type, 12, 159–61, 188–89, 248–49; aid dependence in, 161–66; external market conditions for, 166–70; extractivist-oligarchic type and, 136–37; Laos as, 184–86; Mongolia as, 186–88; Zambia as, 170–84
dos Santos, José Eduardo, 148, 150
drug trafficking, 225
Duhalde, Eduardo, 93, 96
Duque, Ivan, 226

Ebenau, M., 77–78
economic development, 32–33; breakdown of consensus on, 35–38; in colonization, 29–30

unions: in Argentina, 97; in Colombia, 225, 300–301n50, 301n51; in Jamaica, 200; in Zambia, 172, 174–75, 291n15, 291n17

UNIP (United National Independence Party; Zambia), 171–74, 292n25

UNITA (União Nacional para a Independência Total de Angola), 148

United Nations Conference on Trade and Development (UNCTAD), 37, 251

United States: aid to Colombia from, 226–27; China compared with, 257; Chinese investments in, 254; decline of, 3; intervention in Angola by, 148; Jamaica and, 199; as model for modernization, 32; neoliberalism as economic policy of, 42; sanctions against Venezuela by, 135; trade war between China and, 235, 253; waning of hegemony of, 36; world dominance of, 22–23

University of Chicago, 39

Uribe, Álvaro, 226, 301n53

Valdes, Oscar, 300n45

Vargas, Getúlio, 108

Vargas Llosa, Mario, 212

Vedanta Resources (firm; India), 182

Velasco, Juan, 207

Venezuela, 70, 105–7, 110–13; economic crisis in, 234; as extractivist-redistributive state, 113–18; oil exports of, 111–13, 134–35; as rentier state, 288n4

Verlarde, Julio, 216

Vietnam, 289n1

Volcker, Paul, 38

vulture funds, 101, 283n25

Wahid, Abdurrahman, 228

Wallerstein, Immanuel, 29, 275–76n7

Warburton, E., 230

water war (Bolivia), 206

Widodo, Joko (Jokowi), 230–31

Winters, J. A., 227

Wittgenstein, Ludwig, 279n5

working class. *See* popular classes

World Bank: neoliberal policies of, 39; participatory agenda of, 289n3; on South Africa, 300n49

world-system, 22, 26–27, 275–76n7; global and local scales in, 278n2

World Trade Organization (WTO), 50; participatory agenda of, 289n3

Yacimientos Petrolíferos Fiscales (YPF; Argentina), 101, 282n24

Yacimientos Petroliferos Fiscales Bolivianos (Bolivian Treasury Oil Fields; YPFB), 120–21, 285n20

Yudhoyono, Susilo Bambang, 229

Zambia, 3, 157, 161, 189; copper in, 164, 166–69; as donor-dependent orthodoxy state, 170–77, 249; mining industry in, 204; nationalization of natural resources in, 34; Patriotic Front in, 177–84; taxes in, 240–41

Zambian Congress of Trade Unions, 172

Zambia Railways (firm), 180

Zamtel (firm; Zambia), 180

Zuma, Jacob, 224